# The State and Business Powers

C000065446

In the nineteenth and early twentieth centuries, the state emerged as a major player in the economies of the Western World and it was confronted with some formidable problems. Were its defence industries strong enough to cope with hostile neighbours – think of France, Germany and Russia? Could it promote industrialisation to match the early leader, Britain? How far was the state willing to go in liberating the serfs on Russian estates and slaves on American plantations? Did the rise of mass production by huge firms, in congested unhealthy urban areas, warrant state intervention? Should railways, and later airlines, be controlled?

This book challenges the traditional story that the scale of state intervention reflected the degree to which each country was ideologically committed to laissez-faire, that is, to free trade and free movement for private sector businesses in manufacturing, mining, railways, plantations, armaments, peasant agriculture. Thus state intervention was deemed to be minimal in Britain and USA because of their laissez-faire philosophy to which Continental Europe and Japan were less attached. A common assumption in that story is that governments were interested in economic growth and raising average living standards. This book gives a rather different perspective, namely that considerations of external defence and internal social and political unification played a major role in the period 1815–1939. Such considerations in turn were crucially shaped by each country's geo-political position and resource endowment.

For the first time, this new text provides an integrated economic history of these state/business relations in the major powers 1815–1939 and offers a completely new perspective on the links between tariff policies, state enterprise in manufacturing, the treatment of the peasantry, regulation of railways, taxation of the business sector, policies on cartels, trusts and competition.

**Robert Millward** is Professor Emeritus of Economic History, University of Manchester, UK.

# Routledge explorations in economic history

Edited by Lars Magnusson
*Uppsala University, Sweden*

# The State and Business in the Major Powers

# Major Powers

An economic history 1815–1939

**Robert Millward**

LONDON AND NEW YORK

First published
2013 by Routledge

Published 2014 by Routledge
2 Park Square, Milton Park, Abingdon, Oxfordshire OX14 4RN

Simultaneously published in the USA and Canada
by Routledge
711 Third Avenue, New York, NY 10017

*Routledge is an imprint of the Taylor and Francis Group, an informa business*

First issued in paperback 2015

*British Library Cataloguing in Publication Data*
A catalogue record for this book is available from the British Library

*Library of Congress Cataloging in Publication Data*
Millward, Robert.
The state and business in the major powers: an economic history,
1815–1939/Robert Millward.
    pages cm
    1. Business and politics–Western countries–History–nineteenth century.
    2. Business and politics–Western countries–History–twentieth century.
    3. Industrial policy–Western countries–History–nineteenth century.
    4. Industrial policy–Western countries–History–twentieth century. I. Title.
    HD3611.M49 2012
    338.0918′2109034–dc23
                                                            2012041259

ISBN 978-0-415-62790-0 (hbk)
ISBN 978-1-138-90404-0 (pbk)
ISBN 978-0-203-53812-8 (ebk)

Typeset in Times New Roman
by Wearset Ltd, Boldon, Tyne and Wear

**For Polly**

# Contents

# Figures

# Maps

# Tables

**Annex tables**

# Preface

Over the last decade I have been trying to develop a systematic framework for explaining differences in government economic policies in the countries of the Western World in the nineteenth and twentieth centuries. My focus has been the "micro" dimensions of policy towards the business sector whether in industry, agriculture or services. It was very difficult to move away from questions about living standards and productivity growth since they have been, understandably, a central element of the economic history literature. They were not necessarily however the main concerns of governments, whether local or central. I came to the conclusion that these concerns lay elsewhere, from pressures associated with external defence and internal unification. These also get a mention in the existing literature but not in any systematic way and thus began the project of this book. Although the method of analysis is inherently international, I have restricted the detailed work to the six major powers, France, Germany, Russia, Japan, the UK and USA. There is therefore little on Southern Europe and Scandinavia. Even then, the task has stretched my range of knowledge and for that reason banking is not covered systematically, or the imperial interests of the great powers. I had initially thought to take the story up to 2000 but quickly realised that, for reasons discussed in more detail in the following chapters, the strategic parameters changed decisively in the 1930s and 1940s so my story ends in 1939. It is hoped this text will provide links with political historians and add to the, at present limited, interchanges between them and economic historians.

I have benefited in this work from the generous help of many scholars, including opportunities to present some of the ideas in seminars and conferences. I would particularly like to thank Peter Gatrell for looking at the Russian chapters whilst much direct and indirect support came from Judith Clifton and Daniel Fuentes in Spain, Jean Pierre Dormois in France, Franco Amatori, Massimo Florio, Andre Giuntini and Pierangelo Toninelli in Italy, Rolf Künneke in Belgium, Janet Hunter and Gerben Bakker at the LSE. I should also finally acknowledge the superb facilities in the library of the University of Manchester, especially in easing the move to our new electronic age.

# Part I

# Industrialisation and the state 1815–70

# 1 Introduction

Industrialisation was the dominant economic feature of the period 1815–1939 and comprised three inter-related elements. First, there were technological advances in manufacturing and mining – cotton spinning machines, new blast furnaces, steam power – which raised labour productivity, lowered costs and raised sales of industrial products. Second, steam power made possible huge advances in rail transport and shipping which, in conjunction with the application of electricity to telegraph transmissions, revolutionised communications. Bigger markets emerged at home and abroad and the supply chain of raw materials and energy for industry lengthened. Third, there was urbanisation. Populations were generally rising and the labour force in agriculture did not fall (except in the first industrialisers, Belgium and Britain) until after the First World War (WWI) but its share of national labour forces did decline with migration from farming and cottage industry to factories. The huge increase in town populations called for new housing, urban transport, water supplies, lighting and heating which, for the large part, were slow to materialise so that congestion, ill health and rising urban mortality followed.

New businesses were set up with capital intensive technologies and the average size of firms increased. The traditional business sector did not however initially decline. Small firms, some still based on households, acted as feeders and finishers for the large new factories. France was the home of artisans and small workshops for much of the nineteenth century and the putting out system in the central Russian industrial region near Moscow continued to produce woollens, linen and cotton goods. As late as the 1870s in USA, industry was dominated by small unincorporated firms in woodwork, metals, chemicals and printed materials. The boom in the world cotton goods industry was, in the early part of the nineteenth century, good for the owners of cotton growing slave plantations in the southern American states whilst the serf labour estates in Russia responded to the rising demand for cereals. Much of the latter came from small demesne farms and peasant plots which, even after the 1860 emancipation, continued to form the basis of Russian agriculture up to the 1930s. So also in France where the peasant's right to land had been confirmed by the Revolution.

The more striking business developments were undoubtedly however in industry and commerce as capital formation took off. Many started off as partnerships with unlimited liability – like Baring Brothers in the City of London – but governance forms and corporate law proved highly adaptable to the rising business need for capital. Many firms remained unincorporated, common in insurance and banks for privacy reasons, but this did not preclude transferability of shares or some form of limited liability.[1] The Schneider brothers' steelworks in Creusot, France, was in the early days a "limited partnership" whilst the Shotts Iron Company in England was an unincorporated joint stock enterprise. Many joint stock companies did see advantages in incorporation as capital requirements rose and so a publicly acknowledged corporate identity was sought, separate from the identities of the shareholders. Some were international in ownership like the *Grande Société des Chemins de Fer* which played a big part in late nineteenth century Russian railway development. Some companies were large in part because they owned shares in other companies, like the holding companies common in Britain – GKN (Guest, Keen and Nettlefold) and AEI (Associated Electrical Industries). Others like the Chicago Gas Trust exploited alternative governance forms to avoid anti-monopoly legislation. In urban areas new utility companies emerged for gas, water, tramways, electricity supply and some of the big firms like *Allgemeine Elektrizitäts-Gesellschaft* (AEG) straddled various sectors supplying electricity as well as tramway services and manufacturing electrical equipment. America was the home of very large integrated enterprises such as Standard Oil and American Tobacco which, alongside price agreements and cartels like the German coal syndicate *Rheinisch-Westfälisches Kohlensyndikat*, heralded the onset of government interest in the regulation of monopoly practices. Government was also directly active itself in producing manufactures (the Yawata Ironworks in Japan, the *Potasses d'Alsace* in France), in trading (the *Seehandlung* in Germany), large-scale water resource development (*Compagnie Générale des Eaux* in France, the US Tennessee Valley Authority) as well as in smaller scale municipal utilities like the Cochitate Waterworks in Boston USA and the Glasgow Electricity Corporation in Scotland.

The subject of this book is the relationship between these businesses and governments in the major powers of the Western World 1815–1939: France, Germany, Japan, Russia, USA and the UK. The word "state" in the book title is merely a short-hand for "government", which itself had both central and local layers. Our period has been characterised as one which saw the proliferation and consolidation of the "nation state" which may be defined as a geographic area over which there is a common element of government (at a minimum for external defence) and within which the majority of the population has a common ethnic or cultural origin. Such a definition does not however easily translate into examples.[2] The multinational (loosely integrated) Austro-Hungarian and Ottoman Empires (see Map 1.1) were populated by Germans, Hungarians, Serbo-Croats, Slovaks, Poles, none of which necessarily dominated any given area. Russia before WWI had a more integrated governance under the Tsar but there were huge differences in history and culture, embracing as it did Poland, Finland, Turkestan, Siberia and Amur Province in the East. France might fit the definition but even the United Kingdom and Belgium had strong cultural sub-divisions – Scots, Irish, Walloons, Flemish.

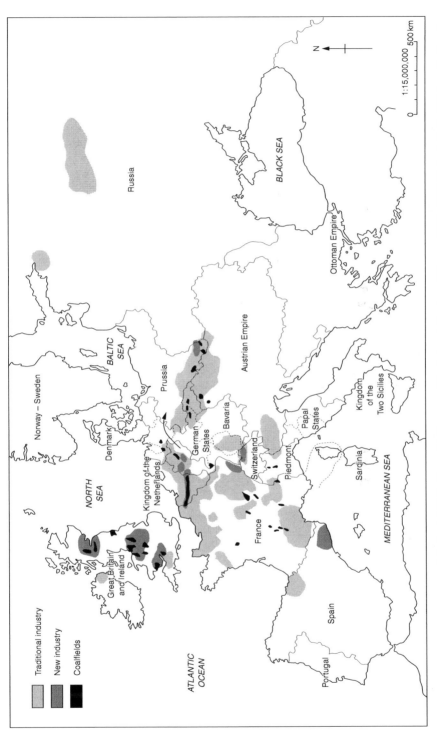

*Map 1.1* Europe in 1815 (source: S. Pollard (1981), *Peaceful Conquest: The Industrialisation of Europe 1760–1970*, Oxford: Oxford University Press).

For purposes of exploring business/government relations however it suffices to focus on two key features of these political structures. First, several important countries achieved a separate status with a unified central government only during our period of study: Belgium 1830, Italy 1860, Germany 1870 quite apart from the states which emerged from the gradual contraction of the Ottoman Empire and the dissolution during WWI of the Russian and Austro-Hungarian Empires – Romania, Bulgaria, Yugoslavia, Poland, Finland, Lithuania, etc. Second, the distribution of powers as between central and local government varied considerably. Whilst local government had important functions in the UK and France, both countries had vested strong powers in central government, as did Japan after the Meiji Restoration of 1868. It took the American Civil War of the early 1860s to provide some sort of inter-state settlement but strong internal differences remained a distinctive feature of USA government. The two layers of local (Pittsburgh) and state (Pennsylvania) government were topped by the Federal which, in the nineteenth century, had limited powers. Whilst the states had few taxation rights, they had been endowed with strong rights of regulation, including regulation of local government. Some rights to taxation were ceded by the German states (Baden, Wurtembourg etc.) to the new Reich on its foundation in 1870 but up to WWII the large states like Prussia and Bavaria wielded considerable influence.

Our interest then is on how these governmental entities related to the business sectors and to answer equations like: how far did governments differ in their support for defence industries; did manufacturing in nineteenth century Continental Europe warrant protection in the face of the huge technological lead of Britain; where and how were cartels restricted; how far were governments willing to intervene to liberate slaves in USA and serfs in Russia; what was the role of business and government in the problems of congestion and ill health in the burgeoning urban areas; where and why were railways and later airlines controlled? Such questions will be confronted in the course of exploring, quantitatively and qualitatively, the following topics: (a) patterns of industrial growth and business development, (b) tariff policy and protection, (c) cartels and monopolies, (d) state enterprise in manufacturing, (e) regulation and ownership patterns in energy, telecoms and transport, (f) government expenditures and revenues.

One broad answer to the above questions might be that the differential responses across countries reflected different ideological commitments. A common view has been that in the early modern period, 1500–1800, various versions of mercantilism were prevalent: the state and its rulers, rather than "the people", were the focus of economic policy; the accumulation of wealth by the state required state monopolies and other trade restrictions, aided by the merchant class. Such mercantilist policies were criticised by Adam Smith whose support for free trade and laissez-faire was adopted strongly in the Anglo-Saxon world of the UK and USA and with varying degrees of intensity in the other nation states of the nineteenth century. Then came socialism from the end of the century again with a varied impact across countries.

That way of thinking is now rejected as too simplistic but certain elements are relevant for the themes pursued in this book. Mercantilism was never a living doctrine like liberalism or Marxism in the sense of being explicitly espoused in active politics.[3] It was strongly associated with German writers conscious of how the state might play a role in getting rid of guilds and other medieval institutions and promoting the unification of the German states. A strong state required economic strength which, in the early modern period, necessitated military strength. For this the state needed loans and tax revenues for which the merchant class was a prime source, in exchange for exclusive overseas trading rights, restrictive navigation laws, tariffs and running state monopolies of tobacco, salt and alcohol. In this light trade was a zero sum game with the accumulation of gold and silver bullion a key objective. Exports were favoured over imports since otherwise bullion would be lost, perhaps to hostile nations like France. Whilst Adam Smith's economic analysis is much more clearly linked to individual well being, rather than to the health of the government, his attack on government interventions and trade restrictions is seen by some modern writers more as a critique of mercantilist practices than simple promotion of laissez-faire. He argued that the state needed tax revenues to finance defence and other public services and to provide aid to the poor and underprivileged. For some writers these two elements mean Smith's analysis cannot be invoked as an all-embracing critique of state intervention.[4] Magnusson (2009) moreover has argued that 1500–1800 was a formative period for the modern state which did intervene actively in progressive support for economic growth under capitalism, providing a civil administration and regulatory framework of law, order and property rights. In the nineteenth century, there were factions and leaders, like some of the Prussian bureaucracy and Napoleon III, who did invoke the virtues of free trade but, as we shall see, their impact was limited whilst the more obvious support in the UK and USA was adopted or abandoned as it suited their national interests. Indeed it is highly questionable whether "average living standards" and "economic growth" were central items on government agendas in our period 1815–1939. What then also becomes questionable is whether, as in many textbooks on economic history, it is meaningful to evaluate government policy towards the business sector in terms of its success in raising living standards and economic growth, even setting aside the modern terminology.[5]

## The core argument

The core thesis advanced and evaluated throughout this book may be briefly stated. The dominant concerns of governments in this period were external defence and internal unification. A range of policy instruments (tariffs, regulation etc.) were used to (a) develop manufacturing so as to enhance military strength, (b) ensure infrastructure industries in energy, telecoms and transport supported manufacturing and provided key strategic communications for military needs and internal unification, (c) minimise social unrest from urbanisation by promoting public health programmes, controlling monopolies and settling land rights.

Each government was influenced by powerful interest groups but it was not until the end of our period that extensions of the franchise had gone far enough for the promotion of economic growth and average living standards to become central policy elements. The differences in policy across Europe at any point in time reflected political geography, political constitutions, resource endowments and stage of economic development. Japan readily fits into that framework as do the external economic relations of USA which however otherwise does stand out in the relative independence of its constituent states and the governance problems which resulted.

## Notes

1  See Freeman *et al*. 2012.
2  Hobsbawn 1990.
3  On mercantilism see the excellent collection of articles in Coleman ed. 1969 and for a good flavour of German writing see Schmoller 1910.
4  Staziani 2012. See also Coleman's own essay in Coleman 1969.
5  See Supple 1963; Milward and Saul 1973, 1977; Trebilcock 1981; Kemp 1989. It is also paradoxical that these texts are organised around chapters on different countries even though the defining features of countries relate to geo-politics and resource endowments which are not the major areas of interest for these authors. It makes more sense with such an approach to study economic history in terms of economic regions as in Pollard 1981. The new *Cambridge Economic History of Modern Europe* (eds Broadberry and O'Rourke 2010) eschews any discussion of government policies, concentrating instead on the quantitative dimensions of economic change. It is thereby possible, and meaningful, to have chapters on economic sectors and economic topics, rather than on countries.

# 2 France, Europe and the Napoleonic legacy

## The Western World in 1815

The starting point in the early nineteenth century is a Europe recovering from the Napoleonic Wars, Japan still basically feudal and USA about to embark on the expulsion of Mexico and its European friends from the southern territories. The Russian Tsar and his Empire have repelled Napoleon and appear to be a stable force in Europe, albeit autocratic, and populated by an enserfed peasantry. Both Russian and German leaders are highly distrustful of France, its revolutionary inclinations and indeed of all aspects of modernisation, democratisation and urbanisation. Britain is the most advanced nation economically and, though this is not necessarily apparent in the early years, has the industrial strength together with assured naval and mercantile power to be dominant militarily. The laissez-faire which emanates from Adam Smith's teaching provides some intellectual background for a society with a thriving private sector and public sector limited to law, order, defence but also with limited local health and sanitation facilities, about to be exposed by rapid urbanisation.

The political geography and key resource endowments reveal many underlying tensions in the early nineteenth century. As Map 1.1 in the previous chapter shows, Germany was a hotchpotch of small principalities (like Berg) and merchant towns (like Hamburg) adjacent to the huge territories of Prussia and Bavaria. Internal and external trade was frustrated by guilds, tolls, differential tariff systems and fragmented transport links. Prussia after 1815 started to forge a path to German unity. It was well endowed with coal, iron and skilled artisans in the Ruhr and Silesia but had limited access to the cheapest form of international transport – the sea. It continued to perceive a threat from the eighteenth century hegemonic, France, and, on the east, from Russia. The latter's hard climate, especially in the central areas around Moscow, was associated with low land yields so that constant additions to the extensive margin were vital. Prussia and Sweden blocked further gains westwards so the more likely options were southwards in the Ukraine and Turkestan where the Turks would have to be confronted. Colonisation eastwards was the easiest option though, in all such expansion, given the autocratic nature of the government, more extended bureaucratic power would be needed. Strengthening the military, it would eventually be

learned, required industrialisation, but that clashed with Tsarist fears of urbanisation and modernisation with their democratic threats, so that in the early part
of the nineteenth century, few reforms were undertaken. As an island economy,
Britain had no threats from contiguous nation states, certainly now that Ireland
was part of the United Kingdom. It was well blessed with coal and its navy was
dominant. There were no immediate strategic concerns about resources or communications so the private sector was allowed to prosper with a continuing eye
on the old French enemy who now faced a growing land threat from Prussia.
France was well endowed with iron ore but the location in Lorraine was not
ideal. So also for its limited coal supplies. Its merchant fleet was small relative to
Britain's and the French economy, though advancing reasonably well, lagged
behind Britain's and the shelter afforded by the Continental System during the
Napoleonic wars, took a new form after 1815, but still gave significant protection to domestic manufactures.

To be more specific, Table 2.1 shows that in the early nineteenth century
Russia had the largest population and, with probably more than 80 per cent of
this in low productivity agriculture, its income per head was, with Japan, the
lowest of the countries due to dominate as major powers in the nineteenth and
twentieth centuries. The extension of its huge land area had not yet come to an
end: hence the 836,000 military personnel recorded for 1830, more than the rest
of the combined strength of the other major powers. These absolute magnitudes
are therefore strategically important and explain why France with a large population and large total national income, though not the most economically developed nation, had a huge army and a merchant fleet which was inferior only to
Britain's. (Comprehensive data on warships are not available for these years but
probably mirror the merchant fleet pattern.) Moreover the absolute total of
French industrial output in 1800 was no less than the UK – both accounted for
about 4.2 per cent of world industrial production.[1] Thus France was a force to be
reckoned with though it did have a lower share of its population in industry than
the UK and income per head, coal output and pig iron production were well
below the UK level. One related feature was that the population, that core source
of France's strength, was destined to grow very modestly in the nineteenth
century (cf. Chapter 6). Fertility control set in earlier in France than anywhere
else so the size of its military and industrial labour force declined relative to
other major nations. USA in the early nineteenth century was not yet a major
power. It did have a sizable fleet but with a population of only ten million, a total
of 11,000 military personnel and 70 per cent of its labour force still in agriculture it was not a strategic worry even though average living standards were relatively high, below those only in the UK.

## France and the Napoleonic legacy

The focus of our analysis is the relation between business and the state and the
hypothesis is that geo-political factors were a central element in economic
policy. The economic history literature on this period has been dominated by a

*Table 2.1* Strategic instruments and resources of the major powers 1820 (contemporary boundaries)[a]

|  | France | Germany | Russia | UK | USA |
|---|---|---|---|---|---|
| Military personnel ('000) | 259[b] | 130[bc] | 826 [b] | 140[b] | 11[b] |
| Merchant fleet ('000 net reg. tons) | 680[d] | 265[e] | n.a. | 2439 | 260[f] |
| Land area ('000 square miles) | 213 | 108[e] | 6775 | 142 | 1798 |
| Population (million) | 31 | 15.1[c] | 50 | 21 | 10 |
| Coal output (million metric tons) | 1 | 1 | 0.2[g] | 18 | 0.3[h] |
| Pig iron output ('000 metric tons) | 113[i] | 85[j] | 135[g] | 374 | 20 |
| % Labour in industry and services | 39 | 36[e] | n.a. | 62.4 | 30 |
| % of World industrial production | 4.2 | 3.5 | 5.6 | 4.2 | 0.7 |
| Income per head in dollars[k] | 1135 | 1077 | 618 | 1706 | 1257 |

Sources: Annex tables; Kennedy 1988; Bairoch 1982; Mitchell 2003a, b, c.

Notes
a  See Annex Table A1.
b  1830.
c  Prussia only.
d  1838.
e  1829.
f  Gross tonnage.
g  European Russia, excluding Poland, Finland, the Caucasus.
h  Includes brown coal, lignite, etc.
i  1819.
j  1823.
k  Gross domestic product per head in 1990 Geary-Khamis dollars, 1989 boundaries.

set of questions which are not central to the analysis here though they certainly enter at several points. The 1815–70 period is one which started with most of the industrial plants with new technology, in textiles, iron and coal, located in Britain. The new technology spread across Europe, mechanisation beyond cotton to wool and iron smelting, labour productivity in manufacturing was rising and railways and steamships emerging so that by 1870 a significant industrial sector existed in USA, Western Europe and parts of Eastern Europe. There is a huge literature on why the industrial revolution started in Britain, the latest themes linking it to the enlightenment and Britain's cheap coal and skilled but expensive labour.[2] Whilst we shall draw on some of these ideas the question of "why Britain" is not our central concern. Nor will there be much discussion of whether, why and where there were marked "take-offs" into self-sustaining growth nor whether leading sectors like cotton and railways had a decisive role in all economies. Finally the industralisation of Europe in the nineteenth century has often been examined in comparison to the economic development of the Third World in the late twentieth century and whether any policy prescriptions emerge from the European experience but again this is not the issue here.[3]

Rather, such themes enter part of the analysis of the relation between business and the state, but, as Chapter 1 stressed, the focus here is on explaining the role of geo-politics and ideology in the way economic policies towards business were developed. Some economic historians, in attempting to capture the role of the state in the French economy have focused heavily on the role of the bourgeoisie and nobility but without invoking the geo-political factors used here which provide a basis for comparing the different tools of economic policy in different countries.[4] The central elements in the French government's attitude to industrialisation were, first, a clear commitment to protect French industry from British competition by tariffs and related restrictions on imports. Second, there was a commitment to planning the economic and social overhead network – transport, energy, telecommunications, buildings. Third, a strong role for the elite bodies of engineers and officials in the central *Ecoles* and *Corps* in promoting technical progress, efficient work patterns in manufacturing and mining as well in the infrastructure sectors. These features constitute a strong contrast with Britain and the reasons lie, not so much in France's level of economic development or wholly in the role of the bourgoisie and nobility, but in its fundamental geopolitical position and resource endowment. This argument will be developed by examining in detail tariff and fiscal policies, policy towards business organisation and industrialisation and the planning process in infrastructure sectors. Much of the means for executing these policies lay in institutions developed under Napoleon, some inherited from the *Ancien Regime*, and this we now first address.

The distinctive institutions in this context were the civil codes, the elite *Ecoles* separate from the universities and the various *Corps* for industry, mining and transport. A strong role for the state was nothing new. For some historians "economic nationalism" was a dominant feature of the *Ancien Regime* – state building, promoting net exports, providing a taxable capacity. Intervention is often traced back to its most articulate defender, the seventeenth century finance Minister Colbert. His so-called mercantalist position was more sophisticated than simply restricting trade to providing bullion and revenues for the Treasury to finance the King's wars. He recognised that a vibrant economy yields good tax returns: "Commerce is the source of finance and finance is the sinew of war".[5] The significance of the Revolution in the present context is, first, that it destroyed the legal and fiscal privileges of the nobility and the church (the latter lost land as well) whilst the confirmation of the land rights of the peasantry guaranteed a future of small plots, low fertility levels and modest agricultural productivity gains in the nineteenth century (cf. Chapter 6). Second, the law of May 1791 abolished guilds and corporations, the key instruments for the regulation of industry and internal trade. Trade unions were banned but unbridled capitalism did not take its place and in particular Napoleon's codification of civil law effectively replaced the old regulatory system and provided a template for much of the rest of Continental Western Europe. This was a revision of Roman Law with its emphasis on a written civil code (in contrast to the tradition in British common law, that is a law which was subordinated to legal tradition and therefore subject to judicial review).[6] The codes were designed to offer unambiguous guidelines, and, amongst other things, extended public property to the sub-soil and ground transport infrastructure. The state then built and operated or built and leased or simply gave concessions for coal, iron and other minerals, shipping, armaments, public services, law enforcement, roads, bridges, posts, canals.[7] The Commercial Code of 1807 was creditor friendly and provided, as we shall see in the fourth section of this chapter, a flexible framework for business organisation, notwithstanding the proliferation of family firms and the views of some who despised large firms, large factories and joint stock companies. The Mining Code of 1810 gives a good indication of the nature of state intervention. It gave (actually restored) to the state the rights to coal concessions in perpetuity; the rights of landowners below ground level were simply not recognised – though the code did restrict the state to fiscal demands, security and rights to forfeiture. Exploring for new reserves and, for example, for surface iron ore deposits, required a licence. This was for one or two years, rents were to be paid to the owner of surface rights and a flat tax per acre to the state which also received up to 5 per cent of the net return whilst overall supervision was by the *administration des mines.*[8]

The supervisors and administrators came from the *Ecoles* and *Corps*. The *Ecole Polytechnique* was established in 1794, specialising in science and engineering, and became the scholarly heart of the highly centralised bureaucratic elite. The *Ecole des Ponts et Chaussées* (established in 1747) and the *Ecoles des Mines* (1783) only recruited from the best graduates of the *Ecole Polytechnique*. So the *Corps* did originate from a longer tradition and in particular from the eighteenth century enlightenment.[9] By 1804 they had emerged with more authority. Napoleon had effectively consolidated them into permanent institutions and over all them and the civil service stood the *Conseil d'État*, the supreme administrative court of the Napoleonic state. Smith's detailed study of the role of the *Corps* suggests that the French "state engineers have promoted the complementary notion of national public administration in the general interest and planning on a national scale. From the beginning they have lived in conflict with the proponents of decentrism, economic liberalism, anti-statism and anti-elitism."[10] The message from France by 1815 was therefore very different from the laissez-faire allegedly underlying British economic growth and, on the other hand, it offered a prospect of planned economic development, urbanisation and modernisation which frightened the Prussian and Russian princes who feared it would be accompanied by the baggage of democratisation and a change in social power.

## Industrial protection, tariff policy and French public finances

In 1815 there was, throughout Europe, a rich variety of industrial forms of which the centralised workshop, the factory and especially the mechanised factory was in the minority. Much was still in the form of cottage industry and outwork, linked to agriculture, and every country had a substantial industrial element. We should not then be surprised to find that the country we think of as being industrially most advanced at this time, the United Kingdom, accounted for less than 5 per cent of total world industrial output and little different from the other major

European countries – France, Germany, Russia (Table 2.1). When expressed per head of population of course the picture changes but the process whereby Western Europe came to dominate world industry had in fact barely begun.

France in 1800 was not untypical of Europe generally in still having over 60 per cent of its labour force in agriculture. Its main industrial growth was in Alsace, Normandy, Paris and Picardy with silk concentrated around Lyons. The technological innovations in Britain from 1760 had been passed on quickly to France though that flow slowed once war started in 1793. In cotton manufacture, mule jennies and water frames spread from the 1780s and the industry developed well up to 1815, especially in Alsace because of its proximity to Switzerland where cotton printing had emerged as a speciality in the eighteenth century (cotton printing having been banned in France before 1785 because of objections to cotton fibre success elsewhere). The Loire coalfield was producing more than the north-east and, given the abundance of forest and timber and the distance to iron ore in Lorraine, coke smelting blast furnaces and steam power showed only modest development in the pre-railway age. Only 15 businesses had steam engines in 1815 and the total number of engines was not much more than 200.[11]

In the early nineteenth century total industrial output in France, like Germany, was well ahead of USA mainly because of a larger population since manufacturing output per head of population was very similar. The French total (Table 2.1) was slightly bigger than Germany and, as noted earlier, about the same as the UK. The latter had a distinctly smaller population but a much bigger share in industry and a higher *productivity of labour in manufacturing*, so that the UK emerges with manufacturing output per head of population nearly twice that of France. Thus by 1815 manufacturing in France and elsewhere on the Continent faced a formidable competitor across the Channel. Matters had not been helped during the Napoleonic period by the Continental Blockade of British goods and shipping. Industry in the eastern and northern parts of France, in Belgium and the Rhine, flourished but industrial activities in the countryside of the south and south-west provinces of Gascony, Poitou, Aquitaine and Maine, which had depended on trans-Atlantic exports, declined and had disappeared by 1815. Moreover once the blockade was lifted, Western Continental Europe was exposed to the full force of competition from British industry and the production gap between France and the UK widened.

It is therefore no surprise that France, as Britain's nearest neighbour, should want to protect its industry by tariffs and import restrictions. Many have bemoaned the mollycoddled French businessman arguing that the full blast of British competition would have stirred manufacturers to greater efforts.[12] France however behaved no differently from USA government towards its own cotton manufacturing industry or from Britain in the twentieth century as it lost its dominance of world trade, as we shall see in later chapters. Kemp is right to say it was "a rationale response to the threat from English and other foreign competition".[13] Tariffs and quantitative restrictions on imported manufactures offered some chance for French industry to grow and modernise. As early as 1816 the Chamber of Commerce in St Etienne said "that the progress of French industry is mainly due to the prohibition of large number of manufactured articles".[14] The opposition to tariffs came from a small group of port merchants and manufacturers of silk and printed cloth. In general, farmers and manufacturers pushed for protection. Internal duties on trade were abolished but in December 1814 a set of protection laws were introduced and 1820, 1822 and 1826 saw more protectionist legislation. Iron import tariffs started at 50 per cent in 1814, steel 45 per cent and both were raised in the 1820s. The duties on cast steel and ropes rose steeply over time. Much of the protection was in the form of quantitative restrictions on imports. Imports of cotton goods, wool fabrics and hosiery, for example, were prohibited whilst fine yarns and worsted yarns came to form routine cargo for the smuggling trade and the navigation laws kept out British shipping. Manufactured goods were more heavily protected than agricultural commodities but a sliding scale for grain was reintroduced in 1819. From 1830 the new July monarchy reduced some duties, relaxed some restrictions and replaced some other restrictions, especially in the tariff laws of 1836 and 1841. Many of these duties were specific in money terms (as opposed to *ad valorem*) and since the period 1830–50 was one of falling prices, the general level of real protection remained intact. By May 1841 the average level of duties on products not restricted was 40–60 per cent. Manufactured goods made up only 6 per cent of imports, falling to 3.8 per cent by 1858–60.[15]

It is true that from 1850, Napoleon III, an admirer of Peel the British corn law repealer, believed that foreign competition would provide a spur to business and duties were lowered on iron, coal, various raw materials and foodstuffs. In 1860 the Cobden–Chevalier Anglo-French Treaty was signed: all quantitative restrictions on trade between the two countries were abolished and all duties on French imports from the UK were less than 25 per cent by 1864. The UK reduced the duties on wine and allowed free entry for many French products. Favoured nation clauses, including reciprocity,[16] featured in the Treaty which was followed by similar French treaties with Belgium, Prussia, Italy, Sweden, Norway, Spain, the Netherlands and Austria in the 1860s. Duties on raw materials imported to France were abolished in a law of 1860 and by 1869 most duties on agricultural products and raw materials had been abolished as had the navigation laws. However the significance of these changes in tariff policy was, first, that they were introduced in the teeth of opposition from many manufacturers and farmers. (Napoleon managed to by-pass Parliament.) There is also the argument that the 1860 Treaty was pushed by Napoleon to mollify Britain's objections to his attempts to force Austria out of Italy. Third, and most importantly, it was not long, the mid 1870s, before protection returned.

It might be objected that French tariff policy had a revenue dimension – that custom duties were levied to support France's fragile public finances. There is no evidence of this however. Given the size of its military, the cost of the Napoleonic wars and the extensive use of tax farming in the *Ancien Regime* one might expect that new tax sources would be exploited. Table 2.2 does display France's sizable military spending which maintained a fairly stable 30 per cent of all central government spending 1815–69. This share was actually not much different from that in the UK and Prussia. Moreover French debt in 1815 was remarkably less than in the UK where it was over £800 million (see Chapter 3). France had financed its war in part by enemy occupation and exploitation. Reparations payments agreed in 1815 were modest and the cost of the public debt had been reduced by currency inflation.[17] Nonetheless, taking income levels into account, the central government's expenditure was higher than in the UK. In France it remained about 9 per cent of national income throughout the period. Whilst the UK figure was initially higher it fell over time to below 6 per cent by 1870. Since it was the aim to avoid the plethora of internal excise duties collected under the *Ancien Regime*, often by corrupt tax farmers, the Revolution outlawed indirect taxes, a policy which Napoleon initially endorsed.[18] The principle of taxation was supposed to be "liberty, equality and justice". Justice was achieved in part because no one was excluded from tax liability – the nobility lost their claim to immunity. Liberty was to be ensured by seeing that in raising direct taxes on income and property only "external" indicators would be used: there would be no investigation of people's income but rather the direct taxes would be levied on land, windows, doors, moveable property etc. In the event the land and trading (business) taxes and those on moveable property did not yield much revenue and total direct taxes fell from 35–40 per cent of total revenues in 1815–29, to 20–25 per cent by 1852–69. Thus the burden fell on the (regressive) indirect taxes which, if stamp duty and registration fees are added, rose to over one-half the total by 1852–69. Napoleon had resorted to many indirect taxes which had existed under the *Ancien Regime* with little concern for "equality and justice". The main internal excise duties were on wine, tobacco, gunpowder, salt and sugar. The significant element was that, despite the replacement of quantitative import restrictions by import duties and their general rise, customs revenues accounted for only 12.7 per cent of all central government revenues in 1813 and 10.8 per cent in 1885, even though all indirect taxes had risen to 57.1 per cent of the total by that date.[19] Even in the UK they were over 30 per cent by 1880 (see Chapter 3). So tariff protection in France can at best be described as an infant industry argument, certainly not as a revenue raiser.

## Business development and the growth of French manufacturing

French industrial development in the nineteenth century has been critically scrutinised by many writers complaining about its protection from foreign competition and about a ruling group suspicious of large firms, limited liability companies and the whole process of mechanisation. In fact the legal system was developed in a way that afforded considerable flexibility for those wishing to accumulate capital beyond the reach of the family firm and the small partnership. Moreover the pace of French industrialisation up to the 1860s was little different from USA and better than Germany and Sweden, let alone Italy and Spain. Germany and USA still had, like France, about one-half of the labour force in agriculture in 1870. The growth of manufacturing per head was significantly

Table 2.2 Central government budgeted[a] expenditures and revenues in France 1801–69 (annual averages in million francs)

Expenditure

|  | Debt service | Military | Education etc. | Public works | Other | Collection expenditure | Total | National income | Total as % NI |
|---|---|---|---|---|---|---|---|---|---|
| 1801–14 | 121 | 506 | 18 | 28 | 45 | 110 | 1003 | 9755[b] | 10.3 |
| 1815–29 | 301 | 302 | 31 | 29 | 84 | 127 | 1020 | 10,503[b] | 9.7 |
| 1830–47 | 348 | 404 | 52 | 104 | 132 | 131 | 1277 | 14,894[b] | 8.6 |
| 1848–51 | 410 | 480 | 67 | 166 | 187 | 149 | 1588 | 17,407[b] | 9.1 |
| 1852–69 | 531 | 691 | 81 | 153 | 246 | 198 | 2089 | 22,824[b] | 9.2 |

Revenue

|  | Direct taxes | Indirect taxes | Stamp and reg. fees | Public lands forests | Other ordinary | Extraordinary | Total | National income | Total as % NI |
|---|---|---|---|---|---|---|---|---|---|
| 1801–14 | 369 | 217 | 147 | 103 | 33 | 102 | 972 | 9755[b] | 10.0 |
| 1815–29 | 357 | 347 | 163 | 35 | 29 | 97 | 1028 | 1053[b] | 9.8 |
| 1830–47 | 386 | 454 | 220 | 37 | 41 | 83 | 1221 | 14,894[b] | 8.2 |
| 1848–51 | 329 | 497 | 224 | 37 | 72 | 239 | 1498 | 17,407[b] | 8.6 |
| 1852–69 | 489 | 751 | 365 | 41 | 121 | 282 | 2059 | 22,824[b] | 9.0 |

Sources: Schremmer 1989, pp. 402–3; Mitchell 2003a.

Notes
a *Résultats généraux des budgets.*
b These are T.J. Markovich's data for respectively 1803–12, 1815–24, 1835–44, 1845–54, 1855–64 (from Mitchell 2003a, p. 837).

worse than Belgium, and of course Britain, but these two countries did have massive coal deposits and less timber and the incentive to develop steam based technology much earlier than France.

French metallurgy was remodelled on English lines after 1815 but only slowly because of the lack of coke for smelting. Blast furnaces were still located near to forests and the number of charcoal blast furnaces kept rising to 1839.[20] The overall index of industrial production in the first column of Table 2.3 shows only modest growth in the 1820s and 1830s. The traditional linen and wool industries were major employers with weaving still dominated by outwork and untouched by steam power before 1850. Nonetheless national total investment rose from 7.2 per cent of national income in 1815–24 to 12.4 per cent in 1855–64. Cotton mechanisation was spreading rapidly. In Alsace the recorded numbed of spindles rose from 0.5 million in 1828 to 1.15 million by 1847 and power looms were coming on stream. Infrastructure, defined to include building, gas and water systems, education, road and rail track accounted for a fairly stable 70 per cent of total annual capital formation with the share of transport rising from 12 per cent to 25 per cent by the 1850s and 1860s.[21]

Cotton's growth was not mirrored in the overall index of industrial production because it was not big enough to dominate the total. So also for silk in the first half of the century. Indeed there were many other sectors which had very high growth rates 1800–70 which had a weight less than even cotton and silk. These included zinc, cast iron, rubber, raw sugar, coal, non-ferrous metals and chemicals.[22] France was excellent in certain niche sectors like cutlery and quality finishing in textiles and it was in printing and bleaching that mechanisation first started. So the leading growth sectors played a rather subdued role in the economy in this period. Indeed it was not until the 1840s and especially the 1850s that the major industrial expansion took off. In part this was linked to the delay in the opening of railway track (see next section), so decisive for linking coal to iron and for transporting heavy cargoes. Table 2.3 shows rail track kilometres rising from 410 in 1840 to 2915 in 1850 but the UK already had 2390 in 1840 rising to 9197 in 1850. Iron and steel expanded markedly in the 1860s through companies like Terre Noire and Schneiders. Rapid changes occurred in sectors such as textile machinery and in the mercantile marine which had been all wood until 1848. The number of blast furnaces using wood was still high, 282 in 1860, but the 113 using coke reflected a rising trend. Caron has estimated that in the period 1835–64 one-half of industrial growth was still craft based and one-half "advanced industry".[23]

How far was business development stifled by the legal forms of business and related aspects of business organisation? Freedom to set up joint stock companies was not encouraged in early nineteenth century France with the state insisting on close scrutiny and on legislative approval for each new company and full liberation did not come until 1863. However this was only some 20 years after the British (where each company had needed a separate Parliamentary Act) and in any case many industrial and commercial companies found other legal forms enabling capital to be attracted and for even the family firms to

Table 2.3  Some key indicators of French industrial output 1820–69

| | Index of industrial production 1913=100 | Cotton ('000 metric tons)a | Linen ('000 metric tons)b | Pig iron output (million metric tons) | Coal output (million metric tons) | Iron ore output (million metric tons) | Rail track open (km) | Beer output ('000 hectolitres) |
|---|---|---|---|---|---|---|---|---|
| 1820 | 20.7 | 19c | 84.7 | 0.1d | 1.1 | n.a. | 17e | 3.0 |
| 1830 | 21.0 | 34c | 100.8 | 0.3 | 1.9 | 0.8f | 31 | 3.1 |
| 1840 | 24.3 | 53 | 113.9 | 0.3 | 3.0 | 1.0 | 410 | 4.2 |
| 1850 | 33.5 | 59 | 118.1 | 0.4 | 4.4 | 1.8 | 2915 | 4.0 |
| 1860 | 39.1 | 115 | 138.8 | 0.9 | 8.3 | 3.0 | 9167 | 6.6 |
| 1869 | 44.4 | 94 | 158.7 | 1.4 | 13.5 | 3.1 | 16,465 | 7.5 |

Source: Mitchell 2003a.

Notes
a  Net imports of raw cotton.
b  Flax and hemp inputs. Average of surrounding years.
c  Average of surrounding years.
d  1819.
e  1828.
f  1835.

expand. That France lagged behind USA in mass production by large companies is a complex issue we shall discuss in Part II and cannot simply be characterised as a product of deficient business forms and timid French entrepreneurs. Natural resources, labour and land supplies were different in Europe from USA and in addition France lacked coal so that concentrating on niche markets in the long run could prove better for France. Businesses that wished to attract financial support with limited liability found a way in the French system. Partly as a consequence of eighteenth century financial crises, the 1807 Commercial Code laid down three seemingly separate forms of business organisation. First, there was the *société en nom collectif*, essentially a partnership which needed only to be registered. With unlimited liability however it was unable to grow and attract risk capital. At the other extreme was the joint stock company, the *société anonyme*, with capital in the form of transferable shares carrying limited liability. The scope for abuse was seen to be extensive and some feared "stock jobbing and monopoly" especially for railway companies.[24] Hence creation of a *société anonyme* required an application via the Departmental Prefect, a very legalistic review by the *Conseil d'État* and the final stamp of a state decree. All existing organisational forms (like partnerships) associated with the applicant business had to be closed, all capital in the company to be paid up and the managerial structure approved. One source estimated that 12 new *sociétés anonymes* were established each year in the period 1817–67; this seems a small figure but it does exclude savings banks (in every town by the 1860s) and the discount houses (*comptoirs d'escomptes*, of which there were 67 by 1849 with 20 per cent of the capital subscribed by the state). Many gas, steamship and bridge companies used this form of organisation but the main examples were insurance companies (188 over the years 1819–67) and railways, the latter numbering only 61 but accounting for over one-half of the capital invested.[25]

Whilst the number of new joint stock companies was not large and the freeing up of the legislation delayed to 1863, this does not mean that large businesses were frustrated by the legislation since many companies found a way of elastically using the third form of business organisation established under the Commercial Code, the *société en commandité*. These were partnerships where some of the partners had limited liability and this proved to be a very flexible and oft used method of attracting capital. It had not been anticipated that such limited partnerships would be popular and all the applicants had to do was register their charter at the local Commercial Tribunal where it was posted for three months.[26] The "sleeping" partners had no managerial role and normally received an agreed share of profits and, in the case where the *société en commandité* was classed as *par action*, their shares could, with certain restrictions, be sold so these companies had many of the attractions of joint stock companies. Many large businesses established in this period took the form of the limited partnership: the Saint-Gobern glass works, Creusot iron (22.5 million francs capital in 1849). From the 1850s more demanding legal requirements were laid on the limited partnerships but, even so, over the period 1848–67 some 14,400 were formed, alongside 307 joint stock companies and 52,800 simple partnerships.[27]

By 1870, France's population had risen only slightly, its coal output was still modest and its pig iron output had been overtaken by Germany. However the picture for the total of manufacturing was better, as may be seen in Table 2.4. Manufacturing output per head of population more than doubled in France 1800 to 1860, less than the UK and Belgium but similar to USA and significantly better than Germany and Sweden who started from the same base. The gap between British manufacturing and the rest was probably at its peak in the 1860s since its manufacturing output per head actually quadrupled 1800–60. The gap in living standards between France and the UK remained roughly constant 1800–50 but had widened by 1870 (at least if we measure only income levels and ignore the quality of life in Britain's industrial towns). Clearly some of the differences over the period relate to that great engine of growth, the railway, and so we finally turn to the policy of the French government to railways and other infrastructures.

## Planning railways, energy and other infrastructure in France

Two elements thread through the French government's policy towards transport, telecommunications and energy. One is the strategic significance of these sectors in the context of potential hostile land neighbours like Prussia. Second, the instruments for external defence and political unification needed to be consciously planned, a process heavily influenced by the Napoleonic legacy. The Napoleonic code

> extended public property to the sub-soil and ground transport infrastructures. This meant that during the early industrial period coal, iron and other minerals, railroads, shipping, armaments and postal services were publicly operated or awarded by the state to private interests.[28]

This provided a key benchmark for the elite corps of the central government although a belief in liberalisation and competition certainly could be found in other circles especially from the July (1830) monarchy onwards and during the second Empire from 1850.[29] The *Corps des Ponts et Chaussées* envisaged an infrastructure planned and operated by the French central government though, again, that stance was constantly challenged throughout the nineteenth century. The outcome was often a planned infrastructure (tracks, waterways etc.) but with services provided by private or municipal or state enterprises: canal barges, train services, gas and water utilities.

Telecommunications were perceived as the most strategically sensitive, a key political instrument. Following the introduction of the Chappe visual hand telegraph in 1797, the extension of the service was financed by the army, navy and the national lottery. Canal development was stimulated by the 1820–21 plan of Becques, the *Corps'* leader though he was unsuccessful in obtaining state construction and the subsequent substantial development by concessionaires was unfortunate in that the peak of the 1830s coincided with the advent of railways;[30] contrast the UK where canals peaked in the 1790s and Germany where political disunity

Table 2.4 Income and industrialisation levels 1800–70 (indexes UK = 100)

| | Manufacturing output per head of population (UK 1860 = 100)[a] | | Gross domestic product per head of population (UK 1870 = 100)[b] | | |
|---|---|---|---|---|---|
| | 1800 | 1860 | 1820 | 1850 | 1870 |
| UK | 25 | 100 | 54 | 72 | 100 |
| Belgium | 16 | 44 | 40 | 56 | 81 |
| USA | 14 | 33 | 40 | 56 | 81 |
| France | 14 | 31 | 38 | 51 | 57 |
| Germany | 13 | 23 | 34 | 45 | 59 |
| Sweden | 13 | 23 | 37 | 40 | 51 |
| Italy | 13 | 16 | 33 | 37[c] | 45 |
| Spain | 11 | 17 | 33 | 36 | 42 |
| Russia | 9 | 13 | 23 | 26[c] | 31 |
| Japan | 11 | 11 | 22 | 22[c] | 22 |
| India | 9 | 5 | 16 | 17 | 17 |

Sources: Bairoch 1982, p. 281; Maddison 1995.

Notes
a 1913 boundaries.
b 1989 boundaries. The index is calculated from Geary–Khamis dollars.
c My interpolation from 1820 and 1870 data.

delayed everything. The development of gas supply was slightly later than Britain with the first public supply for lighting in Paris in 1820 and Lyons 1834 and most gas systems seem to have been concessions.[31] The Paris Water Company was established in the eighteenth century when concessions were free and despite an 1829 edict allowing the Paris municipality to take over, it remained private. It seems there was not a strong demand for water systems outside the major towns and only four new systems were introduced 1800–20. The abundance of aqueducts and wells for domestic use meant that rivers were mainly used for industry. Urbanisation was advancing on nothing like the scale of England with its growing problems of water pollution. The 1830s and 1840s saw the first significant development of commercial water supply, gas supply, telegraph and railways. The state monopoly of telegraph was confirmed by an Act of 1837 which was the basis of all future state claims to exclusive rights in telecommunications and by 1844 there were 534 stations linking Paris to centres. During the 20 years from 1830, some 34 new water systems were introduced and, given the number of municipal water utilities recorded later in the century (and discussed in Part II) we can only assume several were municipally owned before 1850.[32]

Some of the dimensions of French policy towards railways could be found in other European countries, specifically those designed to cope with the natural monopoly features of railways. The government stepped in to facilitate rights of way and then proceeded to monitor the efficiency of the companies, control profits and the configuration of routes but in a more interventionist manner than the UK.[33] Controls were exercised by the *Corps des Ponts et Chaussées* which saw itself as the technical authority. It vetted rail, gas and water companies, assessed their proposals, claimed a right to work inside the companies and exercised continued technical supervision even after the railway, waterworks and gas plants had been constructed. In a classic early example in the 1830s in the proposal for the Paris–St Germain railway, traffic forecasts were made both by the promoter (Emile Pereire) and the *Corps*, and then compared.[34] The *Corps* argued that rail investment had indirect benefits, that routes should be planned with small gradients and curves to facilitate rail's alleged key advantages in speed for passengers and light goods and to economise on France's limited coal supplies. So far as control of fares and freight rates are concerned, the General Highway Council was setting levels as early as the horse-drawn railway era. For the lines opened in the 1830s, leases were often for 99 years but concern over monopoly profits reduced that by the 1840s to an average of 46 years and leases were shorter the greater were expected profits.[35] Some of these leases proved quite restrictive and after 1851 as part of a more general standardisation of conditions, the 99 year lease became the norm and there were government guarantees of returns (often 4 per cent plus 1 per cent for amortisation). On the other hand when rates of return exceeded 8 per cent, half of the excess was to go to the Treasury. These provisions, according to an Act of 1859 were to apply to all new lines. The state had the option of repurchase after 15 years quite apart from the automatic reversion after 99. Such controls on excess profits were finally standardised in the 1883 conventions (cf. Part II).

So the controls on prices and profits were quite intrusive and, if we turn to how the railway network emerged, the state was much more involved than in Britain though several observers like Dobbin have suggested, persuasively, that the state wanted to "orchestrate" rather than manage.[36] As early as 1833 the *Corps* was granted 0.5 million francs to mount a study of the development of the rail track. An Act of 1842 set out nine arteries and, though little followed immediately, it has been seen by some historians as clinching the state's right to control the layout of the system and the companies involved in its construction. The short run effect was to postpone development and by the end of the 1840s only 3000 kilometres of track had been built (one-half of Germany). LeFranc argued that the very postponement made possible the subsequent establishment of a coordinated system such as existed, then and thereafter, in no other country.[37] A plan of six regional networks to absorb 28 companies was agreed in 1850 and became effective during the Napoleonic enthusiasm of the 1850s. Concessions were open to adjudication. Competition between parallel routes ("in the field") was not approved. Competition for concessions, that is "for the field", was encouraged. Competition over the same track between different operating companies, paying access charges, was not forbidden, but very limited in France as elsewhere in the nineteenth century.

The 1850–70 period saw a surge in industrialisation and general economic growth accompanied by a huge expansion of the rail network, strong development of electric telegraph and horse drawn omnibus and street cars and further growth of gas and water supplies. Concession systems continued to dominate the gas industry. The Paris Gas Company emerged in 1855 from a fusion of eight companies that had been supplying the city on a district basis.[38] Urban tram operators were also mainly privately owned in most provincial towns – often parts of industrial conglomerates and railway companies. In Paris there were initially six tram companies but in 1855 the city council gave a 50 year concession to the *Compagnie General d'Omnibus* – closely linked to the Pereire financial empire and instrumental, according to Larroque (1988), in the tram system limiting itself to the wealthiest parts of the city. Much of the famous Haussman rebuilding of the 1850s was by private companies and the *Compagnie General des Eaux*, established in 1853, was awarded the concession for much of the Paris water supply. That same company also won concessions in other towns including Lyons. But many of the 149 new water systems such as that in Grenoble were municipally owned.[39]

These middle decades of the century are however noted more than any other for the large expansion of the rail track which reached 15,000 kilometres by the end of the 1860s, nearly as big as Germany.[40] The restructuring of the 28 companies into six networks was followed by the secondment of the *Corps*' engineers to the companies for technical supervision and the concession system became more standardised, as noted earlier. In each of the networks there was one dominant company. The Act of 1859 distinguished between the old network, basically the trunk lines, and the new network of less profitable secondary lines. The aim was to provide a universal service accessible everywhere. The companies were expected to cross-subsidise the secondary lines and the government interest guarantees were more generous for these lines which however were not always merged successfully into the six networks. In the later part of the nineteenth century as the strategic role of railways was increasingly recognised, especially after the Franco-Prussian War 1870–71, decisions had to be taken about whether such lines would be supported.[41]

## Notes

1  Bairoch 1982.
2  Crafts 1977, 1984; Mokyr 2009; Mokyr and Voth 2010; Allen 2010; Balderston 2010.
3  Landes 1965; Cameron 1958; Marczewski 1963; Crouzet 1972.
4  Keyder 1985; O'Brien and Keyder 1978; Kemp 1989.
5  Wolfe 1969, p. 201; Kemp 1989.
6  Dobbin 1994.
7  Chadeau 2000, pp. 192–3.
8  Parker 1959; Gillet 1969.
9  Margaraiz 1998.
10  Smith Jr 1990, pp. 658–9.
11  Clapham 1961; Fohlen 1973.
12  Gershenkron 1955; Cameron 1958; Fohlen 1973.
13  Kemp 1989, p. 712. Also Sherman 1977.
14  Clapham 1961, p. 72.
15  Bairoch 1989.
16  For example, British tariff concessions to Belgium would also be offered to France as a British favoured nation. Reciprocity required that the benefit to France was not contingent on France making separate concessions to Britain.
17  Schremmer 1989.
18  Ibid., p. 386.
19  Ibid., pp. 377–8.
20  Clapham 1961.
21  Levy-Leboyer 1978, pp. 285–8.
22  Marczewski 1963.
23  Caron 1979; Fohlen 1973.
24  Sherman 1977, p. 724.
25  Freedman 1965, p. 201.
26  Ibid., p. 193.
27  Fohlen 1978, pp. 353–6.
28  Chadeau 2000, p. 192; Barjot 2011.
29  Smith Jr 1990.
30  Geiger 1984.
31  Shaw 1895, ch. 1; Williot 1984.
32  Attali and Stowwdze 1977; Goubert 1988.
33  Parts of what follow can be explored in more detail in Millward 2005.
34  Dunham 1941; Radcliffe 1973.
35  LeFranc 1929/30.
36  Dobbin 1994; Dormois 1999.
37  LeFranc 1929/30.
38  Williot 1984.
39  Pinkney 1957; Goubert 1988. See also Chapter 6.
40  Blanchard 1969.
41  Doukas 1945; Dormois 1999. See also Chapter 6.

# 3   The unifying German states compared to the United Kingdom

## The German economy and geo-politics in the early nineteenth century

An important benchmark for the analysis of industrialisation and the state is Germany, due to become the most industrially dynamic power in Continental Europe, but at the start of the nineteenth century struggling for an identity. In the 1820s it was weak internally and exposed externally. Partly as a result of being at the crossroads of European wars for centuries, it emerged from the Napoleonic period in 1815 still an untidy mixture of small and large states. There was a German political grouping, the German Confederation, established in 1815 to monitor the independence of each state and the internal and external security of Germany. It was however a loose powerless grouping and excluded the eastern part of the largest state, Prussia, and included only the Austrian part of the Austria-Hungarian empire (cf. Map 1.1 in Chapter 1). There was no common external tariff and internal trade was hampered by tolls, custom duties, guild restrictions in and across all the constituent elements. The Stein Reforms of 1806 had promised much and the peasantry had been emancipated but most historians agree that guilds and corporations were still a potent restriction for much of the period up to 1870. The key political groups were court elites with eastern Junkers and the Prussian King dominant forces, suspicious (like the Russian Tsar) of urbanisation and industrialisation associated as these were with democratisation.

Indicative of the obstacles to internal trade was the configuration in the Ruhr, destined to be the centre of German industrialisation. It was

> divided among several virtually independent states. Unna, Soest, Hagen, Witten, Wetter, Herdeke and Bochum were Prussian towns: Essen, Werden, Steele and Recklinghausen lay in ecclesiastical territories: Dortmund was an Imperial City which administered the adjacent rural district (the county of Dortmund), while Mülheim … was owned by a prince of the Hesse-Darmstadt line but was under the protection of the Duke of Berg (the Elector Palatine).[1]

This was the position at the end of the eighteenth century. Napoleonic reform changed matters such that many knightly estates and ecclesiastical domains throughout Germany disappeared but the German Confederation of 1815 still comprised 39 separate Sovereign States and Free Cities (Lübeck, Bremen, Frankfurt, Hamburg). Externally the German states faced one of the chief victors of 1815, Russia, which included large parts of Poland and was a seemingly strong, albeit autocratic state always ready for expansion. Fears of the Napoleonic heritage in France pervaded all Europe but especially the more conservative regimes and France was certainly more united than Germany. Finally there was Britain, now united with Ireland, and completely dominant at sea as well as economically and militarily very strong by any contemporary standards, as Table 3.1 shows.

The final dimension of Germany's geo-political position was its resource endowment. In its climate and agriculture it was much better placed than Russia. It had huge coal and timber reserves and reasonable quantities of iron ore and other minerals and metals. Access to the sea was poor but overall Germany's geo-political problems did not stem from resource endowments – they lay in Germany being at the centre of Europe's military and political conflicts on land and yet with a dysfunctional internal political and economic structure.

The other key starting point in our analysis, alongside geo-politics, is the state of the German economy in the early nineteenth century. It was economically backward relative to several other Western European states. It is the case that Germany had much skilled labour and was industrially very strong in cutlery, printing, silverware and printing.[2] Moreover the delay in shifting to coke smelting of iron partly reflected Germany's comparative advantage in timber and hence charcoal smelting. Coal did not overtake wood as the primary fuel input until the 1860s. Still, the realities were that pig iron output in 1825 was less than the French and only 20 per cent of the British. Textiles had flourished under the protection of the Continental System but by the 1820s were really exposed. Industry was dominated by the putting-out system and there was much hand spinning of linen, outwork and handicrafts in woollens.[3] Recent estimates of overall income levels put British 1820 GDP per head as 50 per cent higher than Germany (Tables 3.1 and 3.2) who also lagged behind the Netherlands, Austria, Belgium, USA and France. Even by 1850 Germany's position in the rankings had not changed – USA swapped positions with Austria. Few Germans wore cotton clothing and, as late as 1840, the level of activity in Germany in this the most advanced sector of capitalism, was little better than Russia, less than 20 per cent France and less than 5 per cent of Britain. Power spinning in linen and woollens, coke smelting, exports of cotton goods did not emerge until the 1840s at the earliest and most historians now see the main industrial acceleration as occurring in the 1850s. Pig iron output then started to shoot up and had overtaken the French by 1870.

The net result of its geo-political position and stage of economic development was, first, that its industrial and hence military strength was low. Its merchant fleet in 1829 was 265,000 tons, less than one-half of the French and less than one-eighth of the British (Table 3.1). True it was more likely to be engaged in land battles but even here if we focus on the one relatively integrated state,

*Table 3.1* Strategic dimensions of Germany and the UK 1820 and 1870 (contemporary boundaries)[a]

| | Germany | | UK | |
| --- | --- | --- | --- | --- |
| | *1820* | *1870* | *1820* | *1870* |
| A *Military and mercantile strength* | | | | |
| Military personnel ('000 persons) | 130[bc] | 430[d] | 140[b] | 248[de] |
| Merchant fleet ('000 net registered tons) | 265[f] | 939 | 2439 | 5691 |
| Warships ('000 tons) | n.a. | 88[c] | 500[e] | 650[de] |
| Defence spending (£ million)[j] | n.a. | 14.4[g] | n.a. | 22.8[e] |
| B *Resources* | | | | |
| Land area ('000 square miles) | 108[e] | 198 | 142 | 142 |
| Population (millions) | 15.1[c] | 39 | 21 | 31 |
| Coal output (million metric tons) | 1[h] | 32[h] | 18 | 112 |
| Iron ore output ('000 metric tons) | 175 | 2918 | n.a. | 14,602 |
| C *Communications* | | | | |
| Railway spread (track miles per 1000 square miles of area) | 0 | 59 | 0.3[i] | 149[i] |
| Telecommunications density (telegrams per 100 pop.) | n.a. | 22.1 | n.a. | 27.4 |
| D *Stages of development* | | | | |
| % Labour in agriculture[j] | 64.0 | 49.5 | 37.6 | 22.7 |
| Incomes[j] (GDP per head in 1990 $) | 1077 | 1839 | 1706 | 3190 |

Sources: Annex Tables; Wright 1942; Kennedy 1988 Tables 8, 20; Hobson 1993.

Notes
a See Annex Table A1.
b 1830.
c Prussia only.
d 1880.
e Britain only.
f 1829.
g 1872.
h Includes brown coal, lignite etc.
i Britain only. The 1870 entry relates to 1871.
j 2003 boundaries for UK. The 1820 entries for Germany relate to Prussia and for 1870 to the contemporary boundaries (i.e. excludes Alsace and Lorraine).

Prussia, military personnel in 1830 totalled 130,000 which was actually less than the British and American totals, about one-half of the French and less than 20 per cent of the Russian. Prussia and the other German states were in a very strategically weak position.

## Tariffs, the *Zollverein* and German public finances

It is this background which largely explains the role of the state in Germany and in particular the relationship between the state and firms in industry and communications. It was the Prussian state which pushed for the establishment of a new all-embracing German customs area, the *Zollverein*, and forged the way to the unification of all the states into an empire in 1870. Led autocratically by the King and the Junkers, it was foremost concerned with Prussia's strategic position. It was this which determined the relations between business and the state, not a commitment to free trade and laissez-faire or promoting economic growth or raising general living standards. The evidence suggests the underlying driving force was to strengthen Prussia, later Germany, industrially and hence militarily. As Tipton said: "Anything that did not contribute to the military power of the state would be given a low priority or rejected."[4]

There were other visions at the time and some historians have stressed a wider range of factors. The Prussian bureaucracy had taken on board some Smithian ideas about the virtues of free trade, seeing British competition as providing a requisite discipline for German industry. The bureaucracy promoted the

*Table 3.2* Income levels in 1820 and 1850 (gross domestic product per head in 1990 dollars, modern boundaries)[a]

|  | *1820* | *1850* |
|---|---|---|
| United Kingdom | 1756 | 2362 |
| Netherlands | 1561 | 1888 |
| Austria | 1295 | 1661 |
| Belgium | 1291 | 1808 |
| USA | 1287 | 1819 |
| France | 1218 | 1669 |
| Germany | 1112 | 1476 |
| Italy | 1092 | 1200[b] |
| Spain | 1063 | 1147 |
| Czechoslovakia | 849 | 1069 |
| Russia | 751 | 850[b] |
| Japan | 704 | 720[b] |
| Brazil | 670 | 711 |
| India | 531 | 547 |

Source: Maddison 1995.

Notes
a  Geary–Khamis 1990 dollars. 1989 boundaries.
b  My interpolation from 1820 and 1870 data.

concept of an all German customs union as an element in the reform of the German Confederation.[5] Frederich List, at a more philosophical level, espoused the importance of economic growth but in a semi-mercantalist fashion, deploring the exposure of German manufacturing by the low Prussian tariff of 1818. He appreciated the virtues of free trade but saw the first priority in Germany was to build a unified state.[6] Some historians have seen the Prussian government as providing an infrastructure and other social overheads within a framework of setting the "right atmosphere".[7] Henderson, more controversially, argued that "the functions of the paternalist state included an active part in fostering the agrarian and industrial expansion of the country"[8] but, as we shall see, there is little evidence of this outside the promotion of military strength and the agricultural economic interests of the Junker landlords. Nor can the Prussian state be easily portrayed as promoting, consciously or not, a take-off into self-sustained growth, a theme which dominated the literature in the 1950s and 1960s.[9]

The *Zollverein* emerged in 1834 as a free trade area of German states with a common external tariff. Prussia, Bavaria, Wurtemburg and Saxony were the dominant elements but altogether there were 18 states involving a total population of 23 million. Given the heavy inheritance of guilds, corporations, customs barriers and duties, there seems little doubt that the *Zollverein* aided trade flows and raised income levels. On the other hand, whatever the net effect on living standards, there are always gainers and losers from the creation of a new customs area and the way the *Zollverein* was set up tended to favour the Prussian state's main power group, the Junkers. In addition, by binding the smaller states more closely to Prussia, it increased that state's overall military and political strength. The customs arrangements were basically taken over from the Maassen tariff introduced in 1818 as a common external tariff for Prussia. This "Prussian system" involved fixed duties related to the weight of the goods and there were transit dues.[10] It was a low tariff by contemporary standards and these features carried over to the *Zollverein*'s external tariff with duties less than 10 per cent on manufactures whilst foodstuffs and raw materials entered free. Quantitative restrictions were abolished and the bulk of the revenue came from duties on luxuries like coffee, tea, beer, wine, spirits and tobacco. The *Zollverein* was welcomed by the eastern Junker grain producers because it eased their supplies to the western regions of Germany and lowered the chance of retaliation from countries to whom they exported.[11] This was clearly not an "infant industry" protection device; manufacturers in the south of Germany complained but were not politically strong. By the 1850s some stronger elements of protection were emerging as fixed tariffs rose in real terms relative to the technologically induced falling supply prices of foreign manufactures as well as some increases in the duties on cotton and iron. The customs area was expanded 1835–42 by the addition of Baden, Nassau, Oldenberg, Luxembourg, Frankfurt and some other small states. In 1852 Hanover and Brunswick joined. In 1866 Prussia itself absorbed a number of German states (including some like Mecklenberg and Schleswig-Holstein who had not been part of the *Zollverein*) whilst the establishment of the German empire in 1870 and the Franco-Prussian

War 1870–71 effectively added Alsace and Lorraine.[12] Whether the *Zollverein* was important in facilitating Germany's industrial and economic growth is not here our main concern and it should be noted that Britain's expanding role as importer of German goods and dominant exporter to the Continent complicates the calculations.[13]

The Prussian state did not benefit fiscally from the *Zollverein*. The abolition of internal custom duties and the low external tariff were reflected in the declining share of customs duties in central government revenues (Table 3.3) and a level distinctly lower than in the UK where they were accounting for over one-third of revenues by the mid nineteenth century. The overall spending commitment of the two countries is difficult to measure but it seems to have been a declining portion of national income falling to about 6 per cent by the 1860s.[14] Army and navy expenditures accounted for fairly stable 30–40 per cent of the totals in both countries. The big differences lay elsewhere, first, in the charges associated with servicing the national debt which, as we shall see later, were huge in the UK in 1820 as an inheritance of the Napoleonic wars. These charges did decline over time in both countries. Second, expenditure on administering the complex Prussian state appears to have been substantial with "public security", according to Schremmer, a large item in the rising total of civil expenditures.[15] The extensive activities of the Prussian state institutions are also manifest on the revenue side. Indirect taxes consisted mainly of general consumption taxes on beverages, tobacco, sugar plus stamp duty and milling and slaughter taxes falling largely on the urban population. In total they were rising but represented only one-fifth of all revenues for most of the period (Table 3.3). Taxation was felt most by the less affluent members of society even though direct taxes were a more important source of central government revenues than in the UK. The period witnessed a fairly vain struggle to develop business and income taxes as well as more efficient tax collection systems. Land and building taxes had a long history but the general liability of the landed aristocracy was not achieved until 1861 and former Princes not until 1891.[16] Where the state influence was especially marked was in its own "productive income", that is from state enterprises in smelting, salt refineries, coal, iron and steel, public lands, forests, post and telegraph, trading and of course the railways. As a revenue source, this had great attraction since these "taxes" did not have to be voted in the normal way. By the 1860s the gross revenues from state enterprises were nearly one-half of all Prussian state revenues[17] though the actual profit inflow is not so clear. In Table 3.3, I have shown the enterprise revenues net of enterprise "administration" costs. They constituted a large part of all revenues but it is doubtful that the interest payments and related capital charges on state enterprise borrowing have been deducted. Even so, if as much as one-half of the debt service charges recorded in Table 3.3 is debited to state enterprises, the net revenues would still average about 20 per cent of total revenues. But was the state simply interested in these profits? We need to examine the role of the state in industrial regulation and ownership.

*Table 3.3* Budgeted revenues and expenditures of the Prussian central government 1821–67 (million thalers)

|  | 1821 | 1847 | 1857 | 1867 |
|---|---|---|---|---|
| *Revenues* | | | | |
| Customs | 19.1[a] | 13.8 | 12.3 | 11.2 |
| Indirect taxes | n.a.[a] | 14.5 | 16.4 | 24.1 |
| Direct taxes[b] | 17.3[c] | 20.3 | 24.7 | 32.7 |
| State enterprises (net)[d] | 11.8 | 13.4 | 19.3 | 42.8 |
| Other | 1.8[c] | 6.8 | 13.8 | 16.3 |
| Total | 50.0[e] | 68.8 | 86.5 | 127.1 |
| *Expenditures* | | | | |
| Defence | 22.8 | 25.7 | 29.5 | 43.4 |
| Debt service[f] | 11.3 | 9.3 | 13.2 | 16.3 |
| Civil[g] | 15.9 | 33.8 | 43.8 | 67.4 |
| Total | 50.0[e] | 68.8 | 86.5 | 127.1 |
| Expenditure as % national income | 8.6[h] | 6.2[h] | n.a. | 6.7[h] |

Source: Schremmer 1989, Tables 68, 78, 79 and p. 436.

Notes
a  Indirect taxes included with customs duties.
b  Taxes on land, buildings, business, graduated income taxes.
c  Net budget values.
d  Entrepreneurial revenues net of expenditures on administration of the enterprises. Covers railways, smelters, salt refineries, public land and forests, *Seehandlung*. Capital charges, such as interest payments on loans, may not have been included.
e  Approximation, according to the source.
f  May include interest charges attributable to state enterprise borrowing.
g  Covers central administration, jurisdiction, administration of the economy and transport, culture and education, fiscal administration, pensions.
h  These are gross actual expenditures as a per cent of national income for 1822, 1850 and 1867.

## The state, industrialisation and communications in Germany

If coal, iron and railways had been left to private enterprise, it would be a good indication of a commitment to free trade, even, given some provision of infrastructure, consistent with the idea of the state limiting itself to social overheads and providing the "right atmosphere". Capital shortages were not a problem even though the Preussche Bank established in 1841 was a conservative institution limited to providing loans for landlords and issuing currency. Investment banking flourished outside Prussian boundaries. It was not shortage of capital that was the problem but rather the demand for it.[18] The state also did little for the textile industry apart from encouraging an inflow of British technical specialists. Rather, the main thrust of the Prussian state was directed to sectors which strengthened the country militarily – armaments, coal, iron, railways, steamships and telegraph. In this sense Hentschel is wrong to say that "[c]oncious industrialisation policy on the part of the state did not exist in Germany … except for … participation in the construction of various railways".[19]

Early interest in coal in the eighteenth century stemmed from Princely royalties but the industrial and military dimensions grew such that by 1850 Prussian state owned mines accounted for 20 per cent of Germany's coal output.[20] It is significant that the state's most direct interventions were in two strategically important border areas. One was Silesia, next to the Hapsburg Empire, acquired in 1741, which saw heavy state involvement in coal, iron ore, lead and zinc. The other area was the Saar, adjacent to France, and acquired after the congress of Vienna settlement of 1815. The state built the Saarbrucken and other rail lines and was the dominant mineowner. Although the Ruhr valley was less geographically exposed and its industry left to develop under private enterprise, sectors like coal mining were run as concession systems with strong supervision from the officials of the Prussian state. Much the most wide-ranging state owned enterprise was *Seehandlung* (Overseas Trading Corporation).[21] Based initially in 1772 on capital from the King, it raised loans, financed road building and factories, exercised the state timber monopoly, engaged in market assessments for Prussian exporters, established model factories and state owned warehouses in Stettin, Hamburg and New York. It had paper, chemical and related manufacturing activities in Bromberg, Hohenofen, Oranienburg and Berlin, engineering works in Dirschau, flour mills in Potsdam, Bromberg, Beutlin and Ohla and textile factories throughout Silesia.[22]

Whilst debate on the unfairness of competition from state owned enterprises was not absent and whilst some have argued that the need for state intervention had declined by the 1850s, many historians agree that the big industrial spurt in the 1850s was helped by current and past aid to railways, telegraph and armaments.[23] This brings us to the attitude of government in Germany to a final important sector of economy, the communications and other network utilities, specifically gas, water, telegraph and railways. Here there are two broad issues. The first is state action on potential market failure in the networks and the second is the extent and causes of direct interventions in these sectors in terms of municipal and state enterprises. The German states and municipalities dealt with the natural monopoly dimensions of network utilities in a manner which was common throughout Western Europe – by arms' length regulation. The technological and economic limits on long distance transmission in gas and water supply in the nineteenth century meant they were essentially local, often town based, networks and had little strategic significance for the state governments. Companies planning to lay gas and water mains needed rights of way and this invariably prompted arbitration by the municipal or state governments. In all countries there was legislation on prices and profit levels applicable both to private and public enterprises. The state also took a view about the configuration of networks – balancing the extra costs of duplicate lines and tracks against the benefits of competition. In the early nineteenth century many towns in the UK, like Birmingham, had more than one gas company. In London private joint stock companies were granted rights to supply water in overlapping areas in the belief that competition was the way to meet the public interest. This was heavily criticised by the famous public health reformer Edwin Chadwick who thought it raised costs, lowered profits and quality of service.[24] All of this "competition in the field" generally gave way in most countries during the nineteenth century to a closer control over the configuration of networks and avoidance of duplication.

What was the relationship between the municipalities and the companies supplying gas and water? The early development of the European gas industry was led by British companies. It started in the late eighteenth century and proliferated both in the form of public lighting and in its use in factories. The Gas, Light and Coke Company initiated public lighting in London in 1814. By 1851 there were 129 (statutory, i.e. Parliament approved) gas undertakings in England and Wales of which 13 were municipally owned. The next 20 years then witnessed a growth rate of supplies which was never subsequently bettered – the number of statutory undertakings in England and Wales doubled and the number of municipal enterprises quadrupled to 56.[25] Public lighting by gas started in Berlin in 1826 where British equipment, engineers and coal were key inputs via English companies like the Imperial Continental Gas Association.[26] Municipal ownership of gas works in Germany started in the 1860s and reached 50 per cent by 1880.[27] The motives and behaviour of the municipal governments become clearer on examination of data on their location and performance but since that data set is fuller for the late nineteenth century we will delay consideration of that issue until Chapter 5. One important point may however be made at this stage. Much has been made by some writers about the socialising activities of German cities and gas and water socialism in Britain and specifically about municipal socialism as a driving force behind the municipalisation of local network utilities.[28] It is clear however that the main currents of this philosophy and of political activity were features of the late nineteenth/early twentieth centuries and cannot therefore account for the initial surge in municipal ownership of gas and water which, as we have seen, dates from the mid nineteenth century.[29]

The *regional and national network utilities* were much more important economically and strategically than municipal networks. In the 1820–50 period the private sector took a strong lead but was regulated by the states, some of whom took to owning trunk railways and telegraph lines, a pattern that grew significantly over time. In some states like Prussia, the private companies held a "regalia", a royal privilege that could be withdrawn at will and which allowed the state governments to draw profits or run the systems themselves. In fact for railways before 1850, the Prussian government limited itself largely to setting the conditions for controlling monopoly power. The state governments could not avoid some interventions, if only to approve rights of way but that meant the governments had been party to the establishment of monopoly conditions, prompting further regulation.[30] The 1838 Prussian Railway Law set levels for passenger fares and freight rates and established a right of the governments to 25–50 per cent of any profits over stated thresholds. One other instrument for controlling profits was the allowance of competition between companies using the same track but this opportunity was apparently not taken up. On the other hand whereas the Law forbade parallel routes, the state chose not to enforce that restriction on competition, at least initially and Fremdling has argued that such liberal elements in the Law allowed Prussian railways to grow more rapidly than the French in the 1840s.[31]

This pattern of regulation was repeated in France, Britain and other Western European countries. But the degree of direct state intervention via state ownership was much higher in Germany – and especially in comparison to Britain – and this reflected the view of some German state governments, Prussia especially, that railways were a security risk which had to be planned and controlled as a tool of military strategy. This was also true of the electric telegraph but in this case Prussia was no different from all the other European countries. In 1849 the Prussian state set up the first electric telegraph line in Germany though there were, shortly afterwards, some private commercial lines elsewhere, along the Taunus and Saxony rivers and indeed in Silesia. Eventually however post and telegraph merged in 1875 in the *Reichpost*. State operation of railways in Prussia was initially weak. In part this was because the National Debt Law of 1820 forbade any borrowing by the state in excess of 18 million thalers without Parliamentary approval.[32] Any state funding would require the approval of the Diet, and the King feared that would be the occasion for a call for electoral reform. So the 1840s saw private enterprise flourishing in Prussia, albeit from 1842 with some government share holdings and guarantees of interest. There was a massive rise in railway construction such that whilst the track length was the same as in France in 1840, it had reached 5856 kilometres by 1850, double the French figure (Table 3.4).

Other states did witness strong intervention. The Bavarian and Wurtemburg governments used trunk railway development to quickly resolve their strategic worries, as did Hanover later. From the 1850s in Prussia the possibilities for

*Table 3.4* Length of railway track 1820–70 (kilometres, contemporary boundaries)[a]

|       | *France*  | *Germany* | *Japan* | *Russia* | *UK[b]*    | *USA[c]* |
|-------|-----------|-----------|---------|----------|------------|----------|
| 1820  | 17[d]     | 0         | 0       | 0        | 43[e]      | n.a.     |
| 1830  | 31        | 6[f]      | 0       | 27[g]    | 157        | 37       |
| 1840  | 410       | 469       | 0       | 144[h]   | 2390       | 4535     |
| 1850  | 2915      | 5856      | 0       | 501      | 9797       | 14,518   |
| 1860  | 9167      | 11,089    | 0       | 1626     | 14,603     | 49,288   |
| 1870  | 15,544[i] | 18,876[i] | 29[j]   | 10,731   | 21,558[k]  | 85,170   |

Notes
a See Annex Table A1.
b Britain only, i.e. excludes all Ireland.
c Length of railways operated, which may involve some double counting.
d 1827.
e 1825.
f 1835.
g 1838.
h 1845.
i Alsace-Lorraine included with Germany.
j 1872.
k 1871.

transporting grains and the strategic needs persuaded the King and Junkers towards a stronger commitment to state railways, including a flow of railway profits to the Treasury "symbolic of the Crown's independence of constitutional fiscal control".[33] Prussia's first publicly owned line was that between Saarbrucken and Neunkirchen in the Saar coalfield (cf. above). By 1870 state railways ran from Berlin to Hamburg, Stettin, Danzig, Breslau, Halle whilst in the west there were state lines connecting the Saar with Luxemburg, Cologne and through the Ruhr to Osnabut and Minden.[34] The logic of the state presence was finalised in Prussia by the decision in 1879 to take all the railways into public ownership.

## The geo-political position of the United Kingdom in the early nineteenth century

Turning now to the United Kingdom, a vivid contrast with Prussia emerges in the much smaller pressure on the British state to intervene as a consequence of its geo-political position and stage of economic development. It was well endowed with the nineteenth century's main energy source, coal. UK output by 1820 was already 18 million tons, more than the aggregate of the rest of the major powers. Data on iron ore are limited but output in 1855 was 9.7 million tons – probably, again, more than the rest of the major powers and certainly so by 1870 when UK output was 14.6 million tons (Table 3.1). Britain is an island economy and, from the early nineteenth century united with Ireland. It had no contiguous hostile nation states. Its main enemies were "overseas", and growing, as the empire during the nineteenth century stretched out across Asia, Africa and the Americas. Security and defence would be clearly linked to naval power. That and most other dimensions of military strength would depend on the state of the economy which by 1820 was the most advanced. The significance of the economy lay not mainly in Britain having the highest income levels; rather it was the structural changes that had already taken place and the degree of industrialisation. The latter was closely linked to urbanisation and by 1800 in England and Wales some 30 per cent of the population was living in towns with 5000 persons or more – France 12.5 per cent, Germany 9.7 per cent, European Russia 4.6 per cent.[35] As early as 1820 more than 60 per cent of the male labour force was working outside agriculture – in manufacturing, construction, infrastructure industries, the commercial sector and public services. Even by 1870 no other country had significantly more than 50 per cent. Britain's manufacturing strength was reflected in its complete dominance of the cotton industry even though the key raw material was imported. Pig iron output at 374,000 tons in 1820 was more than France, Germany and Russia combined.

These three factors – political geography, resource endowment, stage of development – meant Britain was a very powerful military nation. In 1815 Britain had 214 ships of the line (front line warships), France 80, Russia 40, Spain 25. The merchant fleet, at 2.5 million tons in 1820, exceeded the combined tonnage of the other major powers and its military personnel, as noted earlier, was greater than that of Prussia even though a land warfare capability was nowhere near as important as for France, Russia, Prussia and the Austria-Hungarian Empire. We know that, by the end of the 1850s, the admiralty was ordering anything from 20,000 to 50,000 tons of warships per annum (about half of which came from the Royal Naval Dockyards) and 10,000 to 30,000 horse-power of ship engines.[36] Data for 1870 show its warship tonnage at 650,000 exceeding France plus Germany and by 1910 plus Russia. Thus Britain had enough industrial strength to feel secure enough to leave the development of coal, iron and railways to the private sector.[37] There was no reason to think the public sector could do any better or that the private sector could not expand fast enough to meet the country's strategic needs. In the case of warships, for example, the Admiralty in crises like the Crimean war, was able to arrange for the private dockyards in Glasgow and elsewhere to switch work from merchant vessels and treble or quadruple naval vessels, supplementing whatever small increases were possible in the Royal yards.

The British government did not intervene much in the nineteenth century because it had no need to do so apart from posts and armaments. Ireland, a strategic worry, was the exception that proved the rule and here the Public Works Loans Board promoted "economic progress", improving roads, harbours and piers, built colleges, established fish curing stations with loans for land drainage and fencing and to railway companies.[38] For Britain however even arms' length regulation was frowned on by some: "A very extraordinary interference with property" was how the Member of Parliament Edward Baines described it (for railways). Lobbyists to Parliament argued "that nothing which British governments had ever done or left undone made it likely that they would prove good managers; that centralisation was un-English".[39] Yet it is not necessary to invoke a pervasive attachment to laissez-faire to explain why British governments did not intervene more in the economy in this period but did intervene in the twentieth century. The geo-political factors and industrial strength are the key elements in the period 1820–70 distinguishing Britain from continental powers like Prussia and this becomes clear when we examine more fully tariff policy, the public finances and the business/state interface in industry.

## British manufacturing, free trade and the public finances

The major growth sectors of the British economy were manufacturing and transport. From the late eighteenth century, agriculture's share of output and capital formation started a long term decline to the 1920s when it settled to a very small share of Britain's economic activity. Agriculture's share of tradable goods and services was offset, in part by mining and commerce but especially by manufacturing and construction. Its share of total goods and services was also taken up in part by growth in the non-tradable services of infrastructure industries like telecoms, electricity and railways. Figure 3.1 shows how gross fixed capital formation 1820–70 grew fastest in transport, communications, manufacturing and construction. Now in that period public investment was not only small but was dominated by local government. In 1856, for example, out of a total UK investment of £55.8 million, public investment was only £3.5 million of which central government accounted for only £0.5 million (posts, armaments, naval dockyards etc.). It stayed at that level over the next 20 years. Investment by local government was £3 million and trebled to £9 million by 1873. This was education, gas supply but especially water supply, roads and sanitation since, in this era of rapidly growing and disease ridden urban areas, public health was largely left to local government. It was therefore in the remaining private sector of the economy – manufacturing, construction, railways, mining, commerce, agriculture – that most of the investment was undertaken: £52.3 million in 1856 accounting for 93.7 per cent of the total, rising to £115.7 by 1873 and 92.4 per cent of the total.[40]

Much of the economy then was in private ownership and, by the 1860s, tariffs were virtually non-existent on key manufactured goods. Was this due to a firm commitment to free trade and laissez-faire? Many have thought so, and several interest groups in the early nineteenth century certainly took this as their cue, but

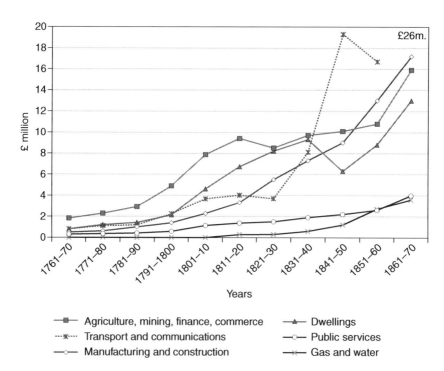

*Figure 3.1* Investment by sector in Britain 1760–1870 (annual average gross domestic fixed capital formation in £ million at current prices) (source: Feinstein and Pollard 1988).

Note
Includes all Ireland 1851–70.

the issue is not straightforward. Indeed O'Brien has argued that the idea that Victorian economic policy, especially with respect to public finances and tariffs, stemmed from an unqualified espousal of "liberalism" is "selective, misplaced and myopic".[41] What one might call the core customs revenue raisers were the tariffs on "luxuries" like coffee, tea, tobacco, sugar: they continued to carry duties and formed a large share of customs revenues throughout the nineteenth century. Raw materials were another important group early on: raw cotton, timber, iron ore and some carried quota restrictions with favoured clauses for imperial links (Canadian timber). These and other devices like the Navigation Acts restricting the use of foreign ships for British goods were generally abandoned during the century. Then there were the clearly protective duties, inherited from the "mercantilist" policies of the eighteenth century, in the form of tariffs on imported linen, Indian cottons, Swedish iron (as well as some which remained throughout like the duties on industrial glass and silk yarn and cloth). Finally of course we have the Corn Laws, entrenched after 1815 when grain prices were falling. By the early 1840s the duty was of the order of 18 shillings per quarter accounting for roughly one-third of the import price. The period 1820–70, and especially from the early 1840s, saw the disappearance or significant reduction in the protective duties. Many at the time like Cobden invoked the moral case for free trade but other pressures and motives seem likely to have been more decisive. By extending her foreign trade, Joseph Hume declared, England could make all the world depend on her.[42]

The removal of the tariffs on imported manufactures was indeed no great sacrifice because Britain by the early nineteenth century was so dominant in this sector. The real cost of exported goods was falling rapidly with technological innovations and the volume of British exports was growing at 4.4 per cent per annum 1821–73.[43] Textiles accounted for three-quarters of the total in the early nineteenth century, about 40 per cent later on. A total of 80 per cent of British cotton cloth was exported by the mid nineteenth century, a half of iron and steel and one-third coal. By the end of our period Britain accounted for nearly 40 per cent of world manufacturing exports and was flooding all markets across Europe with coal.[44] The danger from competing imported manufactures was minimal. In fact the idea that British manufactures were protected in the early nineteenth century is itself misplaced in that duties on imported iron and raw cotton, for example, meant the effective protection of cotton cloth and pig iron was probably negligible. Some idea of Britain's dominance of these markets is that the government did not even bother to exploit the strong monopsonistic power arising from its large purchases of raw materials like raw cotton. The "optimal tariff" in such a situation would raise sufficient tariff revenues to offset any losses to British buyers.[45]

There is also some doubt whether the repeal of the Corn Laws in 1846 was such a momentous economic event. Certainly it reduced the cost of living of the growing body of British industrial workers. But many historians now see the repeal as being significant in reducing chiefly the rent accruing to landlords and hence being, at the time, more a symbol of the reduction in power of the landlord/aristocratic class. To give some idea of the economic impact consider O'Grada's example.[46] By 1888–92 British agriculture was producing about 7.4 million quarters (of eight bushels) of wheat per annum. The tariff in the early 1840s before repeal was 18s per quarter, as noted earlier, and would therefore have raised the import price (and prices for British grown wheat) by that amount. Hence the loss to landlords in 1888–92 would have been $7.4 \times 18 = 133$ million shillings per annum or 177 shillings if we allow for the higher British output which would have been prompted by the tariff. Either way this was less than £7 million which was itself less than 1 per cent of national income in 1890 (5 per cent of agricultural income). The overall net economic gain, as conventionally calculated, was even less. Gains to existing consumers of wheat would have been offset by the loss of landlord rental income and government tariff revenues (and hence benefits via public spending). We are then left with new consumers benefiting from the fall in the price of wheat, and industries elsewhere gaining from the fall in the supply price of those resources released from British agriculture. This is likely to be much less even than the landlords' loss.[47] Hence the significance of the Corn Law Repeal was in the redistribution of income rather than in the overall gain in national income.

The other side of the coin is the public finances where the classic Gladstone fiscal constitution was to minimise spending and levy "acceptable" taxes. Certainly central government expenditure and taxes accounted for a declining share of national income 1820–70 (Figure 3.2). Can this be portrayed as a commitment to laissez-faire? After the Napoleonic Wars in 1815, Britain had a huge national debt – £834 million.[48] Also about to enter the scene were the housing, disease and congestion problems of rapid industrialisation and urbanisation – sufficient to actually reduce even average life expectancy in the middle of the century.[49] The central state turned its back on both these issues. On the one hand it rejected Ricardo's suggestion of a once and for all levy on wealth but instead made national debt interest an annual charge on taxes. Table 3.5 shows national debt charges were some £25–30 million per annum for much of our period 1820–70. Their share of total central government spending declined from over 50 per cent in the early nineteenth century to below 40 per cent by 1870 but the balance was taken up by rising army and navy expenditure. Nor were property and income taxes significant sources of government revenues apart from some short periodic appearances of income tax. Instead customs and excise were the main (regressive) revenue raisers with customs a rising share and excise falling. The implications were that the burden of coping with urbanisation – public health, child labour, sanitation, education – was left to the local government sector. The data for the early nineteenth century are deficient and what we see in Table 3.6 probably underestimates spending at the local level, especially by municipal boroughs.[50] By 1872 when the sources are good, local taxes (rates on property) were £43.1 million – equivalent to nearly three-quarters of the amount which the central government was raising in taxes.

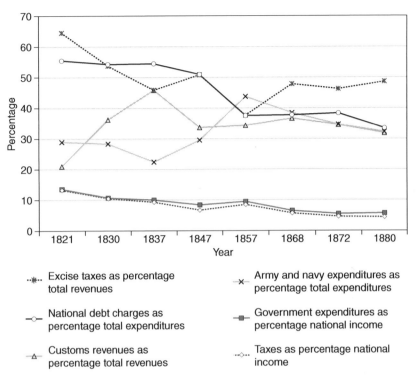

..*.. Excise taxes as percentage total revenues

--o-- National debt charges as percentage total expenditures

--△-- Customs revenues as percentage total revenues

--x-- Army and navy expenditures as percentage total expenditures

--■-- Government expenditures as percentage national income

..◇.. Taxes as percentage national income

*Figure 3.2* UK central government expenditures, taxes and national income 1821–80 (%) (source: Mitchell 1988).

Note
Excludes all capital items. See tables for details.

## British railways and the imperial telegraph

Turning now finally to the national network utilities, was policy for these sectors largely a product of a committed laissez-faire ideology or was that more a matter of *ex post* rationalisation? There were monopolistic elements in all services and potentially important strategic dimensions in the international telegraph, overland and submarine. In the event the railway companies were regulated at arms' length, the domestic telegraph nationalised at the very end of the period and the international telegraph firms, for the time being, left largely to their own devices. The factors involved tell us quite a lot about the motives of governments and about the policy instruments available. The granting of rights of way for railways in Britain was not without considerable local opposition. By effectively granting one company a monopoly status over a given route, it did lead to the threefold control system common in Western Europe. First, efforts were made to ensure several companies bid for provision of railway services on any given route ("competition for the field"). Also the companies bidding for access and permission to lay track were scrutinised

*Table 3.5* UK government spending[a] 1821–80 (£ million)

|  | 1821 | 1830 | 1837 | 1847 | 1857 | 1868 | 1872 | 1880 |
|---|---|---|---|---|---|---|---|---|
| **1  *Central government*** | | | | | | | | |
| National debt charges | 32.0 | 29.1 | 29.4 | 28.3 | 28.8 | 26.6 | 26.8 | 26.1 |
| Army | 10.1 | 9.3 | 7.9 | 9.1 | 20.8 | 15.9 | 14.7 | 15.0 |
| Navy | 6.6 | 5.9 | 4.2 | 7.3 | 12.7 | 11.2 | 9.5 | 10.2 |
| Civil[b] | 9.7 | 9.4 | 4.7 | 10.9 | 13.8 | 16.9 | 18.5 | 24.9 |
| Total | 57.8 | 53.7 | 54.0 | 55.6 | 76.7 | 70.6 | 69.9 | 78.2 |
| **2  *Local government*** | | | | | | | | |
| England and Wales poor relief | 7.0 | 6.8 | 4.0 | 5.3 | 5.9 | 7.5 | 8.0 | 8.0 |
| County expenditure[c] | 0.6 | 0.7 | 0.7 | 0.8 | 1.7 | 2.3 | – | – |
| ***Total Local Authority expenditure*** | | | | | | | | |
| England and Wales | – | – | – | – | – | 30.2 | 31.2 | 30.2 |
| Scotland | – | – | – | – | – | n.a. | n.a. | 8.0[d] |
| Ireland | – | – | – | – | – | 3.1 | n.a. | 3.8 |

Source: Mitchell 1988, pp. 581–638, 822, 831–2.

Notes
a  Excludes capital expenditure but includes interest on national and local authority debt.
b  Includes costs of tax collection.
c  Gaols, bridges, constables, vagrants, prosecution, lunacy, debt charges.
d  1893, including capital expenditure out of loans.

by Parliamentary committees, especially since they were given limited liability status and came to constitute a huge expansion of equity finance and capital formation – as Figure 3.1 shows. There were accounts of Members of Parliament taking bribes and that the whole messy business added greatly to construction costs.[51]

Second, one of the devices for controlling profits initially was to allow competition between different companies on the same track. A Parliamentary Select Committee of 1839 advised against it on safety grounds and such "competition in the field" was ruled out by the 1840 Railway Act.[52] Nor in Britain was there any significant attempt to control the rate of return on capital. Rather the emphasis in the 1840 and 1844 Acts was on ceilings for fares and freight rates in line with long-standing practice for canals. The big difference was that canal tolls were a charge simply for access to the track; there were no controls on the charges for conveyance since competition by canal barges "in the field" was allowed. Railway prices were controlled by Parliament for both conveyance and use of the track with eventually a system of price categories linked to the value of the traffic. This became a problem, as we shall see in a later chapter, when railways faced competition from steamships and road transport.

A third element of the regulatory system related to the configuration of routes. Direct competition between closely parallel routes was not encouraged but different routes between two towns (London to Manchester via Stafford or Leicester) were promoted. Indeed there was no real central planning of the rail network as in France and Germany and here one might argue that laissez-faire principles did have their

Table 3.6 UK government revenues[a] 1821–80 (£ million)

| | 1821 | 1830 | 1837 | 1847 | 1857 | 1868 | 1872 | 1880 |
|---|---|---|---|---|---|---|---|---|
| *1 Central government* | | | | | | | | |
| Customs | 11.9 | 19.2 | 23.1 | 15.0 | 23.5 | 22.7 | 20.3 | 19.3 |
| Excise[b] | 36.5 | 28.4 | 23.1 | 22.7 | 25.7 | 29.7 | 27.2[c] | 29.5[c] |
| Land and assessed taxes[c] | 7.3 | 5.1 | 3.9 | 4.5 | 3.1 | 3.5 | 2.3[c] | 2.7[c] |
| Property/income tax | – | – | – | 3.5 | 16.1 | 6.2 | 9.1 | 9.2 |
| Total | 56.6 | 52.9 | 50.4 | 44.7 | 68.4 | 62.1 | 58.9 | 60.7 |
| National income[d] | 426[e] | 501 | 540 | 662 | 805 | 1079 | 1272 | 1379 |
| Central government revenues as % national income | 13.3 | 10.5 | 9.3 | 6.7 | 8.5 | 5.7 | 4.6 | 4.4 |
| *2 Local government* | | | | | | | | |
| England and Wales poor rates | 8.4 | 8.1 | 5.3 | 7.0 | 8.1 | 10.4 | 11.4 | 12.0 |
| County/police rates | 0.7 | 0.7 | 0.6 | 0.9 | 1.2 | 1.5 | – | – |
| General rates | – | – | – | – | – | 16.5 | 31.7 | 53.0 |
| Scotland rates | – | – | – | – | – | n.a. | n.a. | 2.6 |
| Ireland rates | – | – | – | – | – | 2.3 | n.a. | 2.7 |

Source: Mitchell 1988, pp. 581–638, 822, 831–832.

Notes

a Excludes loans, Treasury grants to local authorities, central government grants to Ireland, receipts of water and gas undertakings.

b Includes stamp duty.

c Land and assessed taxes include land tax and inhabited house duty. Also taxes on servants and carriages but these are included with excise after 1871.

d Gross domestic product at market prices.

e Estimate formed by scaling up Mitchell's figure for Great Britain of gross national product at factor cost of £291 million by the ratio for 1831 between UK gross domestic product at market prices and Great Britain gross national product at factor cost.

way, with probably extra cost to the British system.[53] A large number of entry points to London emerged served by the different companies whilst Manchester had no through route between north and south of the town. However the relatively liberal granting of charters certainly facilitated rapid growth of the track. The trunk network was almost complete by 1850 at which point 9797 kilometres had been built, more than the rest of the Continental powers put together (Table 3.4).

The railway system created no strategic worries for the British state. In times of war perhaps there was concern about congestion on the traffic to the ports (cf. Chapter 8) but nothing like the concerns of the Prussian state. The same cannot be said about the domestic telegraph. Rights of way were granted alongside railway track and nearby roadways so that competition both for and in the field was initially not forbidden. The telegraph indeed saw much unregulated tariff competition. At the very beginning of the electric telegraph in the 1840s the market was served only by the Electric and International Telegraph Company. Competition for routes grew from businesses like the UK Telegraph Company but several market sharing agreements emerged. In the period 1851–68 the number of stations owned by the Electric rose from 257 to 1249 but its market share fell below 60 per cent and revenue per message to one-fifth of the 1851 level. The British press, a big user of the telegraph, were forever complaining about services and the industry was nationalised in 1868. The precise reasons have never been satisfactorily resolved in the historical literature. Most European rulers felt the electric telegraph was not secure and, for Britain, Ireland was a continuing worry. It is significant that the new publicly owned undertaking was not a joint stock company with government shares, not even a state enterprise with its own Act of Parliament like those in the early twentieth century. Rather it was absorbed into a government department as part of the Post Office.[54]

Turning finally to the international telegraph, it transpires that the potentially significant strategic and monopoly dimensions did not trigger much state intervention in the nineteenth century – for reasons that had little to do with laissez-faire ideology. The telegraph was a major new form of communication not unlike the internet in our day. It greatly eased diplomatic links, was especially suitable for commercial transactions (important for Britain's City and Empire) and proved eventually useful for the army in times of war. Overland cables required rights of way and were not therefore very secure, despite the deliberations of the International Telegraph Convention in Paris where governments agreed to ensure the non-interruption of international traffic.[55] The first overland cables were laid in the 1840s but the submarine cables took a long time to emerge until a good sea resistant insulator became available in the form of gutta-percha in 1851. Britain dominated the early cable market. The Atlantic (later Anglo-American) Telegraph Company commenced services across the Atlantic to USA in 1865/66 at roughly the same time as an overland route to India was completed by the Indo-European Telegraph Department (a British company). In 1868 the British owned Eastern Telegraph Company developed a submarine route to India (and hence to the Far East). Indeed the Eastern came to dominate the international cable market and British companies had the field to themselves in these early years.[56] Thus here we have a service which was both strategically important and containing significant monopoly elements. The latter stemmed in part from the natural monopoly conditions in this sector – huge sunken investment in charting a route, employing ships, winches, reels and cables and providing shipping capacity for rescue, repair and maintenance.[57] But the monopoly position stemmed also from, first, the fact that Britain's extensive empire gave it many landing rights in, eventually, Malta, Alexandria, Aden, Karachi, Ireland, Newfoundland, Cape Town, Durban, etc. Also, for much of the nineteenth century, Britain alone with its massive coal, shipping, iron industry and technology was capable of developing these communications networks. Despite then these monopoly conditions and the strategic dimensions, all the British government did was to set up in 1862 a Joint Committee on Submarine Cables with representatives from the Atlantic Telegraph Company and the Board of Trade. It also supported British companies by providing marine surveys and sometimes guaranteeing rates of return on invested capital. The answer to the puzzle is that because the Continental Powers were entirely dependent on Britain for international submarine cables, Britain faced few security worries. Matters changed in the early twentieth century when these other countries developed their own capacity, and so did the British government's scale of intervention (cf. later chapters). For the moment informal links between the government and British companies were enough.

## Notes

1  Henderson 1958, p. 23.
2  Borchardt 1973, 1991.
3  Clapham 1964.
4  Tipton 2003, p. 115.
5  Fischer 1960, p. 68.
6  Cf. also Bairoch 1989, pp. 15, 16, 30.
7  Milward and Saul 1973.
8  Henderson 1958, p. xix.
9  Fischer 1963; Hoffman 1963; Crouzet 1972.
10  Fischer 1960.
11  Borchardt 1991, ch. 1.
12  Marriott and Robertson 1946; Fischer 1960.
13  Borchardt 1973.
14  Cf. below and Hentschel 1989, p. 757.
15  Schremmer 1989, p. 435.
16  Hentschel 1989, p. 761; Schremmer 1989, p. 419.
17  Schremmer 1989, p. 455.
18  Wellhöner and Wixforth 2003; Borchadt 1991, ch. 2.
19  Hentschel 1989, p. 770.
20  Henderson 1958, 1961; Borchadt 1973, p. 151.
21  Henderson 1958, p. 119.
22  Henderson 1975.
23  Fischer 1963; Trebilcock 1981.
24  Select Committee Report 1821; Chadwick 1859; Matthews 1985; Millward 2005, pp. 41–54 and 2007 for detailed discussion of water supply and public health.
25  Millward and Ward 1993.
26  Dawson 1916.

27  Schott 2005.

28  Howe 1913; cf. Hughes 1983.

29  One final point about the German municipalities. They were relatively free of control from the state central governments whether they be Prussia, Bavaria, Wurtemberg apart from some supervision of loan issues and monitoring of debt/income relationships. Indeed the municipalities were very active in independently supporting local businesses. Conscious of the latter's need for finance, municipalities in several regions, from the eighteenth century onwards, guaranteed the capital of local savings banks to encourage and channel savings by the *petit bourgeois* traders and workers. Set up initially to reduce pressure on poor relief funds, they transformed themselves in the late nineteenth century into universal banks such that deposits reached 21 billion marks by 1913 – practically the same as the total for all private German credit banks. See Schott 2005; Wengenroth 2000, p. 109.

30  Bongaerts 1985.

31  Fremdling 1979.

32  Tilly 1966; Henderson 1975, p. 49; Bongaerts 1985.

33  Tilly 1966, p. 493; Goldscheid 1966.

34  Cf. railway map in Henderson 1975.

35  Malanima 2010.

36  Peebles 1987, pp. 168–9.

37  Cf. Bairoch 1989, p. 7.

38  Henderson 1958, p. xv.

39  Clapham 1964, pp. 306, 414, 422.

40  Feinstein and Pollard 1988, appendix tables II and IX.

41  O'Brien 1997, p. 5.

42  Bairoch 1989, pp. 12, 26.

43  Harley and McCloskey 1981.

44  Fremdling 1996.

45  Britain was such a large purchaser of some goods that any increase in its demand would raise world prices. The world supply curve of the imported good was effectively Britain's average cost curve such that increased British purchases would raise the purchase price to Britain. An optimal tariff would be such that Britain's marginal outlays (including the tariff) would just equal the marginal revenues from using these inputs. The resulting tariff revenues would be greater than the decline in consumer plus producer surplus.

46  O'Grada 1994, pp. 168–71.

47  All these statements assume £1 of benefit/loss is the same to whomsoever it accrues. The net gain, in a standard partial equilibrium framework, is in two parts. First is the increase in total British wheat consumption whose average value would be half the fall in the wheat price. A second component is the fall in the output of British wheat producers, valued at half the fall in the wheat price (cf. O'Grada's diagram 1994, p. 171).

48  Daunton 2001, p. 41 and ch. 3.

49  Szreter and Mooney 1998.

50  Millward and Sheard 1995.

51  Gourvish 1980; Foreman-Peck 1987.

52  Barker and Savage 1974, ch. 3; Clapham 1964, ch. 9.

53  Foreman-Peck 1987.

54  Foreman-Peck 1985, 1989b.

55  Silva and Diogo 2006.

56  Headrick 1991; Headrick and Griset 2001.

57  Millward 2011b.

# 4   Free land and unfree labour

## USA and Russia 1815–70

### The expanding frontier

In a characteristically imaginative article, Evsey Domar[1] developed a framework for assessing whether, in countries with lots of land, the labour force would be in servitude. He suggested that an aristocracy, abundant land and free labour could not simultaneously exist – only two of them. Actually he did not use the word "aristocracy" though it was not out of place for Russia, and even southern cotton plantation owners in early nineteenth century America would not have blushed at such a label. What Domar was driving at was that a landlord class could exist when land was scarce for then a rent could be charged to tenants. Such was, classically, eighteenth and nineteenth century England, with its aristocratic landlords receiving rents from tenant farmers who in their turn hired an agricultural wage labour force. If land was abundant as in nineteenth century North America and Russia, rents might be driven down to very low levels so that it might be difficult for a landlord class to survive: enserfment or enslavement of the people could then be highly profitable. Otherwise abundant land could allow the development of free yeoman farmers as in the mid and northern United States, without a landlord class.[2]

One problem with Domar's model is that whether or not a labour force could be restricted in its movements would depend on the social and political climate and the existence of a system for monitoring and supervising forced labour.[3] Serfdom in Russia did not end in 1860 nor slavery at the end of the Civil War in USA 1860–64 because the volume of free labour had reached some critical level relative to the land area. In fact research has suggested that both serfdom and slavery were still highly profitable, in the 1850s, to respectively the Russian nobility and Southern American plantation owners.[4] So abundant land and an aristocratic landlord class are not sufficient conditions for unfree labour. Neither are they necessary conditions; the profitability of tying labour to the soil does not depend on land being freely abundant. A common conceptualisation of the economic effect of enserfment/enslavement is that the labourer's real income is driven down to subsistence level. As long as the labourer's output (the value of his "marginal product") exceeds subsistence requirements it could be profitable to restrict labour movements. Thus in medieval Western Europe there were certain regions with relatively scarce land but where the peasantry were enser-fed. Slave prices in USA in the 1820–60 period reflected the productivity of slave labour and the price of cotton. The sheer size of the increase in cotton growing in America and elsewhere depressed world cotton prices but as new lands were opened up, slave productivity rose and was enough to keep slave prices buoyant in the 1850s.

So Domar's analysis provides neither necessary nor sufficient conditions for the existence of unfree labour. Nonetheless his ideas provide useful insights on economies with abundant land and certainly USA and Russia fell into that category in the nineteenth century. In our period 1815–70, each country expanded by roughly one million square miles – Russia slightly less, USA slightly more. This proved enough to accommodate a huge increase in population. As the American frontier moved west the population quadrupled but population density only doubled. In Russia the annexation of Kazakhstan, Turkestan (modern Central Asia) and regions in the Far East near to the Pacific meant that population density rose less than the 60 per cent increase in population. It was the way in which each country expanded in this century and earlier which determined the very different paths of economic development. True, in both, a significant part of the labour force was tied to the soil – much more in Russia than in USA – but the opposition to the territorial expansion was different. When added to the superior natural resources of America, especially the richer land yields, the choices available diverged significantly.

Most historians see the origins of modern Russia in that state, Muscovy, which, from the fourteenth century, proved the state best able to expand, fighting off the nomadic Asian Mongols and Tartars.[5] Expansion was largely by annexation of territories long occupied by large well-established communities not like the American frontier moving from the eighteenth century over land inhabited mainly by Native Americans. The Russian central government established regional governments or came to terms with autonomous military communities. It absorbed Cossacks and fur trappers in the drive through the Urals, Western Siberia in the sixteenth century and Eastern Siberia in the seventeenth. Land yields in the central Muscovy area were never high and access to ice-free ports was important. From the early eighteenth century therefore the drive was to the west and south. Wars with Sweden lead eventually to the establishment of St Petersburg in 1803 and the occupation of (modern) Latvia and Finland. As may be seen in Map 4.1, Poland was partitioned 1772–95 by Russia in conjunction with the two great central European powers Prussia and Austria with Russia absorbing the central and eastern parts, named Congress Poland in 1815 and absorbed as a full Russian province after the unsuccessful 1830/31 Polish uprising. Finland had been fully absorbed in 1809 and in the nineteenth century the advance swung south into Kazakhstan 1853/54 and Turkestan 1864–78. In the Far East the Amur and Coastal provinces were annexed in the 1850s and 1860s. There was of course also pressure to expand southwards to the Balkans and to dominate the Dardanelles as a link through the Black Sea to the Mediterranean but the Crimean War defeat put an end to that.

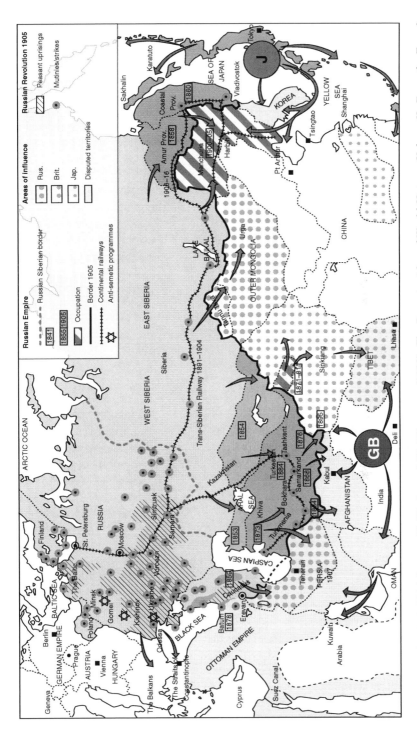

*Map 4.1* Russia 1815–1914 (source: H. Kinder and W. Hilgemann (2003), *The Penguin Atlas of World History: Volume II: From the French Revolution to the Present*, London: Penguin, p. 112).

*Table 4.1* Population of Russia 1762–1859 (million persons)

|       | *1762 area* | *Areas annexed after 1762* | *Total* |
|-------|-------------|----------------------------|---------|
| 1762  | 19          | –                          | 19      |
| 1796  | 29          | 7                          | 36      |
| 1815  | 31          | 14                         | 45      |
| 1851  | 39          | 28                         | 67      |
| 1859  | 45          | 29                         | 74      |

Source: Kaser 1978, p. 446.

A good indication of the significance of these annexations is Kaser's estimate of population change in the annexed territories (Table 4.1). The population of Russia in 1762 was 19 million. By the end of the Polish partitions the population in the original area was 29 million and there were seven million in the annexed regions, making a total of 36 million. Thereafter the original area's population rose by 1859 to 45 million and the population in the annexed regions (including new annexations) to 29 million yielding a total population of 74 million. Neither did matters end in 1860. The tottering Ottoman Empire was a very dispersed territory and it faced the influence and pressure of Russia in the Balkans and the Caucasus from the 1870s and military incursions in Afghanistan and Persia. Further east, Sinkiang and Mongolia were occupied 1900–05. The advance of the Russian frontier required naval vessels as well as huge armies. It required a close control of the population to provide tax revenues, man the military, provide sustenance for the military and provide a labour force for the agricultural estates of the nobility who provided military leadership and regional governors.

We shall explore the implications of this later. Russia in this sense proved a strong contrast with North America, which, in 1815 constituted the settlements on the eastern coastline with much of the rest largely unoccupied, albeit not unclaimed. The essential feature of USA is that it grew up from the settlement towns and states with the Federal government emerging from that late eighteenth century base. There was immense scope for an expansion westwards where the battles were between the settlers, leading eventually to the Civil War 1860–64, rather than the annexations of areas with established populations and institutions as in Russia.

The major settlements did of course have a long history with the French colonising Quebec in the seventeenth century, occupying Louisiana territory with the English in Virginia and Spain in the south-west. By 1775 the main white settlement was still on the Atlantic border area from Georgia to Nova Scotia. Whilst the Declaration of Independence in 1776 of the 13 United States might have been followed by a Confederacy – a joining together of the states and no more – the outcome in the Constitution issued in 1787 was a Federal government given clear responsibilities in foreign affairs, posts and money supply with President Washington, who started in 1789, as the chief executive. Following the acceptance of American independence by Britain, in the Treaty of Paris 1783, settlement pushed across the Appalachians 1790–1812. Much of the south-west was still New Mexico and the Vice-Royalty of New Spain but from 1836 Americans living in Texas were independent and in 1848 Mexico lost all territory north of the Rio Grande (see Map 4.2). The 1840 Oregon Treaty established the 39th parallel as the Canadian border. With a lag, many of the settled territories became states – 33 of them by 1860. Alaska was purchased from Russia in 1868 but did not become a state until 1958.

So this expansion involved relatively unoccupied territory and the eventual establishment of a country with very clear boundaries. The securing of these borders did require the establishment of outposts, battles with Native Americans and a clear role for the Union Army. But the way was open for market sales of land. The Federal government was a huge landowner and could sell land cheaply without being unduly worried about aggression from contiguous nation states and well-established communities as in Western Europe and Russia.

## Public finances, tariff policy and industrialisation in Russia

The political geography of Russia in 1815 yields a picture of a country a long way from the flourishing Atlantic trade of Western Europe, with the Arctic Ocean as its only natural border and access to ice-free ports a priority. Centuries

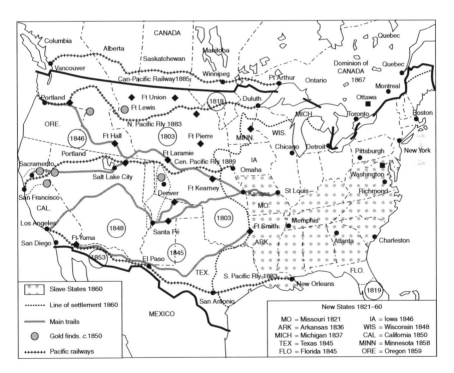

*Map 4.2* USA 1867–75 (source: H. Kinder and W. Hilgemann (2003), *The Penguin Atlas of World History: Volume II: From the French Revolution to the Present*, London: Penguin, p. 94).

of expansion had resulted however in a nation which was a major military entity and, having repelled Napoleon and absorbed Poland and Finland, it was recognised as a strong and, seemingly, stable political force. Its history was also reflected in its political structure, dominated as that was by the Tsar and his nobility. This was not a vassal system. There was no reciprocal recognition of duties and rights as feudal lord and king. The nobility's land was not part of some contract of homage to the Tsar who in return recognised the noble's role in providing regional governance and military leadership. Russia was, as Pipes has clearly argued, a patrimonial state.[6] The Tsar was an autocrat who claimed sovereignty over all land. The noble's tenure was not like a fief. The noble was a "servitor", an agent of the state. Personal gentry service for the state had been a central feature up to the late eighteenth century when it was relaxed by Peter II, a measure endorsed by Catherine the Great, as had the nobility's liability for personal taxation.

Labour and the army were provided by serfdom, perceived as necessary in a country where labour was scarce, a huge army vital and where much of industry was located in inclement areas like the Urals. Serfs on noble estates plus state peasants (cf. later) accounted for over 80 per cent of the population in contrast to American slavery which accounted for less than one-fifth of the US population in the early nineteenth century. How business coexisted with serfdom is a central issue which is taken up in the next section. Regional assemblies in the form of the *volost* and the village *mir* raised revenues for infrastructure development but were also, in an important way, tax raising institutions to support the bureaucracy and the military. Serfdom was therefore not a "noble privilege" but rather an essential part of the hierarchy. The final dimension of Russia's geo-political position was its rather mixed resource endowment.[7] Land was abundant but yields poor except in the Ukrainian black soil areas. Tables 4.2 and 4.3 indicate a reasonable endowment of copper, gold and silver but good access to coal, iron ore and oil was limited, certainly relative to USA and Western Europe. Russian economic development was, in 1820, way behind the major powers. Probably about 90 per cent of labour still worked in agriculture and measured GDP per head was barely one-third of the UK, one-half of France and USA and even less than Japan (Tables 4.2 and 3.2). The eighteenth century had seen, following Peter the Great's initiatives, much state effort to developing roads, canals, markets, mines, metals and textiles as well as ports in the Baltic and Arctic but a large slice of economic activity was still subsistence agriculture and exports were a very small percentage of GDP.[8]

How far then did these geo-political factors and the historical legacy determine relations between business and the state? If anything, economic policy fitted some of the strands of mercantilism described in Chapter 1 but with the additional element of distrust of industrialisation because of the urbanisation and democratisation with which it was associated. The main features were public finances very much geared to supporting the military and bureaucracy, an ambivalent attitude to the development of manufacturing and railways and clear state support for what proved a fairly successful adaptation of serfdom to the growth

*Table 4.2* Strategic dimensions of Russia and USA 1820 and 1870 (contemporary boundaries)[a]

| | Russia | | USA | |
|---|---|---|---|---|
| | *1820* | *1870* | *1820* | *1870* |
| **A Military and mercantile strength** | | | | |
| Military personnel ('000 persons) | 826[b] | 909[c] | 11[b] | 36[c] |
| Merchant fleet ('000 net registered tons) | n.a. | 260[d] | 260[e] | 3438[e] |
| Warships ('000 tons) | n.a. | 200[c] | n.a. | 169[c] |
| Defence spending (£ million) | n.a. | 0.5[f] | n.a. | 16.3 |
| **B Resources** | | | | |
| Land area ('000 sq.miles) | 6775 | 7643 | 1788 | 3022 |
| Population (millions) | 50 | 82 | 10 | 40 |
| Coal output (million met. tons) | 0.2[g] | 0.7 | 0.3[h] | 37[h] |
| Iron ore output ('000 met. tons) | n.a. | 135[g] | n.a. | 3893 |
| **C Communications** | | | | |
| Railway spread (track miles per 1000 sq. miles of area) | 0.01[i] | 1.1[i] | 0.1[b] | 18 |
| Telecommunications density (telegrams per 100 pop.) | n.a. | 3.3 | n.a. | 24.1 |
| **D Stage of development** | | | | |
| % Labour | n.a. in agriculture[j] | 81.0 | 70.0 | 50.0 |
| Incomes[j] (GDP per head in 1990 $) | 618 | 943 | 1257 | 2445 |

Sources: Annex tables; Kennedy 1988, Tables 8, 20; Hobson 1993.

Notes
a See Annex Table A1.
b 1830.
c 1880.
d Excludes vessels less than 25 tons.
e Gross tonnage.
f 1885.
g Relates only to European Russia and also excludes Poland, Finland and the Caucasus.
h Includes brown coal, lignite, etc.
i Excludes local lines. The 1820 entry relates to 1838.
j 2003 boundaries except Russian share of agriculture for 1870 which covers territory of the Russian empire.

*Table 4.3* Production of metals and minerals in Russia and USA in 1870 (metric tons)

|  | USA | Russia |
| --- | --- | --- |
| Copper | 13,000[a] | 99,200[b] |
| Manganese | 580 0[c] | – |
| Mercury | 1044[d] | – |
| Gold | 75[e] | 35[b] |
| Silver | 385[e] | 15[f] |
| Sulphur | 1000[g] | – |
| Platinum | – | 4[b] |
| Zinc | – | 82[b] |
| Soda ash | – | 1320 |
| Lead | – | 1630 |
| Coal ('000) | 37,000[h] | 700 |
| Iron Ore ('000) | 3893 | 135[i] |
| Oil ('000) | 701 | 33 |

Sources: Mitchell 2003c for USA and 2003a for Russian oil and iron ore. For the rest of the Russian data, thanks are due to Olya and Nat Moser and Peter Gatrell for supplying me with data and guidance to Kafengaus 1994 and Nutter 1962.

Notes
a  Estimated recoverable Cu content of domestically mined ores.
b  1887.
c  Relates to 1880 shipments of ore of more than 40% Mn content.
d  Hg content.
e  Production at refinery stage.
f  1887 Belikivvy produced metal ores.
g  1880. Excludes ferro-alloys.
h  Includes brown coal, lignite, etc.
i  European Russia excluding Poland, Finland and the Caucasus.

of industry. Serfdom was still profitable for the nobility and the emancipation in 1860 is seen now by most historians, not as reflecting an unprofitable system but rather a product of fears of revolution and social unrest that could not be controlled.[9] Defeat in the Crimean War undermined self-confidence and shifted government economic policy more towards competition and promotion of railways and modern factory industry.

Russia's huge army is a key benchmark. Table 4.2 records 836,000 military personnel in 1830, more than the rest of the major powers combined. The data on warships relate to the late nineteenth century but if they are at all typical of all the century, the figure of 200,000 tons, exceeded only by the UK and France, suggests a strong commitment to ships of the line bearing in mind Russia's limited access to the sea. The consequence was a defence budget which was, again if the late nineteenth century figures are a guide, in excess of all the other powers, even allowing for the economic resources available: Hobson's estimate of ordinary war expenditures plus extraordinary expenditures excluding debt interest, indicates 4.1 per cent of GDP was allocated to defence – much higher than all the other major powers.[10] Indeed the total of all central government spending was possibly about 5 per cent of national income in 1820 (Table 4.4),

*Table 4.4* Russian central government spending and revenues[a] 1820–70 (million roubles)

| | A | B | C | D | E | F | G |
|---|---|---|---|---|---|---|---|
| | Expenditure | Revenues total | Custom | Excise[b] | Direct | National income[c] | Revenues as % national income |
| 1820 | 145[d] | 130[d] | 16[d] | 46[d] | 38[d] | 2694 | 4.8 |
| 1830 | 124[d] | 114[d] | 19[d] | 32[d] | 34[d] | – | – |
| 1840 | 188 | 155 | 26 | 44 | 42 | – | – |
| 1850 | 287 | 202 | 30 | 65 | 45 | – | – |
| 1860 | 438 | 278 | 34 | 128 | 58 | – | – |
| 1870 | 564 | 460 | 43 | 175 | 110 | 5779 | 8.0 |

Source: Mitchell 2003a; Maddison 1995; Gregory 1994.

Notes

a Russian Empire.

b Includes profits from the state spirit monopoly.

c A rough estimate obtained by, first, deriving, from Maddison 1995, an index of Russian GDP per head in 1990 dollars for 1820 and 1870 with 1890=100 and applying it to Gregory's estimate (1991) of 1890 net national product. It was assumed prices rose about 5% 1820–70 and 2% 1870–90 to yield the final estimates of national income at current prices.

d Paper roubles multiplied by 0.29 to obtain silver as implied by 1839/40 entries in paper and silver roubles in Mitchell 2003a.

similar to that other autocratic state, Prussia, though much lower than the UK where national debt, and debt service charges (cf. Chapter 3) inherited from the Napoleonic Wars, were huge. Contrary to all the other major powers we are studying, Russian central government expenditures then appear to have risen 1820–70 relative to GDP.[11] Moreover the limited scale of market transactions, and especially overseas trade, meant that customs and excise were a smaller part of tax revenues than in other countries. Customs revenue averaged 12–16 per cent of total central government revenues 1820–60 and declined even further in the 1860s as tariff rates fell slightly. A major element in government revenues was direct taxation, a much bigger share than in other countries, save Prussia. The poll tax, introduced by Peter the Great, was dominant and responsibility for collecting it fell on the village *mir*. By nature this was a regressive tax and was topped up by additions for serfs located away from their estates (paying a quit rent, the *obrok*, to their landlords) and with exemptions for the nobility.

Although customs revenues were not an especially large part of total taxes, Russian industry was strongly protected for much of our period. The main industrial centres included the Urals' iron, gold and copper smelting, much originating from Peter the Great's early eighteenth century initiatives. The Central Industrial Region was dominated by artisan occupations, putting-out systems in woollens and linen, and cotton factories, especially in the Ivanovo region near to Moscow. Sugar beet was located in Kiev whilst St Petersburg developed metallurgy and textiles. These regions were separated by huge distances and often a long way from deposits of coal – imported in the case of the St Petersburg area.[12] Practically all labour was enserfed but in an amazingly complex wide range of settings, not simply manorial factories but in Urals mining and factories, wage labour in the new cotton industry, cottage industry and putting-out systems, sometimes far away from the serf's home estate. How the serf system was able to adapt to these varied needs is discussed in the third section of this chapter.

In the meantime, the other significant dimensions of industrialisation were the scale of tariff protection, the limited role of the state and the slow pace of advance. An 1816 tariff may have been a step to liberalisation but it was still highly protectionist.[13] The import of many manufactured goods was prohibited. New tariff structures in 1822, 1824 and 1841 have been characterised by some historians as revenue raising, the main driving force of Kankrin, the Minister of Finance 1823–44, who seemed unwilling to commit himself either to state intervention or laissez-faire. Whatever the revenue effect, duties were averaging 24 per cent of import values in the period 1851–56. Under the 1851 tariff, duties on manufactures were 50–75 per cent.[14] Russia did not participate in the set of favoured nation set of treaties (see Chapter 2) until an agreement with France in 1874. The more positive attitude of the state to economic development and industry from the late 1850s saw duties fall by 30 per cent on manufactured products. By the years 1867–78 duties averaged over all commodities were 17.6 per cent, a trend supported by the nobility, who wanted now to buy farm machinery and rail lines, and by industrialists in St Petersburg, Poland and Riga who were involved in making up semi-manufactured imports. Nonetheless this was but a short relapse in a basically protectionist regime since imports rose at the rate of 9 per cent per annum in the years 1866–77 so that high duties were re-imposed in 1877.

The factory labour force in our period was never more than one million workers. At the turn of the century the major factory employers were in wool-lens, linen, mining and metallurgy. The cotton industry grew very quickly but, as Table 4.5 shows, it was not typical, rising nearly tenfold 1804 to 1830 and then doubling to 1860. The woollen industry and iron and steel also expanded strongly but, for the rest, only sugar beet sticks out. By European standards factory development was slow; in 1860 Russia imported 47,000 metric tons of raw cotton for its cotton textile industry but this was less than Germany, less than one-half of France and less than 10 per cent of the UK.[15] In part the slow progress of industry reflected the delay in railway construction which was vital for linking up the industrial regions and ports. Kankrin typified much of the noble elite in viewing railways like factory industry as a harbinger of urbanisation, democratisation and revolution. By 1850 only 501 track kilometres had been opened and the Crimean War highlighted Russia's severe limitations in communications. The Moscow–St Petersburg line started in 1852 and by 1854 it was only this line and that from Warsaw to the Austrian border which could be classed as important – and more for strategic reasons than commercial. Both lines were state aided. By the same decade the Post Office was reorganised and a telegraph network established – though the 2.72 million telegrams sent in 1870 represented the lowest level in all the major powers. The state raised its commitment to rail development and over the whole period 1836–75 over 80 per cent of rail construction received state help in one form or another.[16] There had been

*Table 4.5* Russian factory labour force[a] 1804–60 ('000)

|                          | 1804  | 1830  | 1860  |
|--------------------------|-------|-------|-------|
| Woollens                 | 28.7  | 67.2  | 120.0 |
| Cotton                   | 8.2   | 76.2  | 152.2 |
| Linen                    | 23.7  | 76.2  | 17.3  |
| Silk                     | 9.2   | 14.0  | 14.3  |
| Paper                    | 6.0   | 10.3  | 12.8  |
| Leather                  | 6.3   | 10.5  | 14.2  |
| Soap etc.                | 0.7   | 6.3   | 12.1  |
| Iron and steel           | 4.1   | 19.9  | 54.8  |
| Copper smelting          | 0.5   | 3.1   | 8.5   |
| Other manufacturing      | 7.5   | 16.3  | 94.0  |
| *Sub-total all* Manufacturing | 95.0  | 252.3 | 565.0 |
| Mining etc.              | 130.0 | n.a.  | 295.0 |
| Total                    | 225.0 | n.a.  | 860.0 |

Sources: Crisp 1978, p. 321; Falkus 1972, p. 33.
Note
a  Manufacturing plants with at least 16 employees.

many delays in the construction of the Moscow–St Petersburg line so that thereafter there was more reliance on private contractors with the state providing financial guarantees. A planned increase of 4000 kilometres was drawn up with heavy involvement of Rothschilds, Barings, the Pereire brothers and French entrepreneurs. The *Grande Société des Chemin de Fer Russes* was established in 1857 with the Russian government guaranteeing a 5 per cent return. Some 1700 kilometres were finished by 1862 but generally the project was riddled with difficulties, including obstruction by the Russian military and bureaucracy who had opposed the use of private contractors. Thereafter the state intervened more directly and by the end of the century the *Grande Société* had been taken over by the state.[17]

## Business organisation, serfdom and the Russian state

In USA the slave population was nearly five million in the 1850s on the eve of the Civil War and was noticeably concentrated not only in the south and not only in cotton growing but in southern plantation cotton estates. In contrast over 40 million of the Russian population were serfs and spread over all sections of the economy. Most businesses used or employed serfs. What is important then is to explain how in Russia serfs were used in a bewildering variety of occupations by nobility, factory owners and the state. Many still provided classic labour services in agriculture (the *barschina*); others worked in manorial industrial factories under the supervision of the noble or his manager. Many serfs worked on canals, roads and railway construction; others in mines and metallurgy and in modern textile factories as well as in more traditional cottage industry settings. Since some of this work was rewarded by wages and took place well away from the serf's home village and his estate noble, the question arises as to how the nobility and the state managed to secure an income from enserfment and what incentives and/or coercion was used. Serf working conditions were often those of the forced labour conditions found with convict labour. In other settings they were given more discretion, were paid wages by a person other than the noble or his manager and sometimes even set up business themselves as serf entrepreneurs. Away from his base agricultural estate, the serf often paid a quit rent, the *obrok*, whilst at the other extreme, on the estate, serfs worked their *barschina* without payment but were allocated land to work up their own sustenance.

Our main theme is that where the work in question was familiar, long established and sometimes with economies in scale in supervision, the serf in Russia supplied labour services under supervision. Where a greater output was possible by giving the worker more latitude in response to uncertainty, the *obrok* rental system was used, often therefore in settings where innovative methods and new products were involved. In such circumstances, since there was no close monitoring of the serf's work, the noble's income (from *obrok*) was less assured than in, for example, cereal cultivation which came from three days' work on the lord's demesne. However the uncertain income often proved profitable for the noble.

Estimates of the number of serfs give a clear indication of how dispersed they must have been. The population may be divided into the serfs of private landlords (the *pomeschik* serfs), state peasants, *udel* peasants (serfs of the imperial family) and others. The status of state peasants was subject to much contemporary confusion and to historical debate. They were by 1838 administered at the very top by a new Ministry of State Domains. Crisp traces their origins to people in petty service, peasants cultivating land for Siberian garrisons but, by 1831, nearly two-thirds of them were descendants of former free peasants on black soil lands acquired by Princes and so-called *yasak* (a tax on furs) paying Tartars.[18] They could be assigned to industrial or agricultural work and their status was little different from the serfs of private landlords though never descending to chattel status as did some of the latter. Note that some merchants acquired so-called possessional factories worked by serf labour. Such possessional serfs were attached to the factory not to the owner of the factory and could then have been state or *pomeschik* serfs.

At the tenth revision of 1858 the total population of Russia was 73 million. Information on how many were serfs is rather shaky. A minimum estimate is that *pomeschik* serfs accounted for some 40 per cent of the population classed as rural ("peasant") with state peasants and *udel* serfs another 40 per cent, each totalling at least roughly 22 million or 44 million in total.[19] How were these serfs allocated across different kinds of work?[20] The argument advanced above is that where production methods were simple and well established, forced labour conditions would prevail. Estate agriculture continued with long established production techniques using serf labour services on the lords' demesne. Such forced labour extended also to domestic service, building and maintenance work, culling timber, building dikes and clearing rivers and ponds. More significant for present purposes are the particular manorial industrial activities which flourished when in the eighteenth century the nobility became increasingly active in production for sale, that is, in coarse woollen and linen cloth, writing paper and distilling. That the nobility were able to obtain special market privileges by way of government contracts, subsidies or extensive protection explains why they became involved in marketing these products but not why they were also involved in production. The answer is that the commodities chosen for production were ones requiring only simple traditional techniques using familiar raw materials. Flax thread, linen, woollen yarn and cloth, shingles, socks, sail cloth, spirits, soap and utensils had for a long time been produced on the estates. As long as the noble's interest in these commodities was minor, mainly that is, as items of personal consumption, there would be little advantage in supervision of this work. Hence the serfs' obligation took the form of quotas of craft products to be surrendered to the lord, produceable that is in peasant cottages without supervision.[21] In essence these were forced rents in kind which were transformed into forced labour under supervision once the precise volume of serf labour input became of stronger economic interest to the lord when market sales of some of these products rose in the eighteenth century.

Thus landlord woollen factories of eighteenth century Russia produced, to a large extent, cheap military cloth on government contracts, in some cases subsidised, and were essentially a centralisation of a peasant craft. It is symptomatic of the relatively secure market and the primitiveness of techniques that the quality was often a source of complaint and of government investigations. By the early nineteenth century most woollen factories (78 per cent in 1813–14) were still owned by nobles and largely located on estates. Even by 1825 the proportion of gentry serfs in the total factory labour force was higher in woollens than in any other manufacturing industry (60 per cent) and a further 20 per cent were assigned or possessional serfs. But the nineteenth century also saw the emergence, outside the gentry framework, of a better quality cloth and in the 1840s worsted production started in Moscow province. Gentry production and forced labour thus declined as a proportion of the industry's activities.[22] Analogously in the production of alcohol, the nobility in all areas had long had an interest, especially where transport costs significantly affected the costs of selling grain, and a market was protected in one way or another. Serf labour services were recorded in the eighteenth century in Prussia, Poland and Estonia. In Russia proper, state purchasing favoured the gentry in distilling, which used grain and later potatoes, and a decree of 1754 granted a noble monopoly so that by the later parts of the eighteenth century the competition from merchants waned. Much was small scale until the nineteenth century when the average size of plants rose dramatically, as it did in sugar beet refining. By the 1850s serf labour services still accounted for over one-half of the sugar beet labour force. Steam-driven refineries were however by this date producing over 50 per cent of the Russian output and significantly there are increasing signs of the use of freely contracted labour time; in part this reflected the heavy seasonal nature of work in the refinery mill but the precise wage conditions in this setting are not clear.[23]

There were also many cases where the serf worked away from his owner with the direct user of his labour contractually linked to the serf owner. Here again one finds that forced labour was used essentially in the more traditional simple tasks. Thus the serfs in railroad construction were involved in digging and hauling earth, rock breaking, cutting trees, swamp clearance and in the 1840s up to 60,000 were being used in some periods on the St Petersburg–Moscow railway. Living conditions were crowded and unsanitary while food and clothing were often insufficient. Symptomatic of the unattractiveness of the work was that other parts of the labour force included prisoners and soldiers. There is evidence also of similar forced labour in canals and highways. "Farmed-out" workers in Russian factories tended to be found in traditional industries (such as woollens) where widespread labour shirking was reported.[24] Since the serf in all these activities was working away from the holding, part of his annual "income" took the form of wages in kind or in money. There were two broad ways by which the product of the serf's work was channelled as income to the lord with the serf kept at a subsistence level. In some cases on the St Petersburg–Moscow railway the local landlords supervised their own serfs, saw to their subsistence and got the fee for the contract from the government. In other instances, especially one would imagine where the work was located well away from the home estate, the lord, or government official in the case of state peasants, would not be involved in supervision. This would be done by the contractor who would pay a fee to the lord and government official, having agreed to pay specified wages to the serf. Similarly the factory owner would pay, direct to the lord, the farmed-out worker's *obrok* quit rent. In some cases, there were intermediaries (labour contractors) between the lord and the employer, again possibly a function of the location of the work. It was common for lords in the populous infertile western provinces of White Russia to hire out their serfs to contractors who herded them to the Central Industrial zone where they were rented out to factories.

In contrast to all the above cases were activities which were new or required particular care and attention and here one finds not forced labour but serfs freely contracting their labour time. They performed work in settings sometimes a long way from their home estate, received wages from an employer who need not be their noble owner to whom they paid the *obrok* quit rent. There is clear evidence of this in early nineteenth century textiles where new products, designs, and materials in *small-scale production* were common. Much emerged from the expropriation of techniques initially developed in late eighteenth century factories which had a short life.[25] Cotton weaving using cheap English yarn saw a considerable growth in the nineteenth century with much division of labour and putting-out systems developing, some with thousands of weavers, especially around Moscow and Ivanovo. The weaving of fine linen, as opposed to coarse linen, saw a similar pattern with small manufacturers playing an important role, especially in Vladimir and Kostroma; they bought flax yarn, put it out to weavers in villages and then finished the raw cloth in workshops which later developed into mechanised factories. Yatsounsky's data on Ivanovo cotton printing show it was replacing linen printing in the late eighteenth century and early nineteenth century.[26] Most enterprises were small family businesses, though there were a few very large enterprises which combined finishing with the putting-out of yarn for cottage weaving, and over the period 1808–49 the average size of establishment increased considerably with an accompanying rise in freely contracted wage labour. The silk industry was one of the first to use freely contracted labour. Large mills were established in the early eighteenth century, but skills developed in linen weaving could readily be adapted and the large mills increasingly put-out weaving to cottages especially in silk winding and twisting.[27] Similar developments of peasant industry for sale, based either on skills acquired in factories or on materials supplied by a putter-out, were to be found in the use of hempen cloth for sails, sacks, tarpaulin and, outside textiles, in the metal trades, fur dressing, decorative clothing, brushes, hats and furniture. Emerging often from the interstices of the putting-out system were also peasant factories, operated by serf entrepreneurs and employing serfs as hired labour, both employer and employee paying *obrok* to their lords. Tugan-Baranovsky characterised them as all being in growing industries especially in cotton, producing inexpensive chintzes and calicoes, and in fine and medium woollens, especially shawls; they were also to be found in silk (especially ribbons), muslins, curtains, rope, leather goods and hats. St Petersburg saw peasants in luxury trades and as building contractors. Finally the major new technology, mechanical cotton spinning, which developed rapidly from the 1840s once the English ban on machinery exports was lifted, used entirely freely contracted labour.[28]

In the possessional factories of the central industrial region, a wide range of wage levels was used for different kinds of work while adscribed state peasants were often on piece wages at rates similar to freely hired labour.[29] In the Urals no more than 3 per cent of the labour force, other than that in transport, was externally hired if measured in man-days. Most labour came then from *pomeschik* serfs and adscribed state peasants but their wage income was as differentiated according to the quality and intensity of work as one might find in a modern factory. Pay rates at the state owned plants varied between foreman and shop worker. At the Vysokogorsk iron mine, piece rates were used and varied according to the skill requirement and location of work. Data from a blast furnace in the same complex indicate generally higher rates than at the mine. As a more precise indication of piece rates, data for the fiscal year 1851–52 for the pig iron refining furnaces in the Niznij Tagil complex indicate that wages were paid per pud of iron, and the rate per pud varied as between foreman, journeyman and assistant and it varied according to whether it was slab iron, bar and assorted iron, or slabs for plate and sheet iron. Moreover, there was one rate per pud for production within a certain absolute quantity of iron and one for production above that quantity; finally there were bonuses for savings in charcoal usage. Thus there were clear incentives here for labour to work with care and attention without constant supervision; this benefited the owners but it also benefited the workers because the product was shared. Similar elements of a wage incentive system can be found in the other sectors which were both capital intensive and of an increasingly complex technology. In the 1840s and 1850s the state owned Alexandrovsk Machine Works at St Petersburg was engaged in the production of locomotives and cars for Russia's infant railroad system. The main labour force was adscribed state peasants. The producers using the plant, Winans Bros, had contracts with the government which specified a minimum wage for the workforce but also that cash bonuses would be paid for individual performance and the quality of output.[30]

In summary, Russia's slow industrial development in the first half of the nineteenth century cannot simply be attributed to an inflexible serf labour system. It is clear that in both state and private iron works and coal mines, in putting-out systems and new cotton factories, labour was paid wages with many incentives for work effort. The institutional framework which gave serfs some security over their earnings and property rights and which facilitated the movement of labour away from their estates, often part time, have recently been fully set out by Dennison.[31] The source of Russia's economic difficulties lay then not in the inflexibility of the serf system but in the huge bureaucracy and military dimensions of the state together with the tying of serfs to their estate noble either in the form of the obligation to pay quit rents or in many cases still as direct labour services on the estate. By the late 1850s the Russian state was supporting economic development but the aim was not some modern notion of raising living standards or the social condition of the peasantry. The fear was serf revolt and so it was better that choice came from above. The objective was military and strategic – to increase military strength and protect the Empire and the Tsar.

## The American Constitution, the military and land policy

The crucial features of the isolated US economy in our period were the open frontier, a huge land area relatively free of inherited institutions and population, plus a slave labour force in the south. This allowed a fairly minimal military expenditure by the new Federal government and a strong cotton-led economic growth with manufacturing protected from outside competition. The political tensions were internal rather than external as the "slave power" sought recognition in new states, leading eventually to the Civil War whilst the scramble for an expanding transport infrastructure took the form of competition between municipal governments and between states. It was a society liberal and laissez-faire only in certain ways: it was not laissez-faire externally and the internal market was free for whites only.

During the 1820–70 period, the political geography of USA was settled. Following the treaty with Canada and the securing of the south-west from Mexico, the country emerged, as we saw earlier, with well defined boundaries of the Atlantic, Pacific, Gulf of Mexico and the 49th parallel. From the 1820s the United States faced nothing like the contiguous nation states threatening France, Germany and Russia. There was no need for large regional governments headed by large landholders as in Russia. Apart from the Native Americans, the land was largely empty. The political structure grew from the towns and states upwards, not from the centre as in Moscovy. In the end however the government structure was not a simple joining up of state power – it was not a Confederacy, much as some would have liked. Rather the Constitutional Convention of 1776 delivered a Federal government of the "people" not of the "states". The Constitution gave powers to the Federal government over the monetary system, taxation, foreign policy, war, patents, post and inter-state commerce conferring clear powers to make laws to execute such policies. This was highly contentious but the Constitution was the "supreme law of the land". The constituent states retained strong regulatory powers which, in the long run, proved more important than their taxation capacity. Finally, and crucially in this period, the Constitution on the one hand underlined freedom of movement and human rights but did not mention the word "slave". It did clearly forbid states to revoke labour contracts and this was precisely how slavery implicitly appeared in the constitution.[32]

The final dimension of USA's geo-political position in 1815 was its resource endowment. Some idea of the scale of the open frontier is that in 1815 the population was less than ten million or less than three persons for each square mile of the final territory of the United States in the twentieth century. The Russian population approached 50 million, nearly six per square mile. America was well endowed with copper, gold, silver, sulphur, iron ore, manganese, mercury (Table 4.3). Its recorded coal output at the start of our period was modest (300,000 tons in 1820, similar to Russia) but the reserves were there, in the north-eastern industrial region, so that by 1870 output was exceeded only by the UK. Its soil was agriculturally superior to Russia and included the scope for profitable cash crops of tobacco and cotton in the south. Slave imports were outlawed from 1808 but the slave population was over 1.5 million and growing rapidly as was the number of white immigrants whose annual inflow was nearly 10,000 in 1820 and over 20,000 by 1830.[33] USA had already registered itself as a land of opportunity. Even with an impoverished black population and even though it still had 70 per cent of its labour force in agriculture, average real incomes were already higher than in France, Germany, Italy, Spain and nearly double Russia (Table 3.2).

This then was America's geo-political position and stage of development in 1820 and the first implication is that military expenditures were unlikely to be a drain on the country as it was in some European countries, especially Russia. Starting with the Land Ordinance Act of 1795, the Federal government developed a clear land grant policy in confronting the Native Americans as the frontier spread west. Here it was important for military purposes to provide a chain of outposts and rapid settlement of the land. Land was abundant but much of it, in the early nineteenth century, was still in Federal hands. Policy was to sell off the land cheaply, initially $2 per acre in 1796 and lowered later, and to set smaller and smaller minimum sized holdings. By the time of the Homestead Act of 1862 settlers with five years' residence could obtain 160 acres free. Although it does not look like it, this was a massive set of business–state transactions. For much of the nineteenth century, fear of Federal power constrained federal activities but as Galambos has reminded us, in the context of agricultural business, "managing US federal public lands was the single largest SOE [state owned enterprise] in any of the capitalist countries of the West".[34] The result was that, at the level of central government, the US public sector was small but this was not so obviously laissez-faire as a product of the modest budget for the military and war debts. In 1830 military personnel totalled some 11,000, less than 10 per cent that of most European powers. Even its war fleet was probably smaller early on (and certainly by 1880, see Table 4.2) than those of Russia, France and the UK. USA did have debt charges hanging over from the War of Independence but nowhere near the levels in Europe. Thus army and naval expenditures accounted for some 40–50 per cent of Federal government spending 1820–70 (Table 4.6) but this amounted to only 1 per cent of national income in 1820 – the UK figure was 4.2 per cent albeit falling later. Hobson's estimate (1993) for the end of our period suggests US defence spending, even with the huge rise in debt charges after the Civil War, was only one-third of Russia's and 1.3 per cent of national income. Total Federal government spending was generally less than 2 per cent of national income. It was financed mainly from customs duties which had been taken over in 1789 from the individual states. The Civil War's military expenditures of course changed all this and the 1860s saw the introduction of income taxes and a huge rise in excise taxes on alcohol, tobacco, stamp duty and indeed increases on all consumer and manufactured goods.

Table 4.6 USA Federal government spending and revenue[a] 1820–70 (million dollars)

Expenditure

| | Army | Navy | Debt interest | Veterans | Other[a] | Total | National Income[b] | Expenditure as % national income |
|---|---|---|---|---|---|---|---|---|
| 1820 | 2.6 | 4.4 | 5.1 | 3.2 | 2.9 | 18.3 | 656 | 2.8 |
| 1830 | 4.8 | 3.2 | 1.9 | 1.4 | 3.8 | 15.1 | 933 | 1.6 |
| 1840 | 7.1 | 6.1 | 0.2 | 2.6 | 8.6 | 24.3 | 1672 | 1.4 |
| 1850 | 9.4 | 7.9 | 3.8 | 1.9 | 16.6 | 39.5 | 2586 | 1.5 |
| 1860 | 16.4 | 11.5 | 3.2 | 1.1 | 30.9 | 63.3 | 3839 | 1.6 |
| 1863 | 599.3 | 63.2 | 24.7 | 1.1 | 26.3 | 714.7 | 7355 | 14.0 |
| 1870 | 57.7 | 21.8 | 129.2 | 28.3 | 72.7 | 309.7 | 7355 | 4.2 |

Revenue

| | Customs | Internal revenue | Sales public land | Other | Total | National income[b] | Revenues as % national income |
|---|---|---|---|---|---|---|---|
| 1820 | 15.0 | 0.1 | 1.6 | 1.8 | 17.9 | 656 | 2.7 |
| 1830 | 21.9 | 0.1 | 2.3 | 0.6 | 24.8 | 933 | 2.3 |
| 1840 | 13.5 | 0.1 | 3.3 | 2.7 | 19.5 | 1672 | 0.8 |
| 1850 | 39.7 | 0 | 1.9 | 2.0 | 43.6 | 2586 | 1.5 |
| 1860 | 53.2 | 0 | 1.8 | 1.1 | 56.1 | 3839 | 1.4 |
| 1863 | 69.1 | 37.6[c] | 0.2 | 5.8 | 112.7 | 5096 | 2.2 |
| 1870 | 194.5 | 184.9[c] | 3.4 | 28.4 | 411.3 | 7355 | 2.6 |

Source: US Bureau of the Census 1976; Mitchell 2003c.

Notes
a Includes interest payments by government commercial enterprises like post.
b Gross national product at current prices.
c Includes income tax $2.7 million in 1863 and $38 million in 1870 but mainly stamp duty and excise taxes on alcohol and tobacco.

## American cotton, slavery, tariffs and industrialisation

USA was well endowed with land, metals, minerals and other natural resources but short of labour and, relative to Europe, capital was also scarce. The capital intensity of its production methods overcame European levels in mid century and as mass production methods came on the scene, large business corporations emerged. We shall examine, in a later chapter, how far such changes in business organisation had effects on Europe. In the meantime the striking feature of our period 1815–70 was that because of the scarcity of labour and capital both wage rates and interest rates were high and US industry was able to overcome the threat from cheap imports in part because of the large transport costs which foreign manufacturers faced and also because American industry was protected by tariffs. The major growth impetus in the period was in fact agriculture and in particular cotton growing and in particular plantation cotton.[35] Anyone doubting the centrality of cotton and slavery to economic growth in this period should reflect on estimates that the total capital value of all slaves in 1860 ranged between $2.7 billion to $3.7 billion, that is, in excess of all the capital in manufacturing and mining combined.[36]

The population did grow immensely as Table 4.7 shows. No restrictions were placed on immigration until the 1880s so we see that by 1850 (partly as a product of the Irish famine) the immigrant inflow was 1.5 per cent of the population, of whom nearly 10 per cent were already foreign born. Even without slave imports, the black population grew strongly and on the eve of the Civil War some four million were slaves, 90 per cent in the Confederate states, 10 per cent in the free Union states and 10 per cent in the "border states" of Delamere, Kentucky, Maryland and Missouri.[37] The long-standing debate on the economic efficiency of slave agriculture is not an issue we need explore. A telling point was made by Fenoaltea that both sides of the argument could be reconciled: those who estimated that productivity was high but that the slaves' treatment was not so bad as had been thought seem to have been involved in a contradiction mirrored by

*Table 4.7* USA population 1820–70 ('000)

|      | White   | Black  | Total[a]  | Foreign born | Annual inflow of immigrants[b] |
|------|---------|--------|-----------|--------------|--------------------------------|
| 1820 | 7867    | 1772   | 9638      | n.a.         | 8                              |
| 1830 | 10,573  | 2329   | 12,866    | n.a.         | 23                             |
| 1850 | 19,553  | 3639   | 23,192    | 2245         | 370                            |
| 1860 | 26,923  | 4442   | 31,443    | 4139         | 154                            |
| 1870 | 33,589[c] | 4880[c] | 38,858[c] | 3007         | 387                            |

Source: US Bureau of the Census 1976, pp. 14, 106.

Notes

a  Total includes other races: 79,000 in 1860 and 89,000 in 1870.

b  Excludes returning citizens 1820–60.

c  These figures involve some under enumeration in the southern states. Revisions for this and other factors indicate a total of 34,337,292 whites and 5,392,172 blacks.

opponents who argued that slaves were worked excessively but that their productivity was not especially high.[38] A difficult question is whether the huge expansion of American cotton could have occurred without slavery. It is significant that, after emancipation, many cotton growers had great difficulties persuading blacks to return, as free wage labour, to the plantations. The gang labour work which no doubt did produce large outputs was clearly disliked. Almost all blacks in the south remained in agriculture after the Civil War but they wanted less hours, as wage earners, and preferred to set up their own farm; this proved difficult without capital, and share-cropping followed. In the decade following the Civil War there was a 50 per cent fall in the number of large cotton farms whilst those of 50 acres or less doubled.[39]

That the southern states fought against emancipation and indeed pushed for the admittance of slavery in new states in our period is not surprising. The data in Table 4.8 show how wealthy were the plantation owners. Whereas the average wealth of the owner of a free farm in 1860 varied from $2632 in the south to $4620 in the north-east, the southern slaveholder averaged nearly $34,000, of which some $20,000 was the "personal estate". In addition of course whites everywhere feared the impact on wage levels should black labour spread outside the south. When added to general racial prejudice and the fear of northern politicians that the "slave power" would dominate Congress and Senate, this made for a strong opposition to allowing slavery in new states. The economic significance of cotton for the American economy is not in dispute. The huge growth in world demand for raw cotton is shown in Table 4.9 with the UK leading the way followed by USA itself. Agriculture generally remained a dominant part of the American economy, growing threefold 1819–70. American cotton textile manufacturing grew strongly in this period but it was clearly not in the same ball game as the UK industry. The number of cotton textile wage earners grew from 10,000 in 1810 to 122,000 in 1860 but it was not cotton manufacturing which dominated the non-agricultural labour force but rather construction, commerce, iron and steel, agricultural processing and other manufacturing (Table 4.10). Nor did

*Table 4.8* Average farmer's wealth in USA in 1860 ($)[a]

|  | *Personal estate* | *Value of farm* | *Total* |
| --- | --- | --- | --- |
| North-east | 1104 | 3694 | 4620 |
| Old north-west | 682 | 2524 | 3176 |
| West | 532 | 1672 | 2212 |
| Southern slave farms | 19,828 | 11,818 | 33,906 |
| Free southern farms | 1188 | 1568 | 2632 |

Source: Ransom 1989, p. 63.

Notes

a  Sample of 643 farms in the South and 9794 farms in the rest of the country.
North-east: Connecticut, Maine, New Hampshire, New Jersey, New York, Pennsylvania, Rhode Island, Vermont. Old north-west: Illinois, Indiana, Michigan, Ohio, Wisconsin. West: Iowa, Kansas, Minnesota. South: Alabama, Georgia, Louisiana, Mississippi, South Carolina, Texas.

*Table 4.9* Cotton manufacturing industries: consumption of raw cotton 1820–70 ('000 metric tons)

| Year | France[a] | Germany[a] | Japan | Russia[b] | UK[c] | USA |
|------|-----------|------------|-------|-----------|-------|-----|
| 1820 | 19[d]     | n.a.       | n.a.  | 0.6       | 54    | n.a. |
| 1825 | 19        | n.a.       | n.a.  | 1.0       | 76    | n.a. |
| 1830 | 34[e]     | n.a.       | n.a.  | 1.9       | 112   | 74  |
| 1835 | 39        | 8.9[f]     | n.a.  | 3.6       | 144   | n.a. |
| 1840 | 53        | 8.9[f]     | n.a.  | 5.8       | 208   | 50  |
| 1845 | 60        | 13[g]      | n.a.  | 20        | 267   | n.a. |
| 1850 | 59        | 16[h]      | n.a.  | 20        | 267   | 151 |
| 1855 | 76        | 26[i]      | n.a.  | 27        | 352   | n.a. |
| 1860 | 115       | 67         | n.a.  | 47        | 492   | 186 |
| 1865 | 61        | 46         | n.a.  | 26        | 328   | 75[j] |
| 1870 | 59        | 81         | 22    | 46        | 489   | 175 |

Sources: Mitchell 2003a, b, c; Copeland 1912.

Notes
a  Net imports.
b  Total imports.
c  Estimates of consumption.
d  Average 1820–27.
e  1831.
f  Average 1836–43.
g  Average 1844–48.
h  Average 1849–53.
i  Average 1855–57.
j  USA figures are from Copeland 1912 (using 1 million pound weight=439 metric tons) except for 1865 which is taken from Mitchell 2003c where the entries for 1860 and 1870 are close to the Copeland figures.

textile manufacturers have a strong presence in exports. Raw cotton accounted for one-half of all American merchandise exports 1821–60.[40] Manufactured exports grew but were at most 15 per cent of all exports by 1870. Indeed America's export performance was generally weak relative to many other countries. By 1870 its merchandise exports were 2.5 per cent of GDP – as against 4.9 per cent France, 9.5 per cent Germany and 12.0 per cent UK. Even Russia was 2.9 per cent (in 1913).[41]

American manufacturing did flourish in the home market and a significant contributory element was tariff protection. This was favoured by northern manufacturers but not by southern planters (cf. the Prussian Junkers) who feared retaliation from countries consuming their exported cotton and in any case, and quite understandably, wanted to keep down the cost of manufactures consumed by the south. "Not until the collapse of world trade in the 1930s did the United States turn away from protectionist trade policies" said Sylla reviewing the nineteenth century experience.[42] Agriculture itself had seen significant protection since 1789. By 1830 the duty on raw cotton was 30 per cent, hemp 26 per cent and sugar 37.5 per cent. Under the 1816 tariff, import duties were about 35 per cent for most manufactured products, rising to about 40 per cent by 1832.[43] By 1845

*Table 4.10* USA employment by industry 1810–70 ('000 persons)[a]

| | 1810 | 1820 | 1830 | 1840 | 1850 | 1860 | 1870 |
|---|---|---|---|---|---|---|---|
| Agriculture | 1950 | 2470 | 2965 | 3570 | 4520 | 5880 | 6790 |
| Construction | n.a. | n.a. | n.a. | 290 | 410 | 520 | 780 |
| Cotton textiles[b] | 10 | 12 | 55 | 72 | 92 | 122 | 135 |
| Iron and steel[c] | 5 | 5 | 20 | 24 | 35 | 43 | 78 |
| Other manufacturing | 60 | n.a. | n.a. | 404 | 1073 | 1365 | 2257 |
| Trade | n.a. | n.a. | n.a. | 350 | 530 | 890 | 1310 |
| Ocean vessels | 60 | 50 | 70 | 95 | 135 | 145 | 135 |
| Railways | n.a. | n.a. | n.a. | 7 | 20 | 80 | 160 |
| Other services including government[d] | 245 | 598 | 1090 | 848 | 1435 | 2065 | 1285 |
| Total | 2330 | 3135 | 4200 | 5600 | 8250 | 11,110 | 12,930 |

Source: US Bureau of the Census 1976, p. 139.

Notes
a  10 years old or more.
b  Cotton textile manufacturing wage earners.
c  Primary iron and steel wage earners.
d  For 1810–30 includes employees not elsewhere classified.

the nominal tax rates were 47 per cent on manufactured textiles, 36 per cent on bar iron, 92 per cent on refined sugar and estimates of the effective rate of protection (that is after allowing for duties on the inputs to these industries) did not lower the rates by large amounts, except for refined sugar.[44] Pottery, coal, vinegar, candles and paper all enjoyed tariff rates of 50–60 per cent in our period. There was some tendency for rates to fall by the 1850s but the financial crisis of 1857 and a decade of declining customs revenues led to the 1861 Morrell Tariff Act which substituted specific duties by *ad valorem*, generally raised rates and heralded a period when all sorts of demands for protection were met.[45] Some like Taussig and David have argued that the early nineteenth century tariffs, bearing in mind transport costs to USA, did not undermine the basic ability of US manufacturers to meet foreign competition.[46] Others more recently have disagreed and Harley felt able to conclude that the cotton textile industry "without protection ... could have attained no more than a fraction of its actual size".[47] We will return to this matter in later chapters in the course of comparing US and European business structures.

## Government and the expansion of the US transport infrastructure

As the settlement line crossed the Appalachians and railways took off from the 1830s, each town and state was keen to secure connections to major transport facilities. Early turnpike development was by private sector investment. The period 1820–40 saw major involvement by the state governments in canals, roads and railways with $200 million raised in loans, christened "rivalistic state mercantilism" by Dobbin.[48] Railway track rose from 4535 kilometres in 1840 to 85,170 in 1870 by which time over nine million telegrams were being sent annually. The railway development per square mile of territory was still quite modest when compared with the UK but relative to population it was massive. Following several debt defaults by the state governments, the municipalities stepped in, competing for rail development and other transport forms as well of course as investing heavily in paving, lighting, water supply, sewerage, schools, hospitals and other urban improvements (cf. Chapter 9). Municipal debt rose from $25 million in 1840 to $82 million by 1880. The Federal government played only a limited role. Congress charged the army to study possible long distance rail routes for which, some argued, federal financial support could be defended on strategic grounds to enhance military protection and aid the conveyance of mail. In the 1860s charters were granted for four trans-continental routes: the Pacific Railroad for Omaha to Sacramento, the Northern Pacific, the Atlantic and Pacific, the Texas and Pacific. Rights of way and land were granted by the Federal government (as had state and municipalities) and loans guaranteed in some cases. Credit scandals followed and in 1872 Congress "foreswore further land grants to railways".[49]

By 1871 government ownership accounted for over one-half of all US railway capital. Several economic historians have argued that transport developments for much of the period before then reflected not simply market forces but an accepted freedom for municipalities and states to promote collective action as they saw fit. There was not a constant insistence on private enterprise nor is the story one of the simple rise, corruption and fall of government involvement.[50] The municipalities were directly involved in canals, roads and railways whilst the state governments were also active in grants, licences, charters, loans, stock purchases, land grants and public bonds. New York State funded the early nineteenth century $6 million Erie Canal, provoking competition from other states and protests from towns within the New York State that they be able to enjoy similar state financed projects: Galambos called it "urban centred mercantilism".[51] State and municipalities competed with each other to attract transport links and much it, on some counts, reflected real transport demands not speculative ventures.[52] The development of long east–west routes generated competition on a scale unheard of in Europe. Several parallel routes emerged in the Netherlands, Germany and the UK but by the end of the century competition was limited to multiple bidding for contracts.[53] By the early nineteenth century, Britain already had a transport network and population that was dense by contemporary standards so there was little "opening up" the territory whilst the countries of Continental Europe, as we have seen, saw more route planning and state support reflecting the key role of railways for national defence.

As long then as action by the US Federal government was inhibited by a fear of the concentration of power, the need for regulation fell initially on the states and municipalities. For companies building and running canals and turnpike roads, regulation could be limited to controlling tolls for the track, letting competition between carriers secure the public interest with respect to conveyance. For railways, competition between carriers on the track was unsafe so some regulation of conveyance rates was required. But that had to involve inter-state traffic yet the regulatory bodies were at state not federal level. The companies wanted to charge low rates where competition from other routes or modes existed and give discounts for big customers like Standard Oil. They wanted high rates where they had some monopoly power, often short distance. Both tendencies reflected the railways' ability and desire to discriminate in pricing because they were providing a service (not a commodity) with high fixed costs and low variable costs. Dobbin has argued that local and state governments lacked a professional civil service to enforce the law so enforcement was post hoc by the judiciary.[54] In the 1840s, as competition between routes mounted, business customers turned to the courts but they could do little because the legislation referred only to high rates whilst they were often complaining about the low rates offered to other competing firms in their industry. Thereon to the 1880s, the railway companies resorted to the state courts to challenge regulation.[55] The 1870s saw the passing, in four states, of laws (the Granger Laws) facilitating more intervention in inter-state rates but the railway companies challenged this in the federal courts. Then in 1886 the Supreme Court ruled explicitly that states could not regulate inter-state traffic and this prompted Congress to pass the Inter-State Commerce Act in 1887. From this period started the great expansion of private investment in railways but it also heralded a growing involvement of the Federal government.

## Notes

1 Domar 1970.
2 Cf. Temin 1991.
3 Engerman 1973; Millward 1982.
4 Domar and Machina 1984; Conrad and Meyer 1958.
5 For example Vernandsky 1969; Pipes 1977; White 1987.
6 Pipes 1977. See also Rosefielde and Hedlund 2000 for links to Soviet and Putin Russia.
7 Baykov 1954.
8 Kahan 1965.
9 Gershenkron 1965; Seton-Watson 1967, pp. 334–7; Milward and Saul 1977, p. 363; Gatrell 1986; Domar and Machina 1984.
10 Hobson 1993.
11 Gatrell (2012) estimates revenues as 12 per cent of national income by 1860 but these data include revenues (not just profits) of state enterprises.
12 Portal 1965.
13 Bairoch 1989, p. 18.
14 Crisp 1972, p. 29; Gatrell 1986; Bairoch 1989, p. 32.
15 Mitchell 2003a.
16 Mitchell 2003a, c.
17 Cameron 1961, pp. 275–83.
18 Crisp 1959.
19 The population total is confirmed in Berelowitch *et al.* (1998, p. 493) and Kaser (1978, p. 466). That the total number of serfs may have been much more than 44 million is suggested by the following. Crisp (1959, pp. 73–5) suggests 75 per cent of the total population were serfs implying a total of 54 million serfs. If 80 per cent of the rural population were serfs, this in turn suggests some ten million were assigned in the census to urban areas, that 11 million non-serfs lived in rural areas and eight million in urban areas. Alternatively if all serfs were classed as rural this would be another reason why the 44 million figure implied in Gershenkron (1965, pp. 717, 722) and Blum (1961, pp. 421, 477) may be an underestimate.
20 The next few paragraphs follow closely some paragraphs in Millward (1984) and thanks are due to Academic Press for granting this author's right to automatic reprint with permission.
21 Lyashenko 1949, pp. 313–14; Rosovsky 1953, p. 214; Esper 1980, p. 66.
22 Kahan 1966, p. 56; Lyashenko 1949, pp. 323–3; Tugan-Baranovsky 1970, pp. 22, 249; Blackwell 1968, p. 27.
23 Kahk and Ligi 1975, p. 145; Tugan-Baranovsky 1970, pp. 22, 249; Blum 1978, p. 296; Blum 1961, pp. 298, 403; Crisp 1967, p. 147; Kahan 1966, p. 58; Blackwell 1968, pp. 36, 53–6; Pintner 1967, p. 263; Lyashenko 1949, p. 318.
24 Crisp 1978, p. 318; Kahan 1966, p. 58; Blum 1961, pp. 319–20; Blackwell 1968, pp. 292–307; Tugan-Baranovsky 1970, pp. 72–4.
25 Tugan-Baranovsky 1970, translated 3rd edition, ch. 7.
26 Yatsounsky 1965, pp. 367–75.
27 Portal 1965; Lyashenko 1949, pp. 135, 353; Tugan-Baranovsky 1970, pp. 193–9.
28 Blum 1961, p. 299; Kaser 1978, p. 447; Blackwell 1968, p. 210; Strumilin 1969, p. 165; Yatsounsky 1974, pp. 114–19.
29 Tugan-Baranovsky 1970, pp. 90–100; Esper 1978, 1980, 1981.
30 Zelnik 1965, pp. 513–16.
31 Dennison 2011.
32 Sylla 2000, p. 488; Ransom 1989, ch. 2.
33 US Bureau of the Census 1976.
34 Galambos 2000a, p. 284.

35  Broadberry 1994b; Temin 1991; North 1961, 1965.
36  Hummel 2007, p. 192.
37  US Bureau of the Census 1976.
38  Fenoaltea 1981; Genovese 1965; Fogel and Engerman 1974; Gutman 1975; David *et al.* 1976.
39  Ransom 1989, pp. 220–5.
40  US Bureau of the Census 1976; Lipsey 2000, p. 701.
41  Maddison 1995, p. 38.
42  Sylla 2000, p. 527.
43  Bairoch 1989.
44  Lebergott 1984, p. 152.
45  Lebergott 1984, p. 152.
46  Taussig 1888; David 1970.
47  Harley 1992, p. 580.
48  Dobbin 1994, p. 86.
49  Ibid., p. 56.
50  Lively 1955; Goodrich 1960; McCraw 1975; Dowd and Dobbin 2001, p. 66.
51  Galambos 2000a, p. 277.
52  Fishlow 2000.
53  Fremdling 1999; Fremdling and Knieps 1993.
54  Dobbin 1994, pp. 45–6.
55  Dunlavy 2001.

# Part II

# Business growth and the nation states 1870–1939

# 5 German business in the world economy

## Cartels to autarky

### The political and economic geography of the new German Reich

The new German Reich of 39 million people which emerged in 1871 was, by contemporary standards, economically strong, still very vulnerable strategically and its constitution gave only vague guidance and limited powers to the central government. It did now have a relatively unified internal market though direct tax systems varied across the different states. It was not especially well endowed with a wide range of resources but by 1870 had achieved a stage of economic development ranking it in Europe below only the UK and Belgium. Its population and land area were now very similar to France. So also were its average income levels, iron production, merchant fleet and telegraph density. Roughly one-half of the labour force was still in agriculture, and manufacturing output per head had caught up to French levels. Germany did have a large coal industry and good potassium salt resources whilst the spread of its rail network, relative to land area, was one-third greater than France's (Table 5.1). It was weak in metals, minerals and oil and of course had to import most of its raw cotton and wool. It was also still relatively weak in military resources with warship tonnage only some 42,000 in 1870 (including wooden vessels) as compared to France 457,000 and the UK 633,000. As a major land power, the size of its army was even more vital and, with 410,000 military personnel, exceeded the British level but it was still below France at 454,000, let alone Russia at 716,000. By 1881 the German figures were higher but so were all the others.[1]

Whilst then by 1870 Germany was developing well economically, its rather mixed resource endowment and inferior military strength was especially significant in the light of its economic and political geography. It had limited access to the sea and as yet no colonies. Following the Franco-Prussian war its position in the centre of Europe was strategically dangerous. With France still resentful and, on its eastern flank, Russia wary, Germany could look for friends only at the two multinational Austria-Hungary and Ottoman empires to its south and south-east. Moreover the German economy was heavily involved in foreign trade and was encircled on land by attractive sales markets and raw material sources in Bohemia textiles, Romanian oil, Polish coal, Alsace textiles and Lorraine iron

Table 5.1 Strategic dimensions of France, Germany and the UK 1870–1929 (contemporary boundaries)[a]

| | France | | | Germany | | | UK | | |
|---|---|---|---|---|---|---|---|---|---|
| | 1870 | 1913 | 1929 | 1870 | 1913 | 1929 | 1870 | 1913 | 1929 |
| **A Military and mercantile strength** | | | | | | | | | |
| Military personnel[b] ('000 persons) | 454 | 910 | 666 | 410 | 891 | 115 | 345 | 532 | 443 |
| Merchant fleet ('000 net reg. tons) | 680 | 1582 | 2007 | 265 | 3320 | 2042 | 2439 | 12,120 | 11,369 |
| Warships[b] ('000 tons) | 457 | 900 | 406 | 42 | 1305 | 157 | 633 | 2714 | 1269 |
| Defence spending (£ sterling)[c] | 23.9 | 72 | 103 | 14.4[d] | 93 | 33 | 22.8[e] | 73 | 105 |
| **B Resources** | | | | | | | | | |
| Land area ('000 square miles) | 213 | 208 | 213 | 198 | 204 | 172 | 142 | 142 | 117 |
| Population (millions) | 38 | 39.8 | 41.2 | 39 | 67.0 | 64.7[f] | 31 | 45.6 | 45.7 |
| Coal output (million metric tons) | 13.3 | 40.8 | 53.0 | 32[g] | 277.3[g] | 337.9[g] | 112 | 292.0 | 262.0 |
| Iron ore output (million metric tons) | 2.6 | 21.9 | 50.7 | 2.9 | 28.6 | 6.4 | 14.6 | 16.3 | 13.4 |
| **C Communications** | | | | | | | | | |
| Railway spread (track miles per 1000 square miles) | 45 | 122 | 123 | 59 | 193 | 209 | 149[h] | 226 | 226 |
| Telecom density (telegrams per 100 population) | 14.9 | 131[i] | 118 | 22.1 | 78[i] | 48[f] | 27.4 | 191 | 155 |
| International telegraph cables[j] (length in '000 kilometres) | n.a. | 44.5 | 64.9 | n.a. | 34.0 | 3.3 | n.a. | 266.0 | 297.8 |
| **D Stage of development** | | | | | | | | | |
| % Labour in agriculture[k] | 49.2 | 41.1 | 35.6 | 49.5 | 34.6 | 29.0 | 22.7 | 11.7 | 6.0 |
| Income levels[k] (GDP per head in $1990) | 1876 | 3485 | 4710 | 1839 | 3648 | 4057 | 3190 | 4921 | 5503 |

Sources: Annex Tables plus Wright 1942, Appendix XXII; Hobson 1993, Appendix 2; Headrick 1991, Tables 6.1 and 11.4; Kennedy 1988, pp. 261, 362, 382, 429; Mitchell 1988.

Notes

a  See Annex Table A1.

b  The 1913 data are from Kennedy (1988) whilst the 1870 and 1929 figures are from Wright (1942) and the entries for military personnel include navies and colonial troops.

c  The 1870 and 1913 data are from Hobson (1993), covering ordinary war expenditures plus extraordinary, excluding debt interest. Hobson gives military expenditure as % national income in 1913 as 4.8 France, 3.9 Germany, 5.1 Japan, 5.1 Russia, 3.2 UK and 1.0 USA. The entries for 1929 relate to 1930 and are from Kennedy (1988, Table 27) which I have converted to sterling by using the New York rate of $4.857 for one pound sterling in 1930 given in Mitchell (1988, p. 702).

d  1872.

e  Britain only.

f  Population of the area occupied by the Reich in 1835, i.e. includes Saarland.

g  Includes brown coal, lignite etc. The 1929 figure includes Upper Silesia and Saarland.

h  Britain only 1871.

i  The French entry relates to 1914 and excludes official telegrams, Alsace and Lorraine (included with Germany).

j  Company plus government cables for 1908 and 1923. The German entry for 1908 includes the Netherlands. After WWI the status of some former German cables stayed undefined for several years.

k  See Annex Tables A4 and A3. In general corresponds to 2003 boundaries. The 1929 entries for agriculture for France and the UK relate to 1930. The German entries for 1913 relate to Prussia only and to the 1870 frontier and hence excludes Alsace and Lorraine; the 1929 entries relate to 1936 German frontiers.

ore. German merchants had long been resident in many of the towns and ports like Danzig, Budapest and Bratislava. These were not secure markets, located as much of this periphery was in the crumbling multinational empires. Then the First World War (WWI) and the Versailles Treaty of 1919 exacerbated Germany's dilemma for two reasons. First, Germany lost Poznan, part of Silesia and West Prussia to what came to be called the Polish Corridor. Alsace and Lorraine were returned to France whilst Upper Silesia became a plebiscite area, Danzig a Free City and the Saar put under the administration of the United Nations for 15 years. This was about one-eighth of Germany's land area and one-tenth of its population. Second, the collapse of the multinational empires at the end of WWI and the withdrawal of the Russian boundary eastwards by the 1917 Treaty of Brest-Litovsk heralded the arrival of a host of new nation states: Poland, Czechoslovakia, Yugoslavia, Lithuania, Latvia and Estonia quite apart from Austria, Hungary and Finland each of whom had a long history of some separate identity, and Bulgaria, Greece and Romania who had detached from the Ottoman Empire in the nineteenth century. The whole of Germany's economic periphery had been "balkanised".[2]

Finally of note, again more a matter of frustration, was Germany's overseas empire. It dated from 1884 and eventually covered territories in Cameroon, Togo, East Africa and South Africa plus New Guinea, several Pacific Islands and Kaiochow in the Far East. These regions were developed in classic British fashion from trading companies to protectorates with the aim of self-government. They received loans and subsidies from the Reich, especially for railway development. By 1913 this empire covered 2.9 million square kilometres but in terms of population and trade was tiny relative to the home population and economy and to Britain's empire. Taken away by the 1919 Treaty of Versailles, its relative failure was an element in pushing Germany's interests to central, eastern and southern Europe.

Turning now to those political institutions of the Reich of relevance to the analysis of business/state relations, the new constitution of 1871 did provide an assignment of functions and tax revenues as between the centre, the states and local government. But the democratic power of the centre was weak. The new Parliament (*Reichstag*) was elected on universal suffrage and the Reich centre had responsibility for defence, foreign policy, posts and telecoms and central banking as well for unifying and standardising the currency, law, traffic, customs, patents, weights and measures and also took on basic social welfare provision for old age and disability from 1881. To finance these functions, the Law of December 1871 assigned to the Reich all indirect taxes – customs, excise, stamp duties – leaving all direct taxes on income, business and property to the states who were allocated responsibility for justice, police, economy, culture, education, other welfare plus transport and other infrastructure. On the surface the Reich blossomed with new imperial institutions: the central bank (*Reichsbank* in 1871), Post Office (*Reichspost* in 1874), the new mark currency and gold standard, a revised legal system, an Audit Office, Statistical Office, National Debt Administration and Health Department.[3]

The problem was that the key decisions were made by the Federal Council (*Reichsbund*) which comprised representatives of all the German states. The sovereign had always been active in defence and foreign policy and especially so was Kaiser Wilhelm II who came to the throne in 1888. His role and power were ambiguous. He had the power to make appointments to imperial government and civil service posts, "the single most important instrument of monarchial power".[4] He could himself declare war but only when the Reich was threatened. Otherwise he had to obtain the assent of the *Reichsbund* which controlled all bills going to the *Reichstag* and had responsibility for executing and administering the legislation. The whole structure was in any case dominated by Prussia which had 17 of the 58 seats on the *Reichsbund* and several of the other states were beholden to Prussia for economic and political support. The sovereign and Reich office had only limited staffing support for which it looked to the Prussian bureaucracy. The Prussian Prime Minister, initially Bismarck, was also the Reich Chancellor and since representation on the Prussian Diet (*Landtag*) was highly skewed to the nobility in a three class system, much power remained with him plus the East Elbian Junkers and now on the scene, as we shall see, the leading industrialists and the heads of cartels, often from Rhineland Prussia. Historians are prone to say the Kaiser was no more than the first among equals; a German Emperor not the Emperor of Germany. The Constitution of 1871 mentioned the office of the Kaiser "under the modest rubric 'presidency of the Council' ".[5]

The idea of a "rye and iron" group (*Sammlungspolitick*) dominating the Reich has long been debated with any concordat seen to be disrupted by clashes between the interests of the Rhenish coal and iron barons and the East Elbian Junker estate owners.[6] There is no dispute however that these two groups had a dominant influence, via the power of the Prussian state, on German economic policy. Whereas the main fears of the Junkers were electoral reform and the rising tide of grain imports from Russia and America, the industrialists felt more the competition from British manufacturing exports and the threat of labour power as the country took to factories in the rapidly urbanising economy. The influence of Germany's agricultural and industrial elites did not disappear with the new Weimar Republic. Nonetheless the 1919 constitution did take power away from the states. The new Republic was to be the central authority, including for taxes. The aim was one country, one government. Everyone over 20 had a vote for the new President and Parliament. The latter had two chambers, the *Reichstag* and the House of States. The Chancellor, as head of the central government, was appointed by the President and was responsible for the legislature and advised the President on the choice of Reich ministers. All direct taxes were now under the control of the Reich though some revenues were redirected to the states. All of this was a considerable advance on 1871. There were potential dangers in the role of the President but Hitler's appearance as Chancellor in 1933, his Nazification of government policy and the subsequent collapse of democracy was a force that could have defeated many constitutions.

The aim now is to examine in detail how Germany's political and economic geography affected business/state relations in tariff policy, cartel development, the growth of transport and other infrastructure, the public finances and the shift to a command type economy in the 1930s. The broad trend is of the centralisation of power, initially a democratically sponsored economic change, including in the 1920s a move to a more self-sufficient economy, but culminating in business subjection to Nazi economic controls in the 1930s. There is certainly continuity in the economic instruments used by German governments, none of which however can explain the commitment to war, racism and violence by the mid 1930s.[7]

## The distinctive character of German business growth

Germany experienced several trends in the growth of industry and agriculture common to Continental Europe and USA, including tariff protection of home industry and agriculture. Its distinctive features were, first, that its major initial industrial spurt coincided, in the second half of the nineteenth century with the tendency for the leading sectors to be in capital intensive heavy industries. Second, industrial leaders showed a strong proclivity to form cartels. Third, public enterprises were more extensive in Germany than in other Western European countries. The aim now is to outline and explain the first two elements whilst the third will emerge as part of the discussion of infrastructure development and the public finances in the fourth and fifth sections of the chapter. National output grew throughout the Western World at about 2 per cent per annum in the 1870s and 1880s, slightly lower than in the previous decade. But from the late 1890s the pace accelerated up to WWI and then flattened out in the 1920s, picking up again after the depression of the 1930s. Whilst USA led economic growth in the period up to WWI, Germany was not far behind (Table 5.2). In the 1920–38 years of peace, Germany also performed well though now the leader was Russia, followed by Japan, and Germany's growth in part reflected its low starting point after WWI. Indeed if the devastations of two World Wars are included, German national output 1913–50, absolutely and per head of population, exhibited only small advances whilst USA and Russia showed massive increases.

Steel, engineering and chemicals were the heavy manufacturing industries which, together with the older coal, railway and iron sectors, played a central role in economic growth in Western Europe and USA in this period. These were very capital intensive activities with high fixed costs, and the average size of firms grew accordingly. Technological change was rapid with business research and development especially important in electrical engineering and chemicals such that horizontal integration to spread R&D and other overheads and vertical integration to lower the risks of raw material failure and secure upstream markets became common. High fixed costs meant low short run marginal costs so that cut-throat competition and dumping were attractive. International trade increased market size, encouraging the shift to mass production of homogeneous products. Monopolistic markets were emerging through enterprise mergers and joining hands in cartels. Smaller scale artisan production was on the decline though the different inheritance of skilled labour supplies in different countries, together with different endowment of natural resources meant that the spread of mass production might, as we shall argue later, be more economical for USA than for Europe.

Three further general points. First, the 1860s and 1870s marked the apogee of British economic power. Its manufacturing could undercut the prices of many European products – even coal with huge transport costs was competitive up many river arteries of Continental Europe like the Saone, Rhine and Oder.[8] The temptation to erect tariff barriers was strong. Second, agriculture's share of the labour force was everywhere falling. In Europe including the Balkans, probably about two-thirds of the labour force were still in agriculture in 1870, falling to just over a half by 1913 and down to 40 per cent by 1950.[9] Mortality rates had started their long term decline from the mid nineteenth century and this more than offset rising emigration to the new world and the onset of the decline in marital fertility from the end of the century. Consequently, Europe's population continued to rise to nearly 500 million by 1913 and, despite the two World Wars, civil wars in Russia and Spain, famines, economic depression, population displacements and ethnic cleansing, it reached nearly 600 million by 1950. So although the share of agriculture was falling, the agrarian labour force remained large in absolute terms everywhere except Britain, the Low Countries, northern France and the Rhineland. Finally of note are the opening years of our period when the agricultural sectors of Western Europe were about to experience a massive grain inflow from North America and Russia. The spread of railways and steamships together with mechanisation in USA and cheap labour and land in Russia heralded a large decline in food prices. Indeed since technological advances were lowering real unit costs also in industry, the absence of any

*Table 5.2* Growth of income 1870–1950 (average annual % growth rates)[a]

|  | France | Germany | Japan | Russia | UK | USA |
|---|---|---|---|---|---|---|
| *National income*[b] | | | | | | |
| 1870–1913 | 1.63 | 2.90 | 2.34 | 2.40 | 1.86 | 3.94 |
| 1920–38 | 2.21 | 4.26 | 3.45 | 5.60[c] | 1.86 | 1.60 |
| 1913–50 | 1.15 | 0.30 | 2.24 | 2.15 | 1.19 | 2.84 |
| *National income per head*[d] | | | | | | |
| 1870–1913 | 1.45 | 1.72 | 1.38 | 0.93 | 1.01 | 1.81 |
| 1920–38 | 1.81 | 3.00 | 2.04 | 4.90 | 1.40 | 0.55 |
| 1913–50 | 1.12 | 0.17 | 0.92 | 1.76 | 0.93 | 1.61 |

Sources: derived from data in 1990 Geary-Khamis dollars, 1989 boundaries, in Maddison 1995, pp. 180–200.

Notes
a  1989 boundaries.
b  Gross domestic product.
c  1928–38.
d  Gross domestic product per head.

massive increase in the world money stock meant all prices were falling in the 1870s and 1880s. There was a short blip 1888–92 and then a flattening out followed by a slow rise in prices to 1913 as national outputs expanded rapidly.

Within this context, German economic growth was distinguished in being focused on the heavy industrial sector which, given a rapidly rising population, allowed an expansion of its military capacity. At the same time, the power of the Prussian Junkers ensured that agriculture, and especially its grain sector, was not sidetracked so that farms remained a large part of the economy. Over the 70 years from 1870, the population rose by two-thirds. Most of it was in the years up to 1913 since, after WWI, the loss of Alsace, Lorraine and West Prussia levelled out the total at about 67 million. Even that increase was significant in the light of the low fertility and stagnation of the French population such that by 1913, as Table 5.1 shows, Germany's military personnel had practically caught up with the French, whilst the tonnage of its warships and merchant fleet, aided by Germany's expansion of heavy industry, ran ahead. Total defence spending in 1913 exceeded that in France even though, at 3.9 per cent of national income, it was less of a burden than the 4.6 per cent of France. This pattern reflected a superior growth generally in industry and national output, as indicated in Table 5.2. GDP grew at an average of 2.9 per cent up to 1913 and GDP per head at 1.72 per cent, the latter exceeded only slightly by USA.

Germany's very strong growth in mining, manufacturing and railways was accompanied by significant concentration of industrial control. Railways and industry accounted for one-quarter of the capital stock in 1873 but over 40 per cent by 1913. Annual investment in the economy rose from 9 per cent of national income in 1871 to 17 per cent by 1918, flattening out in the 1920s, prior to a major surge from the mid 1930s. The output of potassium salts, sulphuric acid, steel and pig iron increased more than tenfold up to 1913 and after a dip in the 1920s resumed growth in the 1930s. The labour force in manufacturing had more than doubled by 1925 and by 1939 those in metals and machinery (including electrical engineering) totalled 4.4 million.[10] No less important, as Table 5.3 shows, was the growth in services with the labour force in transport, communications, finance and commerce increasing from nearly two million in 1882 to 11 million by 1935. Coal and transport maintained a strong expansion throughout whilst the cotton industry flattened out after WWI and in the 1930s as consumption goods made way for investment in heavy industry.

The rise in heavy industry was accompanied by an increase in the size of the average business firm, with giants like Krupps, AEG, IG Farben and Thyssen emerging. In manufacturing in 1882, 23 per cent of workers were in factories with more than 50 employees; by 1907 it was 42 per cent. Within firms the product range diversified and by 1907 three-quarters of the largest 100 firms were joint stock companies vertically integrated backwards, especially in chemicals, metals, electrical engineering and machinery making. By WW1 one-half of the German labour force in industry and mining were in enterprises with more than 50 employees.[11] The discovery, for example, that blast furnace gases could be used as a fuel prompted foundries to integrate forward to steelworks and

*Table 5.3* Labour force[a] in Germany 1872–1939 ('000)

|  | *1882* | *1895* | *1907* | *1925*[b] | *1939*[c] |
|---|---|---|---|---|---|
| Agriculture | 8337 | 8293 | 9883 | 9762 | 8985 |
| Mining, etc. | 591 | 821 | 1245 | 1272 | 734 |
| Manufacturing[d] | 4716 | 5916 | 7834 | 10,359 | 11,508 |
| Construction | 946 | 1354 | 1906 | 1708 | 2375 |
| Commerce, finance, etc. | 854 | 1230 | 1800 | 3083 | 3439 |
| Transport and commununication | 437 | 616 | 1036 | 1520 | 1897 |
| Other services[e] | 1616 | 2341 | 2976 | 4156 | 5680 |
| Other | 235 | 201 | 156 | 249 | 0 |
| Total | 17,732 | 20,772 | 26,836 | 32,109 | 34,618 |

Source: Mitchell 2003a, p. 164.

Notes
a Economically active population.
b Excludes Saarland.
c 1937 territory.
d Includes gas, electricity, water and sanitary services. Applying data from Lee (1979 p. 446), suggests the largest sector by 1939 was "metals and machines" (4.4 million) whose growth since 1846 was exceeded only by paper, printing and probably steel.
e Includes armed forces.

rolling mills. This growing concentration of the capital goods sector was common also in USA but in British industry less so and found more in firms like Unilever, Courtaulds, Distillers, Lancashire Cotton Corporation, Cadburys in retailing, food, textiles and other consumer goods. The role of marketing in US firms involved in mass production developed strongly – typewriters, telephones, harvesters, tractors, sewing machines, later motor cars, elevators, pumps and boilers. German businesses tended more to produce heavy equipment close to the requirement of specific customers and with a strong technical input. They were supported by long term credit and the underwriting of industrial securites by an increasingly dominant group of seven large banks: *Schaaffhausenensche-Bankverein, Disonto-Gesellschaft, Bank für Handel und Industrie, Berliner Handelsgesellschaft, Deutsche Bank, Commerzbank* and *Dresdner bank*, all of them formed between 1848 and 1872.

The years 1870–1939 saw Germany catching up very significantly on British national output and manufacturing levels generating a large literature on what was wrong with British management.[12] Of particular interest is Chandler's thesis that the so-called "cooperative capitalism" of mergers, cartels and trusts in Germany, especially in manufacturing, more nearly matched America's shift to mass marketing, professional managers, M form and related new management structures.[13] British family firms and holding companies, in this light, are seen as an inferior product of an earlier start and entrenched attitudes and for some a class based disdain for "trade and industry".[14] Although Chandler's characterisation of emerging management structures has been very insightful for business historians, it cannot account for the relative growth paths of USA, UK and

Germany. In fact British manufacturing productivity growth over the 100 years from 1870 was just as good as Germany and USA. There will be a more detailed comparison of USA and the UK in later chapters. Here the important point about Germany and the UK is that the differing growth rates of productivity are located not in manufacturing but mainly in services and that the role of agriculture is also central to explanations of how Germany's national income per head grew faster than Britain's in our period. It is the case, as shown in Table 5.4, that German GDP per head grew faster than the UK 1870–1928. So also did its manufacturing output per head of population which rose fivefold 1860–1913 and a further 20 per cent 1913–28. However it is clear that a significant element in this was not only the productivity rise in manufacturing but also a structural shift of the labour force out of agriculture. Changes in manufacturing per head of population reflect both the changing share of manufacturing in the country's labour force and productivity advances in manufacturing.

These insights come from Broadberry's research, some of whose results are illustrated in Figure 5.1.[15] Sectoral efficiency is measured in terms of labour productivity, that is, output per employee, though similar findings apply to total factor productivity. None of the process of catching up with the UK, for both Germany and USA, can be attributed to superior productivity growth in manufacturing: there was little long term change in the relative productivity levels in manufacturing across USA, Germany and the UK over the 100 years from 1870 notwithstanding some short term movements. The big German productivity gains up to 1935 were in mining and in certain service sectors, especially transport and communications, whilst the transfer of labour from agriculture to industry involved a shift from a low value added to a high value added sector. Only 22 per cent of the UK labour force in 1871 was in agriculture whereas, as already noted, it was one-half in Germany. That labour force actually grew to nearly ten million by 1907, falling to just less than nine million by 1939 (Table 5.3). Since however the population was rising rapidly, agriculture's share of the labour force had fallen to 30 per cent by the late 1920s. German agriculture was markedly less efficient than British agriculture as may be seen in Figure 5.1. This is part of the old story of Germany holding on to its large grain estates of the East Elbian Junkers. They were certainly large. As late as 1925, 40 per cent of the agricultural land in East Elbia was in farms of more than 100 hectares whereas the figure for the rest of Germany was 8 per cent.[16] With a productivity level only one-half of the British and outcompeted by North America and Russian grain imports, German grain growers kept their position, as we shall see, by tariff protection and bail-outs by the *Reich*. For the moment, the important point is that agriculture employed a declining *share* of the labour force and that Germany's GDP per head could advance rapidly for that reason alone.

The level of productivity in the German manufacturing sector was very similar to Britain's in 1871, fluctuated at about the same level until the early 1900s when it rose above Britain, then dipping after WW1 and recovering in the 1930s. For "industry" as a whole (mining, manufacturing, construction), the German productivity level at the start of each decade from 1871 to 1951 was

Table 5.4 Income and industrialisation levels 1860–1953 (USA 1913=100)

| | Manufacturing output per head of population[a] | | | | Gross domestic product per head of population[b] | | | |
|---|---|---|---|---|---|---|---|---|
| | 1860 | 1913 | 1928 | 1953 | 1870 | 1913 | 1928 | 1953 |
| USA | 17 | 100 | 144 | 281 | 46 | 100 | 124 | 204 |
| UK | 51 | 91 | 97 | 167 | 61 | 95 | 96 | 136 |
| Belgium | 22 | 70 | 92 | 93 | 50 | 78 | 78 | 107 |
| France | 16 | 47 | 62 | 71 | 35 | 65 | 83 | 108 |
| Germany | 12 | 67 | 80 | 106[c] | 36 | 72 | 81 | 102 |
| Sweden | 12 | 53 | 67 | 129 | 31 | 58 | 69 | 134 |
| Italy | 8 | 21 | 31 | 48 | 28 | 47 | 56 | 78 |
| Spain | 9 | 17 | 22 | 25 | 26 | 42 | 53 | 53 |
| Russia | 6 | 16 | 16[d] | 58[d] | 19 | 28 | 26 | 57 |
| Japan | 5 | 16 | 24 | 32 | 14 | 25 | 36 | 45 |
| India | 2 | 2 | 2 | 4[e] | 11 | 13 | 12 | 12 |

Source: Bairoch 1982; Maddison 1995.

Notes
a 1913 boundaries.
b 1989 boundaries. The index is derived from Maddison's estimates in Geary–Khamis 1990 dollars.
c East plus West.
d USSR.
e India plus Pakistan.

below the British level, except for 1901 and 1911.[17] Rather, Germany's productivity raced ahead in transport, communications, electricity supply and mining. The share of the service sectors of all the economies in the Western World was rising in the nineteenth century. Germany was especially good in services associated with office technology and equipment, electricity and railways whilst Britain was better at distribution and finance where it maintained a large productivity lead over Germany.

## Trade, tariffs and cartels

So the distinctive features of Germany's business growth 1870–1938 was a strong concentration of ownership levels in heavy manufacturing goods and mining, robust expansion of transport, telecoms and electricity supply and where the process of catching up to UK income levels was largely to be found in the

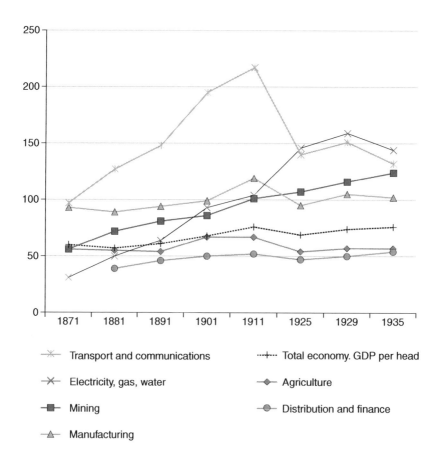

*Figure 5.1* Sector productivity in Germany and the UK 1871–1935 (German output per employee as % UK) (source: Broadberry 1997a, 1998).

structural shift out of agriculture plus a superior productivity performance in parts of the service sector and mining, and with little change in comparative productivity levels for manufacturing. Germany was also distinctive in some of the relations between government and business and, for manufacturing and mining, in the area of cartels, mergers and tariff protection. These policy and institutional changes were not easy to effect and in some other countries were not deemed desirable. Forming cartels and securing tariff protection usually required good cooperation between firms and also effective lobbying of government. The difficulties of doing that in the UK from the late nineteenth century onwards are clearly revealed in the study by Marrison of the various factions involved in the British business sector in its search for protection in the first few decades of the twentieth century.[18] In USA, trusts (mergers) were allowed and tariff protection facilitated by the Federal government. The large transport costs for European goods exported to USA itself limited competition. Internally, competition in USA was promoted, as we shall see later, by the banning of price fixing and related cartel arrangements. The central government in France supported tariff protection because of its proximity to Britain, the world's greatest industrial power. Both France and the UK by 1870 had a considerable industrial history with strong family firms, not especially amenable to cartel formation or trustification.

In contrast, modern industry in Germany was fairly recent and it had only a small merchant class. There was an artisan/guild culture which was sufficiently strong to have a voice in the 1848 revolution. Much was still based on small firms with tailor made products and its manufacturing output per head was not much different from Spain and Italy in 1860 (cf. Table 5.4). The immense industrial expansion into which it now entered meant a very uncertain future, given its limited inheritance. The German politicians therefore acceded to calls for tariff protection and cartels when this accorded with the wishes of the two dominant groups, the East Elbian Junkers and Rhenish industrialists. The state backed cartels and tariffs in so far as they were consistent with Germany's new military requirements and that the requirements of the key interest groups could be reconciled.

Although Germany did, from the 1870s, take the lead in Europe in a protectionism which dominated all Reich and Weimar trade policies, she did successfully expand international trade up to WWI. As Figure 5.2 illustrates, Germany's merchandise exports, at 10 per cent of national output in 1870, were very close to the UK and well above other countries, a position held throughout much of the inter-war period. Her trade pattern was closely linked to her foreign investments which, over the period 1870–1913, were spread evenly over all areas of Europe and USA in contrast to France's strong concentration in Russia as well as Africa whilst the main destinations of UK foreign investment were Australia, New Zealand, North and South America (Table 5.5). These patterns were mirrored in the destination of German exports with a very large share of the exports of steel, iron, coal, machinery, cotton and woollen goods by 1913 going to other European countries, paying for a high proportion of its imports of grain, raw cotton, wool and tea from Asia, the Americas and British dominions.[19]

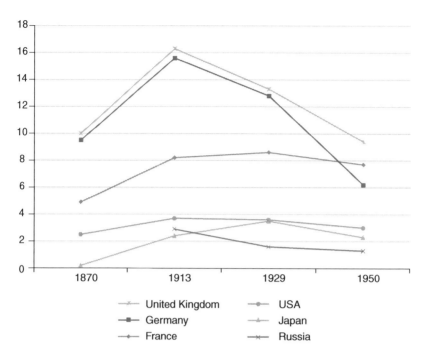

*Figure 5.2* Exports as % GDP in the major powers 1870–1950 (source: Maddison 1995, p. 38) (relates to merchandise exports, 1989 boundaries and 1990 prices).

Support for free trade in Germany had traditionally resided in merchants in ports like Hamburg and Bremen plus those firms in the finishing trades like weaving who wanted cheap yarns and other raw materials and were less concerned about import competition with their products which were less standardised and more tailor made for customers. The East Elbian Junker estate owners had also favoured free trade on the grounds that the countries to which they exported would not themselves set up grain tariff barriers. Producers of industrial raw materials like pig iron and those involved in the early stages of production like soda manufacturers and cotton spinners facing competition from French and Swiss textiles, favoured protection but, within the *Zollverein*, such manufacturers (in Bavaria, for example) were never politically strong. The return to protection from the late 1870s was a result of a growing coincidence of interests across three power groups: the new heavy goods producers, the East Elbian Junker estate owners, the government, specifically the Prussian Chancellor, Bismarck. The iron masters were by the early 1870s becoming increasingly apprehensive about the repeal of iron duties, due in 1878 when a treaty with France expired. Coal, iron and steel producers joined the spinners and soda manufacturers in pressing for tariffs on industrial raw materials and intermediate goods. The early 1870s saw a financial crisis and the onset of the massive grain inflow from

*Table 5.5* Foreign investment by France, Germany and the UK 1870–1914 (% distribution of cumulative investments by destination)

|  | France | Germany | UK |
|---|---|---|---|
| Russia | 25.1 | 7.7 | 3.4 |
| Other Europe | 36.0 | 45.6 | 6.3 |
| USA | 4.4 | 15.7 | 20.5 |
| Japan | 0 | 0 | 1.9 |
| British dominions | 0 | 0 | 20.5 |
| Latin America | 13.3 | 16.2 | 17.7 |
| India | 4.9 | 4.3 | 7.8 |
| Other | 16.3 | 10.5 | 21.9 |
| Total | 100 | 100 | 100 |

Source: Daudin *et al.* 2010, p. 12.

North America and Russia as rail and steamship costs fell. The major German rye and wheat production came from the large East Elbian estates whilst animal husbandry was more common in the small peasant farms in the West. The Junker estates now faced the prospect of declining export markets and threats to their domestic sales. Finally Bismarck and the *Reichsbund* were always conscious of the strategic argument for some minimal ring fencing of agriculture and armaments but now, from the early 1870s, there was a need for military re-equipment, and expansion of the warship fleet and a rise in defence spending and hence a rise in the Reich's tax revenues. As noted earlier and to be articulated more fully later in this chapter, custom revenues were the main tax source for the Reich from the 1870s, given that direct taxes had been assigned to the states and excise taxes on "luxuries" like coffee, tea and wine were not so productive of revenues as they were in the UK.

The years 1877–79 therefore saw the onset of protective policies as a Union of Iron and Steel Manufacturers (established in 1873) pushed for the continuance of iron duties and in 1878 the Central Association of German Manufacturers drafted a tariff for iron, steel and textiles. The agriculturalists were lobbying for a rise in cereal duties and this turned out to be the most important element in the 1879 tariff. Bismarck masked his interest in customs revenues by "playing the part of a convert to protection" arguing that the "German Empire must not take its policies from Manchester".[20] Grain duties were set at ten marks per kilogram rising to 50 marks in 1887 by which time the duties were equivalent to 33 per cent of the wheat import price and 47 per cent for rye, much higher than London prices; oats, turnips and some other vegetables also attracted duties.[21] The tariffs on industrial goods were moderate; ten marks per ton on pig-iron; on finer cotton yarns and the better class of textiles generally the duties were raised, also for oil, tallow, timber but other raw materials were free. Bismarck's successor, Caprivi, saw rising import prices as a danger to living standards and exports. In 1891/92 agricultural duties were reduced and commercial treaties concluded with Austria-Hungary, Belgium, Switzerland, Portugal and Romania. By this stage however a tariff war was breaking out with Russia and the East Elbian Junkers were near revolt. They initiated in 1892 an Agrarian League (*Landbund*) which in 1895 established a formal link with the peasants' association (*Deutsche Bauerbund*) – for long seen by historians as a democratic mask hailing the farmers and agricultural labourers as professional colleagues of the Junkers.[22] The Junker East Elbian estate owners and Rhenish industrialists in the rye and iron alliance (*Sammlungspolitick*) were often at loggerheads but a Committee for the Drafting of a Trade Treaty was established to prepare for the expiry of the commercial treaties signed by Caprivi who was toppled in 1894.

By the late 1890s then the protective drive was fully renewed, encouraged by a rise in duties in USA, with the new Chancellor Bulöw keen to seek support for an expansion of the naval programme. A new Navigation Law was passed in 1898 and a new tariff law in 1902 raising the duty on semi-finished and finished manufacturing goods by 40–80 per cent, on wheat and rye by 55 per cent though several raw materials were still free. Thus raw cotton was free, yarn duties raised and the duties on finished cotton goods raised by 58 per cent. By 1910 German duties on wheat were high by European standards, were "average" for all manufacturing goods and for all imports from Britain.[23] The Bulöw tariff together with a surge in rye export bounties coincided with a rise in world rye prices and generated a big export boom in rye, a commodity which was on decline elsewhere and had little long term future. The First World War of course disrupted all trade and the 1919 Treaty of Versailles did not say much about tariffs save that Germany had to give "most favoured nation status" to all the allies. By 1925 a new reparation plan was in place (the Dawes plan, see the fourth section of this chapter) and Germany, free to make commercial treaties, returned to the Bulöw tariff of 1902. Duties on agricultural and industrial products were reintroduced and followed by several favoured nation agreements. This restoration of protection was nothing compared to the stringent quotas and controls which followed the 1929–31 depression – see the fifth section of this chapter.

Turning now to *cartels*, the support they received from Germany's government at all levels as well as policies for tariff protection and social welfare from the 1880s, has prompted several writers to characterise German's economy as "organised capitalism" or "cooperative capitalism" or even "state socialism".[24] Some have also seen state intervention in industry and agriculture after 1850 as not especially productive given the unwarranted extension to the lives of Junker estates, the boost to rye and the creation of highly protected industrial businesses.[25] The significance of state intervention for our purposes is not the direct impact, conscious or otherwise, on living standards and economic growth. Rather we are concerned to explore the link between Germany's distinctive institutions, its geo-political position and contemporary ideologies. It was argued above that cartels were attractive both to industrial leaders and government and the aim now is to explain, first, how and why they flourished given the inherent difficulties in maintaining such cooperative behaviour and, second, how government responded.

There had been some cartelisation before 1870 in salt works and in the manufacture of tin plate and iron rails. These were invariably simple price agreements as they were for potash 1876, cement 1882, puddling iron 1882, coking coal 1879–81 and coke 1882.[26] Any agreement on prices, to be effective, had to control for quality so that cartels were easier to set up for homogeneous products and, in the case of chemicals and textiles where product differentiation was common, a large number of different cartels for the different products were established in the 1880s. However price agreements on their own are not easy to sustain. The basic economics of cartels suggest that firms come to an agreement to set prices above that level which would operate with unrestricted competitive markets. Unless each firm's output is reduced, the new higher price will be unsustainable since market demand will contract. Hence from the 1880s quotas came into play for cartel members. Theory also suggests that it will be profitable for firms to cheat by producing output levels larger than their quota and for firms to leave the agreement and produce more on their own at the market price level which the remaining cartel members are trying to enforce. Firms in iron and steel who also owned coal mines might escape the coal quota by consuming their own coal and not informing the cartel. Such possibilities were also an incentive to vertically integrate. Hence the pressure to pool the sales and marketing agencies into a "syndicate". For example the Rhenish Westphalian Coal Syndicate (*Rheinisch-Westfälisches Kohlensyndikat*, RKWS) was established in 1893, following two decades of broken agreements, covering 87 per cent of coal produced in the Dortmund region. Likewise, the Potash Agreement of 1876 was followed by the Potash Syndicate of 1880.

Forming cartels was therefore not an easy matter but was helped in Germany by the growing institutional links between firms and by the support of the state. It might seem that cartels were triggered by falling prices and recessions and it cannot be denied that many cartels were formed after the financial crisis of the early 1870s and the onset of falling world commodity prices. However cartels sometimes collapsed in recessions and in recovery. The more important elements were the formation of institutional links and a key starting point was the establishment, in the 1870s, of the Central Association of German Manufacturers, a lobby group for cartels and tariffs. In the same decade the move to tariff protection and the pressure from Junker estate owners were additional forces for cooperation. Fighting ruinous competition was a slogan in many of these campaigns but cartels by the 1900s courted governments and consumers also by emphasising their aim to stabilise prices: such claimed the Steel Union formed in 1904 and RKWS, for which the research of Lübbers[27] provides some empirical support.

The attitude of the Reich and the Prussian state government was very different from government policy in other countries. It was certainly permissive and undeterred by the rise in the number of cartels. The various statistical sources do not give every confidence that they are covering the same phenomenon. Suffice to note that some suggest 14 cartels had been established by 1877 whilst for 1885 it was reported that 12,000 factories were in 385 cartels, a figure repeated in the Ministry of the Interior Enquiry of 1905. In 1925 the Federation of German Industry estimated there were 1500 cartels but two years later a government count registered 3000. For the period 1907–37, a large share of output was reputably governed by cartels in mining, iron, steel, chemicals, glass and cement.[28] Guidance about government policy is not helped by the 1871 constitution which stated simply that "all trade is open to everyone". A Supreme Court ruling of 1897 on the Saxon Woodpulp Manufacturers' agreement invoked that phrase and stated the agreement was in the interest of society because it avoided ruinous competition and that restrictions on the cartel would constitute a limit on freedom of contract.[29] The relevance of an economic enquiry was not established and although the court said cartels might be banned in creating a monopoly, no criterion had been established as to when a monopoly was not in the public interest. The 1905 Ministry enquiry said that the time was not ripe for controlling cartels and in 1910 a Prussian Law actually enforced cartelisation on the potash industry.[30] In 1923 the Ordinance Against the Abuse of Economic Power specified that cartel agreements had to be published and a system for administrating them was established. Cartels became semi-official channels during WWI and in the 1930s, under the Nazis, who however abolished them in 1943.

## Regulation and ownership of businesses in energy, transport and telecommunications

The infrastructure industries have two important technical characteristics: they contain natural monopoly conditions as well as having a strategic value for defence. Natural monopoly conditions, whereby one firm can supply a given service more cheaply than two or more firms, are often found in the grid networks of railways, telecoms, gas and electricity supply. When governments grant rights of way they usually accompany it with conditions and, in Germany, the regulation of fares, tariffs and the bidding process for contracts was not dissimilar to that in other countries, as we saw for the UK, Prussia and France in earlier chapters. The strategic concerns arose in part from the need for communication links to the borders and for secure telecommunication lines to promote social and economic unification, links with overseas colonies and for military operations. In addition coal, gas and electricity represented key intermediate inputs for heavy industry, and could not be easily substituted in the short run. The regulatory regimes in Germany were administered by the states. Gas, electricity, trams and water supply had fairly small town based networks before the 1920s and strategic issues were not the main concern of the states and municipalities. The municipalities were the ones dealing with business firms like AEG (*Allgemeine Elektrizitäts-Gesellschaft*) or running the service themselves through municipal enterprises. They were, as we shall see, often motivated by fiscal considerations. Railways and telecoms, including international telegraph cables, were of direct strategic concern to the Reich government, given its role in defence, though the instruments at its disposal were often owned by the states.

The broad economic trends in these sectors 1870–1938, as shown in Table 5.6, reflected changes in technology, territory and population as well as the demands of industrial and urban growth. The length of rail track trebled up to 1913 but thereafter flattened out in part reflecting the loss of territory. In any case most of the necessary track had been laid, and development thereafter took the form of better, faster services, reflected in the growth of freight traffic which dipped in the 1920s but revived in the 1930s. Inland water navigation was very important in Germany and tonnage carried grew even in the inter-war period but when measured in ton kilometres, there was a distinct flattening out, reflecting the competition from railways. Similarly telegrams gave way to telephones whilst the stagnation of merchant shipping reflected political constraints follow-ing WWI as well as the growing focus on land trade with Central and Eastern Europe. Germany's greatest resource was coal whose output rose sevenfold up to 1913 and continued to rise strongly in the inter-war period, despite the loss of fields in Silesia, Poland and the Saar. Germany never had the strategic worries of France, Spain and Italy about coal though in Prussia, perhaps as a form of state leverage against the Rhenish syndicate RKWS, the state took part ownership of the Hibernia Company. In 1905 a Prussian law ruled that all unclaimed coal con-cessions were to be state property; by the late 1930s probably about one-fifth of all German coal came from state mines.[31]

Coal was the dominant primary energy source for the provision of gas, elec-tricity, tramways and water supply which flourished as local networks in the late

*Table 5.6* Energy and communications in Germany 1871–1938 (contemporary boundaries)[a]

|  | *1871* | *1913* | *1929* | *1938* |
|---|---|---|---|---|
| Rail track ('000 kilometres open) | 21.5 | 62.4 | 58.2 | 58.9 |
| Rail freight traffic (billion ton kilometres) | 6.4 | 67.7 | 53.1 | 89.0 |
| Inland waterway cargo (billion ton kilometres) | 1.7 | 17.9 | 15.1 | 18.7 |
| Merchant shipping (million tons) | 0.9 | 3.3 | 2.5 | 2.7 |
| Telegrams (millions) | 8.9 | 52.3 | 30.9 | 21.9 |
| Telephone calls (billions) | 0.08[b] | 2.5 | 2.6 | 3.2 |
| Mail items[c] (billions) | 0.5 | 7.0 | 7.4 | 7.6 |
| Coal output[d] (million metric tons) | 38.9 | 277.3 | 337.9 | 381.2 |
| Gas supply (billion cubic metres) | n.a. | 1.3[e] | n.a. | 3.4[e] |
| Electricity supply (gigawatt hours) | 1.0[f] | 8.0 | 39.7 | 55.3 |
| Population (millions) | 41.0 | 67.0 | 64.7[g] | 68.6[g] |

Sources: Mitchell 2003a; Matthews 1987; Maddison 1991 for population data.

Notes
a Excludes Alsace and Lorraine 1919–38 and, unless otherwise stated, Saarland 1920–34 and Upper Silesia from 1922.
b 1883.
c Excludes newspapers and registered mail.
d Hard and brown coal.
e 1900 and 1935. Interpolated from chart in Matthews 1987.
f 1900.
g Population of the area occupied by the *Reich* in 1937, i.e. includes the Saar.

nineteenth century. It is true that hydro-electricity emerged also in this period as an alternative to thermal generating plants but even by the late 1930s this accounted for probably no more than 10 per cent of Germany's kilowatt capacity.[32] The growth of huge conglomerates in electrical engineering meant that several large firms – Lahmeyer, Siemen, AEG, Stinnes – became involved in thermal electricity plants and tramways, alongside many smaller enterprises. The municipalities granted concessions to these companies but often at a price, demanding a share of their profits. In some towns the local governments set up their own municipal enterprises in electricity as well as gas, tramways and water supply. By the 1880s one-half of all gas works were in municipal hands and by 1908 all the 50 largest towns; in the latter year some 1240 water undertakings out of 2309 urban districts were municipally owned. The 1880s was the decade when electricity took off and by 1908 only 413 of the 2309 urban district supplies were in municipal ownership but 42 of the 50 largest towns. It has been estimated that by 1913 nearly one-half of electricity power was supplied by plants entirely owned by municipal authorities.[33]

How is one to account for this complex government/private business mix? Electricity was a speculative venture in the 1880s and governments were happy to leave it to the private sector. But that would not explain why towns like Mainz, Mannheim and Darmstadt municipalised their electricity works.[34] Historians of technology such as Hughes have often invoked the long tradition of civic commitment to provision for the "town family".[35] Others have appealed to the rise of municipal socialism. How does that help in explaining the many municipalities that did not municipalise or those like Berlin which stayed private until 1917? A good case can be made that, as in Britain (cf. Chapter 9), some municipalities were driven to ensure that the local utilities generated revenues which the municipalities could use to supplement local tax sources. Such municipalities tended to be in urban areas and especially the large rapidly growing towns facing all the problems of congestion and disease. Public health programmes for sewers, drainage, water supplies and other sanitary works were expensive and even by the early years of the twentieth century water quality in many German cities was still poor, privies were common and there had been only a limited spread of water closets.[36] Means of supplementing local taxes were sought, especially in states like Prussia with its limited privileged electoral roll, with the aim of preventing the finance of public health spending overburdening direct income and property taxes.[37]

Thus two solutions emerged: one was to municipalise and generate from gas, electricity, markets and tramways (but not water supply which was never run for profit) a stream of profits which could be transferred to the general accounts of local authorities. The other was to do deals with private companies as a *quid pro quo* for their concessions. Thus municipalisation was not common in small towns and rural areas, without major public health problems, and much more common in the bigger urban areas. Dawson showed how significant were the profits and transfers generated by municipal enterprises.[38] In 1910/11 in German towns with populations of 100,000 to 200,000, gas trading profits were equivalent to 36 (old English) pence per head of population with £2.6 million accruing in total to towns with more than 50,000. The latter's revenues from electricity worked out at 27 pence per head and tramways ten pence: these were higher than receipts in British towns though it is likely, as we shall see in the fifth section, below, that capital charges have not been deducted from the reported German profits. In striking contrast was the experience of big cities like Berlin which for the period up to WWI received its electricity supply from a private company. The town reaped significant financial rewards and it seems that, like Paris and Copenhagen with their gas supplies, the large city councils were the only ones which were strong enough to obtain lucrative deals from the large electrical companies. AEG and its subsidiaries were heavily involved in electricity supply to Berlin and were able to secure contracts for supplying electricity to the Berlin Tramways Company, as well as for city lighting. The Edison patents were held by *Deutsche Edison Gesellschaft*, a precursor of AEG, whose contract for 30 years from 1884 guaranteed to the Berlin town council one-tenth of gross income and one-quarter of any profits after paying a 6 per cent dividend to the shareholders. In 1889 an even better deal was struck with AEG's foundling, *Berliner Elektritäts*, providing for a 50 per cent share in profits after dividends. Similarly the Berlin Tramways Company paid 8 per cent of its gross receipts and one-half of its profits after a 6 per cent dividend whilst the elevated and underground railway companies had to hand over 2 per cent of receipts and 50 per cent of excess profits.[39]

The inter-war period saw the spread of two key technological innovations in electricity supply. One was the rise in the size of generating plants, lowering unit costs, and the other was the advent of alternating current (allowing electricity to flow both ways on a line) which lowered transmission costs (energy losses) and thereby rendered long distance connections economic. By 1920 Germany was already producing 246 kilowatt hours per head of population, a level exceeded only in Scandinavia with its large hydro-electricity resources. All government levels in Germany took a close interest in promoting further development. On the one hand network integration promised large economic gains but required that generation be concentrated in the largest plants and this would entail the absorption and/or elimination of small enterprises whether privately or municipally owned. Second, electricity was becoming a key intermediate input in the economy with the development of electro-chemical and electro-metallurgical processes in manufacturing. Breakdowns or shortages of electricity supply would have significant effects on industry and military capacity so that electricity had become a service with strong strategic elements. These two issues, network integration and strategic concerns, lead to the deep involvement of government at all levels. There were state owned undertakings like *Preussische Elektrizitäts* and others like *Elecktrowerke* owned jointly by the Reich and local governments. As early as 1929 the Reich and states accounted for one-quarter of all production, the municipalities about the same whilst other public authorities and undertakings with mixed private/public ownership accounted for one-third. In other words only about 15 per cent of total electricity output was produced in purely private businesses.[40] The leverage of government at all levels was both pervasive and complex. The Lahmeyer and Stinnes companies joined in 1890 to form the *Rhenisch-Wetfalisches Elektrizitätswerke*, one-half of whose shares were, in 1914, owned by municipalities. By 1924 it had (it claimed) the largest coal plant in Europe, the *Goldenbergwerk*. It had supply contracts with inter-municipal associations like the United Electricity Works and by 1929 had established lines to a hydro-electric plant in the Alps.[41]

German electricity supply expanded strongly in the inter-war period and, with government help, made some progress towards a nationally integrated system. In 1919 the National Assembly passed a bill which encouraged the development of a coordinated national high tension grid. A model was available in Bavaria where the state system had a grid connecting to municipal undertakings and private companies and sent electricity to Munich and other large towns. In the country as a whole three regional groups were established but real progress towards national system integration was not made until the 1935 strategically motivated law, *Gesetz zur Förderung der Energiewirtschaft*, which ruled that all investment in generating plant and networks had to be approved by the Minister of Economics. It was actually not until 1948 that a unified organisation for a national grid was created but progress in this respect in Germany up to the late 1930s was better than many other countries, except the UK. German output had trebled to 843 kilowatt hours per head of population – still higher than every country in Europe except Norway and Sweden.[42]

In telecommunications, the Reich exercised a very close grip on business activity, continuing the strict security levels perceived to be important for this sector. Post and telegraph were merged in the *Reichspost* in 1875. So also the telephone where the Rathenau and Bell companies were refused concessions. A *Reichspost* monopoly was confirmed in 1892. In general the pace of telephone development was similar to the European average with 19 telephones per 1000 population in 1913, rising to 46 by 1932, levels exceeded in Europe only by Scandinavia.[43] Regional interests were accommodated and peripheral areas subsidised. The development of the telegraph in the late nineteenth century was rather weak by European standards and especially as compared to Britain's international cable network. Germans sent 78 telegrams per 100 population in 1913 and 33 in 1939. The falling off in part reflected the growth of the telephone but the development was the worst in Europe. An important element was the lack of imperial connections and the limited spread of international cables before the late 1920s. Overland cables developed from the 1840s but the more secure submarine cables not until the 1860s. Britain was the only country with the technology, shipping and industrial capacity to mount the capital intensive projects which international cables needed and it had the additional advantage of colonial links throughout the world to secure landing rights (see Chapter 8). Germany was therefore frustratingly dependent on using the international cables of British companies. An important overland cable going through Germany to the Ottoman Empire and Iraq was completed in 1865/66 but it originated in the UK and was a British/Indian company. So also for the overland cable from Germany through Russia, Armenia and Iraq to India owned by the British company Indo-European Telegraph. There were no German company owned international cables and in 1892 the total length of Germany's (government) cables was a mere 1541 kilometres, less than 1 per cent of the British.[44] During WWI Germany's vulnerability was exposed when the British cut off Germany's few submarine cables and in the immediate aftermath of the war the status of the cables was unclear. Only from the late 1920s was development renewed but the Reich retained a strong grip on the whole sector. The assets and turnover of the *Deutsche Reichspost*, established under the budget law of 1924, were to be separately identified and it could issue its own bonds. Close control continued under the Nazis and in 1938 the Reich Defence Act placed the *Reichspost* under the supreme military command.

In the case of *railways*, the regulatory framework for prices, service quality and the award of contracts was similar to other European countries but in other respects there was much more government intervention in Germany. Some of the practices associated with the Prussian legislation of 1838 (cf. Chapter 3) carried through to the late nineteenth century. In the tariff structure of most states, the freight and passenger traffic services were placed, in the classic practice of discriminating monopolists, in groups reflecting their "value" rather than the cost to the railways of supplying these services. An Imperial Railway, the *Reichsbahn*, was formed, under Article 92 of the Federal Constitution of 1919, from all the existing state railways. Whilst the tapering of rates for volume traffic was allowed it was still a system based on the value rather than cost and hence became vulnerable, like all railway systems at this time, to competition from the new road transport charging cost based rates.[45]

Otherwise however German railways after 1870 did differ from those elsewhere, certainly UK and USA, in the degree of government intervention and ownership. Bismarck's aim of creating an imperial railway had been thwarted in the 1880s but the nationalisation of Prussia's railways was started in 1879 and, by 1906, 93 per cent of Germany's railways were state owned.[46] This spread of public ownership was the highest in Europe and reflected Germany's geo-political position and the strong perception of its army and political leaders that railways were vital for military defence and offence. Some have argued that public ownership was simply a vehicle for raising state revenues from the general population rather than via direct taxes on income and property which the Prussian Junkers and Bismarck wished to avoid. Certainly the railways were profitable – the average rate of return on capital 1880–1913 was 5–7 per cent, well above the rate on government bonds, though the examination of Germany's public finances in the next section suggests the fiscal impact may have been exaggerated. The profits were sizable in Prussia but, rather more significant, was that at the time of nationalisation in 1879, they were not expected to be large and hence cannot have been so decisive.[47] Nor is the argument that nationalisation was a device for lowering freight rates. The Junkers complained that Prussian railways offered cheap rates for imports of Russian grain. The rate issue was typical of what happened in many countries following the decline in world commodity prices and the influx of American and Russian grain in the late nineteenth century. To dissuade importers from shipping cargoes on the Baltic or on the Irish Sea, the railway companies offered attractive rates to move the goods overland by rail from Smolensk to Berlin or from Liverpool to London.[48] Why that should lead to nationalisation in Prussia and not elsewhere is not clear especially since Prussian railways were not loss making. Strategic issues were constantly mentioned by the leaders of the German army which even had a "Railway Section" and railway directors were often army generals. Through lines to the borders were vital; there were nine such lines in 1871 and 13 by 1913. The rail track trebled in length up to 1913 and the establishment of the Imperial Railway, *Deutsche Reichsbahn*, from a merger in 1919 of the seven state networks gave Germany a centralised communications network. With 193 rail track miles per 1000 square miles of territory in 1913, and 209 in 1929, Germany had a better spread than any other European country except Britain.[49]

In the inter-war period German railways faced financial difficulties, especially after the depression of 1929–31, but in this respect they suffered like every other European system. The rationalisation of structure in 1919 also included economic aims not much different from Britain and France. It was hoped that economies of scale would ensure future profitability, mirroring the expectations from the 1921 establishment of four regional private monopolies in Britain and the agreement between five companies and two state owned railways in France. The ability of German railways after 1919 to be profitable was partly undermined by the new universal suffrage. The new voters, unencumbered by the three class Prussian *Landtag*, were less inclined to allow public expenditure to be financed by the purchase of railway tickets and shifted the burden to direct taxes. Profits were also squeezed because some of the reparation payments due to the allies of WWI were assigned by the Dawes Report to *Deutsche Reichsbahn*. Under the Federal Railway Act of 1924 the reparation trustees were to sit on the board of a *company*, the *Deutsche Reichbahngesellschaft*, which was expected each year to pay 650 million *reichmarks* as interest on and redemption of 40 year reparation mortgage bonds as well as 38 per cent of its transport tax payments. In fact the company did remarkably well, earning enough revenue up to 1929 to cover operating costs, taxes and all capital charges. Matters deteriorated thereafter but this was due to the depression rather than reparations which, following the Lausanne Conference 1931, were replaced by a once and for all payment of 3000 million *reichmarks* of German government bonds. By 1937 the "company" label had been dropped and the Director-General of the revived *Deutsche Reichsbahn* was the Minister of Transport.

It is true that, reparations aside, German railways were treated by their government more favourably than railways in other countries.[50] By the 1920s, inland navigation, albeit still huge by European standards, had exhausted its competitive threat to railways, for whom the threat from road transport, so strong in Britain and France, had barely taken off. In 1924 there were only 3000 motor vehicles per million population, the road surfaces were poor, an excise tax was supplemented by an annual car tax and a law of 1927 prohibited the use of car tax revenues for road construction. This success of German railways in fighting off the growing road lobby, including the road transport association, is usually attributed to their strong traditional support in the civil administration of Prussia and now the Reich. It was actually not until the 1930s that the road programme took off with the well-known support given by the Nazi government to roads and other public works during the depression years. The military by then had recognised the importance of motor engines, lorries and tanks and road transport took off as transport planning came to be centralised in state and Nazi party agencies.[51]

## Public finances, state enterprises and the move to autarky

Public expenditures in Germany are part of the ingredients of the horrendous inflation of the early 1920s and of the size and length of the depression of the early 1930s. These issues are outside our brief here.[52] The focus rather is on three issues. The first is how the changing dimensions of public spending and the associated means of financing it affected the private business sector. Second, there is the question of the scale of public enterprise in mining, manufacturing and the infrastructure industries and how that affected the public sector budget. The third issue is the impact on business of the shift in the economy as a whole to self-sufficiency from the 1920s and to Nazi economic planning in the 1930s.

The broad trend of total public sector spending in Germany was a rise in allocations for social welfare and defence and a shift from the states to the centre: the data of Andic and Veverka in Table 5.7 cover current and capital spending, transfers, loans and subsidies but excludes funds moved from one level of government to another. It was the central Reich level of government which had responsibility for defence and the aim of increasing defence spending was partly frustrated in the years up to WWI by the Reich's reliance on indirect taxes, relieved after WWI by the transfer of authority for direct taxes from the states to the Reich. The latter's share of total public expenditure rose from 30 per cent before WWI to 75 per cent by the late 1930s. Total public expenditure rose from 10 per cent of national income to a staggering 42 per cent by 1938. The rise before the 1930s reflected both welfare spending and defence and their levels were not much different from those in France and the UK. It was in the 1930s that defence started to dominate spending and grew much more rapidly than elsewhere: 24 per cent of national income in 1937, very similar to Japan and Russia but well above France at 9.1 per cent, the UK 5.7 per cent and USA 1.5 per cent.[53]

Up to 1913, German taxation was still linked closely to the agrarian economy. The industrial sector, which grew quickly from the mid nineteenth century, bore little of the burden since there was heavy reliance on indirect taxes but the shift to income taxes in some states like Prussia was a real modernisation of the tax system as also was Germany's early expansion of social insurance. The 1871

Table 5.7 Government expenditure[a] in Germany 1872–1938 (million Marks)

| | 1872 | 1881 | 1891 | 1901 | 1913 | 1925 | 1930 | 1938 |
|---|---|---|---|---|---|---|---|---|
| *Reich government* | | | | | | | | |
| 1 Debt service | 1 | 11 | 54 | 86 | 182 | 8 | 259 | 1200 |
| 2 Defence | 295 | 446 | 725 | 1007 | 1909 | 633 | 755 | 15,850 |
| 3 War damage | 0 | 0 | 0 | 0 | 0 | 1674 | 2175 | n.a. |
| 4 Social services[b] | n.a.[c] | n.a.[c] | 158 | 424 | 994 | 4079 | 8961 | 4634 |
| 5 Other[d] | 1084 | 79 | 106 | 154 | 333 | 749 | 1046 | 7625 |
| Total | 1380 | 536 | 1043 | 1671 | 3418 | 7143 | 13,196 | 29,309 |
| *States* | | | | | | | | |
| 1 Debt service | n.a. | 62 | 64 | 172 | 169 | 33 | 214 | 325[e] |
| 2 Social services[b] | n.a. | 108[f] | 179[f] | n.a.[c] | n.a.[c] | 1822 | 1967 | 1618[e] |
| 3 Other[d] | n.a. | 641 | 1007 | 1578 | 2915 | 1841 | 2223 | 839[e] |
| Sub-total | n.a. | 811 | 1250 | 1750 | 3084 | 3696 | 4404 | 2782[e] |
| *Local government* | | | | | | | | |
| 1 Debt service | n.a. | n.a. | n.a. | n.a. | 50 | 50 | 106 | 208[e] |
| 2 Social services[b] | n.a. | n.a. | n.a. | n.a. | 1253 | 3064 | 4456 | 2623[e] |
| 3 Other[d] | n.a. | n.a. | n.a. | n.a. | 1270 | 1790 | 2347 | 2341[e] |
| Sub-total | n.a. | 480 | 780 | 1431 | 2523 | 4904 | 6909 | 5172[e] |

| Grand total | | | | | | | | |
|---|---|---|---|---|---|---|---|---|
| National income[g] ('000 million) | 16 | 18.2 | 23.3 | 32.5 | 54.7 | 63 | 73.1 | 87.6 |
| Reich expenditure as % NI | 8.6 | 2.9 | 4.5 | 5.1 | 6.2 | 11.3 | 18.1 | 32.5 |
| Grand total as % NI | n.a. | 10.0 | 13.2 | 14.9 | 13.7 | 25.0 | 33.6 | 42.4 |
| | n.a. | 1827 | 3072 | 4852 | 7476 | 15,743 | 24,528 | 37,159 |

Source: Andic and Veverka 1963.

Notes

a Includes current and capital expenditure plus loans. Excludes transfers between levels of government. The expenditure of public trading enterprises is excluded, except before 1913 when the entries include their capital expenditure. The classification scheme changes 1913–25.

b Includes social assistance, social insurance, health, housing, education, etc.

c Included in other.

d Includes law, reparations, trading services, economic services, environmental services.

e 1937.

f Education only.

g Gross national product at current prices.

Constitutional settlement left direct taxes to the states, indirect taxes to the Reich. Some welfare spending was shifted from the states to local authorities whilst the Reich itself took responsibility for age and disability pensions from 1881. Customs revenues were about one-half of the Reich's tax revenues in 1872, rising slowly up to 1913, with the yield from agrarian tariffs more important than those on "luxuries" (tea, coffee, cocoa and rice) and industrial goods. Excise taxes were mainly on liquors, sugar, beer, salt and tobacco – about 35 per cent of Reich revenue in 1913, more if duties (stamp, etc.) are added (Table 5.8). The Reich's finances were aided initially in the 1870s by the reparations due after the Franco-Prussian war. Thereafter there were the payments by the states to the centre due as part of the 1871 constitutional changes (the "matricular contributions"). However the prospect of rising customs revenues for the Reich as tariffs rose were frustrated for a time by the so-called Frankenstein clause of 1879 which capped Reich customs revenues at 139 million marks, any surplus to go as "remittances" to the states in proportion to their populations. The Reich remittances fluctuated above and below the level of matricular contributions but did finish up lower in the 1900s when the Reich also received the proceeds of an inheritance tax (not called so because the Reich was not supposed to receive direct tax revenues). Overall Reich finances were not healthy, with expenditure net of revenues at 167 million marks in 1881, rising to 770 million marks in 1901 and continuing to rise thereafter. The balance was met by borrowing and these persistent trends were an element in the early 1920s inflation.

No uniformity was imposed on direct taxation by the states: the south German states chose mainly revenue taxes whilst Prussia and Saxony moved more to the British personal tax system. The Prussian income tax, introduced in the 1880s, was heralded by many as a classic modern fiscal system with a general liability, a duty to disclose and abatement for family circumstances. Land, property and business taxes were left to the local authorities and the revenues were modest.

*Table 5.8* Reich government revenues[a] 1872–1938 (million marks)

|            | 1872 | 1881 | 1891 | 1901 | 1913 | 1925 | 1930 | 1938 |
|------------|------|------|------|------|------|------|------|------|
| 1 Customs  | 95   | 181  | 378  | 494  | 679  | 591  | 1083 | 1818 |
| 2 Excise   | 74   | 165  | 263  | 323  | 660  | 1371 | 1980 | 2828 |
| 3 Income   | n.a. | n.a. | n.a. | n.a. | n.a. | 2440 | 3211 | 7769 |
| 4 Turnover | n.a. | n.a. | n.a. | n.a. | n.a. | 1416 | 996  | 3357 |
| 5 Other    | 13[b] | 21[b] | 34[b] | 83[b] | 326[b] | 0[c] | 0[c] | 1940 |
| Total      | 182  | 367  | 675  | 901  | 1665 | 4818[c] | 7270[c] | 17,712[c] |

Source: Mitchell 2003a.

Notes

a  The definition of tax revenues was extended in scope after 1913.

b  Includes income and turnover taxes, if any.

c  The totals shown here from Mitchell 2003a are less than the sum of the parts, some of which are not "tax revenues".

The incidence of direct taxes on higher incomes was no more than 15 per cent. Local authorities were able to surcharge state taxes and the Junker estate owners, holding police authority and other rights and duties, were still receiving revenues like other local authorities. The major change after WWI was that the Reich became the main legislative power for taxation. A turnover tax had been introduced and the rate rose, as did income tax rates, in the 1920s, with some of the proceeds transferred to the states. Schremmer suggests that only 5 per cent of incomes were likely to be subject to tax rates which would significantly affect income distribution and by the 1920s only about 4 per cent of national income accrued as income tax.[54]

A distinctive feature of Germany's public sector was the large role played by public enterprises, not only in infrastructure industries (which were discussed in the last section) but also in mining, manufacturing and commerce. On some counts for Prussia they generated more revenue than taxes. Whilst, as will be argued below, the actual net profit inflow accruing and hence the fiscal impact has been exaggerated by some writers, there is no doubting they were a larger sector than anywhere else in Europe before the formation of the USSR. Public authorities played "a significant role in promoting the expansion of industry, agriculture, forests and commerce" said Henderson. They "were responsible – either entirely or in part – for the provision of communications, energy, land improvements, educational instruments and health facilities. Public undertakings included railways, iron works, shipyards and various manufacturing enterprises".[55] Henderson is not always very clear about the motives for this activity,

*Table 5.9* German public revenues in 1913 (million marks)

|  | Reich | States | Local | Total | % |
|---|---|---|---|---|---|
| *Taxes* |  |  |  |  |  |
| Income tax | 0 | 609 | 781 | 1390 | 22.6 |
| Property tax | 41 | 155 | 430 | 626 | 10.1 |
| Business tax | 0 | 18 | 162 | 179 | 2.9 |
| Customs | 641 | 0 | 0 | 641 | 10.4 |
| Consumption taxes | 655 | 62 | 64 | 781 | 12.7 |
| Stamp duty, etc. | 247 | 112 | 76 | 434 | 7.0 |
| *Other revenues* |  |  |  |  |  |
| Public enterprises | 176 | 538 | 279 | 973 | 16.1 |
| Fees etc. | 84 | 388 | 642 | 1133 | 18.1 |
| *Grand total* | 1846 | 1883 | 2432 | 6160 | 100 |
| % | 30.0 | 30.6 | 39.4 | 100 | – |
| *Inter-government transfers* |  |  |  |  |  |
| Matricular contributions from States to Reich | 52[a] | – | – | – | – |
| Remittances from Reich to States | – | 199[a] | – | – | – |

Source: Schremmer 1989, pp. 468, 282.

Note
a Annual average 1912–13.

merging Bismarck's concern about military capacity and curbing labour power with more doubtful aims about raising living standards. Here we are focusing on public enterprises (not health, education, welfare etc.) the establishment of which at municipal level we have attributed to fiscal concerns and at state or Reich level to considerations of defence.

It is possible to give some orders of magnitude of the impact of public enterprise on municipal, state and Reich finances using Schremmer's cross-section of total government revenues for 1913 shown in Table 5.9. The enterprise revenues are shown net of certain expenditures which will likely include only operating costs. Thus they are gross operating profits and the total of such public enterprise gross profits in 1913, over all government levels, was 973 million marks, that is 15 per cent of all revenues or 34 per cent if fees and other non-tax entrepreneurial receipts are included. This is about 4 per cent of national income, suggesting that if wages and salaries are added in, public enterprise net output was 10–20 per cent of national output, likely therefore to have been much bigger than in other European countries.

For municipalities the activities include gas, electricity, trams, water, markets etc., and totalled 279 million marks, that is over 10 per cent of total municipal revenues or 38 per cent if fees and the other non-tax entrepreneurial type revenues are included. At the other end of the government spectrum, the productive activities of the Reich itself were limited mainly to post, telecoms and shipping though up to 1913 it also owned the Alsace-Lorraine railway system acquired after the Franco-Prussian war. Defence considerations induced the Reich to subsidise state owned shipyards. Shipping lines were subsidised if they used ships built in German yards and also were given preferential status for coastal traffic and post. In 1913 the Reich's public enterprise gross profits were 176 million marks, that is 10 per cent of all its revenues or 14 per cent if fees are included.

The most extensive entrepreneurial activities were undertaken in the states. Prominent amongst these was the Prussian state which included the activities of *Preussische Elektrizitäts AG*, the *Preussche Bank* and all of the railway system. Many of the states were involved in canal construction and operation. Prussia had a state monopoly (for strategic reasons) of tugs on the Kiel canal connecting the Baltic and North Seas and in 1905 for example the Prussian Diet approved the equivalent of £17 million for canal construction.[56] It had extensive interests in mining and manufacturing: in 1899 17 coal companies, eight lignite, seven iron ore, four saltworks, four copper and silver mines, ten smelters and six salt refineries, not to mention various breweries, amber works and tobacco factories.[57] Total public enterprise gross profits of all the states in 1913 were 538 million marks, that is 29 per cent of all the state revenues or nearly 50 per cent if fees are included, a level somewhat less than is sometime quoted. A broader and deeper insight is in Table 5.10 which shows budgeted revenues and budgeted operating expenses separately for the Prussian state for the whole period 1875–1913. Restricting ourselves to the ordinary budget, the total turnover of public enterprises was 385 million marks in 1875, at first blush a massive figure, more than all the other revenues in that year, a pattern repeated for all the other years recorded in Table 5.10 up to WWI. After deducting operating costs of 241 million marks this yields gross profits of 144 million for 1875, a figure which rose to 605 million by 1902. But these estimates also do not reflect the fiscal impact since interest payments and other capital charges attributable to these state enterprises have not been deducted but rather are included as part of the debt service entry in Table 5.10. As a rough guide, if half of this is attributed to public enterprises the net profit yielded by public enterprises comes out at 124 million marks in 1875 rising to 497 in 1902 which was equivalent to 44 per cent of all Prussian state ordinary tax revenues in 1875 and 55 per cent in 1902. This

*Table 5.10* Prussian state revenues and expenditures 1875–1913 (gross budget values in million marks)

|  | 1875 | 1882 | 1892 | 1902 | 1913 |
|---|---|---|---|---|---|
| *Ordinary budget* |  |  |  |  |  |
| Revenues: |  |  |  |  |  |
| Direct taxes | 146 | 147 | 180 | 225 | 459 |
| Indirect taxes | 46 | 50 | 71 | 91 | 124 |
| Public enterprise | 385 | 622 | 1217 | 1786 | 3331 |
| Reich remittances | 0 | 51 | 218 | 341 | 150 |
| Other | 87 | 130 | 129 | 341 | 353 |
| Sub-total | 665 | 1000 | 1816 | 2685 | 4418 |
| Expenditures: |  |  |  |  |  |
| Administration and judiciary | 203 | 236 | 344 | 388 | 605 |
| Debt service | 40 | 125 | 274 | 295 | 463 |
| Public enterprise | 241 | 422 | 787 | 1141 | 2441 |
| Culture and education | 39 | 48 | 101 | 149 | 292 |
| Reich payments | 32 | 52 | 193 | 355 | 158 |
| Other[a] | 50 | 71 | 103 | 191 | 212 |
| Sub-total | 605 | 954 | 1802 | 2520 | 4172 |
| *Extraordinary budget* |  |  |  |  |  |
| Revenues: |  |  |  |  |  |
| Entrepreneurial | 82 | 121 | 107 | 168 | 1371 |
| Surpluses | 129 | 65 | 111 | 205 | 307 |
| Other | 97 | 27 | 45 | 0 | 0 |
| Sub-total | 307 | 214 | 263 | 374 | 1678 |
| Expenditures: |  |  |  |  |  |
| Entrepreneurial | 17 | 5 | 13 | 249 | 731 |
| Debt service | 85 | 134 | 106 | 0 | 796 |
| Other | 105 | 45 | 73 | 109 | 218 |
| Sub-total | 207 | 184 | 192 | 358 | 1745 |
| *Grand totals* |  |  |  |  |  |
| Revenues | 972 | 1214 | 2078 | 3059 | 6096 |
| Expenditures | 813 | 1138 | 1994 | 2878 | 5917 |

Source: Schremmer 1989, pp. 460, 462.

Note
a Including increase in debt.

is less than sometimes quoted and Prussia is probably not typical of other states. Nevertheless the pattern in Germany is of a much bigger spread of public enterprises and contribution to government revenues.

The strong element of government enterprise and intervention continued after 1913 and was reinforced by the experience of WWI and the drive to self-sufficiency which started in the 1920s. At one level of discourse, in the 1930s the resort of the Nazis to tariffs, quotas, price fixing, control orders, currency restrictions and economic nationalism generally was symptomatic of all the crisis management that occurred in that decade throughout the world in response to the great depression 1929–31.[58] It was the commitment to military aggression which really distinguished Germany and its resort to civil violence, racism and slave labour. Several historians now argue that the lesson drawn by the Third Reich of what went wrong in the First World War was focused on the performance of the economy, that is, the ill-preparedness of the defence sector, the vulnerability to blockade and the inability of Germany's overseas empire to help, all signposting central and south-eastern Europe as the source of raw materials, labour and food.[59] At the start of WWI no thought had been given to rationing and how to divert resources to the military – the federal structure was not really attuned to that sort of economic management and it was some time before market transactions were suspended. The output of the armaments sector actually declined to 1915 and then recovered from 1916 as controls were tightened and a new armaments programme initiated. The output of non-armaments suffered and, staggeringly, national output per head fell by 20 per cent during 1914–18.[60] Germany had acquired 150 billion marks of war debt by 1918 but the manner in which it had financed the war was little different from Britain – about 80 per cent by bonds of which 15 per cent was monetised. The navy could defend the coastline but was otherwise, despite heavy investment in the fleet, helpless to fight the allied blockade which damaged Germany more than Britain was damaged by the blockade of the UK. The food shortage was not relieved by Germany's overseas empire and with the experience of the territory forcibly released from Russia by the 1917 Treaty of Brest-Litovsk, expansion to eastern and south-eastern Europe rather than the colonies was the message for the future; there was the living space, *lebensraum*, that Germany needed. The policies necessitated during WWI by the blockade and its resource constraints led Germany to devise a more extensive set of controls than other countries. A War Raw Materials Department (*Kriegrohstoffabteilum*) was established to supervise 20 raw material components and food supply from 1916 whilst the cartels became semi-official arms of government. By 1918, suggests Overy, "Germany had, despite wartime failures, a form of command economy unthinkable only a few years before."[61]

After the war, the powers of the centre in the Weimar Republic were enhanced with the number of employees rising to over one million. Disillusion with capitalism after the early 1920s inflation and the suspension of the mark in 1923, became widespread so that self-sufficiency and contacts with other countries to form trade blocs were on the agenda. Import substitutes were developed by large private firms such as the chemical giant IG Farben and by state holding companies like *Vereinigte Industrieunternehmen AG* (VIAG, established 1923) and *Vereinigten Elektrizititäts u. Bergwerk AG* (VEBA, established 1929) which had extensive interests in tin, lead, oil, coal, electricity.[62] The pressure to adopt autarkic policies was increased by the depression years 1929–31. As grain prices fell in the late 1920s, German tariffs doubled and further restrictions and tariffs followed USA 1930 tariff.[63] Where Germany differed in economic policy was that its shift to autarky was stronger than elsewhere; it developed corporate institutions to act as conduits of policy and became committed to a war economy footing by the mid 1930s. The initial emphasis of Chancellor Bruning in 1930/31 to the depression was on "sound finance". Even at this point, Junker influence had not disappeared; 8 per cent of the Reich's spending 1930–32 was devoted to reducing the eastern estate owners' debt.[64] The advent of Hitler and Nazi personnel in many branches of government saw the development of a closely regulated economy which became the basis of an expanding defence sector and a war economy. Initially the lead was taken by a financial technocrat, Hjalmar Schacht, appointed President of the *Reichbank*, who brought a whole raft of regulations under one roof, especially in banking, but more generally in his 1934 New Plan. This included restrictions on imports and foreign travel with 25 agencies for controls on exports. Supervisory boards were established for complete control over goods and foreign exchange. Special *reichmarks* were developed for special purposes, for example the Aski for imports, especially from South America.[65] Schacht headed the State Supervisory Office for Banking, established under the bank law of 1934: given new powers of regulation, it forced out "uneconomic banks" by revoking their licences. Several banks were taken over (and reprivatised later) but the main thrust initially was to change business policy; only the *Dresdner* bank saw forced personnel changes, leading to an influx of Nazis to management positions.[66] The *Reichsbank* directed the flow of capital formation to facilitate increasing government expenditure and debt. About one-half of German banks disappeared, mainly small and Jewish but from 1936, when Schacht was dismissed, large Jewish banks were also forced to close and the main non-Jewish banks benefited. Nazi economic policy was pragmatic about the ownership of firms. Some historians have argued Hitler viewed profit driven entrepreneurs as egotistic and with the wrong motivation for developing the kind of economy he wanted. Hence the shift to a set of corporate institutions which could act as a channel for Nazi policy. The Reich Economic Chamber overlooked 18 "chambers" or corporations responsible for different parts of the economy, exploiting the tradition of the cartels. For agriculture a Reich Food Estate was established (*Reichsnährstand*) to manage food production, price controls and markets. There was a German Labour Front, emasculating the role of trade unions. Nazi leaders were appointed to all sectors of the economy. A Four Year Plan under Göring was established in 1936 with the Prussian planning team fused with the Reich Ministry of Economics in 1937. Much state investment was directed to developing import substitutes – oil, textiles, rubber – and to the expansion of aluminium, chemicals and iron ore.[67] By the end of the 1930s, a large proportion of employees in manufacturing, construction and raw material production were working on orders for the armaments industry, financed by the rise in public spending and debt, recorded earlier in this section. The economy, its inherited and new institutions were directed to the service of the state. It was in Germany however, by the late 1930s, a war economy and the label of a "people's economy" showed that it differed from other command economies in that it was not separate from race.

## Notes

1   Wright 1942, Appendix XXII; Kennedy 1988, Tables 8 and 20.
2   Brady 1943.
3   Tipton 2003.
4   Clark 2009, p. 100.
5   Clark 2000. See also Carsten 1989; Marriott and Robertson 1946.
6   Hentschel 1989; Trebilcock 1981; Gershenkron 1966b; Bowen 1950; Rosenberg 1943.
7   In Hayek's 1944 *Road to Serfdom*, the rise of fascism is explicitly linked to the rise of government intervention in German economy and society. This is a classic text but this particular argument in retrospect looks weak given the many different outcomes in European countries all experiencing a growing role for the state. See Caldwell (2007) for details of the history of Hayek's fascinating book.
8   Fremdling 1996.
9   Broadberry and O'Rourke 2010, vol. II.
10   Tilly 1978; Tipton 2003, p. 124; Mitchell 2003a.
11   Kocka 1978, 1980; Trebilcock 1981.
12   Cf. Elbaum and Lazonick 1986.
13   Chandler 1976, 1984, 1990; Lazonick 1991; Hannah 1976; Kirby 1992; Feldenkirchen 1999.
14   Wiener 1985.
15   Broadberry 1993, 1997a, 1998, 2006.
16   Gerschenkron 1960, p. 23.
17   Broadberry 2006.
18   Marrison 1996.
19   Woodruff 1973, annex tables.
20   Clapham 1961, p. 317; Hentschel 1989.
21   Bairoch 1989.
22   Rosenberg 1943, p. 103.
23   Clapham 1961; Bairoch 1989 p. 71.
24   Borchardt 1973; Bowen 1950; Lübbers 2004; Maschke 1969.
25   Trebilcock 1981, p. 87; Bowen 1950.
26   Maschke 1969.
27   Lübbers 2004.
28   Clapham 1961; Maschke 1969; Marburg 1964; Trebilcock 1981; Feldenkirchen 1999.
29   Cf. Marburg 1964 who pointed out that the Association had been resisting the introduction of steam power.
30   Hentschel 1989; Maschke 1969; Marburg 1964.
31   Vinck and Boursin 1962, pp. 309–10.
32   Hughes 1977, 1983.
33   Dawson 1916; Messager 1988, p. 288; Schott 2004.
34   Schott 2004.

35  Hughes 1969, 1977, 1983; Hughes and Pinch 1987.
36  Evans 1990; Hennock 2000.
37  Cf. Kuhl 2002b.
38  Dawson 1916, pp. 190–1.
39  Brooks 1916; Meyer 1906; Hughes 1983.
40  Mulert 1929; Schott 1997b; Falk and Pittack 1986; Wengenroth 1987.
41  Hughes 1983, p. 409.
42  Schneider and Schulz 1980; Oeftering 1953; Millward 2005.
43  American Telegraph and Telephone 1913; Gunston 1933; Thomas 1978; Wengenroth 2000.
44  Headrick 1991.
45  Mierzejewski 1990, 1999; McMahon and Dittmar 1939/1940; Leyen 1926.
46  Foreman-Peck 1987.
47  Fremdling 1979, 1980, 1996, 1999.
48  Cain 1973; Hawke 1969.
49  Table 5.1 and Stevenson 1999.
50  Mierzejewski 1995, 1999; Leyen 1926; McMahon and Dittmar 1939/1940; Yago 1984.
51  Mierzejewski 1999, vol I, pp. 355–7 and vol II, pp. 29–45; Overy 1994, pp. 69–71.
52  See Balderston 1993 for an extensive discussion.
53  Wright 1942.
54  Schremmer 1989, pp. 447–50, 781.
55  Henderson 1975, pp. 175–7.
56  Hentschel 1989.
57  Schremmer 1989, p. 457.
58  Overy 2003a.
59  Ritschl 2005; Overy 2003a, b.
60  Ritschl 2005.
61  Overy 2003b, p. 255. See also Wengenroth 2000.
62  Oeftering 1953; Wengenroth 2000.
63  Kindleberger 1989.
64  Hentschel 1989.
65  Kindleberger 1989.
66  Wellhöner and Wixforth 2003.
67  Overy 2003a.

# 6    Peasant farms, industrial growth and national defence in France

## Introduction: strategic and economic problems

A very large part of French foreign investment went to Russia in the two decades before the First World War (WWI). These investments were endorsed by both governments and reflected in part a strong political entente between the two countries. From 1870, between France's eastern border and Russia's western, was the newly unified state of Germany, economically and politically imperialist in its desire for markets and space and unequivocally therefore more of a potential enemy to France and Russia than any other country, including Britain. This was not all they shared. For nation states to be successful militarily, it was clear by the mid nineteenth century that armaments, naval power and communication lines had to reflect changing technology. Modern arsenals, steamships, railways, cables, later tanks, destroyers and aircraft, became as important as the crude size of army manpower. Industrialisation was necessary and in the nineteenth century that meant coal, iron, metallurgy, machines and later electricity. Apart from the need to keep abreast of technology innovations, industrial expansion required a much bigger manufacturing labour force and that would have to come from falling mortality in urban areas, immigration or, most likely in this period, a shift out of agriculture. In both France and Russia this was a major economic problem: the slow decline in agriculture's share of the economy and slow rural–urban migration was common to both, albeit in very different contexts.

In the case of France 1870–1939, the literature on the economic history of business/state relationships has been dominated by debates about the performance of the economy and, in some cases, of the inadequate responses by the various coalition governments of the Third Republic. Income levels, it is alleged, remained lower than the UK and grew more slowly than in Germany and USA, carrying strong criticism of protective tariff policy, of an unenterprising business culture and only a slow movement towards the modern form of business organisation found already in late nineteenth century America. Some features of this performance will figure here but the treatment of business/state relationships in the existing literature is limited by viewing the state through the prism of the promotion of economic growth, modernisation and average living standards. It is a moot point whether the French state had that agenda during the Third Republic and the thrust of the approach here is that much industrial policy can better be understood as reflecting strategic worries which arose from the geo-political position of France and its resource endowment. There are three key issues.

The first is political geography. By 1870 Germany was united, had absorbed Alsace and Lorraine and was a constant military threat. Colonial competition in Asia and Africa was mainly about relations with Britain whose navy and merchant marine were dominant, challenging also in the Mediterraneum and Suez. France's main military hope was Russia. The second element was the political constitution. The life of the Third Republic was littered with short lived coalitions as the far right and far left gathered strength. However the most important constitutional feature was still the Revolutionary and Napoleonic heritage. The various civil codes for mining and infrastructure development continued to structure business links in these sectors but what became a particular problem was the emphasis on human rights and equality. Peasant rights to land were strengthened, thereby encouraging the continuance of small plots, slow release of labour to industry and some dampening of productivity growth in agriculture. In addition the right to decide family size strengthened prevailing trends to smaller numbers of children via falling fertility, reinforced by the partible inheritance systems confirmed in the Revolutionary legislation. Hence population growth was slow affecting the size of the army and of the domestic market and again the size of the industrial labour force. The third element is resource endowment. The coal and iron reserves were still limited in size and location and exacerbated by the loss of Lorraine iron and Alsace textiles. The importance of coal cannot be exaggerated. It was the key primary resource, with no ready substitutes in the nineteenth century, and was often a fixed industrial necessity given the rise of steam power. Balderston has recently shown how the many scattered coalfields in Lancashire sustained large numbers of cotton firms, coexisting in agglomerations which exploited external economies and allowed the Lancashire industry to maintain world leadership throughout the nineteenth century.[1] This points also to the final element of France's strategic problems, namely its stage of development or rather the fact that France faced the dominant world industrial power on its doorstep. Those involved in French industrial policy were faced with the threat that most French manufacturing could be completely outcompeted by Britain.

Thus the French problem, which coloured all business/state relationships, had two dimensions. On the one hand, there was the geo-political pressure that the nation's defence required industrial strength and a larger population. On the other hand, there were socio-political pressures working the other way, tending, that is, to freeze population growth and, as compared to UK, Germany and USA, to slow down agricultural modernisation and release labour more slowly to industry.

## Stagnant population and agriculture?

The structure and size of the agricultural sector and the trend of population were central elements in the fortunes of French economy and society throughout the

Third Republic. In the early nineteenth century there was a huge number of small farm businesses, over five million less than 25 acres, accounting for 90 per cent of the total. These businesses were active in market sales but an element of family self-sufficiency still survived in many of the peasant farms. Moreover the structure changed little during the nineteenth century, agriculture's share of the labour force declined more slowly than in other Western European countries and has thereby been seen as something of a drag on economic development. A closely related factor was the slow growth of the population which had reached 36 million by 1870. Its size was important for business because it affected the size of the domestic market and the labour supply to industry and for the state because it affected the size of the army and the ease of recruitment. It is worth spending some time examining the population trends in some detail for they were at the heart of France's problems in the nineteenth and early twentieth centuries.

The population rose by 14 per cent over the years 1700–50, 19 per cent 1750–1800 and 25 per cent 1800–50.[2] Falling mortality rates were a significant element in the eighteenth century but flattened out in the early nineteenth century as industrialisation and urbanisation increased. Birth rates had been falling in some regions from at least the eighteenth century and fell decisively in the nineteenth, much against the trend in other countries. From 1870 to WWI the birth rate and death rate tracked each other so the population grew only modestly as Figure 6.1 shows. By 1913 it had reached 41.7 million and the population in the area which France occupied in 1913 (that is excluding Alsace and Lorraine) then actually declined, despite rising immigration in the 1920s, to 41.5 million in 1938.[3] All of this, moreover, needs to be viewed in the context that France lost only a tiny number of people through emigration. From France, emigration out of Europe averaged 5300 person per annum 1901–10 (the peak year for European overseas emigration), bigger only than Switzerland, Belgium and the Netherlands. Germany was 274,000, Italy 361,000. Then over 1921–40 all rates fell but the French figure at 450 persons per annum was the smallest in Europe.[4]

The role of the state in relation to the development of farm businesses and to the population trends was largely indirect. There was support for agricultural cooperatives and for natality programmes, as we shall see later, but it was the political changes in the years 1789–99 which crucially confirmed and enhanced the tendency to small farms and smaller families. The revolution, claimed Murphy, "shattered the traditions that sustained the passive role in family planning",[5] effectively by enshrining the right of each person and household to decide the size of the family, irrespective of the teachings of the church. It also reinforced the practice of partible inheritance (justice for all siblings) providing an economic incentive to reduce birth rates. However the story is rather more nuanced than that. To start with, the decline in the birth rate was strongly linked to a decline in marital fertility since average marriage rates (the traditional method of controlling family size) did not fall in the nineteenth century. The fertility index favoured by demographers expresses the number of children per

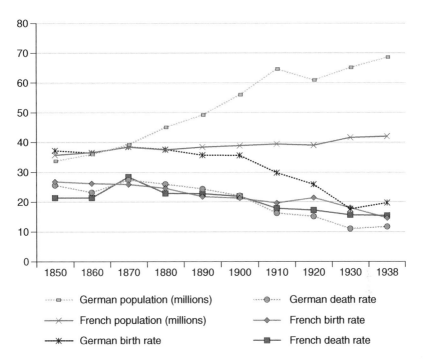

*Figure 6.1* Population trends in France and Germany 1850–1938 (sources: Mitchell 2003a; Maddison 1991).

Note
Birth, death and marriage rates expressed per 1000 population.

mother as a percentage of known maximums, with 70 per cent a benchmark below which it was likely family size was being controlled via marital fertility.[6] Walle reported 48 per cent for France 1831 as compared to 78 per cent for Belgium and 83 per cent for the Netherlands.[7] This is why the birth rate was down to 30 per 1000 population, and falling, whilst Germany was still at 40. That the low French birth rate was not simply a one-off reaction to the Revolution is revealed by pre-Revolutionaray trends as well as the regional patterns in the nineteenth century. Nor can the eighteenth century examples be written off simply as practices of a few nobles. French literature provides clear evidence of the general problems which arose when all siblings had a legal share in family estates so that "the initial motives must probably be sought in the peculiar set of family settlements, inheritance systems and status seeking gentry of the aristocracy and upper bourgeoisie".[8] The nobility was important in inducing imitation and there is evidence of low marital fertility rates before the Revolution throughout urban areas like Meulan and Châtillon-sur Seine near Paris. Bardet estimates marital fertility in France 1740–80 as 77 per cent, falling steeply to 64 per cent by 1800 and of fertility levels in Rouen falling by 40 per cent over the period 1680–1789.[9] By 1801–10 birth rates were at relatively low levels in Normandy, Paris and the Loire.[10] Moreover these early falls in marital fertility seemed to have occurred in a Malthusian setting. Wrigley in particular has argued that the large unprecedented fall in mortality in the late eighteenth century was followed, in classic Malthusian fashion, by a decline in the birth rate, in response to the threat to living standards from larger family size.[11] In contrast the decline in birth rates across all Europe in the late nineteenth century occurred when living standards were rising. The twist in the birth rate story in France in the late eighteenth century was that the traditional device of postponing marriages was not working because illegitimate births were rising.

So the French had, before the Revolution, accultured themselves in part to a new mode of family planning. Contraceptive practices were to be found even in regions with high birth rates like Brittany, Alsace and the Nord. This becomes clear from the early nineteenth century evidence that regions of high marital fertility were often associated with late marriage dates, and vice versa. Walle found for 1831–51 a strong negative correlation across *departements* between levels of marital fertility and the proportion of the population who were married.[12] Lot et Garonne had early marriage and low fertility, Manche late marriage and high fertility. Murphy's data for 86 *departements* for the period 1876–96 suggest the birth rate patterns reflected both the cultural heritage of the eighteenth century and the Revolution, and the economic inducements from employment, inheritance systems and urban life.[13] Thus *departements* with low fertility tended to have low child mortality, were more urbanised, had higher income levels, partible inheritance systems and smaller concentration of land ownership. The population of such *departements* was better educated, less religious and more republican politically. In sum the cultural willingness of the French population to change family planning practices did exist before 1789 but was extended by the Revolution which reinforced the role of economic factors as evidenced by the differential speed at which marital fertility declined across *departements*. By 1870 then, as Figure 6.1 illustrates with Germany, the growth of the French population was lagging behind other countries. Just before WWI, French women were giving birth at a rate equivalent to 2.5 children during their normal child bearing years of 15–49. As Figure 6.2 shows this was well below the four+ children in other parts of Continental Europe. Given contemporary child mortality rates in France, that meant no more than two children would survive and the population was not sustainable. These numbers continued to decline but at a smaller rate in France such that by the 1930s the basement reproduction levels of fertility and hence stationary populations had been reached in most Western European countries. France had lost its singularity.

The significance of the stagnant population was not lost on French governments both in terms of the potential size of the army and the speed with which industrial production could be expanded. An alarmist pro-natalist literature emerged from the mid nineteenth century with fears of domination by Germany and Italy.[14] Hypocrisy abounded as the professional elites (doctors, politicians,

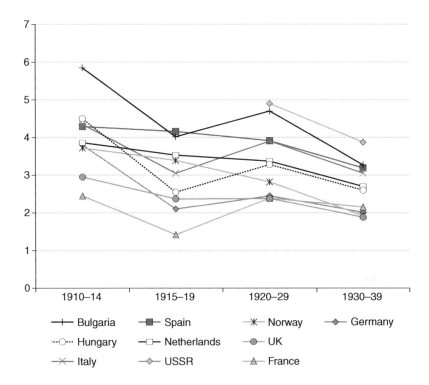

*Figure 6.2* Fertility in Europe 1910–39 (source: Chesnais 1999: the UK entries exclude S. Ireland and are estimates as is the entry for Italy, 1910–19).

Note

For each period, such as 1920–29, the data refer to the number of children which a woman would have borne during her childbearing years (15–49) if she bore them at the same rate as, on average, women did in 1920–29.

moralists) controlled their own family sizes but invoked the people to multiply. A common method of birth control was abortion for which five to ten years' imprisonment was laid down in a law of 1810 but never implemented.[15] The strategic importance of the issue for the government was enough to induce a big propaganda campaign during WWI: appeals to the virility of men, crude *double entendres* about "firing a shot", fighting for women and children and extensive use of postcards to ensure literacy was not a barrier.[16] For the 1870–1939 period the state response, understandably, was too little too late. It was actually business firms who were at the centre of the family allowance systems in the nineteenth century, especially in textiles and metallurgy.[17] The Catholic church and Catholic business owners were active: they preferred the vehicle of firms over state regulation, fearing modernisation, trade unions and threats to family agriculture and peasant ownership. Often the schemes took the form of "equalisation funds" whereby cash grants paid by firms and other donors went to a fund rather than the worker, to minimise the chance of firms favouring married men.[18] Although strong pro-birth control and eugenics movements did exist in France, the family movement generated many associations including in 1896 the *Alliance National pour l'Accroissement de la Population Française*, the Fecund Fathers Association of Saone and Loire 1908 and the *Federation des Associations de Familles Nombreuses de France* in 1921. An extra-Parliamentary commission on depopulation was established in 1901 and its first report damned family planning but there was little effective government action before WWI. In 1919 a *Conseil Superieur de la Natalité* was attached to the Ministry of Health, a 1920 law prescribed jail for anyone promoting birth control (though condoms were not banned because of their use in controlling VD) and a 1923 law moved rulings on abortion out of the hands of juries. In the early 1930s equalisation funds became mandatory but only in 1939 was a comprehensive *Code de la Famille* introduced. Government policies had helped the pro-natality movements in grants for child support, pregnant women, breast feeding, bottled water confinement allowances.[19] Overall however the family allowances had little effect. Glass estimated that they were about 3 per cent of national income in the 1930s, that few workers qualified for the allowances which ranged from 4 to 12 per cent of earnings and that, with three children, a family would have needed an allowance of 22 per cent. At most, concluded Glass, the fall in fertility might have been slightly bigger without the allowances.

All of this was of course important in the context of the shift of labour out of agriculture as urbanisation and industrialisation advanced. Despite advances in techniques, agriculture was a relatively low productivity sector and the pace at which economies changed their balance away from agriculture to industry was a significant ingredient in the rise of national outputs. Britain was the vivid contrast to France. Manufacturing productivity did rise in Britain but its industrial revolution was marked more than anything else by the shift of resources out of agriculture whose share of total employment was less than 40 per cent as early as 1820 whilst France's was still at that level in 1913 (Annex Table A4). Of course Britain was exceptional in this respect but after 1870, when Germany, France and USA still had one-half of their labour force in agriculture, the subsequent decline was distinctly faster in the other two countries (Germany 34.6 per cent by 1913, USA 27.5 per cent). It was not that the absolute size of these labour forces was falling. Germany's did rise to nearly ten million by 1905 and USA to 12.3 million by 1910.

In France the labour force in agriculture in the mid nineteenth century was of the order of 7.5 million. Thereafter it rose slightly and then declined in the twentieth century, but more slowly than Germany and USA. The agricultural product mix remained heavily weighted to grain, the ownership and concentration of farm businesses were remarkably stable, productivity growth was modest and the state, apart from tariff protection, did little to disrupt that pattern. All the more remarkable that, given the slow release of resources to industry and services, the performance of agriculture 1870–1938 was perfectly respectable as we shall see. It was however in a context of tariffs on agricultural imports, whose main features can now be outlined. A major element in protection of the French economy was the tariff of 1892 named after its author, Meline, subsequently the French Prime Minister. Before that, protection was constrained by various treaties which France had made with the UK (1860) and other countries. Agriculture was not covered in these treaties so that, from the 1870s, tariffs rose relentlessly especially on wheat and other grains. The fall in agricultural prices, as American and Russian grain imports mounted, led to a tariff campaign by the *Société des Agriculteurs de France*. In the 1881 general tariff, changes in duties were limited and imports continued to flow – German and Austrian sugar, Japanese silk, Scandinavian timber, American wheat and cattle. Then in 1885–87 duties on cattle, flour, rye, barley and oats were raised and those on wheat to three francs per 100 kilograms.[20] Imports of wheat continued – 21 per cent of home consumption 1876–92. Then in the 1890s duties were raised on wine, eggs, butter, silk. Across all agriculture the Meline tariff raised duties by 25 per cent; this excluded wheat but in 1897 the wheat duty was up to seven francs. Imports of grain then fell sharply 1898–1905, wheat imports from 15 per cent of home consumption 1886–92 to 6 per cent 1896–1902 and 8 per cent 1902–12. By 1913 the wheat tariff was 38 per cent and wheat prices were about 45 per cent higher than in free trade Britain.[21] The protection of French grain producers had been "successful": self-sufficiency in bread had been achieved. Nor did matters change much in the inter-war period where France's protectionist policy differed little from that of other countries. As grain prices fell in the 1920s, tariffs rose and France had grain quotas by 1929 and on most agricultural goods by 1932.

Under this protective shield, the labour force in agriculture had risen, on most estimates, to about 8.5 million by 1896. Carré, Dubois and Malinvaud's careful analysis of part time and support labour suggests an absolute decline to 5900 by 1938 – an earlier decline and lower level than in other studies.[22] The striking feature of French farm business was its stable structure. As Table 6.1 shows, by 1892 there were still 2.2 million farms less than 2.5 acres. The number of farms in the 2.5–24 acres range remained fairly stable at 2.5 million or thereabouts

*Table 6.1* Number of farms in France 1862–1929 (millions)

| Size of farms in acres | 1862 | 1882 | 1892 | 1908 | 1929 |
|---|---|---|---|---|---|
| Less than 2.5 | – | – | 2.2 | 2.1 | – |
| 2.5–24 | 2.4 | 2.6 | 2.6 | 2.5 | 1.9 |
| 25–99 | 0.64 | 0.73 | 0.72 | 0.75 | 0.97[a] |
| 100+ | 0.15 | 0.14 | 0.14 | 0.15 | 0.1[b] |

Sources: Clapham 1961; Milward and Saul 1977; Carré *et al.* 1975.

Notes
a  26–125.
b  Over 125.

from 1862 to 1908, falling only in the 1920s. Here were the property owning peasants of Burgundy, Garonne and Normandy. The average size in England in the late nineteenth century was 66 acres. Of course the much smaller number of farms greater than 24 acres in France did occupy at least one-half the total acreage. Here were Bordeaux wine, forest areas, the north of Paris grain fields. However the main point is that this structure did not change much throughout the nineteenth century.

France was a flourishing exporter of food, wine and flowers with niche production of sugar beet, dairy products, flour, often for specialist markets. Labour productivity in agriculture was lower in France than in the UK. Broadberry, Federico and Klein estimated the French level as 74 per cent of the UK in 1913 with Germany 52.4 per cent and USA 108.5 per cent.[23] The higher level in Britain was in part due to its abundant pasture land allowing more animal husbandry, fertiliser, horsepower and meat production and hence greater yields per acre.[24] The productivity advances throughout Europe 1870–1939 were a result of the disappearance of fallow, improvements in tools and equipment, more machines and fertilisers. France experienced all these developments and indeed the rise in the productivity of French agriculture was about the same as Germany.[25] At the heart of the lower French productivity *level* was the extensive cultivation of grain. The opportunity for grain exports 1855–75 afforded by English free trade, the retention of small peasant plots and an element of chosen self-sufficiency at farm and national level meant that French grain production was raised to an amount three times that of Germany and exceeded in Europe only by Russia. In Britain, grain cultivation was concentrated on specific suitable soils whereas in France it was widespread with much finishing up on poor quality land and lower yields. As the grain imports from Russia and America rose in the 1870s, the state erected tariff barriers and French grain production mushroomed.

In sum, on the one hand, French farming was nowhere near so bad nor reluctant to change has sometimes been argued.[26] It did not benefit from the same abundance of pasture and therefore animal husbandry as Britain and its chief weakness was excessive cultivation of grains. The cooperative movement from the late nineteenth century proved useful, especially for providing credit but the major stumbling block was the persistence of small plots and the slow decline in their share of the economy. Indeed the rural exodus that did occur 1870–1939 consisted more of journey men, day labourers, cottage industry and women. This also affected the pattern of urbanisation, the growth of consumption and of industry to which we now turn.

## French business and the growth of manufacturing

State intervention in industry during the Third Republic has often been discussed in terms of the interplay between a desire for economic stability in the economy, a liberal attitude to the private sector whilst confronting the threat to the "little man" of the new industrial barons, which followed the wide male electoral suffrage introduced by the 1875 constitution.[27] The outcome is then seen as a rather uncoordinated set of pragmatic industrial policies that did little to promote economic growth and some have argued the state lacked resources.[28] It will be argued here that the development of French manufacturing was perfectly respectable by contemporary European standards and that the various strands of industrial policy can be better understood as reflecting France's concerns about national defence. The first issue then is to assess the performance of French manufacturing, paving the way for an examination in later sections of the role of state intervention in manufacturing and the infrastructure industries.

Criticism of the French manufacturing performance in the nineteenth century has often alluded to the absence of competition because of tariff protection and that there was a culture biased towards holding companies and family firms which did not exploit the economies of scale and integration which characterised the new species of business organisation in USA – research divisions, M form product line organisation, specialist staff.[29] There is little doubt that the industrial structure was different from that in USA and that tariff protection of manufacturing was substantial. The benchmark is often the large US firm like Standard Oil, US Rubber, du Pont, the American Sugar Refining Company, Western Union, US Steel, catering for mass markets in oil, rubber, food, railways, later airlines. These "modern" business organisations achieved economies by diversifying across product ranges, integrating forward to distribution and marketing and devoting considerable manpower to marketing. Security of raw material supply was achieved by integration backwards into iron, steel and coal firms whilst the development of specialist staff in marketing, personnel, research was fostered in the multi-divisional business form and eventually came to be trained in the American business schools. Some said France had a "management gap" and up to WWI "remained ... a ... home of artisan trades, of *ateliers*, of small workshops, many of which made no use of power".[30] In 1896 an industrial census recorded 575,000 establishments which employed no more than 5.5 workers on average. There were large firms like Saint-Gobain in glass and chemicals and Alsthom in electrical equipment but they were only about 6 per cent the size of ICI or IG Farben. A limited degree of backward integration in chemicals, aluminium, steel, motor cars and light machinery occurred as well as forward integration to distribution and marketing in bicycles, small arms, sewing machines and motor cars, Renault being a classic example. Mergers came in the 1920s – Schneider, Kuhlmann and Westinghouse in electrical machinery for example. The new industries of the late nineteenth and early twentieth centuries saw the emergence of some large firms but out of the top 25 firms by size in 1930 only a few were in these new industries – Péchiney, Air Liquide, Rhône-Poulenc (chemicals), Citroen (cars), Standard Française (oil). Some 80 per cent of the top ranking firms originated in the nineteenth century. Many large firms were large because they were holding companies and/or held a large financial portfolio. Of the 30 largest firms in 1913, those in chemicals held financial assets equivalent to 30 per cent of the value of their real capital assets, a figure that rose to 50 per cent in 1927 and 80 per cent in 1937, by which time the rest of the 30 firms recorded more than 50 per cent except for cars, machines and coal.[31] Financial holding companies held 6 per cent of all stock in 1919, 14 per cent in 1937, flourishing not via the exploitation of economies of scale but because other companies needed external finance.

So whilst "modern business organisation" did proliferate in France after 1945, during the Third Republic the industrial structure was more one of small works, family firms, large holding companies and some mergers. Moreover industry was protected from foreign competition by tariffs. The free trade era of the 1860s saw treaty agreements with other countries for industrial goods, much against the wishes of French manufacturers (cf. Chapter 2) who were frustrated by the enforced wait for the expiry of these treaties. Even though the tariffs on manufactures averaged only 12–15 per cent in the 1870s, they were higher than in Germany at 4–6 per cent. In the meantime in the 1880s, bounties for shipping and shipbuilding were extended and greater scope given in treaty deliberations to raise the duties on manufactures. It was however the Meline tariff of 1892 which "put an end [until the 1960s] ... to the free trade interlude in France".[32] A maximum/minimum range was prescribed to constrain the government in its treaty negotiation but a "Padlock Act" of 1897 allowed government to raise certain duties without the permission of Parliament. The aim of the Meline tariff was to exempt Empire commodities and all products in which France was deficient, usually raw materials, coal and generally the early stages of production. Nevertheless though flax, hide, oil seed were exempt, timber, bricks, cement, paving stones, coal and iron compounds became subject to duty. The rate of duty on textiles was higher the nearer was the product to the finished article – zero on worsted and woollen yarn rising through wool and jute fabrics, linen and cotton goods. There were duties on rubber, paper, furniture, china, glass and leather goods, large increases for fine steel goods and other metals whilst bounties were extended for silk, hemp, sugar and shipping. By 1913, tariffs on imported manufactures averaged 20 per cent whilst the figure for all British imports was 34 per cent.[33] Protection continued after WWI, tracking price movements and France benefited from the favoured nation status which the Treaty of Versailles forced Germany to confer. This only lasted to 1925 after which it became difficult to sell Alsace textiles and Lorraine iron ore. It was not long after the introduction of quotas on agricultural imports in 1929 that quotas were extended, in the early 1930s, to manufactured goods.

In sum French industry and agriculture were heavily protected, certainly by the standards of most European countries, whilst its industrial structure and business organisation did not appear to be progressing along the lines of American industry. However, as for Germany (cf. Chapter 5) and the UK (Chapter 8), America's abundance of land, natural resources and the scarcity of labour cast doubt on whether it is an appropriate comparator. Prices of factors of production were different in Europe so different techniques of production were warranted.[34] Niche production with skilled labour could survive to exploit the different factor endowments, even though technical progress turned out to be faster in the mass production methods of USA. What moreover is the evidence that French industrial performance was poorer than other European countries? How far if at all did the gap between labour productivity in manufacturing in France and USA actually change from the one that existed already in the mid nineteenth century? One measure of the rate of industrialisation is the size and growth of manufacturing output relative to the size of each country. This is what Bairoch measures in his 1982 study of world industrial trends and Table 5.4 showed the key markers. The measure for each country for each year is manufacturing output per head of population, expressed as a percentage of USA 1913. It is useful to reproduce some of the figures here:

|         | *1860* | *1913* | *1928* |
|---------|--------|--------|--------|
| USA     | 17     | 100    | 144    |
| UK      | 51     | 91     | 97     |
| France  | 16     | 47     | 62     |
| Germany | 12     | 67     | 80     |

France's manufacturing output per head of population was well below the UK in 1860 but did catch up to some extent in the years up to WWI and in the 1920s. Germany did even better, especially in the 1860–1913 period. If one were to widen the scope to national income per head (cf. Table 5.2) the growth rate in France was not far behind Germany and USA and over the whole period 1870–1950 was exceeded only by USA amongst the six major powers. By all European standards then the French performance was perfectly respectable as Crafts concluded in a different context.[35] Nor do the above indicate anything about productivity in manufacturing which becomes clear once one recognises the three key elements in the change in manufacturing output per head: these were the demand for French manufactures, the ease with which labour was released from agriculture to manufacturing and, third, the changes in labour productivity in manufacturing. Clearly the rise of large homogeneous mass consumption markets inside America was a strong inducement for the emergence of assembly lines and large firms. In France the slow growth of population and the rural exodus, recorded earlier, were reflected in the slow pace of urbanisation and hence in big urban markets. As Table 6.2 shows, although France in 1830 had more of its population (15.8 per cent) than Germany in towns of 5000+ inhabitants, the gap had disappeared by 1870 and in 1913 the French figure was just below 40 per cent whilst Germany was over 50 per cent. France had the lowest level of urbanisation in Western Europe, more like Italy and Spain. In 1911 it had five towns with a population greater than 200,000 whilst Germany had 16, Russia ten, UK ten, Italy seven, Poland seven: thereafter we find that 44 per cent of the French population who lived in towns of at least 2000 inhabitants had risen only to 52 per cent by 1931 and 43 per cent by 1946.[36]

A relatively weak growth of domestic demand may tell part of the story but there were also export markets open to every country. France's merchandise exports were 4.9 per cent of GDP in 1870 rising to 8.2 per cent in 1913 and 8.6

*Table 6.2* Urbanisation in Europe 1830–1913 (% of population in towns with 5000 or more inhabitants)

|  | 1830 | 1850 | 1870 | 1890 | 1900 | 1913 |
|---|---|---|---|---|---|---|
| UK | 27.5 | 39.6 | 53.3 | 64.0 | 67.4 | 69.7 |
| Belgium | 25.0 | 33.5 | 38.8 | 48.0 | 52.3 | 58.0 |
| Netherlands | 35.7 | 35.6 | 38.5 | 46.3 | 47.8 | 51.3 |
| Germany | 10.0 | 15.0 | 24.5 | 34.5 | 42.0 | 51.0 |
| France | 15.7 | 19.5 | 24.7 | 30.7 | 35.4 | 39.5 |
| Switzerland | 7.5 | 11.9 | 17.5 | 24.5 | 30.6 | 39.3 |
| Total = "Western Europe" | 17.6 | 24.1 | 32.8 | 42.2 | 47.6 | 53.4 |
| Italy and Spain | 18.1 | 20.5 | 23.2 | 29.3 | 33.1 | 38.3 |
| Scandinavia | 7.5 | 7.9 | 111.2 | 17.3 | 21.1 | 24.3 |
| Balkans | 7.6 | 10.5 | 11.8 | 12.5 | 19.8 | 22.6 |
| Russia | 6.0 | 7.2 | 9.2 | 11.6 | 13.2 | 14.6 |
| All Europe | 12.8 | 16.3 | 20.6 | 26.4 | 33.2 | 33.6 |

Source: Bairoch 1998, Table 23.

*Table 6.3* Sectoral distribution of the French employed population 1896–1938 ('000 persons, contemporary boundaries)

|  | 1896 | 1913 | 1929 | 1938 |
|---|---|---|---|---|
| Agriculture | 8350 | 7450 | 6600 | 5900 |
| Energy and mining[a] | 180 | 270 | 420 | 380 |
| Construction[b] | 830 | 960 | 1120 | 780 |
| Manufacturing |  |  |  |  |
| Food processing | 470 | 520 | 550 | 580 |
| Building materials | 260 | 290 | 350 | 250 |
| Textiles[c] | 2790 | 2850 | 2300 | 1800 |
| Metallurgy | 80 | 120 | 230 | 200 |
| Mechanical and electrical | 660 | 870 | 1400 | 1160 |
| Chemicals | 70 | 110 | 210 | 210 |
| Other manufacturing | 660 | 730 | 850 | 700 |
| Total | 4990 | 5490 | 5890 | 4900 |
| Services |  |  |  |  |
| Transport and communication | 600 | 750 | 1150 | 1000 |
| Finance | 60 | 110 | 220 | 200 |
| Domestic service | 950 | 930 | 780 | 750 |
| Trade | 1000 | 1250 | 1500 | 1650 |
| Government[d] | 1110 | 1290 | 1100 | 1450 |
| Other services | 1150 | 1400 | 1520 | 1750 |
| Total | 4870 | 5730 | 6270 | 6500 |
| Grand total | 19,220 | 19,900 | 20,300 | 18,760 |

Source: Carré *et al.* 1975, Table 3.4.

Notes
a  Solid mineral fuel, gas, electricity, water, petroleum and oil production.
b  Building and public works.
c  Includes clothing and leather.
d  Includes armed forces draftees.

per cent in 1929, well below the UK and Germany and the latter did not have any intrinsic advantages in such markets.[37] So demand factors do not tell us much. More revealing is the supply side where changes in manufacturing output per head were a product of two elements, the rise in manufacturing's share of the population and, second, the change in output per head of the labour force in manufacturing. Table 6.3 is based on the methods and classification of Carré *et al.* and displays the decline in the agricultural labour force after 1896 noted earlier.[38] Manufacturing plus construction, energy and mining constitute "industry" whose share of the economy is slightly lower in Table 6.3 than in other studies (cf. Annex Table A4) but does rise in a similar fashion to 32 per cent in 1913, 33 per cent in 1930 falling back slightly in the 1930s. The service sector's share of employment is slightly higher in France than Germany and that gap does not change much. Within manufacturing the big growth sectors were chemicals, metallurgy, machinery and electrical equipment, as in Germany. By how much was the rise in manufacturing output per head of population due to the rise in the labour force in manufacturing, as opposed to productivity change in manufacturing? An attempt to answer this is provided in the Appendix to this chapter using data for 1860–1928. The French labour force in manufacturing rose from 9 per cent of the population in 1860 to 15 per cent in 1913, remaining roughly constant thereafter. The trend for Germany was from 7 per cent to 13 per cent in 1913 and then a rise to 16 per cent by 1928, reflecting the expansion of the German manufacturing labour force in the inter-war period, up to 10.4 million in 1925 and 11.5 million by 1939. It is shown in the Appendix that, first, the contribution of the rise in the labour force in manufacturing is very similar in France and USA and concentrated in the years up to 1913; in the UK there is no effect because the manufacturing share remains unchanged after 1870 whereas in Germany there is a big change and concentrated in the inter-war period. Second, the productivity contribution of Germany is only slightly bigger than France and concentrated wholly in the years up to 1913. In both countries, that contribution is much less than the productivity contributions in the UK and USA.

In summary, the stagnant population and modest changes in agriculture are at the heart of the differences between the French economy and others. The growth of labour productivity in manufacturing was only slightly behind Germany; rather it was the shift in the balance of the German economy from agriculture to industry which yielded the faster progress of industrialisation, that is in manufacturing output per head of population.

## Industrial policies and national defence

The central government provided tariff protection, intervened in several manufacturing sectors and closely regulated businesses in the infrastructure industries. Economic historians have had some difficulty in making sense of French industrial policy. Some writers have wanted to stress that there was no simple gradual extension of state intervention and no obvious signs of a planned programme, until the 1936–38 Popular Front programme which in any case was unambitious.[39] Many have evaluated industrial policy, implicitly or explicitly, in terms of how far it raised "economic growth", average living standards and/or accelerated economic and techological modernisation.[40] Certainly one can see some elements of this but they are not very powerful. From Fontvieille's presentation (1976) of the central government's expenditure, it is possible to identify an "economy" category which varied between 3 and 10 per cent of total spending for much of the period, before rising to 15 per cent in the late 1930s (Table 6.4). About one-half of government subsidies were for industry though not much went on capital equipment. The gross turnover of various state enterprises (tobacco, matches, gunpowder, post and telecoms) also rose considerably over

*Table 6.4* French central government revenues and expenditures 1870–1938 (annual averages, billion francs)

|  | 1870 | 1880 | 1890 | 1900 | 1913 | 1920 | 1930 | 1938 |
|---|---|---|---|---|---|---|---|---|
| *Revenues*[a] | | | | | | | | |
| 1 Direct taxes | 0.3 | 0.4 | 0.5 | 0.5 | 0.6 | 1.9 | 10.5 | 9.2 |
| 2 Customs | 0.1 | 0.3 | 0.4 | 0.4 | 0.8 | 1.9 | 6.1 | 8.8 |
| 3 Excise | 0.3 | 0.6 | 0.6 | 0.7 | 0.7 | 1.9 | 2.0 | 5.1 |
| 4 Registration fees[b] | 0.3 | 0.6 | 0.5 | 0.6 | 0.8 | 2.7 | 4.9 | 4.1 |
| 5 Turnover and transport taxes | 0 | 0 | 0 | 0 | 0 | 1.8 | 8.7 | 9.8 |
| 7 Other[c] | 0.7 | 1.1 | 1.2 | 1.6 | 2.2 | 12.3 | 13.5 | 17.5 |
| Total | 1.7 | 3.0 | 3.2 | 3.8 | 5.1 | 22.5 | 50.8 | 54.6 |
| National Income[d] | 26.5 | 27.2 | 27.3 | 29.1 | 38.0 | 187.9 | 288.5 | 314.0 |
| Revenue as % NI | 6.4 | 11.0 | 11.7 | 13.1 | 13.4 | 12.0 | 17.6 | 17.3 |
| *Expenditures*[e] | | | | | | | | |
| 1 Debt service | 0.4 | 0.9 | 1.0 | 0.9 | 0.8 | 9.4 | 11.7 | 15.4 |
| 2 Defence | 1.2 | 0.9 | 1.0 | 1.1 | 1.6 | 11.2 | 9.4 | 37.4 |
| 3 Colonies | 0.1 | 0.1 | 0.2 | 0.2 | 0.3 | 1.5 | 2.1 | 3.3 |
| 4 Social etc.[f] | 0.1 | 0.1 | 0.2 | 0.3 | 0.5 | 2.4 | 5.2 | 8.2 |
| 5 Public works | 0.1 | 0.2 | 0.1 | 0.2 | 0.1 | 0.8 | 2.1 | 5.1 |
| 6 Economy | 0.1 | 0.3 | 0.1 | 0.2 | 0.5 | 2.0 | 3.2 | 14.1 |
| 7 Other[g] | 0.3 | 0.5 | 0.4 | 0.5 | 0.6 | 14.8 | 6.7 | 12.4 |
| Total | 2.3 | 3.0 | 3.0 | 3.3 | 4.4 | 42.1 | 40.4 | 95.9 |
| Expenditure as % NI | 8.7 | 11.0 | 11.0 | 11.3 | 11.6 | 22.4 | 14.0 | 30.5 |

Notes

a  Mitchell 2003a.

b  Registration fees and stamp duties.

c  The rise after WWI seems mainly to be consumption taxes for tobacco, brandy and motor cars (cf. Schremmer 1989, p. 397).

d  Gross domestic product based on data for 1865–74, 1875–84, 1885–94, 1895–1904, 1905–13, 1920–24, 1925–34, 1935–38. See Mitchell (2003a, p. 838). There will therefore be some underestimating for 1913 and 1938 and overestimating for 1920.

e  Thanks are due to Jean-Pierre Dormois for pointing me to Fontvielle (1976) for these expenditure data.

f  Includes education, culture and social welfare activities.

g  Includes general administration, foreign affairs, justice, local activities and extraordinary expenditures. The rise after WWI seems to be due initially to extraordinary expenditure and in the 1930s to general administration.

the period and Dormois characterised much of this state intervention as "erratic, unconvincing and superficial" with armaments programmes playing only a minor role in promoting economic growth and even the rise in military spending in the 1930s had little economic expansionary effects because of bottlenecks.[41] There was some tendency for the spending to be counter-cyclical like the Freycinet Plan 1876–82 and the Baudin Plan for 1908. Indeed the major peacetime successful venture, in this light, was the reconstruction programme in the 1920s. By 1931, 7700 factories, 500,000 houses, 25,000 farm buildings were built or restored and 300 mines recovered. New financial institutions were established to help small and medium sized businesses – *Banque Populaire* (1913), *Crédit National Hôtelier* (1924), *Credit National* (1919). In sectors like iron and steel, concentration and rationalisation were fostered and state orders for aircraft and ships were restricted to rationalising firms.[42]

Much of state intervention in industry can be better understood in terms of the state's desire to strengthen the country's national defences, not only in terms of the tariff protection already discussed and the regulation of infrastructure industries (next section) but also in terms of manufacturing. Contemporary observers during the Third Republic were aware of the strategic dangers facing France and so were the governments. Kemp, though characterising 1870–1939 as the apogee of French liberalism with few social welfare schemes, did view the state as quintessentially active in a strong regulatory and military role; not a police state but, as he put it, *l'état gendarm* in the supervisory sense.[43] For manufacturing the key elements were a consistently rising demand from government defence requirements, the build up of armaments and aircraft industries and the support for business development by the avoidance of direct taxes. How successful were these activities is a big question for military historians and the fact that France was overrun by Germany in 1870–71, 1914–15 and 1940 could be counted as the key

*Table 6.5* Military spending of the major powers 1870–1938[a]

|  | 1870–1913 | | 1920–38 | |
|---|---|---|---|---|
|  | As % national income[b] | As % central government expenditure | As national % income[b] | As % central government expenditure |
| Japan | 5.0 | 32.2 | 5.7 | 20.1 |
| Russia | 3.9 | 27.9 | 7.1 | 11.9 |
| France | 3.7 | 25.9 | 4.3 | 22.4 |
| Germany | 2.6 | 54.1 | 3.3 | 23.8 |
| UK | 2.6 | 37.5 | 3.8 | 17.6 |
| USA | 0.7 | 29.4 | 1.2 | 22.4 |

Source: Eloranta and Harrison 2010.

Notes
a  Contemporary boundaries, except that USSR boundaries are used for Russia 1870–1913.
b  Gross domestic product.

verdict were it not for the fact that France's geo-political position and resource weaknesses meant that only drastic political changes would have altered the outcome (cf. the post 1945 move to European union). In the meantime the various strands of industrial policy do make some sort of sense in the context of national defence. Note first of all that central government spending was about 9 per cent of national income in the 1870s rising to 12 per cent by 1913 and even to 30 per cent by 1938 (Table 6.4). Whilst some have speculated that the French state lacked revenues, it is not the case that defence suffered from lack of resources. The French military system involved a standing army with conscription of personnel for long periods (by lottery but with paid substitutes allowed) in contrast to the volunteer recruitment in Britain and universal military obligations in Prussia.[44] Germany was spending more in the few years before WWI but not earlier and, as Tables 6.4 and 6.5 show, over the whole period 1870–1938, France devoted more of its national income to defence (excluding the WWI years) than Germany, the UK and USA.[45] Rather, the issue was the role of strategic resources and industrial strength in armaments.

State activity in the manufacture of armaments had a long history. The Revolutionary decree of March 1791 proclaimed the right of everyone to trade freely but the September Law ruled that explosives should continue to be a state monopoly. The Napoleonic code ruled that private property and the private economy were subject to the law so that armament production (as well as transport etc.) became state enterprises or subject to state regulation. The Third Republic in the 1870s inherited 64 state arsenals as well as the explosives monopoly. About 12–15 per cent of military spending was on armaments and both the army and the navy promoted competition across their suppliers such that by 1913 there were 1531 suppliers for the army and 348 for the navy. Warships were built in state or private yards and in shipbuilding generally 1881–1900 the state ensured that 60 per cent of the market was reserved for domestic yards, the modernisation of which was later fostered by the state.[46] Artillery and other armaments were also made both in state enterprises and in private metallurgical businesses like Schneider and Firminy. State controls stretched also to exports such that an 1895 law allowed the Minister of War to prohibit the export of arms "of any type". By 1934 Renault was exporting 24 different armoured combat vehicles fitted with Schneider firearms but a 1935 decree prohibited the export of any war material without the permission of the state.[47] During WWI there had been much reliance on private firms like Renault for shell casings and trucks. The early loss of the eastern regions in 1914 called for a reaction but it was not until 1916 that a strong lead was taken (France was not alone – Britain also did not wake up until 1916). The war brutally exposed French weaknesses not only by being overrun by Germany 1914–15 but because the eastern regions contained much of France's coal and iron and thereafter France was heavily reliant on allied supplies of coal, iron, raw materials, machine tools and explosives.[48] Imports were regulated, production in part organised by the existing cartels and "Consortiums" of firms were made purchase agents at prices agreed by the government. The capacity of the state arsenals and shipyards were deemed inadequate and so the merchant marine, shipyards and factories like those owned by Michelin were requisitioned. A new huge state arsenal was opened in Roanne but proved a disaster and was closed in 1917. In the end the 1918 Spring Allied expeditionary force used French armaments and light vehicles plus British heavy guns and vehicles.[49] There was an expectation in some quarters that the strong state intervention in the economy in the war years might herald a new phase of state intervention in industry. Some like socialist Clementes wanted to retain controls after the war to strengthen France's access to core raw materials. In the 1920s the state strengthened its grip on transport and energy (cf. next section) and in manufacturing the *Potasses d'Alsace* became a state owned enterprise rather than being left to private chemical firms like Saint-Gobain, Kuhlman and Péchiney.[50] But for the large part controls were relaxed and the state retreated until the 1930s with the advent of the Popular Front and the spectre of another war.

The state takeovers in armaments and aircraft manufacture in the late 1930s have been seen in part as an attempt to control the "cannon merchants" as well as limit the influence of the 200 rich families in the "great trusts".[51] The mixed motives have also been seen to explain why the nationalisation programme was limited. In fact its significance lay in taking place in industries that were of central strategic significance and not in other industries and that, given German rearmament, there was a desire that urgent attention be given to securing "long runs" and stability for the manufacturers. Munitions and tank producers were the core elements. The decree of October 1936 nationalised Renault armoured vehicles and assembly lines at Issy-les Moulineaux to be followed by 39 other takeovers which included some of the assets of Oscar Brandt, Schneider (guns), Saint-Chamond (tanks) and plants at Mans and Vernon, and Havre, Creusot and Saint Priest in 1937. These were divisions of companies, the rest left untouched. Thus Hotchkiss owned the Levallois plant but also produced motor cars; Schneider-Creusot owned the Havre and Creusot plants but also manufactured mainly steel products. Compensation for the takeovers was paid and the programme was limited to large plants.[52] All armament suppliers left in the private sector were subject to strict licensing. Some have judged the programme was a success in that tank production had trebled by 1939 and the army had learnt how to construct and test for itself. So also for the aircraft industry where initially the military ranks had even less ability to design what they wanted, let alone construct and test.[53] The industry was in an artisan stage, concentrated around Paris, and the Air Ministry had no arsenal of its own. A Company of Conjoint Management was established in 1936 and the state was allowed to buy whatever assets it needed short of buying out a whole company. Five new national aircraft companies were established and one for engine manufacture. They were joint stock companies subject to commercial law. Some of the existing private sector directors sat on the boards but the state owned 67 per cent of the assets and the board members also included magistrates and trade union members. By 1939 France claimed to have the "best bombers".[54] There was a symmetry here with what was happening to airlines. Most European countries were determined to have their own airline even if privately owned. Each claimed sovereign airspace and so the European airline industry developed as a set of many small companies in each country – in contrast to the trans-continental airlines in USA. Air France was set up in 1935 with one-quarter of the shares owned by the state which also provided a 78 per cent subsidy on turnover.[55]

Some have argued the industrial interventions of the Popular Front were constrained by limited funds. France did spend heavily on defence, as already noted, but revenues proved more of a problem. They tracked expenditures in the period before WWI but fell behind thereafter creating significant debt problems (Table 6.4). In many respects the philosophy behind the tax systems inherited from the Revolutionary and Napoleonic regimes (cf. Chapter 2) did not change much before WWI. "Liberty" was to be assured by avoiding inquisitorial tax regimes like the British income tax whilst "equality" was to be attained by proportional rather than progressive systems. The business and propertied classes were effectively protected in the nineteenth century by a light tax burden. There were direct taxes on buildings, doors, windows, moveable property, land and income from securities but they fell from 42 per cent of all revenues in 1815 to 23 per cent in 1870 and 14 per cent in 1913, though local government did levy direct tax surcharges, at 75 per cent of the central government taxes in 1885.[56] During WWI a new income tax system was introduced replacing all the existing direct taxes. One element was the so-called general comprehensive tax on incomes above 7000 francs, a proportional system as were the five new "partial" income taxes on business, agricultural, earned and professional incomes plus that on capital revenues. They included minimum thresholds and allowed for family size. This new income tax system took some time to develop and direct taxes still accounted for only 20 per cent of revenues in 1925 and 16 per cent by 1938 (Table 6.4). The bulk of revenues therefore came from indirect taxes, including customs revenues (about 15 per cent of all revenues up to 1913), new turnover and transport taxes in the 1920s, alongside enhanced consumption taxes on tobacco, brandy and motor cars. From the beginning in the early 1870s, this system of taxes lagged behind expenditures. The legacy of the Franco-Prussian War 1870–71 was a large debt and an annual debt service above other countries, about 30 per cent of total spending. By 1913 the French national debt was 33 billion francs – 86 per cent of national income as compared to the UK 25 per cent and Germany 9 per cent. Further debt was amassed during WWI reaching a staggering 533 per cent of national income in 1919 with the UK at 133 per cent and Germany at 99 per cent.[57] These debts were important for the macroeonomy, the franc and the financial system. They did not seem to constrain public spending sufficiently to put France at a lower spending level than other Western European countries. The welfare system was not as well developed as Germany, and France did not face the same urban problems as the UK but the strategic dimensions of industrial policy which have been outlined here and the degree of intervention by the state do not seem to have been unduly limited by the public finances.

**The concession system in energy, transport and telecommications**[58]

Business in the infrastructure industries developed in the nineteenth century within the framework set out in the Napoleonic codes outlined in Chapter 2. Coal, gas, water, electricity, railways, tramways, telegraph and telephone firms operated under a concession system supervised by the *Conseil d'État* which set standards, whilst bodies like the *Corps des Mines* monitored and regulated detailed business operations. The operating enterprises could be private companies, municipal enterprises or state owned, but all operated as concessionaires. There were two key factors affecting business/state relationships and they stemmed from the two central characteristics of the infrastructure industries. One was the monopoly element in transport, telecoms and energy grids; the other was the importance of the infrastructure industries for national defence. It is useful first to show how the network utilities were regulated and then examine the way structures did or did not emerge in response to the needs of a national defence in coal, oil, telecoms, railway and electricity supply.

Gas and water supply remained essentially local utilities during the Third Republic and in economic terms were in a very different position from these sectors in the UK and Germany. The availability of gas depended crucially on coal supplies and the output of French mines, as late as 1912, was only 41 million tons, constituting, per head of population, only one-third of German supplies and less than one-fifth of the UK. Gas supplies rose from 0.6 million cubic metres in 1913 to 1.7 million by 1935 (Table 6.6) but again these were modest amounts. The improvement of water supplies was not unimportant in France in the nineteenth century but was of a different order of magnitude to the position in the UK and Germany where rapid urbanisation, unclean water supplies and limited sewerage capacity put the issue at crisis levels for many of the large cities with appalling health problems. The slower pace of urbanisation in France has already been documented (Table 6.2). Wells and aqueducts were also abundant reducing the need to rely on rivers which became polluted in many parts of Europe. In the early nineteenth century only four new local water supply systems were built in France, 34 in 1830–50, 315 between 1850 and 1900, much less than the UK and Germany. Only a small number of households were actually connected to water supplies in 1900 (18 per cent in Paris) even though more than 350 towns with populations of 5000+ had a water system.[59]

Both water supply and gas businesses had to deal with a regulatory system which stemmed from central government. The main unit of local government, the commune, was small and rarely became directly involved in gas, or later electricity supply, even though a law of 1884 allowed them to regulate local community matters. They were subject to the tutelage of central government, via the prefect system, with engineering and financial parameters laid down by the *Conseil d'État.*[60] Municipalisation of gas and electricity was rare. Of 844 gasworks in 1905 only 20 were municipally managed and for electricity it was "exceptionnelle".[61] It is argued in Chapters 5 and 8 that municipalisation in

*Table 6.6* Communications and energy in France 1871–1938 (contemporary boundaries)[a]

|  | *1871* | *1913* | *1929* | *1938* |
|---|---|---|---|---|
| Rail track ('000 kilometres open) | 15.5 | 40.8 | 42.3 | 42.6 |
| Rail freight traffic (billion ton kilometres) | 5.5 | 25.2 | 41.8 | 31.8[b] |
| Inland waterway cargo (billion ton kilometres) | 1.6 | 5.9 | 6.8 | 8.3 |
| Merchant shipping (million tons) | 1.1 | 1.6 | 2.0 | 1.5 |
| Telegrams (millions) | 5.0[c] | 50.5[c] | 48.4 | 36.4 |
| Telephone calls (billions) | 0.02[d] | 0.4 | 0.8 | 1.0 |
| Mail items (billions) | 0.6 | 3.7 | 6.1 | 5.7 |
| Coal output[e] (million metric tons) | 13.3 | 40.8 | 55.0 | 47.6 |
| Gas supply (billion cubic metres) | n.a. | 0.6[f] | n.a. | 1.7[f] |
| Electricity supply (gigawatt hours) | 0.3[g] | 1.8 | 15.6 | 20.8 |
| Population (millions) | 36.2 | 39.8 | 41.2 | 42.0 |

Sources: Mitchell 2003a; Matthews 1987; Maddison 1991 for population data.

Notes
a  Excludes Alsace and Lorraine 1871–1913.
b  1937.
c  Excludes official telegrams and radio telegrams. The 1871 figure excludes telegrams from railway stations. The 1913 entry relates to 1911.
d  1892.
e  Hard coal and lignite.
f  1900 and 1935. Interpolated from chart in Matthews 1987.
g  1900.

Britain and Germany was very much a feature of the growing industrial towns whose councils used trading profits to ease the strains on local property taxes from growing public health programmes. In France the nearest to that was the case of the capital where the Council came to an agreement with the privately owned Paris Gas Company for a slice of the profits. Established in 1855 under a charter which was renewed in 1870, the company paid the Council 0.2 million francs per annum for the right to lay pipes plus two francs for every cubic metre of gas produced. In the case of water supply the concession for Paris was held from 1857 by the *Compagnie Général des Eaux* but across the whole country municipalisation was more common. It grew from the mid nineteenth century and by 1913 three-quarters of all communes ran their own system.[62] A common problem in both Europe and USA was that standards for water quality were rising. Demands on the water undertakings were increasing whilst any decline in costs through technological improvement in reservoirs and piping was offset by the classic diminishing returns in the use of a resource, water, with all the same features as land. Faced with controls on water prices, private companies often floundered and the municipality took over.[63]

The regulatory regime in nineteenth century France for electricity supply and tramways has also been regarded as tough. Initially the concession periods were very short, and in 1887 there were only seven public electricity systems (and none in Paris) with total output only one-third of Germany. Even by 1889, the six concessionaire companies in Paris were on 18 year leases. At Le Havre the leases were only for five years, and even the cables had to be submitted for the approval of the mayor.[64] The horse-drawn tramways had developed strongly from the 1850s and especially from the 1870s as the world price of fodder fell. In Paris, there were six horse-drawn omnibus companies in the early 1850s, but in 1855 the *Compagnie Général d'Omnibus* (linked to the Pereire financial empire) was awarded a 50 year concession, and horse-drawn trams flourished, although there were criticisms that they kept to the most profitable routes.[65] By the 1890s, electric trams were operating in many large towns throughout Europe – Turin in 1891, Düsseldorf in 1892, parts of Tuscany later. By 1896, however, in France only 2.5 per cent of the tram network was electric. The main operators were equipment manufacturers like Thomas Houston, which was one of ten companies granted concessions in Paris in 1899 after that of the *Compagnie Général d'Omnibus* had been revoked. Fares and routes had been closely regulated from the 1890s. The mileage of electric trams was only 12.6 kilometres per million population but it did grow to 51 by 1905 – only slightly behind Germany and Denmark, though minuscule as compared to USA where however street layout and available land made route planning and regulation much easier.[66]

Strangely enough, the telephone in France also developed rather slowly in part as a product of being constrained within a concession system more suited to local utilities than the national networks towards which telephones were developing. The state claimed rights to all telecommunications, so the telephone was simply added to the telegraph, which had been merged with post in 1878. Local post offices were careful to guard their interests against the telephone newcomer, who was regarded with suspicion. In the municipalities it was initially seen as a simple one-way extension of the telegraph, and links, such as those between the town hall and the excise office together with the "wire to Paris", dominated attitudes. Business firms, including vineyards, had connections with the major cities – often close-circuit with no external links. During the Belle Epoque, the telephone had a rather licentious image for its non-professional uses. Parliament refused to grant funds.[67] Since it appeared to be mainly a short distance means of communication, it was treated like gas, electricity and water, with concessions granted to firms such as the *Société Générale de Téléphone* for Paris. Municipalities who wanted approval for telephone connections had to advance funds to the central government, a practice similar to that which had applied earlier in the nineteenth century, in the initially private telegraph system. Nor were local leaders eager to extend the number of telephone subscribers, concerned as those leaders were to avoid congestion on the wire to Paris. The result was that telephone development was very slow, and the whole system was nationalised in 1889. Some have ascribed the slow development partly to France's low rate of urbanisation, but this cannot explain the lag behind Scandinavia. There were lots of exchanges in France, indeed more than in many other European countries, but the number of telephones per exchange was very small.[68] The telephone was simply not treated very seriously in France: the 30,000 telephones in 1900 might be compared with 27,000 in New York hotels alone. In 1913 there were seven telephones per 1000 population, well below Britain, Scandinavia and Germany. By 1932, it was 30 per 1000, still among the lowest in Europe.

Turning now to the major national network of communications, regulation of the *railway* companies had been, as explained in Chapter 2, somewhat tighter than in other countries whilst government support via the guarantee of rates of return was meant to ensure France had a railway network which would unify the country and provide vital links for national defence. That emphasis on the security dimensions of railways continued in the Third Republic and expanded as the threat from Germany increased. The aim in France was to provide a universal service, accessible over all French territory. In each of the six networks that emerged in the 1850s there was one dominant company, but outside the basic trunk routes were "secondary lines", which did not always prove financially viable. The 1859 act distinguished between the old network (the *ancien reseau*, basically the trunk lines) and the new network. The interest guarantees were more generous on the new network and, in addition to subsidies per kilometre of line, the French state expected that such lines, if unprofitable, would be subsidised by the profits on the trunk network. Traffic grew healthily in the 1860s, but many of the secondary lines were not being merged successfully into the six basic networks. It was only when such lines were unprofitable and had military value that the state stepped in – specifically first for lines in the Paris–Orleans and Western networks. The Franco-Prussian War of 1870–71 was decisive in convincing the French government "that an adequate system of communications was indispensable to the successful pursuit of military operations".[69] The law of 1878 made provision for the finances of the new state lines to be incorporated in the budget of the Ministry of Works and financed through government bonds ("rentes").

The strategic factor was therefore decisive in prompting state ownership, but note that this was the solution only when the lines could not be sustained by subsidies. The government subsidised a number of small companies especially in the west and south-west. The scale of the subsidies throughout the system in the latter part of the nineteenth century caused some, later, to claim that the "tremendous increase in trackage and rail traffic was to a very large extent due to the lavish contributions made by a bountiful state".[70] Moreover, in what came to be called the "scoundrelly" conventions of 1883, the government committed itself, for new lines, to building the substructure and part of the superstructure, with companies doing the rest (in the form of paying to the government a number of francs per kilometre). This was a massive subsidy – the substructure was to be effectively provided free, like highways. But it was not a state takeover as in the cases of the Paris–Orleans and Western lines. It would seem that supporting unprofitable lines that were not of significant military value took the form of subsidies, and there was some (unspecified) level of subsidy at which the government would let the line close. In the case of France before the First World War, the situation was such that some parts of the railway system could not be sustained without a subsidy. Thus the whole of the Western network was taken over in 1906 because it was not proving financially viable yet was important militarily. Under the 1883 conventions, lines that were perceived to contribute to national defence "could not be discontinued even though unprofitable without the approval of the Minister of War".[71] As early as 1882, 26.4 per cent of railway capital was being supplied by the state, with only 16 per cent accounted for by equity shares – the rest were railway bonds. By 1913, 90 per cent of company capital was in the form of bonds, and close to 9000 kilometres of track were in public ownership.[72] Much of the basic trunk network was still in private owner- ship, so that the French government must have felt that it could, during a war, take control of these lines and commandeer resources sufficiently to achieve its military objectives.

There is indeed some evidence that French planning of the railways was as good as anywhere in Europe. By the early 1900s, in the War Ministry, there was a consultative commission of railway chiefs and departmental representatives whilst a national commission (*commission des reseuax*) provided military liaison with the big six railway companies. They were required by legislation of 1873 to place their resources at the disposal of the state for military movements. Steven- son suggests that the bureau of the general staff (*État-major de l'armée*) was as good as the German army's railway section. In 1870 there were five through lines in France (i.e. to the borders) and nine in Germany. By 1913 Germany had 13 and France 16 and the French lines all had double transit independent current giving great adaptation when the armed forces had to be concentrated.[73]

In the years running up to WWI, the railways' financial position deteriorated, as did many in Europe. By 1913 the cumulative debt to the French state was 617 million francs.[74] They had become common carriers (required to supply services on demand), had to publish all their prices and in response to complaints about their semi-monopoly positions, they were required to offer services in kind, like transport of mail. During WWI, as elsewhere, equipment was run down and price increases delayed. Net profits over the whole system had been 72 million francs in 1913 turning to a deficit of 1206 million by 1921 and operating costs were 124 per cent of revenues.[75] Although thereafter the track was not extended by any significant amount (apart from the return from Germany of the Alsace and Lorraine lines), the broad stance of the state was to maintain a strong railway system, to continue the old pattern of rates and fares but to attempt some ration- alisation of the structure. In 1921 an agreement was made with five major private companies, the state owned western network and the Alsace–Lorraine railway which had been placed in public ownership. A new *Conseil Supérieure des Chemins des Fer* was set up to act as an advisory body on all financial and tech- nical issues. All the net profits of the seven railways had to be pooled into the *Fonds Commun*. The aim was that customer prices would be so set as to provide a "users' guarantee" with the more profitable Nord, Est and Paris–Mediterrané networks cross-subsidising the less profitable Midi, Paris–Orleans and the two state enterprises.[76] This would underwrite the state's continuing guarantee to shareholders. The likelihood of success was reduced by the rise in coal prices and wages and in the introduction of an eight hour day from 1918 but some sort of financial normality was achieved by 1926 when a net profit of 542 million francs was earned.

However the advent of competition from road transport together with the 1930s depression made for more financial problems such that by 1933 a deficit of 3860 million francs was recorded rising to 5934 million in 1937. The economics of rail and road transport created huge problems for the railways which cannot be discussed here.[77] Suffice to record that France suffered as much as the rest of Europe. Rail freight traffic rose at the start but fell off in the 1930s as road vehicle numbers increased from 14 per 1000 population in 1924 to 54 by 1938 (i.e. to 1.5 million vehicles).[78] Tough regulation followed but, as in other countries, it was not the railway pricing structure that was adapted but rather constraints were put on road transport, starting with a decree of 1934. There was some recognition of a "transport" issue so that the *Conseil Supérieure de Transport* replaced the one for railways. Few then demurred when the railways were bought out by the state in 1937. It was a rather odd takeover, not so much a nationalisation as a centralisation since the (despised) shareholders retained their legal rights to the concessions and to interest payments. All franchise and assets were transferred to the new *Société National des Chemin des Fer Francais* (SNCF) and the shares were to be amortised by 1982 although any interest payments on the shares held by the five private companies did not have to be paid until 1955.

The other key strategic resource was energy where a key issue in the interwar period was the extent to which the new grids using hydro-electricity might alleviate France's poor endowment of primary energy resources. Coal output reached 50 million tons by 1930 but was still way behind the UK and Germany. At least, as noted in Chapter 2, the rights enshrined in the Napoleonic codes, including the Mining Code of 1811, gave the government rights over the sub-soil and a concession system that allowed state leverage when necessary. Nor had France yet realised any workable oil or natural gas so, like other Western European countries, it secured shares in the international oil giants and took a strong grip on refining and distribution in France. Oil import quotas were established in the 1920s and only companies authorised by the state were allowed to import oil and they were required to develop refining facilities. A *Compagnie Française de Raffinage* was set up in 1924 whilst the *Compagnie Française des Pétroles* was started in 1927 vested with the state's financial holdings in oil companies, including some of the German shares (assigned as part of the war settlement) in the Turkish Petroleum Company. CFP controlled one-half of French oil imports and refining capacity by 1939 and 88 per cent of all oil requirements were controlled by CFP and other companies in which the state held shares.[79]

France's most hopeful prospect however was that hydro-electricity (HEP) resources might overcome the deficiencies in coal and oil. During the early years of the twentieth century, technological developments had made possible very large electricity generating stations, however powered, whilst the introduction of alternating current made longer distances transmission lines economically viable. The first 60 kilovolt line was completed between Grenoble and the Loire in 1909 and by 1932 the *Chemin de Fer de Paris–Orleans* had introduced a 220 kilovolt line.[80] Especially promising was the exploitation of water dams in the Massif Central and the Alps with high tension lines to Paris, saving precious coal for other uses, especially in time of war. Consumption of electricity grew from 149 kilowatt hours per head of population in 1920 to 495 in 1938 but this threefold increase was no more than the European average (Annex Tables A11 and A12). By the end of the 1930s many observers were dissatisfied with the limited nature of the national network and support to rural areas. The beginning of the inter-war period had witnessed a very strong surge in output. The capacity of HEP plants grew rapidly – at 9.1 per cent per annum in the period 1925–32 – such that it overtook thermal capacity, which was growing at 7.1 per cent. By the early 1930s, the three major plants in Paris had an average capacity of 300 MW (which may be compared to 5 MW for St Denis in 1905), whilst the HEP plants at Kembs, Brommart and Marèges averaged 140 MW. By this stage five major holding companies had emerged, each dominating generating capacity in their region. In Paris the *Union d'Electricité* (the Mercier group) had built the large Gennevihiers plant in 1922. It came to control, in conjunction with the Empain Company, most of the thermal supplies in Paris and became the largest public utility in France. *Energie Electrique du Littoral Méditerranéen* (the Cordier group) was created in 1900 with the backing of Thomas Houston. The others were *Loire et Centre* (the Giros group), *Pechiney et Ugine* (the "electrochem-ists") and *Energie Industrielle* (the Durant group). These five groups controlled three-quarters of all French capacity by 1938, and the situation had not changed by the end of the war.[81] Each of these companies commanded regional networks of considerable size within which there was extensive, albeit variable, degrees of interconnection. A different matter was that of joining up the regional networks. This required agreements between the companies or perhaps state intervention when there was intransigence. In a 1922 law the state had taken powers to influ-ence the structure of the national networks. Little progress was made, and the governments largely accepted what emerged from the bargaining process of the companies.

Pooling agreements between companies and the development of long-distance high tension lines proceeded with reasonable success. The importance of inter-connection can be gauged from the fact that HEP in the Massif Central would only be viable if long distance links were established, since it had no local indus-try. In the early 1920s, it still awaited such links. By the 1930s, there were six major groups transporting electricity over long distances. From 1926 the *Union des Producteurs des Pyrénées Occidentales* acted as transporter for its six con-stituent companies, including the railway company for the Mediterranean area (*Chemin de Fer du Midi*). The *Union de l'Energie Electrique* was financially linked to the Paris based company *Union d'Electricité*, and had established Paris–Alps lines by the mid 1930s. Other transport groups were *Société de Transport d'Energie des Alpes*, STAD (for the Alpes Durances) and TERA for the Auvergne.[82] It is not easy to assess quantitatively how successful different countries were in achieving system integration. The length of the high tension transmission network, even when allowing for population and area covered, may not be an adequate reflection of system integration, especially when, as in France, the distribution of population was very uneven geographically. The scale of construction was quite impressive. By 1930, there were already some 4000 kilometres of high tension transmission lines. The next eight years saw the system double in size. Expressed per head of population, this measure of network spread shows France in a better position, by 1938, than Britain, whose system development has usually been seen as a success story. The length of line per square kilometre may be a better guide and, by that measure, France was less successful than Britain. The distinctive feature of Britain's network, as we shall see in Chapter 8, was that it was managed as an integrated system, so that the benefits of low cost sources could be passed through the country as low prices. This was not the case in France whose average consumption levels remained low. Consumption was 197 kWh per head of population in 1924, rising rapidly to 327 kWh in 1930, but then there was stagnation in the depression years, and the 1930 figure was not achieved again until 1936.[83] In truth, the French network had served industry and traction well, since the consumption levels in these sectors were equivalent to those in the same sectors in other parts of Europe. By the end of the 1930s, Paris consumption levels attained the levels in Berlin. Only when Paris was fully connected was a national network seriously considered. It was the household sector, especially in rural areas, which lagged behind with consumption levels in the centre-west as low as 28 kWh per inhabitant, some of which was public lighting.

There were plenty of schemes for a unified network mooted in the 1920s. Initially, the focus was a plan for connecting the liberated territories in the north-east coal mining area and the iron regions in Lorraine. It was soon learnt that the main likely benefits from interconnection lay elsewhere and involved HEP. The hopes for "white coal" to ease the dependency on coal had already prompted a 1919 law which separated riparian rights in rivers from the energy associated with water flows, which were vested in the state and thereby obviated the burden on HEP producers of buying out such riparian rights. Then a 1922 law stipulated that all new high tension lines had to be approved by the state. This prompted a state commission to propose a national plan ensuring that the Paris and Lyons urban areas would be joined to the HEP regions of the Pyrenees, the Alps, the Massif Central and Alsace, and all joined to the coal region in the north-east. Another plan was devised by engineers with a five-network scheme envisaged, including proposals for closing all thermal plants in HEP areas.[84] The state, however, did not impose a national plan. It did intervene and invest in specific areas. It had set up the mixed enterprise *Compagnie Nationale du Rhone* to develop water supplies and electricity in the Rhone valley. In other regions, the electricity supply companies were expanding supplies to the railways, several of whose networks were subsidised or owned by the state. From the 1920s the government was subsidising the electrification of certain rail tracks and the spread of electricity to rural areas. It was not however until 1937 that anything decisive happened about an integrated system. A revamped *Conseil Supérieur de l'Electricité* produced a 3000 million franc plan for expansion of capacity. It envisaged new HEP dams, a 220 kV line to Paris and the completion of integrating lines. Rearmament diverted the funds, but during the war, the Vichy government's *Comité de l'Organisation de l'Electricité* made some progress. Most important it recognised a role for the state in securing a firm link between the HEP and thermal areas. Thus, in seeming contrast to the case of the railways and the activities of the *Corps du Ponts et Chaussées*, the French government's involvement in planning the electricity infrastructure seems weak.

## Appendix: sectoral shares and productivity growth in manufacturing in the major powers 1860–1928

An important dimension of industrialisation in the Western World was the rise in manufacturing output, both absolutely and relative to population. Bairoch's indexes of manufacturing output per head of population have often been used as a measure of the differential spread of industry across countries and over time (cf. Tables 2.4 and 5.4). They indicate that the level in 1860 in USA was 17 per cent of the 1913 level reflecting huge American industrialisation over these years. France's manufacturing output per head in 1860 was also about 17 per cent of the 1913 USA level but rose to only 47 per cent by 1913. France did however catch up to some extent with the UK, and Germany did even better. Russia changed from 6 to 16 per cent which tells its own story. In the 1913–28 period it rose no more. Nor did the UK as it lost its export markets in the 1920s whilst Germany and especially France continued to grow, albeit still not faster than USA.

The aim here is to try to disentangle the two elements in the changes in manufacturing output per head of population, that is, (a) the share of the population working in manufacturing and (b) output per head of labour in manufacturing. Data on (b) are not readily available. However since total population figures are available, it would be possible to derive, from Bairoch's indexes, estimates of output per head of the manufacturing labour force (relative to USA) if data can be assembled on the size of the labour forces in manufacturing. In Table 6.a.1, estimates are given for 1860, 1913 and 1928 of the labour force in manufacturing for the major powers (except Japan). They are not all strictly comparable since the German figures include labour in gas, electricity, water and sanitation, USA figure for 1860 includes the construction industry, the Russian entry for 1928 and the German entry for 1860 involve some extrapolations and some of the figures do not correspond to the precise year in question (see notes to Table 6.a.1). They are however all close enough to give a good guide.

The method by which estimates of labour productivity in manufacturing were deduced can be explained by the example of Germany in 1860. The labour in German manufacturing as a share of the whole population (0.07) is shown in row C, Bairoch's (1982) measure (12 per cent) is in row E which allows the derivation in row F of labour productivity in German manufacturing as 15 per cent of USA 1913 level. Similar figures are derived and shown for 1913 and 1928 and for the other countries. It is now possible to assess how much of the change in manufacturing output ($M$) per head of population is due to changes in the share of the population ($P$) accounted for by labour in manufacturing ($L$). Here

Table 6.a.1 Labour shares and productivity change in manufacturing 1860–1928[a]

| | France | Germany | Russia | UK | USA |
|---|---|---|---|---|---|
| **1860** | | | | | |
| A Labour in manufacturing (millions) | 3.3[bc] | 2.52[cd] | 1.7 | 4.3[e] | 1.9[f] |
| B Population (millions) | 36.6 | 36.0[e] | 72.1[g] | 29.0[e] | 31.5 |
| C Share A/B | 0.09 | 0.07 | 0.02 | 0.15 | 0.06 |
| D Share relative to USA 1913[h] | 1 | 0.78 | 0.26 | 1.7 | 0.66 |
| E Man. output per head of pop. as % USA 1913 | 16 | 12 | 6 | 51 | 17 |
| F Man. output per head of man. labour as % USA 1913 (=E/D) | 16 | 15 | 23 | 30 | 26 |
| **1913** | | | | | |
| A Labour in manufacturing (millions) | 6.1[ci] | 7.8[cj] | 6.1 | 6.6[k] | 8.2[l] |
| B Population (millions) | 39.6[i] | 62.0[j] | 156.2[g] | 45.3[k] | 92.4[l] |
| C Share A/B | 0.15 | 0.13 | 0.04 | 0.15 | 0.09 |
| D Share relative to USA 1913[h] | 1.6 | 1.4 | 0.43 | 1.7 | 1 |
| E Man. output per head of pop. as % USA 1913 | 47 | 67 | 16 | 91 | 100 |
| F Man. output per head of man. labour as % USA 1913 (=E/D) | 29 | 48 | 37 | 54 | 100 |
| **1928** | | | | | |
| A Labour in manufacturing (millions) | 5.9[cm] | 10.4[cn] | 6.6[o] | 6.7[p] | 11.0 |
| B Population (millions) | 40.9[m] | 63.2[n] | 169.3[g] | 45.8[p] | 120.5 |
| C Share A/B | 0.14 | 0.16 | 0.04 | 0.15 | 0.09 |
| D Share relative to USA 1913[h] | 1.6 | 1.8 | 0.4 | 1.6 | 1 |
| E Man. output per head of pop. as % USA 1913 | 62 | 80 | 16 | 97 | 144 |
| F Man. output per head of man. labour as % USA 1913(=E/D) | 39 | 44 | 40 | 61 | 144 |

Sources: Bairoch 1982; Carr and Davies 1969; Crisp 1978; Maddison 1991; Mitchell 1988, pp 111–13; Mitchell 2003a; Trebilcock 1981; US Bureau of the Census 1976.

Notes

a Contemporary boundaries (see Annex Table A1) unless otherwise stated.

b Average of 1856 and 1866.

c Includes gas, electricity, water and sanitary services.

d This is a rough extrapolation backwards from the 1913 entry of 7.8 million using Trebilcock's estimate (1981) that "industry" share of the population rose from 23 to 43% 1860–1913 and so it is assumed here that the 1860 figure is $7.8 \times 23/43$.

e 1861.

f Includes construction.

g Relates to the population in 1860 within an area corresponding to the USSR's 1989 boundaries.

h The USA 1913 share is 0.09.

i 1911. The source data (Mitchell 2003a) include construction which I have estimated as 0.6 million and deducted.

j 1907.

k 1911.

l 1910.

m 1926.

n 1925.

o Carr and Davies (1969) report Census Industry as having 3.4 million employees for 1928/9 and say that the "relative weight [of census industry and small industry] was approximately the same as it was in 1913" (p. 291). Crisp (1978, p. 332) estimates employment in small scale industry as only slightly less than census industry in 1913 which suggests we can use a figure of 6.6 million for total industrial employment in 1928/29.

p 1930.

and henceforth all symbols refer to values relative to USA 1913. Note that manufacturing output per head of population may be defined as:

$$M/P = (M/L) \times (L/P)$$

Hence a change ($\Delta$) in $M/P$ may be written as:

$$\Delta M/P = [M/L \times \Delta L/P] + [L/P \times \Delta M/L] + [\Delta L/P \times \Delta M/L]$$

The first component is the rise in $M/P$ due to the change in manufacturing
labour's share in the population, evaluated at the starting level of labour productivity in manufacturing. The second is the rise due to the change in labour productivity in manufacturing, evaluated at the starting level of manufacturing
labour's share of the population. The third term allows for interaction between
the two change elements, which would disappear (mathematically) if only small
changes were involved. For example for Russia 1860–1913:

$$\Delta M/P = 23(0.43 - 0.26) + 0.26(37 - 23) + (0.43 - 0.26)(37 - 23)$$
$$= 3.91m + 3.64 + 2.38 = 9.93$$

This corresponds closely to the actual total increase of 10. The rest of the results
rounded out are given in Table 6.a.2.

The Russian advance is very moderate though it is of note that labour productivity in manufacturing in 1860 is estimated to have been higher than in
France and Germany underlining the considerable development of industry by
that date, reflecting perhaps the large element of contributory inputs from land,
minerals and other resources. The trouble was only 2 per cent of the population were in manufacturing in 1860; this rose to 4 per cent by 1913 but then
stayed at that level in the 1920s. At the other extreme was the UK where there
was a very large proportion (15 per cent) of the population in manufacturing
already in 1860; future changes were minor and the UK advance in $M/P$ was
solely due to the large rise in labour productivity in manufacturing 1860–1913.
This was the case also for USA 1913–28 but in the earlier period both the
change in sectoral shares and rising labour productivity contributed to the
huge increase in American manufacturing output per head of population. The
French pattern was similar to USA but with smaller increases. This leaves
Germany where the growing labour force in manufacturing contributed in the
period 1860–1913 to industrialisation in a manner not too different from
France and USA whilst its labour productivity increase in that period lay
roughly halfway between France and USA. In the years 1913–28 however
there was no rise in labour productivity and all the change was due to the rise
in the labour force in manufacturing. There was a sizable increase in the manufacturing labour force in absolute terms (similar to USA) but relative to population it was even much more dramatic – a doubling of the share, quite out of
line with the experience of the other countries in these years.

Table 6.a.2 Contributions to changes in manufacturing output per head of population 1860–1928 (relative to USA 1913)

### 1860–1913

| | Labour share | Labour productivity | Interaction | Total |
|---|---|---|---|---|
| France | 10 | 13 | 8 | 31 |
| Germany | 9 | 26 | 20 | 55 |
| Russia | 4 | 4 | 2 | 10 |
| UK | 0 | 41 | 0 | 41 |
| USA | 9 | 49 | 25 | 83 |

### 1913–28

| | Labour share | Labour productivity | Interaction | Total |
|---|---|---|---|---|
| France | 0 | 16 | 0 | 16 |
| Germany | 19 | –6 | –1 | 12 |
| Russia | 3 | –2 | –1 | 0 |
| UK | –5 | 12 | –1 | 6 |
| USA | 0 | 44 | 0 | 44 |

### 1860–1928

| | Labour share | Labour productivity | Interaction | Total |
|---|---|---|---|---|
| France | 10 | 29 | 8 | 47 |
| Germany | 28 | 20 | 19 | 67 |
| Russia | 7 | 2 | 1 | 10 |
| UK | –5 | 53 | –1 | 47 |
| USA | 9 | 93 | 25 | 127 |

Aggregating over the whole period 1860–1928, it emerges that:

a The contribution of a rising share of employment in manufacturing is very similar in France and USA and concentrated in the 1860–1913 period. For the UK there is little effect whilst for Germany it is very large, much of it in the 1913–28 period.

b The contribution of manufacturing labour productivity in Germany, including the interactive term, is not much different from France. Both are less than the UK and well below USA.

## Notes

1 Balderston 2010.
2 Walle 1979.
3 Bardet 1999.
4 Mitchell 2003a.
5 Murphy 2006.
6 The known maximum being the practice in the North American Hutterite tribe. See Coale and Treadway 1986, p. 33.
7 Walle 1979.
8 Walle 1978, p. 263.
9 Bardet 1998.
10 Walle 1978.
11 Wrigley 1985.
12 Walle 1978, 1979.
13 Murphy 2006.
14 Quine 1996.
15 Glass 1967.
16 Huss 1988.
17 Quine 1996.
18 Glass 1967.
19 Ibid., pp. 166–7.
20 Clapham 1961.
21 Clapham 1936; Milward and Saul 1977; Bairoch 1989.
22 Carré *et al.* 1975; Lequin 1978; Mitchell 2003a.
23 Broadberry *et al.* 2010.
24 O'Brien and Keyder 1978.
25 Broadberry *et al.* 2010.
26 Clapham 1961; Trebilcock 1981.
27 Thomson 1958.
28 Dormois 1999; Keyder 1985.
29 Caron 1979; Cameron 1958; Landes 1949, 1950; Trebilcock 1981; Clapham 1961; Chandler 1984, 1990. See also Chapters 5 and 7.
30 Clapham 1961.
31 Levy-Leboyer 1978.
32 Bairoch 1989.
33 Clapham 1961.
34 Broadberry 1994a.
35 Crafts 1984.
36 Bardet 1999; Leonard and Ljundberg 2010.
37 Maddison 1995.
38 Carré *et al.* 1975.

39 Margairaz 1998.
40 Cameron 1958; Dormois 1999; Milward and Saul 1977; Trebilcock 1981.
41 Dormois 1999.
42 Margairaz 1998.
43 Kemp 1989.
44 Whitaker 1991.
45 Cf. Ferguson 1994; Eloranta and Harrison 2010.
46 Margairaz 1998.
47 Clarke 1977.
48 Chadeau 2000.
49 Dormois 1999.
50 Margairaz 1998.
51 Doukas 1939.
52 Clarke 1977; Chadeau 2000.
53 Chadeau 2000.
54 Doukas 1939; Milhaud 1939.
55 Niertz 1998.
56 Cf. Table 6.4; Schremmer 1989.
57 Eloranta and Harrison 2010.
58 Some of the following paragraphs follow closely some paragraphs in parts of Millward 2005 and thanks are due to Cambridge University Press for granting this author's right to automatic reprint with permission.
59 Goubert 1986, pp. 195–6; Goubert 1988, pp. 116–36.
60 Fernandez 1999; Freedman 1961.
61 Caron and Cardot 1991, pp. 299, 399.
62 Goubert 1989, pp. 186–7.
63 Jacobson 2000; Millward 2007.
64 Levy-Leboyer 1978, pp. 245–62; Lanthier 1979; Caron and Cardot 1999, p. 400.
65 Larroque 1982.
66 MacKay 1976.
67 Bertho-Lavenir 1978.
68 Gournay 1988.
69 Doukas 1945; Dormois 1999, pp. 37, 41, 52.
70 Doukas 1945, p. 25; Clapham 1961, pp. 340–1.
71 Doukas 1945, p. 35.
72 Caron 1987, p. 91.
73 Stevenson 1999, p. 175.
74 Bressler 1922, p. 212.
75 Doukas 1945.
76 Doukas 1945, p. 298.
77 See Millward 2005, ch. 9.
78 Mitchell 2003a.
79 Noreng 1981, p. 133; Lucas 1985, p. 9; Dormois 1999, p. 67.
80 Levy-Leboyer 1994.
81 Ibid., pp. 254–7; Morsel 1987; Ramunni 1987; Schwob 1934; Frost 1981.
82 Ramunni 1987; Morsel 1987.
83 Levy-Leboyer 1994; Morsel 1987.
84 Doukas 1938; Lanthier 1979; Schwob 1934; Ramunni 1987.

# 7 Peasant economy, industrial growth and national defence in Russia 1870–1939

Tsarism has proved to be a hindrance to the organisation of up to date efficient warfare, that very business to which tsarism dedicated itself so wholeheartedly, of which it was so proud, and for which it offered such colossal sacrifices.

V.I. Lenin 1905

## The Russian problem

The period of Tsarist rule which ended during the First World War (WWI) saw considerable economic development with a mainly private industrial sector. From 1870 to 1913 the population doubled, average income levels rose by about 50 per cent and the share of the labour force in agriculture fell by about 15 per cent. The output of agricultural products grew at nearly 2 per cent per annum whilst manufacturing output per head of population more than doubled and the pace of the major industrial surge in the 1890s has been seen as comparable to earlier spurts in France and Germany. Of course, even by 1913, absolute levels were still dreadfully low: incomes less than one-third USA, the manufacturing index less than one-sixth, agricultural productivity higher than only Spain and Italy whilst less than 15 per cent of the population were living in towns of more than 5000 inhabitants. Still, a seemingly strong start had been made, especially since energy resources in the form of coal, electricity, petroleum and natural gas were being harnessed and the country more integrated as the rail network expanded to exceed that in all other European countries. A strong effort was made to balance the government's budget if only to give confidence in the Russian rouble and to foreigners contemplating loans and engaging in direct investment. A massive inflow of foreign capital in the 1890s was given a final confidence boost by Russia joining the gold standard in 1897. Then in 1917 came the Revolution and Civil War so that even by 1927 and the "New Economic Policy", the 1913 levels of economic activity had barely been regained. However in the next decade Stalinist planning engineered a huge advance in heavy industry and the output of pig iron and crude steel more than trebled (Table 7.1).

Our major question concerns the role of the state in all this, at least up to the 1920s, after which Stalinist planning entailed the disappearance of any semblance of a business sector in the sense in which that term is used here. Before the Revolution, the autocratic regime was driven by fear of an increasingly resentful peasantry and a concern to keep on board the unpredictable nobility. It is by no means clear that state policy was aimed directly at promoting economic growth in the sense of raising average living standards. It was argued in Chapter 4 that Russia's history, geo-political position and resource endowments yielded a distinct state policy which was very much directed to external defence and internal peace. In his review of Tsarist policy, Laue suggested the state's aim to protect sovereignty and expand its frontiers echoed the states of Western Europe but that if

> there was an ingredient peculiar to Russian state ambitions, it was not the reckless sweep of her global pretensions ... [as in Britain, France and Germany] but the hypersensitivity concerning all threats to her power, a sensitivity conditioned over the centuries very largely by the tremendous disparities between the material and cultural resources of Russia, on the one hand, and those of her rivals on the other.[1]

Hence it needed a strong army and, given its geographic area, this meant in fact a huge army relative to the country's GDP. A volunteer army would have been prohibitively expensive so it had to be a conscript military, financed by taxation. Securing the supply of recruits and the tax base required close control of the peasantry since escape and evasion were facilitated by the huge land area. This was the basis for enserfing the peasantry to the land with the village as tax base. Enforcing serfdom and collecting taxes entailed a large bureaucracy and a loyal nobility. Hence the high costs of government with the gentry as servitors. Finally Russia's history meant this autocracy took the form of the patrimonial Tsarist regimes outlined in Chapter 4.

By 1861, the peasantry had been emancipated but Russia's geo-political position exhibited most of the same tensions with the added dimension that Western Europe had been industrialising rapidly. As Figes has recently argued, the Crimean War in the 1850s was probably a key turning point in political alliances as Russia broke with conservative Austria whilst two Christian nations (France and Britain) supported the Muslim Ottoman Empire.[2] Poor communications and health supplies devastated both sides but Russia could see, by 1870, that it was technologically backward. For a nation state to be a successful military power, naval power, armaments and communications had to reflect the rapidly changing industrial technology – steamships, railways, telegraph, cables, modern arsenals. This was now becoming more important than sheer numbers of military personnel. Significant industrialisation was necessary and this meant coal, pig iron, metal manufacture, machinery and, later, electricity. It would not be good enough to rely on imports of equipment of strategic significance; domestic industry had to be developed.

What were the options? Russia required more capital and entrepreneurship and it needed a bigger industrial labour force with a strong skill element. One

*Table 7.1* Russian economic development 1870–1938 (contemporary boundaries)[a]

| | 1870 | 1913 | 1929 | 1938 |
|---|---|---|---|---|
| *General* | | | | |
| Land area ('000 square miles) | 7643 | 8379b | 8176 | 8176 |
| Population (millions) | 82c | 163 | 172 | 188.5 |
| Military personnel ('000) | 716 | 1352b | 1285 | 1324d |
| Warships ('000 tons) | 363 | 40b | 401 | 267d |
| GDP per head (% of USA 1913) | 19 | 28 | 26 | 40 |
| *Agriculture* | | | | |
| % labour in agriculture | 81.0 | 70.0 | 60.0e | 54.0e |
| Area sown in hectares 1913=100 | | | | |
| a Wheat | 35f | 100 | 89 | 124 |
| b Rye | 88f | 100 | 81 | 70 |
| Grain output[g] 1913=100 | 49 | 100 | 96 | 121 |
| *Energy* | | | | |
| Coal output (million metric tons) | 0.7 | 36.1 | 40.0 | 133.3 |
| Electricity supply (gigawatt hours) | 1.95h | 6.22 | 39.40 | – |
| Crude petroleum (million metric tons) | 0.03 | 10.3 | 13.7 | 30.2 |
| Natural gas (billion cubic metres) | 0.03h | 0.33 | 2.20 | – |
| *Communications* | | | | |
| Rail track open[i] ('000 kilometres) | 8.28 | 70.17 | 76.93 | 84.98 |
| Rail freight traffic (billion ton kilometres) | 0.003j | 0.07h | 0.12 | 0.37 |
| Merchant fleet[k] (million metric tons) | 0.26 | 0.78 | 0.44 | 1.27 |
| *Industry* | | | | |
| Manufacturing output per head of population (% of USA 1913) | 61 | 16 | 16m | – |
| Pig iron output ('000 metric tons) | 0.36 | 4.64 | 4.02 | 14.65 |
| Crude steel (million metric tons) | 0.01 | 4.92 | 4.85 | 18.06 |

Sources: Annex Tables; Bairoch 1982; Crisp 1972; Gatrell 1986; Kennedy 1988; Nove 1972; Maddison 1995; Mitchell 2003a; Wright 1942.

Notes

a Unless otherwise stated the data for 1870–1913 relate to the Russian Empire and 1929–38 to the 1923 boundaries of the USSR.

b 1910

c Interpolated. See Annex Table A1.

d 1937.

e The 1929 figure is a rough interpolation from 1913 and 1950 data. The 1938 figure is based on Crisp's observation (1972) that 54.5% of employment was in agriculture in 1937.

f European Russia excluding Poland, Finland and the Caucasus

g The entries for 1870 and 1913 relate to the data for 1861–75 and 1911–14 in Gatrell (1986, p. 101). The other entry for 1929 is based on the figures in Nove (1972, p. 94) for the grain harvests of 1926 and 1937.

h Territory of USSR in 1923.

i 1870 and 1913 entries exclude local lines and relate to the average length of line open during the year. Thereafter the entries relate to all lines open at end year.

j 1872. Covers European Russia excluding Finland. Mitchell's data for tons have been converted into ton kilometres using the ratio between the two in the 1898 figures.

k The 1870 entry relates to 1872 which, together with the 1913 entry, excludes vessels less than 60 net tons and also excludes Finland. The 1929 and 1938 entries relate to gross tonnages.

l 1860.

m 1928.

option might be to induce enhanced output from industry and agriculture by freeing up market transactions. Such a liberalisation would entail reducing the nobility's privileges in trade and industry, reforming the village commune in agriculture and reinforcing competition by low tariffs on imported foods and manufactured products. The hope would be that existing or only slightly modified tax rates would generate enough government revenue to finance the Tsar's defence expenditures and that rising productivity in agriculture would allow a growing urban labour force to be fed. A strong liberal stance would be very disruptive so some element of tariff protection would not be very inconsistent with what was happening in France and Germany. A modest increase in the amount of government intervention could take the form of guarantees of the interest on private sector bond issues. This might induce more domestic saving but had the greatest potential for attracting foreign capital, especially if the currency and government budget could be stabilised. Finally industrialisation could be speeded up more directly by direct state participation in industry: state owned enterprises in heavy industry and railways; subsidies and capital for industry via increased taxation of the peasantry. The forced nationalisation of industry and agriculture – that is expropriation of the private business sector without compensation – was clearly not an option for the Tsarist state but emerged under the "War Communism" of 1918–20 and retained in the 1920s New Economic Policy with the state owned enterprises operating with a certain freedom in markets for goods, service and labour.

Many of these options confronted both the Tsarist and Soviet regimes but they both also faced some central socio-political constraints. The 1861 Emancipation Act had heralded the release of labour to industry in urban areas and this was later helped, as we shall see, by the Stolypin reforms of 1906. However a freed peasantry and a rising urban population brought the prospect of democratisation and threat to the patrimonial Tsarist state. Second, using taxes to finance the shift of the balance of the economy towards a capital intensive industrial sector, and doing it effectively, required relatively free markets to minimise the burden of rising money taxation on the peasantry. This was anathema for the Soviet state – or rather it was for the Bolsheviks if not the Mensheviks. Third, and crucially for Russia given its unwillingness to surrender its great power status, there was no guarantee that using taxation and relatively free markets to strengthen industry would operate quickly enough for the Tsarist state in the early 1900s as it watched the growing power of Germany, nor in the 1920s for the Soviet state as it became politically isolated.

## Finance and protection for defence: the public finances and tariff policy

At the heart of both its obligations and its power, the state's budget was a central instrument for securing external defence and promoting industrialisation. Armaments and warships, some of which were in state factories and dockyards, generated, together with army and navy supplies and pay, a large claim on the government's budget. The state did also support industry by subsidies to the private business sector. There is a strong theme in the works of Gershenkron, Laue and others,[3] that the state promoted industrialisation through such subsidies, supplementing its own enterprises in iron works, shipbuilding, ports, mines and railways. Indeed for Gershenkron the state was the prime mover in the late nineteenth century industrial spurt substituting for the backward Russian economy's alleged lack of entrepreneurship and capital. That state activity was financed, so the story goes, by squeezing the peasantry through taxation and burdening them with the redemption dues arising from the land transfers of the Emancipation Edict of 1861. How far then did the state actually use its budget to promote industrialisation, how far was it linked to defence requirements and in what sense was industrialisation and defence financed on the backs of the peasantry?

Russia's defence programmes, as we shall see, were a significant burden on the economy but overall government spending was, in two respects, very similar to other European countries. First, in the years up to WWI, expenditures invariably exceeded revenues so state borrowing was a constant feature and the need to secure foreign loans pushed the Tsarist regime to stabilise the currency by joining the gold standard in 1897. A distinction was made between the expenditures expected to be incurred every year and those associated with emergencies. In order to hide its tight financial position the Tsarist regime often resorted to assigning expenditures to the extraordinary category so that as well as the costs of the Russo-Japanese War (2595 million roubles) and the rearmament expenditures (463 million) the extraordinary box also included for 1900–13 items like debt repayment (942 million) and state railways (463 million).[4] Extensive borrowing and some obfuscation in government accounting could be found in some other European countries in this period. Perhaps Russia was different in that, desperate for revenue, it sought to structure tariff policy to generate revenues rather than protect industry. Russian industry was in fact heavily protected. Those historians disputing that protection was the main driving force, argue that tariffs under a protectionist regime would have fallen on finished manufactured goods rather than raw materials and intermediate inputs for Russian industry. Yet, they point out, tariffs were levied on wool, cotton and iron as well as yarn and other semi-manufactured goods and that the 1880s and 1890s saw large increases in tariffs on tea, alcohol, tobacco, salt, herring – that is on foodstuffs irrelevant to the problems of Russian industry.[5] Protection of industry will be analysed in detail later on. The important point to note now is that, as Table 7.2 shows, if revenue raising was dominant it did not achieve much. Customs revenues were a fairly small part of total revenues averaging about 10 per cent in the 1870–1913 period. They rose from 9.2 per cent in 1870 to 10.3 per cent by 1913, levels which were lower than those found elsewhere in Europe and in part reflected Russia's smaller involvement in international trade (exports less than 3 per cent of GDP generally).[6]

Second, government expenditures and revenues, again like the rest of Europe, accounted for a rising share of national income throughout the period. Table 7.2

shows expenditures rising consistently from 9.8 per cent of GDP in 1870 to 16.7 per cent in 1913 and 19.5 per cent in 1926/27. These figures include the expenditures of state owned enterprises (SOEs) which were relatively large in Russia even in the nineteenth century and such items are not usually included in that form.[7] Excluding state enterprise suggests that central government expenditures were 10.3 per cent of national income in 1885 rising to 11.4 per cent by 1913 and 13.3 per cent by 1926/27. Such levels are no higher and sometimes below those that can be found in international studies of public spending though these

*Table 7.2* Russian central government spending and revenues[a] 1870–1927 (million roubles)

|  | 1870 | 1885 | 1891 | 1900 | 1913 | 1926/27 |
|---|---|---|---|---|---|---|
| *Expenditure*[b] | | | | | | |
| Debt interest | – | 310 | 257 | 317 | 424 | 0[c] |
| Defence | – | 240 | 296 | 483 | 970 | 634[c] |
| Subsidies[d] | – | 50 | 56 | 147 | 188 | 1022[c] |
| State enterprise | – | 49 | 101 | 570 | 1064 | 1509[c] |
| Health and education | – | 23 | 26 | 46 | 154 | 356[c] |
| Administration and other | – | 194 | 247 | 326 | 583 | 1117[c] |
| Total | 564 | 866 | 962 | 1889 | 3383 | 4698[c] |
| *Revenues* | | | | | | |
| Customs | 43 | 95 | 128 | 204 | 353 | 289 |
| Excise[e] | 175 | 265 | 312 | 572 | 1254 | 1026 |
| Direct taxes[f] | 110 | 131 | 87 | 132 | 273 | 431 |
| Other[g] | 132 | 271 | 365 | 796 | 1537 | 3228 |
| Total | 466 | 762 | 892 | 1704 | 3417 | 4974 |
| National income[h] | 5779 | 7904 | 7917 | 13,227 | 20,266 | 24,000 |
| Revenues as % NI | 8.0 | 9.6 | 11.3 | 12.9 | 16.9 | 20.7 |
| Expenditures as % NI | 9.8 | 11.0 | 12.2 | 14.3 | 16.7 | 19.5 |

Sources: Mitchell 2003a for expenditure totals 1870 and 1926–27 and all revenue entries; Davies 1991, Table 41 for 1926–27 expenditure components; the rest comes from Gregory 1982, 1991, 1994.

Notes
a  Russian Empire (excluding Finland) to 1913, USSR thereafter.
b  Includes extraordinary expenditure.
c  The entries for defence, debt interest, education and health ("social and cultural") and administration etc., are taken from Davies (1991, Table 41). The subsidies entry is c "total on national economy" less net expenditure on transport and posts. The difference between the total of all these items and the total expenditure in Mitchell (2003a) (4698 million, an average of 1926 and 1927) is taken to be expenditure by state enterprises, 1509 million.
d  Includes subsidies to private railway companies, ports, shipyards, iron works, agriculture, housing, electrification etc.
e  Includes revenues from the state spirit monopoly.
f  Includes poll tax up to 1886 and redemption dues of peasantry to 1905.
g  Includes government royalties and gross revenues of state enterprises in railways, telecommunications, ports etc.
h  The 1885–1913 figures are net national product at current prices from Gregory (1994). The 1926/27 figure is a rough reduction of the 1928 estimates in Table 67 of Gregory (1991). For the 1870 figure see footnote 3 to Table 4.3.

often include local government spending (cf. chapters on France, Germany and the UK). The available data for central government only expenditures in Belgium, the Netherlands and Spain averaged 9.1 per cent of national income in 1870, 12.7 per cent in 1913, 18.7 per cent in 1920 and 22.8 per cent in 1937.[8]

So, as a burden on national income, the Russian public finances look very similar to those elsewhere. Where they differed was in the defence component and in the more extensive use of poll and other direct taxes. The role of defence in Russian public spending reflected clearly the importance of the military in all the Tsarist state's policies on the economy. A strong military commitment can be seen in the late nineteenth century but especially with the re-equipment of the army with new rifles in the 1890s and the building of a large fleet of battleships, armoured cruisers and destroyers at the turn of the century. The 1904/05 Russo-Japanese War involved much loss of warships and military equipment and a very ambitious programme for fleet, arsenals, weaponry and roads followed. As early as 1885 defence was 27.2 per cent of total spending or 30 per cent if state enterprise spending is excluded from the total, rising to 41.8 per cent by 1913. The rest of central government spending was dominated by debt interest which in part reflected past state borrowing for war. Defence spending was equal to 3.0 per cent of national income in 1885 rising to 4.8 per cent by 1913, a much bigger burden than in other countries. Indeed Eloranta and Harrison's estimates for the whole 1870–1913 period put Russian defence spending at 3.9 per cent of national income, larger than USA (0.7), the UK (2.6), Germany (3.6) and France (3.7) and exceeded only by Japan (5.0).[9] In the other peacetime years, 1920–38, they estimate Russian defence spending at 7.1 per cent of national income, larger than all the other major powers – more than double the levels in Germany and the UK.

A potentially important role for promoting industrialisation was government subsidy of private companies in industry and transport. Gerschenkron included this as one of the elements of the state's role in substituting for the enterprise and capital lacking in Russia.[10] For Laue the aim of the Tsarist state was to sustain its status as a "great power".[11] State expenditures on railways and other heavy industry would, the story goes, generate an industrial expansion since the heavy industries would in turn stimulate lighter industries like chemicals and mechanical equipment and raise the demand for textiles and foodstuffs with benefits for agriculture. Laue claimed two-thirds of government expenditures in the years 1894–1902 were devoted to economic development, echoing Babkov's claim in 1912 that state revenues (to finance the expansion) trebled from 1890 to 1910 despite the 1891 crop failure, the Russo-Japanese War of 1904 and the 1905 Revolution.[12] There are two issues here. On the one hand a large chunk of these expenditures and revenues relate to SOEs in railways, posts, telegraph, ports etc. Babkov noted that revenues from royalties and state owned enterprises increased sixfold in the two decades. These are income generating state assets – the gross receipts of the state railways alone were 362 million roubles in 1900, rising to 814 million by 1913.[13] Their expenditures do not generate a claim on tax revenues, apart from any financial losses they made. So they should not be included in any assessment of state financial support for industry; the state did help secure and generate loans, especially for railways but even here much of it was for troop movements rather than economic development. Moreover Laue uses a very generous interpretation of the phrase "economic development" in including debt interest as well as the budgets for a wide range of Ministries. Long ago, Kahan suggested that "only a minute part of its budget expenditures were devoted for the purpose of developing the industrial sector" and this is confirmed by the data in Table 7.2.[14] In 1885 subsidies and transfers by the state were 50 million roubles, that is only 6.1 per cent of total spending (net of SOE spending), 6.5 per cent in 1891, 11.1 per cent in 1900, 8.1 per cent in 1913. A vivid contrast is revealed by the figure of 32.0 per cent for 1926/27 showing the scale of financial support under the New Economic Policy.

Government expenditures were therefore not out of line with other European counties but were heavily skewed to national defence rather than industrialisation itself. The state's role in industrialisation did also include direct operations of railways and other SOEs, generous contracts for industry and guarantees of loans but these will be discussed later. The other main question about the public finances is how far the revenue raised by taxation hit the peasantry and/or the industrial business sector. Since over four-fifths of the population lived in rural areas it was inevitable that much of taxation would have to fall on that sector. Russia was also distinctive in the extent of direct taxes so we find that in 1870 the tax system was largely geared to rural activities and direct taxes accounted for about one-quarter of tax-only revenues. The poll tax originated in 1724, was levied on all male peasants and no other social group and was an intrinsic element in the link between the village *mir* and the autocratic state's military requirements.[15] In addition in 1861, following the Emancipation Edict, the transfer of land to the peasants was accompanied by a requirement that they pay redemption dues to the state to finance the government bonds issued as compensation to the nobility for their loss of land. From 1864 the peasant had to pay taxes to the new parallel institutions of local government, the *zemstvos*. Finally there were passport dues.[16] Some historians have painted a fairly bleak and worsening picture of the peasant's lot in the late nineteenth century. There is little dispute that the redemption values were inflated to secure the support of the nobility. A village member wishing to pay off his debt was not able to count the redemption dues already paid and an Act of 1866 reinforced the obstacles to the division of property within the household. As late as 1893 an Act was introduced preventing the peasant from redeeming his allotted land unless two-thirds of the commune agreed. Land prices were rising and even the Peasant Land Bank established in 1872 was limited because loans could only be made via the *mir*.[17]

Doubt has been cast on this portrait of a heavily burdened peasantry. Some breakdowns of the peasant's direct tax liability for 1877 show a total of 197 million roubles of which the poll tax was 42 million, land tax and redemption dues 95 million and others 60 million.[18] Whilst the Tsarist government saw direct taxes and the 1861 Emancipation arrangements as central to the continuance of the traditional social structure, by the 1880s the threat of peasant discontent was growing. Minister of Finance Bunge abolished the poll tax from 1886, reduced the annual redemption dues and started to shift the fiscal balance towards indirect taxes and to some direct taxation of industrial businesses. Direct taxes and arrears became the responsibility of the individual peasant from 1893 and in 1906 the restrictions on division of property within households were abolished. In 1904 arrears of the land tax and redemption dues were written off (benefiting especially the state peasant who started repayments later) and these dues were scheduled to be abolished from 1907. Taxes on business profits, patents and equity were increasing in the late nineteenth century which saw a rise in the number of businesses liable for tax. An industrial tax was levied on all commercial and industrial enterprises (which also had to be licensed) and it yielded 150 million roubles in 1913.[19] The net result was that direct taxes fell from 23.6 per cent of total revenues in 1870 to 8.1 per cent in 1913 or 11.6 per cent if tax-only revenues are counted (Table 7.2).

This shift in emphasis from rural to urban areas was also an element in the large rise of indirect taxes, which was consistent with what was happening elsewhere in Europe. At the same time it hit urban dwellers and poor peasants more than the average (and wealthiest) peasants whose general standard of living may have actually been rising in the late nineteenth century. The traditional targets for the excise were sugar, kerosene, matches, tobacco, beer, vodka and the tax rates rose significantly on all these items. Indirect taxes rose from 37.1 per cent of all tax-only revenues in 1885 to over 50 per cent by 1913. Some of these increases were due to the rise in consumption per head of kerosene and sugar whilst the vodka revenues rose as the state monopoly was extended to new parts of the Empire. But peasants could manufacture many of these commodities themselves and tended to pay cash for them only if they moved to urban areas where they were luxury items. Together with the relaxation of direct taxes, this gives some support to the notion that the peasant's lot might actually have been improving in the late nineteenth century. Rising land prices are usually a sign of growing demand for land and in any case reduced the real cost of the redemption payments. Wheatcroft suggests that about 0.5 million tons of grain per head of population were being produced annually just before WWI and that the share of the crop remaining in rural areas was increasing, indicating rising living standards.[20] Some of the peasant's consumption of the cheaper cereal, rye, was being replaced by the superior wheat. All the evidence is that national output per head was growing, albeit slowly on average each year and since most of the population lived in rural areas, it is unlikely, suggests Gregory, that peasant living standards were not improving.[21]

In sum the main driving force in Russian public finances was not industrialisation per se but rather the ever growing defence programme, financed initially by a larger dose of direct taxation on the peasantry than elsewhere in Europe, but increasingly on a wider base of indirect taxes falling on all money transactions, especially in urban areas. That defence element threaded also through tariff policies by affecting which sectors were the targets and ensuring that tariffs contributed to the finance of the defence programmes. Indeed historians have dwelled, perhaps unnecessarily, on the idea that manufacturing was not singled out for protection and that raising revenue was the prime mover. It is certainly possible to point to elements that suggest protection for manufactured goods was no stronger than for raw materials and intermediate goods. As mentioned earlier, in the late nineteenth century there were large increases in the rates on industrial inputs like iron and yarn and on foodstuffs, and where manufactured goods did carry tariffs the effective rates of protection were lowered by the higher prices which manufacturing firms had to pay for raw material and intermediate good imports. On the other hand in the 1890s some imports were exempted from tariff increases and they included agricultural machinery, flax, tallow and hemp and tariff revenues were only a small portion of total fiscal receipts, as noted earlier.

The thread of much government policy was to gear tariffs to aid defence via the development of domestic industry.[22] There can be no doubt that Russian industry was heavily protected even though policy may have lacked refinement and discrimination.[23] The scale of protection was such as to prompt Bairoch, in his exhaustive study of tariff policies, to conclude that Russia finished up with a system which was "probably the most protective in Europe before the First World War".[24] The main features of Russian tariff policy were, first, that it was both revenue raising and protective and, second, the protective element was directed to promoting military strength through the development of mining, metallurgy, oil and railway equipment. Indeed this latter element was sufficiently strong that policy was directed to protecting "inner" Russian industry in the Donets, Ukraine and Urals as opposed to Poland and the other strategically exposed Baltic regions whose political allegiance was also in doubt.

The brief flirtation with free trade noted in Chapter 4, including the 1874 treaty with France which drew Russia into the international trade and treaty networks, had disappeared by the end of the 1870s. A Law of 1877 had required customs duties be paid in gold which effectively raised rates by 30 per cent and by the end of the 1870s tariffs on manufactured goods were already in the 15–20 per cent range.[25] An industrial lobby was emerging and the 1880s saw an intensive propaganda campaign by the Congress of Metallurgists and by the Stock Exchange Committees of Moscow and Kharkov.[26] The general tariff level was raised by 10 per cent in 1881 and 20 per cent in 1885, including iron and coal and the years 1884–87 witnessed similar changes for pig iron, steel and machinery. For all commodities carrying tariffs, the rate had risen from 17.8 per cent of import value in 1868 to 28.7 per cent by the end of the 1880s.[27] The protectionist surge was very strong in the 1890s starting with the "prohibitive monster tariff" of 1891, introduced by Minister of Finance Mendeleyev, which allowed free entry for only 14 minor products whilst Witte (Minister 1892–1903) openly proclaimed his economic nationalism. The rise in tariff rates on cotton, tea, coffee and other foodstuffs, noted earlier, occurred in the 1880s and 1890s. By the end of the century the duties on raw materials and food were 31 per cent of import value, 28 per cent for manufactured goods.[28] The duties on pig iron and coal illustrate the strategic regional dimension in that the metallurgical industries of Poland and the north-west, drawing imported materials overland from Germany, were affected more than the industries of southern Russia and the Urals which used their own coal and iron.[29] By the early 1900s the duties on foodstuffs were 89 per cent of import values, 5–30 per cent for raw materials and semi-manufactured goods and 9–26 per cent for manufactured goods. By 1913 the duties on exports from Britain were 131 per cent and import duties in total were 29.5 per cent of import values.

## Emancipation and reform: peasant agriculture to 1913

Since agriculture employed over two-thirds of the labour force, even by 1913, the agrarian policies of the Tsarist government had the potential to secure great changes in the economy.

The two major legislative developments were the Emancipation Edict of 1861 which abolished serfdom and hence the peasantry's servitude to the gentry and the state and the reforms of Stolypin of 1906 which severed the peasants' obliga-tions and freedom of action with respect to the village commune, the *mir*, and its agricultural system, the *obschina*. The traditional Marxist view was that the *obschina* was no longer important at the end of the century whilst the Slavo-philes and populists bemoaned any undermining of what they saw as a key institution for advancing Russian economic development on a communal basis. The classic view from the 1960s about the Emancipation Edict was that it tied the peasant to the village commune, thereby impeding the flow to the urban labour force and dampened the incentive for productivity gains in agriculture which would have fed a growing urban labour force. Such was Gershenkron's argument which then led to the proposition that the state was forced to squeeze the peasantry to generate tax finance for state promotion of industry. Doubt has already been cast on one part of this argument in the section on public finance: there is little evidence of declining living standards in the last decades of Tsarism.

What then of the impact of the Edict on the release of labour to industry and on agricultural development? From the start it needs emphasising that it is not clear that the Tsarist governments were interested in agricultural development itself. Even though the Gerschenkron hypothesis about the release of labour to industry and the economic mechanisms of industrialisation will be questioned, this is not to challenge his broad judgement that "political and social expediency ... prevailed over considerations of economic efficiency". The Edict was strongly driven by the self-preservation of the autocracy which was "eager to lay the ghost of peasant rebellion; it was unwilling to conjure up the menace of urban revolution" and the economic individualism promised by the Stolypin reforms of 1906 was aimed at strengthening the peasant opposition to rebellion.[30] Indeed in this light the success of Tsarist policy would have to be judged by how far it delayed or muted peasant rebellion rather than by its direct economic impact.

The Edict certainly did not ease *permanent* departures from the village and the 1860s and 1870s saw no major economic developments in agriculture. The state had to carry the gentry with it so that loss of noble land without compensation was unthinkable. All land was deemed to be owned by the noble landowner, the *pomeschik* (or the state in the case of state peasants). That did not mean that the abolition of serfdom and of compulsory labour services would lead to a completely landless rural proletariat, along the lines of the "Prussian road" to capitalism. Rather the Edict required that the peasants (via the *mir*) be allotted enough land and farmstead to make a livelihood. The peasants had to pay compensation, 20 per cent directly to the noble landowners and the rest (via the *mir* over 49 years) as redemption dues to the state to finance the government bonds issued to the nobility. The initiatives in the land transfers and allotments could not be taken by the peasants, only by the noble landowner. For the state peasants (cf. Chapter 4) there was effectively no initial change in that they continued to pay poll tax and rent and their release from the legal status as serfs was accompanied only by being granted "possessional entry" for the land.[31] The state peasants only did well where, as in Poland, the Tsarist state wanted to secure their allegiance against what it saw as a hostile local gentry, and their rents were converted into redemption payments, thereby granting those peasants full ownership. The peasants everywhere hated the whole idea that, historically, all this property was legally owned by the nobility or the state. Historians now also seem to agree that the peasants gained little economically from the settlement. As compared to the land they used before 1861, the subsequent allocations constituted a decline in area of 13 per cent (if Poland is excluded), greatest in the rich black earth territories and by the early 1880s with population growth, the extent of land available per head had fallen by a further 25 per cent.[32] The land transferred also seems to have been overvalued, especially in the less fertile non-black earth regions which saw the largest release of land. Lyaschenko once estimated that one-quarter of peasant farms finished up with insufficient land for sustenance.[33]

All land transactions were between the nobility, the *mir* and the state. The system continued whereby the commune supervised land repartitions and was responsible for taxes. The three field system remained and some common land was incorporated into the lord's demesne though that classic system only occurred in certain grain specialist areas. It was largely absent in Byelorussia, the south-west and Kharkov.[34] The individual peasant could demand a separation of his land only if he had paid off all his debt (with no credit for previous redemption payments) and even then the permission of the commune was needed; the peasant could not even walk off his land without paying off one-half of his debt. These obstacles to movement were reinforced by an 1868 act which limited the division of property within households and as late as 1893 an Act stipulated that repartition could take place only with a gap of at least 12 years and that a peasant could only redeem his land if approval was given by a two-thirds majority of the commune.

When added to the requirement that peasants could only move with passports (valid only for one year), this all seemed to be a significant obstacle to an expanding urban labour force. Whether industry really suffered from labour shortages is questionable. The complaints were mainly from the newly industrialising regions of the south.[35] Nor is it credible to argue that because Russian industry was short of labour it was unable to expand industrially with a labour intensive technology, causing it to adopt a capital intensive technology in sectors like cotton and metallurgy.[36] It was not until well into the twentieth century that labour intensive technologies were developed to exploit the vast pools of relatively unskilled labour in the Third World. In any case, whatever obstacles the Edict placed in the way of permanent movements, short term movement and part time participation in industry were not affected and indeed had been common for a very long time. Serfs had residence in rural estates but travelled widely for industrial work as outlined in Chapter 4; not just as corvée labour on railway construction, road works, manorial distilleries and woollen factories supplying the army but as freely contracted labour in sugar beet steam driven factories, the Urals state mining and iron works, cotton spinning factories around Moscow and Ivanov, the silk industry, St Petersburg luxury trades and locomotive works. In all these examples, serfs often worked for piece wages. Work in both *kustar* and factory industries had a long history and the data in Table 7.3 suggest each group had about 800,000 wage earners in 1860 rising to three million by 1913. Over time some of the obstacles to permanent movement were removed. Passports became available after 1894 for five years and the level of redemption dues was reduced in 1881. In the early 1900s, when worries about peasant rebellion multiplied, there was a relaxation of the restrictions on division of property within households (1906), free access to passports (for five years) and to choice of residence so that the juridical power of the *mir* was broken. In the same year, Stolypin's reform act established the right of heads of households to demand transfers of allotted land to peasant ownership and to consolidation of strips. During 1906–15 some 22 per cent of all heads of households were separated out as owners, often with small plots, and mainly in the south, south-west and west. The *mir* was given the right to abandon the open field system though there is not much evidence of land sales and within the open field system only 10 per cent of peasant holdings had been consolidated by 1917.[37]

Agricultural technology and methods did change, before the Stolypin reforms as well as after. The overall trend was of a slow decline of the subsistence economy with land becoming more of a commercial asset. The tenfold rise in the length of railway track facilitated trade encouraging regional specialisation and narrowing inter-regional price differences.[38] Grain was shipped to Moscow, Riga and St Petersburg whilst population growth in the central industrial region and the north-west outstripped the growth of agricultural output and increased the market for black earth agricultural foods. The main technological changes, at least up to 1900, were in hand tools like ploughs since mechanisation was rare in the nineteenth century. Table 7.1 shows the area sown with the traditional crop, rye, rose by about 15 per cent 1870–1913 whereas for wheat the rise was nearly threefold, again reflecting the rise in living standards. Grain output doubled and total agricultural output increased at about 2 per cent per annum up to WWI. Given the rise in population, the increase in output per head was modest though Gregory has identified two strong bursts, with labour productivity in agriculture rising by 2.55 per cent per annum in the period 1883/87 to 1897/1900 and 3.0 per cent per annum for 1897/1900 to 1905/13, only slightly below industrial productivity growth.[39]

The Emancipation edict therefore created obstacles to permanent moves out of agriculture but not short term or part time assignments which continued on a large scale. The Stolypin reforms pushed the system more towards individual ownership but had little effect before WWI. The patchy growth of productivity which did occur arose therefore despite rather than because of government reforms which were prompted in 1861 and 1906 by fears of peasant rebellion, the threat of which did not disappear since gentry ownership was still pervasive:

*Table 7.3* Labour force in Russia 1860–1937 (million persons; contemporary boundaries)[a]

| | Hired labour | | | | Gainfully occupied | | |
|---|---|---|---|---|---|---|---|
| | A | B | C | D | E | F | G |
| | 1860 | 1913 | 1917 | 1929[b] | 1913 | 1926 | 1937 |
| 1 Agriculture | 0.70 | 4.5 | 5.0 | 3.69[c] | 55.5 | 71.73[d] | 57.0 |
| 2 Industry | | | | | | | |
| a Construction | 0.35 | 1.50 | 1.50 | 0.92 | 0.97 | 0.36 | 1.6 |
| b Factories and mines | 0.86 | 3.1 | 3.6 | 3.4[e] | 2.82 | 2.79 | 11.6[f] |
| c Small scale/cottage | 0.80 | 3.0 | 3.5 | 3.2[g] | 3.59 | 1.87 | – |
| Industry sub-total | 2.01 | 7.60 | 8.60 | 7.52 | 7.38 | 5.02 | 13.2 |
| 3 Services | | | | | | | |
| a Railways | 0.01 | 0.82 | 1.90[h] | 1.30[g] | 0.71 | 0.89 | 1.5 |
| b Waterways | 0.50 | 0.50 | – | – | 0.14 | – | – |
| c Other services[i] | 0.80 | 4.07 | 4.47 | 4.55[j] | 8.75 | 8.58 | – |
| Services sub-total | 1.41 | 5.39 | 6.37 | 5.85 | 9.60 | 9.47 | – |
| Grand Total | 4.02 | 17.48 | 19.97 | 17.06[k] | 72.48 | 86.22 | – |

Sources: Columns A, B and C, Crisp 1978; Column D, Carr and Davies 1969; Column E and F (December census), Davies 1991; Column G, Davies 1989.

Notes
a Unless otherwise stated these boundaries relate to the Russian Empire up to 1913 and the USSR for 1929.
b Annual averages 1928–29.
c This is the figure for 1929 in Table 23 of Carr and Davies (1969).
d Davies (1991, p. 45) suggests different treatment of children, women and the aged account for the difference between the census figure and other sources for 19242/5 which come out in the range 55–57 million for 1913 and 1937.
e "Census industry".
f All "industrial production".
g A rough estimate based on the statement by Carr and Davies (1969, p. 291) that the relative weight of census and small industry was similar to 1913, for which Crisp (1978) said census industry was slightly bigger.
h Includes waterways. The 1929 figure is for "transport" as a whole.
i Calculated as a residual and may include persons who should be classified elsewhere.
j This is the number classed as "state establishments" and "other employed persons".
k This is the total in Carr and Davies (1969, Table 22) plus my adjustments for agriculture and small industry (cf. Notes c and g above).

some 57 million hectares have been recorded as late as 1905, with huge estates in the Urals, the south-west and Don regions still intact or indeed enlarged as the smaller estates were sold to the more affluent elements.[40]

## State enterprise and direct intervention in industry and transport

Direct state participation in industry and transport was the clearest manifestation of the Tsarist government's commitment to industrial development. Expansion of the rail track was initially modest after 1870 but then grew rapidly from the mid 1880s to 1900 with strong state involvement coinciding with a major surge in industrial growth at 8 per cent per annum. Whilst state participation in railways then tailed off slightly the programme for armaments and naval expansion (including the build up of the Black Sea fleet which had started in 1882), ensured that state activity continued on a large scale through to WWI. Whilst these decades were undoubtedly periods of rapid industrialisation, it is debatable whether the government saw industry as a means to economic growth and rising living standards as opposed to providing the industrial muscle for military strength. Government support leant towards heavy industry, railways and other transport and the projects which had no defence dimensions are hard to find. Whilst light industry, including textiles, developed strongly, these were not the sectors which the government targeted.

State involvement took basically four forms. One was the wholly state owned enterprise (SOE) in railways (like the Trans-Siberian), shipbuilding and naval dockyards (as in Izhara), ports (Sebastopol), armament factories (Tula) as well as the mining and iron works in Perm and other parts of the Urals which had a long history as noted in Chapter 4. Some indication of the growth of the SOEs is suggested by the fact that their operating expenditures in 1885 were equivalent to 6 per cent of central government spending on debt interest, defence, subsidies, education, health and administration, rising to 12 per cent in 1890 and over 40 per cent by 1900–13 (Table 7.2). Second, the government took equity shares in joint stock companies in all these sectors (such as the *Grand Société des Chemins de Fer Russes*). It also, third, exerted preference in the award of generous contracts to domestic private industrial firms producing and supplying iron, rails, rolling stock and coal to the various SOEs and to the companies in which the government had some share ownership. Similar preferences were used in allocating the military budget on clothing and armaments supplied by private sector firms and it should be recalled that the military budget accounted for 30 per cent of all central government spending (excluding SOEs) in 1885 rising to 42 per cent by 1913. Finally the state often guaranteed interest on the substantial loans made by domestic and foreign suppliers of credit and capital to Russian private companies and SOEs, as well as granting loans of its own to such enterprises.[41]

Well before the arrival of railways, the Russian state from Peter the Great's time onwards had invested in and operated ports, ships, metallurgical plants and mines. By the mid nineteenth century the state still owned several mines and metallurgical plants, many in the Urals. It was granting loans for factory construction and of course, as outlined in Chapter 4, provided a stream of orders for guns, shells and clothing, often from manorial factories. From this point, military personnel numbers shot up: 716,000 in 1870 to 878,000 in 1890 and over 1.3 million by 1910 (Table 7.1). By 1900 there were 14,000 employees in government shipyards, 25,000 in Urals ironworks, 27,000 in arsenals and related factories, 9000 in private sector defence companies. This total of 75,000 rose to 86,000 in 1908 and 120,000 by 1913.[42] The years from 1870 saw the Ukraine coming to the forefront in industrial development, dominating the production of railway equipment, rich in iron ore and coal and developing very strongly after the so-called "Catherine" railway was completed in 1885 linking the Donetz basin to the Krivig Rog iron ore. A key enterprise was the (tax exempt, English) New Russian Iron Company benefiting from state loans and orders. The railway also helped grain exports via the Black Sea ports. Meanwhile the old, mainly state owned industrial complex in the Urals was dormant; there were 105 factories (13 state owned) linked to the central industrial region only by waterways and only five joint stock companies were set up in the Urals before 1900.[43] The Department of Mines supervised 13 ironworks all but one of which were in the Urals, especially in Perm and Zletoust.[44] The region's revival was prompted by an inflow of foreign capital from the early 1900s.

Government involvement was especially strong in the production of armaments and in shipbuilding, employing some 60,000 workers in 1900.[45] By then there were six state armories, the most important being the one at Tula in the central industrial region (7000 workers). The private sector was small except for one huge firm, Putilov, with 12,400 workers, and in 1900 was linked to the Russo-Asiatic bank. Armaments, military fortresses and barracks were among the big new projects in the years 1896–1900. The six state armories were part of 18 SOEs overseen by the Main Artillery Administration. Dockyards for warships were also dominated by SOEs with Putilov again the main exception. The navy had four shipyards (Admiralty, Izhora, Oakhov and the Baltic) together with wharves and workshops in Kronstadt, Sebastopol and Nikolaev. Some private yards and foreign supplies were used before the Crimean War but many collapsed later. In 1877 the Russian Baltic Ironworks and Machine Company was established, three-quarters owned by the Admiralty who took it over completely in 1894, by which time there was a boom in the industry and by 1900 the Baltic yards were the most important. The state factories and yards tended to dominate over private firms in part from the fear of the bureaucracy being subject to the "whim of the entrepreneur". As WWI approached however capacity was strained and the private sector was used more. The banking sector had been involved all along and in particular the three large banks in St Petersburg: Russo-Asiatic Bank, linked to the Putilov company; International Bank; Private Commercial Bank. All three had strong connections with private sector shipbuilding and armaments especially 1906–13 and attracted financial capital also to Black Sea shipping.

These two sectors, armaments and dockyards, were unambiguously a major focus of government enterprise and intervention, driven by the state's military concerns. The picture for the railways is less straightforward. The growth of track construction was strong throughout the period with the biggest surge in the 1890–1905 period during which annual average track completions peaked at 3235 kilometres in 1898–1902 (Figure 7.1). New financial support had been announced as early as 1867 by Minister of Finance Reutern and the government later promised to purchase all bonds issued by the private companies at 70–75 per cent of normal value mortgaged on railway property. In addition the government sometimes provided subsidies and interest guarantees. There is however a case to be made that in the first more modest phase of development 1860–90 there were more private sector companies. French capital was heavily involved, as in the boost to Donetz coal by the completion of links in 1869 between Kask, Kharkov and Azov. Also in the 1860s several important lines were built serving the central industrial region – Moscow to Kursky, Yaroslav, Varoneeh and Nizhi-Novgorod. The 1870s saw clear economic gains from the Riga-Tsaritsyn lines and that between Perm and Ekaterina. In the south the grain producing areas were linked to the Black Sea and we noted earlier the important links between coal and iron ore created in 1885 by the "Catherine" line.[46] Therefore many private companies were involved in these early developments and much of it could be justified on economic grounds. Indeed Metzer's work on late nineteenth century and early twentieth century data

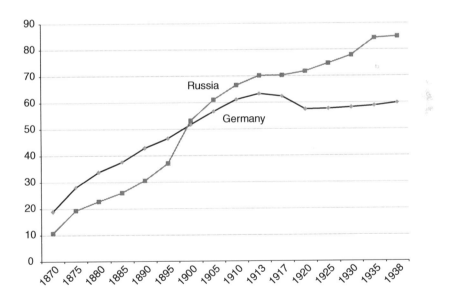

*Figure 7.1* Railways in Russia and Germany 1870–1938 (length of track in '000 kilometres) (source: Mitchell 2003a).

Note
Entries relate to contemporary boundaries and Russian data exclude local lines before 1914.

suggest railway expansion did improve inter-regional trade and that social rates of return of about 5 per cent GDP were good, even though modest compared to USA, reflecting the lower income levels in Russia as well as the more extensive use of waterways.[47] Backward industrial links were also important: in the years 1893–99 the railway accounted for 37 per cent of the market for pig iron.

An important turning point, escalating the government's strategic concern about railways, was the war against the Ottoman Empire in the Danube and Balkan mountain areas, culminating in a diplomatic defeat for Russia at the 1878 Berlin Congress. The Russian state had been reminded of its technological limitations and need for enhanced development of the railway infrastructure. Some historians like Gerschenkron and Portal have stressed that state involvement with railways was only partly linked to strategic concerns which mainly "reinforced" the economic factors. Others like Kahan have argued that at the end of the nineteenth century and early twentieth century, the government inspired railways were "constructed to serve the needs of troop movements, rather than the economic needs of freight and passenger services" whilst Falkus characterises Prime Minister Witte's motives in the 1890s as "unambiguously political".[48] Some idea of the significance of the railways for military strategy and resources is that whilst general mobilisation was estimated to take five months in 1859 this had been reduced to about 15 days as early as 1879. Construction work on the Trans-Siberian railway was started in 1891 and completed by reaching Vladivostock in 1901, with unambiguous strategic targets of links to the Far East given the increasing menace of Japan. The total state financial commitment for this and other new lines in the Urals, Lower Volga and the Caucasus was 3.5 billion roubles.[49] By 1913 about two-thirds of the 72,000 kilometres of rail track were state owned.

The Russian rail track therefore grew rapidly in the 1890s overtaking Germany by 1900 as Figure 7.1 illustrates. That picture obviously leaves out the significance of the immense size of Russia and the limited nature of the network, especially for military movements. The USA network was six times bigger. A comparison with nearer hostile states indicates that the rail track in Russia was just over three kilometres per 1000 square kilometres of territory as compared to Japan 25, France 76, Germany 130 and the UK 141 (Annex Table A17). The limitations of the Russian network were revealed during WWI with much criticism of deficient supplies for the army and poor links between the key industrial areas. Westwood has argued that this criticism is overstated.[50] The problem about supplies to the army was as much about production as delivery and no one had anticipated such a long war and the loss of the Baltic and Black Sea shipping routes. Nonetheless the track linking the Donetz basin, Polish mining, Baltic ports and the central industrial region was inadequate so that if one were to judge Russian state policy on railways in strategic terms, rather than its impact on economic growth, the verdict must be failure. Even though the system was in no sense "in decline" it did not square with the political and military aspirations of the Russian autocracy

## From new economic policy to central planning: Russia 1920–39

For much of the 1920s Russia had a mixed economy of a very distinctive character. Some have called it market socialism to distinguish it from the rigidly planned Stalinist economy which emerged in the 1930s. The puzzle as to how socialism could coexist with markets attracted the attention of economists and, especially in the 1930–70 period, models of market socialism were developed by economists like Lange and Lerner.[51] Such models often lay behind the pricing and investment rules advocated for publicly owned industries in the West in the 1950s and 1960s. The socialist element was deemed to be present in that the assets of such industries were acquired by the state, though not expropriated, and compensation was paid to the previous shareholders of for example private steel and railway companies. The broad idea in the models was that prices, output and investment outcomes should approximate (mimic) that achieved in the perfectly competitive version of pure capitalism, but without its exploitative private capital element. Each sector (like mining, chemicals) was a state monopoly and the industry managers would so set output levels that the freely determined market price of the commodity or service would equal the marginal costs of production. The labour force would be free to move around so that wage levels, given the output rules, would approximate those found in perfect labour markets.[52] Finance for investment would come from the state but industry managers would be expected to engage in only those investment programmes whose rate of return exceeded the rate of interest specified by the state.[53] When the technology of production was such as to generate large economies of scale (railways, telecoms), spillover benefits and costs (road investments) and other potential "market failure" problems, the state would provide subsidies or levy taxes. The practical impact of these economic ideas can be seen most vividly in the research of French engineers and economists working on the *tarif vert* of *Électricité de France.*[54]

These economic ideas can provide a useful, "idealistic" benchmark against which to evaluate the so-called New Economic Policy in Russia of the 1920s. There were three features which rendered the reality very different from the economic model. First, Russia did not develop a coherent plan for market socialism but stumbled into it as a consequence of the Civil War conditions following the 1917 Revolution. Second, market freedom was severely curtailed because of political factors. Third, there was a growing and decisive worry of how far liberal economic conditions would generate quickly enough the heavy industry to combat the military threats which continued to haunt Russia, especially from the mid 1920s onwards.

In the early 1900s many large private industrial firms clustered into trusts and some into syndicates (with a common sales agency). During WWI these were taken over by the state which also engaged in a huge expansion of armaments, subordinating all other sectors to its needs. After the abdication of the Tsar in March 1917, the provisional government took some modest steps to reforming the economic and social system but again this was within the spirit of protecting private property rights. That government was overthrown by the Bolsheviks in October and the ownership of property was then transformed. All land and industrial assets were declared to be the property of the state and scheduled for expropriation. In the next 12 months however chaos ensued. Much territory in western Russia had been lost by the terms of the November 1917 Treaty of Brest Litovsk ending the war with Germany. An initial breathing space in spring 1918 was then followed by Civil War. The counter revolutionaries in the shape of the White[55] Armies, supported by West European states, occupied all of Siberia and the Urals with Kolchak's armies at some point within 100 miles of the Volga. In the south, the Ukraine and Caucasus regions were lost and Denikin's armies advanced to Tula and cut off the lower Volga. In 1920 Poland invaded, advancing through Byelorussia to the east of Minsk and across the western Ukraine, occupying Kiev alternatively with Denikin's armies.[56] The new Russian state had effectively been reduced to little more than the medieval Moscovy state and the customary sources of oil, coal and grain had been cut off. Although the Polish–Soviet War was being resolved by the early 1920s and the White armies repulsed, Russia was left with famine, the rouble all but valueless as the Soviet state financed its spending by printing money, and mounting disquiet about the Bolshevik government.

During this period of so-called "war communism" there was little sign of an overall economic plan.[57] A grain collection mechanism had operated 1915–17 but this then had all but collapsed and from May 1918 a state monopoly of grain acquisitions was decreed, initially in the form of "seizures", later quotas. Private trade in grain was banned and indeed trade in all foodstuffs and the principal consumer goods was deemed to be a state monopoly. Within the agricultural sector, all the remaining large estates had been nationalised by a decree of November 1917 and the peasant was no longer obliged to pay rent to a land-owner (or tax in the case of the erstwhile state peasant). However the transfer of land from the nobility was not in practice to the individual peasant (nor the state) but to the village commune, the *mir*, and the old three field systems continued. This would not have been a problem for the Social Revolutionaries (the SRs) who followed the traditions of the populist Slavophiles (Narovniks) in viewing the village commune as Russia's answer to capitalism.[58] Not however for the Marxists and certainly not the Bolsheviks. Meanwhile the agricultural problem grew and the Bolsheviks blamed it on the *kulaks*, the richer peasants. The amounts demanded in the compulsory grain acquisitions rose consistently from 1918 through to 1921 under the rubric that "grain was in the hands of the rural *kulaks* and the rich". The peasant lacked incentives to produce, sowings fell, the village became more self-sufficient and resentment at the compulsory requisitions increased.[59]

Oversight of the economy rested in a technical sense on the *vesenkha* (VSNKh), established in December 1917 as the Supreme Council of the National Economy, based on the war time planning agencies. It was attached to the (political) Council of People's Commisary and from March 1920 to the Council of

Labour and Defence (STO). To confuse matters further it was not the only high level economic institution. By the end of 1918 the Commissariat of Utilisation was coordinating distribution channels. Moreover whilst VSNKh had responsibility for the whole economy, it effectively was restricted to industry, finance and transport. Nationalisation was decreed for all large-scale industry and in January 1918 for the railways and the merchant fleet. The national debt was annulled, foreign debt was repudiated in February 1918 and all shareholders in banks expropriated. Strictly speaking, industry was not nationalised but rather the very large firms were expropriated, and enterprises with fewer than five employees were initially explicitly left to the private sector. It has been estimated that by the end of 1919 about 90 per cent of large-scale industry was publicly owned. "Control" was both centralised and diffused. On the one hand transactions between factories were essentially book-keeping entries, as VSNKh set orders and targets through its departments (*glavki*). Indeed Nove suggested that large-scale industry was effectively run by VSNKh as a "single firm".[60] On the other hand, many factories had boards of management which included representatives of workers' committees. Only 10 per cent of factories in 1919 had one man management. For Lenin this was problematic and a sign of things to come was the conferment of dictatorial powers over the railways on the People's Commissar for Transport.

The shift to the New Economic Policy was forced by the crisis conditions of famine, the threat of starvation as grain requisitions increased and the strike of the Kronstadt sailors in March 1921. The grain requisition system (*prodrazverstka*) was replaced by a tax in kind (*prodnalog*) on food with the peasant free to trade. May 1921 saw the revocation of an earlier decree which had committed the government to nationalise all small-scale industry and, in June, approval was given to VSNKh leasing out some of its factories. The food tax was the cornerstone of the alliance (*smychka*) between the Soviet regime and the peasants, with trading in the hands of the "NEPmen". For Gregory this was an "attempt to combine the market with socialism".[61]

How did NEP work? In rural areas, the peasants were allowed to leave the land, the hiring of labour was permitted and the large estates were being broken up. On the other hand Bolshevik party membership was weaker than in urban areas and the meetings of the village elders (*skhod*) were more influential than the party officials. The three field system survived and the share of enclosed land grew only slowly. The number of peasant holdings rose from 17 million in 1917 to 25 million in 1927 and the average NEP farm was smaller than the 1913 farm.[62] Structural change to larger more efficient units was therefore slow. Moreover peasant incentives to grow for the market were diminishing. The food tax which had replaced the compulsory grain acquisitions was a specified share of output and progressive in incidence, with the price level set by the government. In 1924 it was converted to a money tax. However the way in which the government set prices meant that the ratio of agricultural prices to industrial prices was persistently below the 1913 level with the gap between industrial and agricultural prices forever rising and falling and then rising again (the scissors crisis).[63]

This reduced the willingness of the peasantry to export to urban areas, induced more self-consumption and more time, effort and other resources to industrial crops like cotton and flax (when not subject to controls) and especially to live-stock. Specialists in Russian history warn us to treat agrarian data with caution but it does seem that although the sown area was rising in the 1920s, as were crop outputs, it was a struggle to regain the 1913 levels, as Tables 7.1 and 7.4 suggest. The sugar beet and potato sown areas seem to have risen by 1929 above the 1913 levels but the grain level was not restored. Outside the requisition and tax systems livestock numbers flourished.

In industry the role of VSNKh as a "single firm" was ended with factories collected into trusts, later into syndicates to coordinate sales. By 1923 there were 478 trusts accounting for 75 per cent of publicly owned industry and one-third of them were controlled directly by VSNKh, the rest by local councils.[64] Whilst all had a certain degree of autonomy, this was particularly true of light industry and consumer goods where prices were left to be determined by consumer demand and the level of enterprise costs, and where each enterprise was given some freedom in employing labour, defining investment programmes and setting output targets. In addition state owned enterprises accounted for only 2.3 per cent of small-scale industry by 1926/27.[65] Heavy industry was a different story, most noticeably and significantly where strategic issues were involved. Apart from continuing old industries, there were many state-led new industrial projects like the Dneiper hydro-electric station and the Turkestan–Siberian railway. The fuel industries, metallurgy, armaments, wholesale trade, communications and banking were deemed to be of strategic importance. They had production quotas

*Table 7.4* Russian agriculture 1913–38[a]

|  | 1913 | 1929 | 1938 |
|---|---|---|---|
| *Area sown ('000 hectares)* |  |  |  |
| Wheat | 33.5 | 29.7 | 41.5 |
| Rye | 30.7 | 24.9 | 21.6 |
| Oats | 19.7 | 18.9 | 17.9 |
| Sugar beet | 0.7 | 0.8 | 1.2 |
| Potatoes | 4.9 | 5.7 | 7.4 |
| *Crop outputs (million metric tons)* |  |  |  |
| Wheat | 28.0 | 18.9 | 40.8 |
| Rye | 25.7 | 20.4 | 20.9 |
| Oats | 18.2 | 15.7 | 17.0 |
| Sugar beet | 12.4 | 6.3 | 16.7 |
| Potatoes | 35.9 | 45.6 | 42.0 |
| Total grain exports (million metric tons) | 9.08 | 0.18 | 2.05 |

Source: Mitchell 2003a.

Note

a The 1913 entries cover the Russian Empire, excluding Finland, whilst the other entries relate to the USSR boundaries of 1923.

and supplies to them of raw materials and other intermediate inputs were controlled. As part of the state budget, they were closely linked to the central allocations of supplies though they were expected to make a profit, albeit sometimes with subsidies.[66] Prices were also controlled as they were for the traditional "revenue sources", the state monopolies in vodka, kerosene and tobacco. VSNKh had from February 1921 been supplemented by a new state planning commission, Gosplan, which, again somewhat confusingly, had the duty to draw up a single plan for the whole economy.

If then we compare the reality of Russia's economy in the 1920s with the market socialism models, huge differences are apparent. It was a mixed economy of sorts, it did involve a "New Economic Policy" and public ownership of the commanding heights, but it was more like a war economy than market socialism. The major industries were given little room, outputs and input supplies were controlled and price levels set by the state. Government intervention in pricing led to problems when, as often, they did not reflect supply and demand factors. This may have been, as Gregory argues, because the Soviet regime did not understand how markets worked or it may equally have been simply reflecting a temporary nod towards some liberation of markets. Either way, by 1926/27 inflationary pressures were building up for non-grain agricultural goods. At the same time there was repressed inflation for manufactured goods, smaller quantities of which were available for the peasantry generating another disincentive to freely sell to urban areas and every inducement to return to cottage industry. The volume of the 1927 state grain procurement was one-half of the 1926 level and over the 1926–29 period only 15 per cent of total grain production is estimated to have been acquired by the state; alongside this goes the statistic that the state determined grain price was in 1928–29 only one-half that in private markets.[67]

Most crucially for what was to follow is that economic recovery was proceeding only at a slow pace. In the 1920s, the industrial share of GDP never returned to the 1913 level. By 1928 total manufacturing output (including all the light industry) per head of population had done no more than achieve the 1913 level and, as Table 7.1 shows, by 1929 the output of pig iron and crude steel had yet to return to 1913 levels. By this stage it is clear that all of Russia's traditional defence worries had reappeared and the industrial performance and military preparedness looked totally inadequate. The West's involvement with the White Armies had not been forgotten, the Chinese Revolution had failed, Japan looked increasingly threatening in the Far East, Britain broke off diplomatic relations in 1927 and the USSR was isolated. By that stage the Red Army had fallen from a peak of 5.3 million to 566,000 and the state armaments output had dwindled. For Russia the "commanding heights" were as significant for military as for socialist reasons and plans were afoot to develop internal regions for national defence programmes.[68] Stalin had been complaining about the inefficiency of small scattered farms as early as 1926 and concluded that controls over markets were inadequate.[69] By the end of the 1920s arbitrary acquisitions of grain were on the rise under the guise of dealing with "speculators".

In the 1930s Russia moved unambiguously to what has been termed "command socialism" or "an administrative-command system".[70] Its main economic features were state planning, rationing, few free market prices, collectivised agriculture and an immense expansion of heavy industry. It was achieved by state coercion and accompanied by famine, brutalities, inefficient production methods and widespread human suffering. In rural areas the *obschina* and *mir* were replaced by the collective farm and the Soviet. Five Year Plans were drawn up by Gosplan with much intervention from the Communist Party. There was no market for producer goods whether in industry or agriculture. Industrial enterprises were overseen by Ministries answerable to the Council of People's Commissars which was effectively a state arm of the Politburo, the central committee of the Party. Since the NEP never approached the ideals of market socialism, the links between the 1920s and 1930s are clear. But what prompted the decisive push? By the middle decades of the twentieth century, in all the major powers, agendas were changing with the widening of electoral franchises, revolutionary pressures from the working classes and the 1930s depression forced governments to put general living standards higher on the list of policy priorities. In some cases this meant governments facing social unrest at home so that, in conjunction with continuing foreign policy and defence worries, military and strategic factors remained at the fore. It is our thesis here that the trajectory of the Russian economy in the 1930s is best understood in these terms; that is, Stalin's "Great Turn" reflected the perceived need to build up heavy industry for securing military strength and to cope, by coercion, with the social unrest that followed from the accompanying impairment of living standards which had added to the after effects, in Russia, of war and revolution 1914–20.[71]

As measured by the overall economic aggregates, the performance was astonishing. Over the whole period 1913–50, the average rate of growth of Russian GDP per head, on Maddison's estimates, was 1.76 per cent per annum, a higher figure than for any of the major powers.[72] Most of this was due to what happened in the 1930s as the industrial sector grew, if not at the 18 per cent annual rate in the Soviet data, at probably just over 10 per cent, and capital formation rose from 13 per cent of national income to 30 per cent.[73] Pig iron, steel and coal output more than trebled, electricity supply and natural gas rose sixfold and the output of crude petroleum doubled (Table 7.1). By 1938 Russia was largely self-sufficient in iron, steel, electrical power equipment, tractors, combine harvesters, tanks and metal aircraft. Finance for the huge capital requirements came from forced bond issues, increases in excise and other turnover taxes, and the money supply (which rose from 1.7 million roubles in 1928 consistently to 8.4 million in 1938).[74] Given the ceilings imposed on the prices paid by government for its grain requisitions and that it sold grain at higher prices, some have said that margin generated surpluses which financed investment. In fact research on the terms of trade suggest prices received in rural areas did not fall, overall in the 1930s, relative to industrial prices. The caps on the prices of grain and other food and commodities, in conjunction with rationing, played perhaps more of a role in ensuring that the large increase in the money supply did not lead to the sort of inflation experienced in Germany in the early 1920s. Some idea of the repressed inflation comes from estimates that black market prices exceeded average prices for bread, grain and vegetables by 60 per cent in 1932.[75]

Astonishing as are some of the industrial growth figures, they were invariably less than those propagated in the planning targets. Indeed a shift of emphasis clearly occurred after crisis and famine hit Russia 1932–33. The sixteenth Party Congress of 1929 had approved a Five Year Plan, more ambitious (more "optimal") than the first drafts. At this stage the vision was for complete public ownership of the means of production, "production communes" in both agriculture and industry, a moneyless economy and an eventual withering away of the state. After 1932 it was explicitly recognised that the economy needed money means of exchange, that public ownership of agriculture did not mean nationalisation but takeover by local communities and the stated rationale for the continuance of a strong state was that Russia was encircled by threatening capitalist powers. During 1930–32 the initial plan targets (if not the "optimal") were met for coal, oil and pig iron but not for others, especially the less strategic sectors like textiles and other consumer goods. Some 55 per cent of peasant households were nominally in collectives by 1930. The relentless spread of forced grain acquisitions, the liquidation of the *kulak* class and other ruthless measures pioneered in the Urals and Siberia, had devastating effects on agriculture. A huge migration from agriculture to industry occurred: it is estimated that numbers gainfully occupied in agriculture fell from 71 million in 1926 to 57 million by 1937 (cf. Table 7.3) not so much from higher productivity or the advance of collectives as simply the product of falling material living standards in rural areas. Grain harvests are estimated to have been 73.3 million tons in 1928 and 83.5 million in 1930 but in each of the next four years fell below 70 million. State procurement of livestock plus that consumed as food by a starving peasantry saw the number of cattle fall from 70.5 million in 1928 to 38.4 million by 1933. Some recovery occurred thereafter but the evidence points to the grain requisitions in the rest of the 1930s rising faster than grain outputs.[76]

The growth of heavy industry in the 1930s was quite distinctive in the way it used capital and labour and by its orientation to the military needs of the nation. Annual military spending was initially modest and Eloranta and Harrison's estimate that it accounted for 7.1 per cent of annual GDP over the whole 1920–38 period, a higher level than in any of the other major powers, reflected largely the surge in the 1930s, towards the end of which the figure had reached 18 per cent.[77] A sound industrial base with engineering capabilities had first to be established. The big increase in capital goods as both inputs and outputs for industry, in conjunction with the new unskilled urban workforce, generated low productivity methods, satirised as capital and labour intensive. There were some huge new schemes like the Dneiper Dam and the Volga-White Sea Canal. Key inputs like machinery, metals and other industrial raw materials were initially imported from Western Europe and financed by agricultural exports. As such foreign trading transactions declined so did economic activity in seaport cities like Odessa and Leningrad whilst the shift of emphasis away from consumer goods meant areas like the Moscow textile region had less prominence. The growth regions were the Donetz basin and Krivog Rog in the Ukraine, the Volga area, the Urals and Siberia. Strategic factors were dominant and these areas, away from border territories, were the centre of Soviet armaments production in the Second World War, though the need for speedy deliveries and for facilities to halt the enemy at the borders meant some industries continued in European Russia.[78]

The planning system was disjointed, full of confusion and contradictions and operating efficiency was low. The massive shift to heavy industry had taken decades in other countries. "There is little doubt that, as so often before, Russian industrialisation in the Soviet period, was a function of the country's foreign and military policies."[79] Such a shift to industry, with all its brutalities, might have no economic rationale, as Gregory suggests, and agriculture might also, as he argues, have performed better without collectivisation.[80] But the problem was not one of economic outcomes but rather it was about how quickly the military preparedness of the country could be developed and whether direct controls would give more certainties than liberal markets. The Soviet Union did survive, unlike Tsarist Russia.

## Appendix: the challenge from the newcomer, Japan 1870–1939[81]

In narrow economic terms, Japan in 1870 was similar to Russia. Average income levels were about the same, there were few rail and telegraph lines, probably three-quarters or more of the labour force was still in agriculture and the limited manufacturing base was strong only in textiles and especially silk and other agricultural processing industries. There were, as in Russia, some potentialities. On its small island economy was a population of 34 million, a considerable urban life and education system. Japan had eschewed contact with the outside world and some idea of the nature of the changes that were needed is reflected in the fact that the central government in the early nineteenth century (the Shogunate or *bakafu*) still maintained a ban on the building and purchase of large ships whilst the indigenous fleet was limited to the coast. There were irrigation systems in rice agriculture but small self-subsistence plots dominated. Provincial lords (*daimyo*) and a military class (*samurai*) existed alongside a strong central state. The need for a bigger military was recognised in several quarters, both before and after the appearance of Commodore Perry in 1853 and the subsequent opening up to the West. Posts and roads were reasonably well developed – despite the continued reliance on corvée labour. Western methods of arms manufacture were monitored and the period 1853–68 saw the development of shipyards, mines and arms factories by the *samurai*.[82]

Geo-politically, Japan was of course very different from Russia and not so well endowed with resources. The central issue was that if Japan was to emulate the major powers, as it so wanted, it would have to develop military strength by industrialisation and this required the securing of raw materials and fuels from the Asian mainland. The political and social structures (analysis of which are beyond the scope of this book) were such that Japan confronted these challenges with much less hesitation than Tsarist Russia. It developed so rapidly and strongly that it won both the Sino-Japanese war of 1894/95 and the Russo-Japanese war of 1904/05, invaded China in 1937 and by 1940 had sufficient confidence, misplaced or not, to contemplate taking on America in what became the great Pacific War.

The auguries in 1870 were not good. With the overthrow of the feudal order and the restoration in 1868 of a central role for the new emperor (Meiji Tenno), reformation of the political structure paved the way for conventional capitalistic development. But Japan had less than 200,000 square miles of territory and, given much mountain and forests, only some 15 per cent of the land was cultivable so there was heavy reliance on intensive rice paddies. Coal deposits were modest (0.2 million tons annual output) as were oil, natural gas and iron ore and there were only tiny amounts of copper, gold and manganese again when compared to Russia. One later testimony to the significance of these factors was the relief that was felt in the 1960s when the development of synthetic products reduced some of the import requirements.[83] In the meantime from the 1870s onwards it had to look to the Asian mainland for raw materials and fuel.

Since commandeering key resources was strategically superior to simply buying them on open markets, this inevitably meant confrontation with the European powers. Britain and France had economic interests in China as well as South-East Asia whilst the completion of the Trans-Siberian Railway in the 1890s advanced the threat from Russia in Manchuria and the Amur Province (see Figure 4.1). Indeed, following Landes, the "steady aggrandisement of Western commercial and political power in the Far East threatened nothing less than the dissolution of the Japanese polity and the reduction of the society to colonial status".[84] Japan did not rush into developing the heavy industry needed for military strength. It continued, for example, to import its main requirements of rails, iron and steel right up to the early 1900s. Instead the focus was on encouraging traditional agriculture and its export products to provide the means of importing modern machinery and tools.[85] Small-scale industry also flourished but it was, as with agricultural sales, greatly helped by a huge state commitment to the development of shipping, inland transport and other infrastructure in the period up to WWI. It was infrastructure development with traditional agriculture and industry which allowed Japan to develop its military strength, in particular to spending more of its national income on defence than any of the major powers. Avoiding involvement in WWI provided further opportunities for export markets and it was not until the 1930s that any of the Western powers, specifically Russia, were able to overtake Japan in the share of economic development allocated to army and navy.

Given its weak resource base and inability to protect its industry by tariffs (as we shall see later), the economic record is truly remarkable compared to Russia. Total national output up to 1913 grew at the same rate but population was increasing more quickly in Russia so that GDP per head grew at 1.38 per cent per annum 1870–1913 in Japan and 0.93 per cent in Russia.[86] By the 1920s Japan had overtaken Russia in both GDP per head and in manufacturing output per head. Electricity supply per head was double that of Russia by 1913 and six times higher by 1929. The merchant fleet was tiny in 1870 but double that of Russia by 1913 and eight times higher by 1929. There were 41 rail track miles per 1000 square miles of land area in 1913 – eight times the Russian level. Even international telegraph cables, which were late to develop, were five times Russia by 1923.

The industrial development up to 1913 was concentrated on traditional small-scale industry in cotton, silk and textiles and, rather than reflecting any great technical strides and productivity growth in manufacturing, took the form of a huge shift of the balance of the labour force within the economy. The occupied population (more than 14 years old) in 1872 totalled 17.1 million and some 14.5 million were in agriculture, forestry and fishing, a figure that, with some oscillations, rose to over 16 million by 1913. However the population by then had risen to 51.7 million so the share of industry and services rose significantly. In fact the growth of industry in this period was not so much a matter of rising productivity in industry as modest increases in productivity accompanied by a huge shift of labour. Some estimates suggest that whilst the labour force in manufacturing in Russia rose from 1.7 million in 1860 to 6.1 million in 1913, Japan's rose proportionately even more from 0.7 million to 4.0 million.[87] That change is enough to explain the whole of the rise in Japan's manufacturing output, relative to its population, even if one were to assume productivity in manufacturing were unchanged at the 1860 level.[88] It was, in one sense, very similar to the classic industrial revolution in Britain 1760–1840 which, notwithstanding the well-known technological improvements, was marked more than anything by a huge shift of labour out of agriculture into manufacturing.[89]

Moreover Japan, unlike Russia, did not rely on foreign capital. Investment in the economy has been estimated at 12.8 per cent of national income in 1907, rising thereafter to 15.1 per cent in 1931 and 20.5 per cent in 1937. These rates are consistent with modern economic development but had two important features. First, the main components were transport, utilities and commerce with manufacturing and construction showing only a slow rise up to the late 1920s, with a big spurt in the 1930s.[90] Second, private domestic investment accounted for roughly one-half of the total but the other half was not foreign capital, which was tiny relative to that in Russia, but was investment by the state. The ability to take on foreign capital was, in part, restricted by Japan's inability to generate, in the nineteenth century, large current account surpluses on its balance of payments. In its trading relations, Japan was, at this time, at the mercy of the major Western powers. Exports were dominated by primary products especially raw silk which still accounted for 50–80 per cent in 1870. Its imports needs were mainly arms, vessels and textiles and it could do little initially to protect its manufactures from fierce competition. Japan "relinquished her commercial sovereignty"[91] in a series of trade treaties agreed shortly after Commodore Perry's visit in 1853 opening up Japan to the outside world. All trade business was dominated by the Americans and Europeans and the treaties gave rights of territoriality to them and set very low import duties. It was not until the 1890s that progress was made in renegotiating the treaties, leading eventually to complete tariff autonomy in 1911. Woollen mills were protected by a 25 per cent duty on foreign woollens from 1899. By 1913 duties averaged 20–25 per cent for machinery and equipment, 20–30 per cent for semi-manufactured goods and 30–40 per cent for all manufactured goods. Duties fell during WWI but in the inter-war period, Japan was embroiled in the worldwide trade restrictions and the 1920s saw duties raised for sectors like chemicals and metals and dyestuffs imports had to be licensed. Japan left the gold standard in the 1920s but restored it at par in 1930 which made itself vulnerable to the 1930/31 liquidity crisis. Raw silk was 36 per cent of total exports in 1929 but the dollar price fell dramatically and the export focus shifted away from North America to Asia and Africa. The Dutch and British reacted to the intrusions in their Asian markets by restricting Japan's exports to their own colonies.[92]

Turning back to our main theme, the key question is how Japan so developed its infrastructure from 1870 to facilitate the growth of agriculture and industry and an industry eventually geared to military strength. Here the Japanese state played a decisive role in subsidising railways, shipping, shipbuilding, armaments and their supply industries and in setting up its own enterprises in these sectors.[93] In 1871 a telegram system was introduced and Japan joined the International Postal Union in 1878. The government regarded "communication as critical to national security and broader economic development" and was opposed to foreign companies in these sectors. It established its own telephone network in 1881 and in 1888 "decided that the Ministry of Communications should have a telephone monopoly just like the telegraph monopoly ... because, for military and administrative reasons, they did not want a foreign company to dominate the market" (though the manufacture of electrical equipment was left to joint ventures with Western Electric).[94] This was the origin of that public enterprise which was later, from 1952, to become the Nippon Telegraph and Telephone Company.

The geo-political setting wherein Japan relied on the Asian mainland for many raw materials and viewed it as territory to be developed and controlled meant that shipping and the shipbuilding industry would be of central importance. They were important in Europe but whereas by 1880 the other major island economy, the UK, had 25,000 sailing, steam and motor merchant ships and even Italy had nearly 8000, Japan had only 210. Support for shipbuilding and subsidies to shipping were modest in Europe, apart from Spain which is a better analogy and where central government support for shipping and the navy programme saw its merchant fleet tonnage climb by 1913 to equal, relative to population, France and Germany. For two centuries Japan had effectively been isolated from the world outside and shipping restricted to coastal waters. At the start of the Meiji era the only vessels of Western design were owned by local notables or the government so they had to be leased out if local entrepreneurship were to be encouraged. The rail network was in no better shape. So if Japan was to expand and dominate economically and militarily, speed in adjustment was essential and this put an onus on the state to push the private sector and/or activate state enterprises. The size of the state subsidies to Japanese shipping and shipbuilding, from the late nineteenth century, has no parallel in Europe or North America. By the late 1880s two major indigenous shipping companies (Nihon Yusen Kaisha and Osaka Shōsen Kaisha) had emerged under government protection and they developed shipping lines to China, Korea and Russia.[95] The Mitsubishi company was the first to benefit from government support. Its Shanghai line was initially the only overseas route serviced by Japanese ships and its shipping interests were merged into NYK in the 1880s and formed part of the big expansion of the merchant fleet to 1913. The first diesel powered ship was built under its auspices in 1923. The Sino-Japanese War of 1894–95 and the Russo-Japanese war of 1904–05 had vividly drawn attention to the need for development in these infrastructure areas. Massive government subsidies effectively allowed risks to be shared between business and the state and the fleet grew from 45,000 tons in 1883 to 1.5 million in 1913. Per thousand head of population this works out at 29 tons, only slightly less than Italy at 33, Spain (45) and Germany (49). In these terms Japan was well ahead of those countries by 1938 and had become the third largest ship owner in the world by as early as 1919.[96]

The first railway in Japan was not open until 1872 – from Tokyo to Yokohoma – and only 283 miles had been built by 1883. There was much private, including foreign, capital involved initially, albeit with government subsidies. By the 1880s the strategic significance of railways for binding the country socially and politically and providing rapid means of troop movements on the long island chain had become apparent. One-third of all central government subsidies went to railways, a portion exceeded only by the allocations to shipping and shipbuilding. The speed of development and the faltering profitability of many private railway companies meant that reliance on subsidies would never be enough. There were pressures for the development of a planned network and after the Russo-Japanese war of 1904–05 there were strong demands for a linked system embracing Manchuria and Korea. Proposals for nationalisation from the military as well as business users was reinforced by the Diet stressing its urgency on military and economic grounds in 1906 at which point 17 private companies were taken over. The railways were subsequently a key element in all Japanese strategies as the state share of lines rose. Symptomatic of the driving force was that the state undertaking, Japanese Railways, was, from 1908, under the control of the Railway Agency which reported direct to the Prime Minister's office – and included railways in Korea and Manchuria. It became a Railway Ministry in 1920 and took all motorised transport under its wing in 1928.[97]

In the case of manufacturing industry, including armaments and shipbuilding, the Japanese government's presence was more direct and longer lasting, the more the sector in question had strategic value. In the non-strategic parts of the economy, the government set up pilot plants, recruited foreign experts, leased out imported machinery and provided subsidies as well as using the business houses, the *zaibatsu* (the "money cliques", Mitsui, Mitsubishi etc.) as a source of loans in exchange for valued industrial contracts. Pilot manufacturing plants were established in the 1870s in cotton spinning in Aichi and Hiroshima, silk reeling in Macbashi and Tomioko, paper, printing, glass, tiles, cement, sodium phosphate and bleaching powder.[98] The success of these ventures is still in dispute and many were sold off in the 1880s. Foreign experts were also used only in the initial phases. There were few permanent immigrants and, for example, by 1920 only one foreign officer in the merchant marine. Success in these non-strategic sectors came often more from regulation rather than direct state production. In contrast to the Chinese, for example, the Japanese government recognised the need for a uniform quality of silk thread, took responsibility for licensing those enterprises raising eggs (from which came the silkworm and its cocoon), enforced concentration of factories ("filatures") in the ports and a pool for silk conditioning. In the more obviously strategic sectors however state owned enterprises were more common. Government woollen factories made most of the army's cloth up to the early twentieth century.

By the 1880s the government owned four shipyards at Nagasaki, Kobe, Uraja and Ishikawa under the supervision of the new Ministry of Military affairs. The shipbuilding elements were sold to the private sector but shipbuilding and navigation subsidy Acts of 1896 and 1899 provided subsidies for vessels made of iron and steel, warships or mercantile, whilst ship owners were given a double discount for buying ships produced in Japanese yards. By the early 1900s there was still a heavy reliance on foreign shipyards but after the Russo-Japanese war of 1904/05, Japan became virtually self-sufficient in new ships – 71 out of 78 warships commissioned 1905–13 were built in Japan, of which one-quarter came from the private sector.[99] By that stage Japan was claiming to be as good as the Western powers in shipbuilding. Several of the state owned shipyards were heavily involved in producing inputs to the industry. As well as Nagasaki, two other units established in 1871 (Hyago, Akabane) by the Ministry of Construction made machine tools and steam engines as well as ships and all SOEs were active in aiding private non-military shipping and factories.

In the armaments sector, the government took over the *daimyo* army workshops and navy munitions factories and by 1880 had five munitions works, including army arsenals in Tokyo and Osaka and navy arsenals at Yokosuka and Tsukiji, the only plants at the time with Western-type blast furnaces.[100] Throughout the Meiji period, iron and steel production struggled to get off the ground and in 1896 some 40 per cent of pig iron was still imported. In 1901 the Yawata Ironworks heralded the state's major initiative which, by the 1920s, was making a significant contribution to indigenous pig iron production, all of which was helped by exemptions from income and excess profits tax. Indeed the inter-war period generally saw much "indirect" state activity, especially on the Asian mainland involving industries of strategic importance with the government directing matters through its South Manchurian Railway Company. Subsidies were extended to chemicals and oil exploration, rice production, land drainage and water supplies. In conjunction with the Mitsui and Mitsubishi *zaibatsu* the government also aided assembly operations in the embryonic aircraft industry.

Allen claims there was "scarcely any important Japanese industry of the western type during the latter decades of the nineteenth century which did not own its establishment to state initiative".[101] It has also been suggested that, by the 1930s, the government was involved in at least one-half of the "modern sector" in the form of the army, navy, bureaucracy, railways, shipping and education. That commitment was facilitated by the initial growth of the traditional industrial and agricultural sectors generating tax and other revenues which financed the government's expanded activities to such an extent that state presence was bigger in Japan than in any of the major powers. A large part of state revenues came initially from the land tax which was based on the value of land. This was a proportional tax on gross income but was effectively regressive because net incomes tended to increase with land values.[102] Most of the tax burden fell then on agriculture and even though excise taxes gradually increased thereafter they fell on rural as well as urban workers – tobacco, sake, soy sauce, beverages, sugar. Customs revenue was small and the central government's share of all tax revenues remained at about 56 per cent over the decades up to WWI: its share of the land tax fell but personal and corporate taxes increased and accrued more to central than local government.

A distinctive feature of Japanese public finances 1870–1939 was that defence spending was higher, relative to national income, than in all the major powers and that government enterprises and state monopolies generated more non-tax revenues than in the other countries. In the Meiji period, some 55 per cent of all government spending was on defence plus administration, policing, foreign affairs and compensation to the nobility for their loss of lands (cf. Russia). Oshima claims this total was unparalleled in the finances of modern nations.[103] More pointedly military expenditure alone took a rising share and increased from 1.4 per cent of gross national product in 1880 to 8.8 per cent by 1910. Eloranta and Harrison estimate the share was 5.0 per cent for all of the 1870–1913 period, considerably higher than in the major powers – even Russia was only 3.9 per cent.[104] Again in the next peace time period 1920–38, Japan devoted 5.7 per cent of GNP to defence, well above Germany (3.3 per cent), France (4.3 per cent) and exceeded only by Russia (7.3 per cent). The amounts spent on education and transport did rise significantly throughout both periods but it was largely as a result of its military spending that Japan finished up with one of the highest public spending totals, rising from 11.4 per cent of GNP in 1880 to 21.2 per cent in 1920 – again much higher than the European powers.[105] Much of the rise in spending appears to have been financed not by taxes but from the surpluses of state monopolies and enterprises – tobacco, rails, post, telegraph, etc. Certainly from 1900 government expenditures and revenues rose rapidly and most of the increase in the latter came from non-tax revenues. The surpluses were 338 million yen in 1910 as compared to 504 tax revenues, that is two-thirds, a ratio about the same in both central and local government. For central government alone the figure rose to 167 per cent by 1939[106] and this use of state enterprise matches closely that in Prussia (Chapter 5). How far all these tax and non-tax revenues affected living standards is still a matter of dispute. Whilst some have seen Japanese living standards depressed for the majority of the population, others have found evidence that whilst the gap in per capita consumption with USA did not fall, neither did it rise, and real disposable income per worker increased, at least until the 1930s. Of course, in the absence of the big military effort, living standards might well have increased even faster. Japan however was, rightly or wrongly, better prepared for war than Russia.

## Notes

1 Laue 1960, p. 210.
2 Figes 2011.
3 Laue 1960; Gershenkron 1963, 1965, 1966a; Falkus 1972.
4 Gatrell 1994, p. 140; Crisp 1972.
5 Kahan 1967; Gatrell and Davies 1991.
6 If the revenues of state enterprises are deducted from the total revenue figures in Table 7.2, we find customs accounted for 13.3 per cent of tax-only revenues in 1885 and 15.0 per cent in 1913.
7 Net profits or losses would be the more conventional way of recording state enterprise activity.
8 Tanzi and Schuknecht 2000.
9 Eloranta and Harrison 2010.
10 Gerschenkron 1963, 1966a.
11 Laue 1960.
12 Babkov 1912; Laue 1960.
13 Gatrell 1994.
14 Kahan 1967, p. 466.
15 Gatrell 2012.
16 Babkov 1912.
17 Gerschenkron 1965; Kahan 1967.
18 Gatrell 1986, p. 198. Gatrell 2012 estimates revenues (including state enterprise receipts) as over 12 per cent of national income by 1860 though his 1913 figure is 16.9 per cent as in Table 7.2. See also the second section of Chapter 4.
19 Babkov 1912; Gatrell 1994.
20 Wheatcroft 1991; Harrison 1991.
21 Gregory 1994.
22 Gerschenkron 1966a; Crisp 1972; Falkus 1972.
23 Cf. Kahan 1967.
24 Bairoch 1989, p. 77.
25 Bairoch 1989.
26 Portal 1965.
27 Ibid.
28 Crisp 1972.
29 Portal 1965; Gatrell 1986.
30 Gerschenkron 1965, pp. 711, 768, 792.
31 Ibid., p. 760.
32 Ibid., p. 730.
33 Lyaschenko 1949, p. 49.
34 Gatrell 1986.
35 Falkus 1972.
36 Gerschenkron 1960, 1966a, p. 9.

37  Crisp 1972.
38  Metzer 1974, 1976.
39  Gregory 1994.
40  Gatrell 1986.
41  Crisp 1976, chs 6–8.
42  Gatrell 1994.
43  Portal 1965.
44  Gatrell 1994.
45  Ibid.
46  Falkus 1972.
47  Metzer 1974, 1976.
48  Kahan 1967, p. 467; Falkus 1972; Portal 1965, p. 813; Gerschenkron 1963, 1966a.
49  Crisp 1972; Falkus 1972.
50  Westwood 1991.
51  Lange 1936; Lerner 1944.
52  That is, for each factor of production like labour, the reward (wage) would equal the value of the marginal product of that factor.
53  This was equivalent to a requirement that long run (as well as short run) marginal cost equal price. See Boiteux 1957.
54  Nelson 1964; Chick 2002, 2006.
55  So called apparently in part because they wore the white uniforms of the imperial army. Cf. Figes 1997, pp. 91 and 559, who also reminds us that *kulak* was a Bolshevik misappropriation of a term initially used to refer to swindlers, usurers, etc.
56  See useful maps in Figes 1996.
57  Cf. Davis 1999.
58  On all this see Nove 1972; Davies 1989; Harrison 1991; Gregory 1994; Davis 1999.
59  Harrison 1991; Davis 1999.
60  Nove 1972.
61  Gregory 1994, p. 86.
62  Nove 1972; Gregory 1994.
63  See Gregory 1994, pp. 92–3.
64  Nove 1972; Gregory 1994.
65  Nove 1972.
66  Gregory 1994, pp. 88–9; Davis 1999.
67  Gregory 1994.
68  Davis 1999, p. 336.
69  Davies 1989, p. 1026.
70  Davis 1999; Gregory 2004.
71  Cf. Gershenkron 1966a. This may be contrasted with Davies' emphasis (1989) that the aim was for a socialist society and is nearer to Gregory's thesis (2004) of Stalin as a stationary bandit (rather than a selfish or refereeing or benevolent dictator), maximising growth and tax revenues to achieve military power and reward allies.
72  See Table 5.2.
73  Davies 1989; Gregory 2004.
74  Nove 1972, p. 209.
75  Ibid., p. 205.
76  Gregory 2004.
77  Eloranta and Harrison 2010. See Table 6.5.
78  Davies 1989; Davis 1999.
79  Gershenkron 1966a, p. 148.
80  Gregory 1994.
81  Much of the data used in this appendix are, unless otherwise specified, derived from the Annex Tables.
82  Mitsuhaya 1958; Allen 1965; Ohkawa and Rosovsky 1978; Yamamoto 1993a.

83 Lockwood 1965b.
84 Landes 1965, p. 111.
85 Ohkawa and Rosovsky 1965; Nakamura 1997; Samuels 1994, ch. 2; Crawcour 1997.
86 See Annex Tables plus Tables 5.2 and Table 8.4 for data sources for this paragraph.
87 Crisp 1978; Ohkawa 1957.
88 That is, using the shift-share analysis in the appendix to Chapter 6, the rise in manufacturing output per head of population is more than wholly accounted for by the rise in manufacturing's share of the labour force, multiplied by the 1860 productivity level in manufacturing.
89 Crafts 1985.
90 Ohkawa and Rosovsky 1978.
91 Bairoch 1989, p. 157.
92 Kindelberger 1989; Macpherson 1987; Allen 1962.
93 Yamamura 1977, 1978.
94 Anchordoguy 2001, pp. 505, 510–11.
95 Mitsuhaya 1958, p. 375.
96 Crawcour 1997, p. 16; Harada 1993; Masuda 1993; Millward 2005; Mitchell 2003c; Valdaliso 1996; Wray 1984.
97 Harada 1993; Aoki 1993; Macpherson 1987 p. 27; Yamamoto 1993a.
98 Smith 1955; Allen 1962; Yamamura 1977, 1978.
99 Samuels 1994; Allen 1962.
100 Yamamura 1977.
101 Allen 1962, p. 34.
102 Oshima 1965; Allen 1965.
103 Oshima 1965, p. 376. Our data in Tables 5.7 and 7.2 indicate that defence and debt interest in Germany exceeded such levels in some decades as they did Russia at least in terms of the share of central government spending.
104 Eloranta and Harrrison 2010; Macpherson 1987. Cf. Table 6.5.
105 Mitchell 2003c data for GNP and Oshima 1965 data for spending.
106 Mitchell's data (2003c) on revenues seem to include the *gross* revenues of state enterprises with gross operating expenses included in expenditures. Comparing these figures with Oshima 1965 suggests that surpluses were about one-fifth of gross revenues and therefore equivalent to 66 per cent of central government tax revenues in 1910 and 167 per cent in 1939.

# 8 The costs of being first

Britain 1870–1939

## Strategic policy instruments and the business sector in the defence of Britain

The British economy was at its apogee at the start of this period. A worldwide empire defended by a huge navy was underwritten by a higher level of income and of industrialisation than any other country. It appeared also to be different in being wedded to free entry to markets both at home and abroad. In the event, when its rulers were tested, as the other major powers had been, they behaved no differently. The crucial factors, both of which stemmed from Britain being the first to industrialise, were the cataclysmic decline in its share of world output and exports of manufactured goods and, second, the cesspits of disease and desperate living conditions which had accompanied rapid urbanisation. By the 1930s local government was deeply involved in the delivery of health and education services with central government closely monitoring and regulating key sectors of the economy and with all the ingredients in place for the state to shortly become the major supplier of energy, steel and transport.

Defence was the major concern of the central government in the nineteenth century and military strength was closely linked to industrial strength. Because of its leadership in manufacturing and mining, Britain could rely on its private business sector to provide the naval and army equipment to match other countries. In coal, shipping and submarine telegraph, the key strategic sectors of international trade and communications, Britain initially dominated the world. There were some sectors where the state felt the need for security of supplies and it therefore actively participated in the production of armaments, warships, airlines and oil. Relative to their income levels, the nations of Continental Europe tended to spend more than Britain on defence and were more directly involved in coal mining, railways, telegraph and indeed manufacturing, stemming from their geo-political position and from the extent to which, for much of the nineteenth century, they lagged behind Britain industrially. Earlier chapters emphasised the importance of hostile neighbours on the borders of France, Germany and Russia and that new nation states were keen to promote internal unification (Belgium, Italy, Germany). Land battles were important and the major powers had considerably more military personnel than Britain (Table 8.1). As an island economy, united with Ireland since 1800,

Britain had no contiguous hostile nations. Its main enemies were "overseas" and growing as the empire stretched across Asia and Africa. Naval power was the key and this plus other dimensions of military strength depended on the state of the economy and its endowment of coal and iron ore. The significance of the economy lay not in Britain having the highest income levels for much of the nineteenth century but in the degree of industrialisation: its manufacturing output per head of population in 1860 more than three times that of France and Germany (cf. Table 5.4). It had 633,000 tons of warships by 1870, bigger than France and Germany combined, thereby already satisfying the two navy rule that became popular in the years leading up to the First World War (WWI): British naval power should exceed the combined forces of the two next most powerful nations. It also had a massive merchant fleet whose size right up to the 1930s exceeded the combined tonnages of France, Germany, Japan and Russia. In times of war both vessels and seamen could be transferred into useful supplies for the navy.

The relatively small army did not mean small defence expenditure. It totalled £21.5 million in 1870 with army expenditure bigger than the navy. As Table 8.2 shows, this was over 30 per cent of all public spending on goods and services rising to nearly 40 per cent by 1913 with much of the increase spent on the navy.

*Table 8.1* Military and naval development of the major powers[a] 1870–1937 (military personnel in '000; warships and merchant fleet in '000 net tons)[b]

|  | France | Germany | Japan | Russia | UK | USA |
|---|---|---|---|---|---|---|
| *Military personnel* | | | | | | |
| 1870 | 454 | 410 | n.a. | 716 | 345 | 47 |
| 1910 | 769 | 891 | n.a. | 1352 | 576 | 127 |
| 1929 | 666 | 115 | 284 | 1285 | 443 | 249 |
| 1937 | 825 | 766 | 957 | 1324 | 645 | 288 |
| *Warships* | | | | | | |
| 1870 | 457 | 42 | n.a. | 363 | 633 | 175 |
| 1910 | 725 | 964 | n.a. | 401 | 2174 | 824 |
| 1929 | 406 | 157 | 618 | 401 | 1269 | 721 |
| 1937 | 552 | 281 | 874 | 267 | 1211 | 1099 |
| *Merchant fleet* | | | | | | |
| 1870 | 1072 | 939 | 16[c] | 260[d] | 5691 | 3438[c] |
| 1910 | 1452 | 2890 | 1234[c] | 723[d] | 11,556 | 6555[c] |
| 1929 | 2007 | 2502 | 3862[c] | 437 | 12,369 | 14,887[c] |
| 1937 | 1664 | 2370 | n.a. | 1254 | 10,553 | 12,382[c] |

Source: Mitchell 2003a, b and c; Wright 1942, Appendix XXII.

Notes

a Contemporary boundaries.

b The entries for warships include colonial navies and cover all vessels in use, including wooden vessels. Military personnel covers only those actively enlisted (not reservists and those inactive) and includes troops of the colonies.

c Gross tonnage. For Japan the data refer to all non-wooden vessels owned by Japanese citizens.

d Excludes vessels less than 25 tons and all Finland. The 1870 entry relates to 1872.

Table 8.2  Defence, public spending and national income in the UK 1870–1938[a] (£ million)

| | 1870 | 1890 | 1913 | 1929 | 1938 |
|---|---|---|---|---|---|
| A Defence | 21 | 32 | 72 | 110 | 353 |
| B Other public spending on goods and services[b] | 42 | 72 | 122 | 448 | 592 |
| C Debt interest | 30 | 30 | 30 | 310 | 220 |
| D Other government cash transfers[c] | 10 | 10 | 10 | 200 | 300 |
| E GDP | 1120 | 1460 | 2520 | 4730 | 5570 |
| Defence as % public spending on goods and services A/(A+B) | 33.3 | 30.8 | 37.1 | 19.7 | 37.4 |
| Defence as % GDP (A/E) | 1.9 | 2.2 | 2.9 | 2.3 | 6.3 |
| Defence plus debt interest as % public spending (A+C)/(A+B+C+D) | 49.5 | 43.0 | 43.6 | 39.4 | 39.1 |
| Defence plus debt interest as % GDP (A+C)/E) | 4.6 | 4.2 | 4.1 | 8.9 | 10.3 |

Sources: Mitchell 1988; Feinstein 1972.

Notes
a  Public spending includes local and central government.
b  Mainly education, sanitation, health, roads and housing.
c  Mainly poor relief, pensions, subsidies and education grants.

It has been estimated that Britain spent £1.18 per head of population annually 1870–1913, a higher level than all the major powers.[1] Allowing for differences in average income levels reveals however a different picture. Defence spending rose consistently from 1.9 per cent of national income in 1870 to 6.3 per cent by 1938, dipping only in the 1920s. As we showed in Chapter 6 (Table 6.5) the UK devoted 2.6 per cent of national income over the whole period 1870–1913, less than the other major powers and over the next peacetime period, 1920–38, the UK again comes out at the lower end at 3.8 per cent compared to Germany 3.3 per cent, France 4.3 per cent, Japan 5.7 per cent and Russia 7.1 per cent. On the other hand Britain did not emerge from its wars in a sound financial position. After the Napoleonic Wars Britain had a national debt of £834 million, twice the level of national income and repaid through regressive indirect taxes. Throughout the period to 1939, annual debt interest accounted for over one-half of government spending on transfers. Adding this to defence spending yields annual outlays of nearly 50 per cent of public spending in 1870, a share that fell only to about 40 per cent in the inter-war period (Table 8.2).[2]

What was the role of the business sectors? The days of mercenary armies were nearly over, given the rise of strong nation states, but that still left several options. As compared to the situation in Continental Europe Britain had more of a voluntary "standing" than a "national" army with recruitment for the King's shilling the classic form for overseas battle and short service terms for those stationed at home. Compulsion was avoided but higher pay was needed for volunteers so that some citizens (especially taxpayers) felt the "burden" was higher with the British system. The wide imperial brief also raised costs and played a part in the figure for the annual costs per annum of £100 per man in the 1870s as compared to £41 for France and £29 in Germany. The production pattern in armaments, railways, telegraph and other strategic goods and services also revealed big differences between Britain and elsewhere. In all countries a bare minimum of armament factories and naval dockyards was maintained. On the Continent, as we have seen, geo-political factors led to state owned mines, railways and metallurgy. In Germany it was concentrated in sensitive border areas like Silesia and the Saar whilst railway finance, route layout and construction were strongly planned and sometimes operated by government in France, Russia, Belgium and Italy. As an island economy with a highly developed industry Britain had few of these worries. It did have its Royal Naval Dockyards (at Portsmouth and elsewhere) and armaments factories (the Woolwich arsenal) and the Post Office was a government department. It could in emergencies call on world leading private companies like Vickers. The Admiralty in the 1870s was each year ordering some 30,000 tons of new warships from the royal dockyards but similar orders were being placed also in the private yards, like those in Glasgow. In the 1890s and 1900s as the threat of war approached, orders for the royal dockyards rose to 70,000 tons per annum but for the private yards even more so, such that during WW1 it was the private yards, switching in a major way from building commercial vessels to warships, that met the bulk of the war requirements, dealing with orders that had risen to over 200,000 tons per annum.[3]

By that stage of course airlines and oil had entered as new strategic instruments. The government took shares, in the early twentieth century, in the Anglo-Persian Oil company which itself held shares in the Turkish Petroleum Company and from these beginnings did British Petroleum emerge with part government ownership. Airspace and airlines were, from the beginning, of strategic concern for all governments, and especially one like Britain which was in the inter-war period still a major power and concerned to forge strong links with its colonies. It was one of the signatories of the 1919 Paris Air Convention which granted sovereign rights to airspace (analogous to oil underground). The embryonic domestic airline industry was unstable, there were several bankruptcies so we find the government subsidising the largest private airline serving domestic and Continental routes, British Airways, and the Imperial Airways Company on its colonial links. In 1940 the two were absorbed and merged into a new state enterprise, the British Overseas Aircraft Corporation. Part of the latter was hived off as British European Airways in 1946 but both were merged into British Airways in 1975.[4] An interesting footnote to all this is Ireland which had been absorbed into the UK in 1800 but was always something of a strategic worry. What emerged, in complete contrast to everything else, was that the British government from the 1870s set up a Public Works Loan Board and to the end of promoting "economic progress", provided loans for railway companies, established fish curing stations and built Colleges quite apart from schemes for improving roads and harbours. Almost as a defensive echo, in the 1920s, the new separate Irish Free State itself immediately set up a state sector with a very wide industrial coverage, to show it could perform better than the faltering economy it had left.

Internal communications did not raise the same problems in Britain as on the Continent. With a trunk network of railways already built by 1850 and no contiguous hostile states, lines to Southampton were, apparently, the only strategic worry and in 1912–14 the Liberal government covertly subsidised lines along this route.[5] Otherwise Britain's main strategic concerns were the empire and financial channels for the City. The case of the telegraph reveals the factors prompting state intervention. The electric telegraph was regarded throughout Europe as a security risk and the domestic service was absorbed in the Post Office in 1868 followed by the telephone in 1907. For international telegraphs the submarine cables were important since the overland cables were unsafe. As suggested in Chapter 3, cables speeded up diplomatic links, were especially suited for communications in numerical form (like the City's commercial transactions) and became a vital form of communications for the army in times of war as was the radio later for ship to shore transmissions. The importance and vulnerability of the submarine cable was demonstrated most forcibly at the start of WWI when the allies quickly and easily cut the German Atlantic cables and linked the ends to their own systems. Prior to that, in the nineteenth century, both Germany and France were heavily dependent on the use of British owned cables. Some indication of the strength of the British position comes from an estimate that, in 1911, to isolate countries like Egypt and South Africa from telegraph connections would require five cable cuttings for each country. For the UK the figure was 49.[6]

International submarine cables involved strong natural monopoly elements which stemmed from the huge investment needed (and very much "sunken") in charting a route, employing massive ships and winches to load, reel and lay the cable and in harnessing ships for the repair, rescue and maintenance needed through the life of the cable.[7] Initially one cable to USA might have sufficed for Europe's commercial demands. Others might be competitive but essentially duplicates (abstracting that is, from national security considerations). These natural monopoly conditions did not stem from any need for governments to facilitate rights of way since the ocean bed was unused space. The only rights needed were for landing and here USA was important in its attempt to refuse landing rights in USA to companies whose home government restricted access on home territory to indigenous enterprises (cf. France). Although rising demand eventually generated incentives for the development of competitive lines, the above economic and technological characteristics of the telegraph did lead, indirectly, to another form of monopolisation, namely the dominance of the British companies and this stemmed, first, from Britain being initially the only country with the industry and capital to promote submarine cables.[8] They required strong shipping support and shipping itself required coal. In the nineteenth century, as Table 8.3 shows, Britain was supremely dominant in both respects. As late as 1892 its coal output vastly exceeded the rest of Europe combined as did its steam merchant shipping fleet. Fremdling has provided us with a very clear picture of Britain's domination of the output and trade in coal with its exporting ships spreading all across Europe's Atlantic, North Sea and Baltic coastlines, reaching via river transport far inland to Paris, Berlin and beyond.[9] Second, as argued in Chapter 3, the far flung British Empire had many strategic outposts and land areas (Malta, Alexandria, Aden, Karachi, Ireland, Newfoundland, Cape Town, Durban) so that it was much better placed for landing rights than were other countries. It also was careful to maintain good relations with Portugal since Lisbon, Cape Verde and the Azores were key staging posts for the Atlantic.[10] Following the establishment in the 1860s of a submarine route to India, 1870 saw the completion of a mainly overland cable by a British owned company (the Indo-European Telegraph Company) through Germany, Russia, Armenia and Iraq to India. Round the Cape routes followed as did a Caribbean network and lines to Brazil, and by 1892 British firms accounted for nearly two-thirds of the 221,000 kilometres of cables in the world and 45 per cent was the business of the Eastern Telegraph Company group. Of the 41 cable laying ships in 1894, 28 were British.[11] Even in the 1890s, the companies and governments of France, Germany, Russia and Japan together owned only 24,000 kilometres of international cables, that is, no more than 15 per cent of the British total.

Despite the dominant part played by one firm and despite the strategic issues involved, the British government's regulation was extremely light. It did support British companies by providing marine surveys and sometimes guaranteed rates of return on invested capital, often in return for favourable rates for government

Table 8.3 Strategic instruments in the major powers: cables, shipping, rail track and coal 1892

| | UK | Germany | France | Russia | Japan | USA |
|---|---|---|---|---|---|---|
| Coal output ('000 metric tons) | 184,704 | 92,350[a] | 26,179 | 6950 | 3176 | 162,686 |
| *Merchant shipping (net registered capacity in '000 metric tons)* | | | | | | |
| Sail | 3080 | 986 | 407 | 323 | n.a. | 2172 |
| Steam | 4565 | 696 | 409 | 206 | n.a. | 2016 |
| Total | 7645 | 1682 | 816 | 529 | 102 | 2188 |
| *International telegraph cables (length in kilometres)* | | | | | | |
| Companies | 155,814[b] | 0 | 13,427 | 0 | 0 | 38,987 |
| Governments | 7804[b] | 1541[b] | 8432[b] | 524 | 0 | 0 |
| Total | 163,618[b] | 1541[b] | 21,859[b] | 524 | 0 | 38,987 |
| *Railway density and spread track mileage open* | | | | | | |
| Per 1000 square miles | 197[c] | 132 | 105 | 2.5 | 12 | 56 |
| Per million population | 527[c] | 546 | 565 | 204[d] | 48 | 2612 |

Source: Millward 2011b

Notes
a Includes 20,978,000 metric tons of brown coal.
b Includes all imperial links.
c Britain, i.e. excluding all Ireland.
d 1897.

traffic. Also, despairing of private British companies crossing the Pacific, the government eventually joined up in 1902 with the Canadian, Australian and New Zealand governments to set up a cross-Pacific link in the form of the Pacific Cable Board. Shortly afterwards, a new private company, the Commercial Pacific Cable Company, was formed which promised competition on the Pacific routes but even here the reality was rather different in that half the shares were owned by the Eastern Telegraph Company group which enforced high tariff rates so that its African–Asian cables were not strongly challenged.

So the British government intervened with a very light touch. This was not because there no market failures – the monopolistic elements were there, leading one Member of Parliament to declare he knew "no monopoly in the world that is doing more injury to trade than the concentrated companies represented in the Eastern Telegraph Company".[12] Nor was the light touch due to the British government's ideological commitment to laissez-faire. There were security issues but the government had little to worry about because the industry (and the same was true of radio early on since Marconi had British nationality) was dominated by British firms whose cables could be readily commandeered in times of crises. As early as 1862 the government had set up, as noted in Chapter 3, a Joint Committee on Submarine Cables with representatives from the Atlantic Telegraph Company and the Board of Trade. For the time being informal links were enough. The underlying issues were revealed once Britain lost its dominant position in the 1920s by which time German, French and American cable capacity had developed considerably (Table 8.4). The British government then promoted and subsidised the establishment of two companies. One was Cable and Wireless, a holding company with shares in the Eastern Telegraph Company group and also in Marconi. Second, there was Imperial and International Communications Ltd, consisting of operations in the Post Office's non-domestic radio and cable assets, the Pacific Cable Board, the Eastern Telegraph system and the Marconi system. Then in 1938 the Treasury acquired £2.6 million shares in Cable and Wireless. In 1944 there was an agreement with all Commonwealth countries that all telecommunications companies with international commitments should be publicly owned and in 1946 the Treasury acquired the remaining £27.4 million shares, followed in 1950 by the transfer of all Cable and Wireless assets to the Post Office.[13]

## Government and business investment in the urban infrastructure

Apart from national defence, there were two main factors that brought government intervention in the economy, both linked to Britain being the first industrial nation. One was that Britain was so far ahead in the early nineteenth century that it dominated world industrial exports and the business sector set a technological lead that strengthened Britain's relative military standing. Once it lost that lead the central government started to intervene in the economy. Those issues are considered in the next two sections of this chapter. Attention now is directed to

*Table 8.4* Strategic instruments: cables, shipping, rail track and coal 1923

| | UK[a] | Germany | France | Russia (USSR) | Japan | USA |
|---|---|---|---|---|---|---|
| Coal output ('000 metric tons) | 280,430 | 180,474[b] | 38,566 | 12,700[c] | 29,106[d] | 596,841 |
| *Merchant shipping (net registered capacity in '000 metric tons)* | | | | | | |
| Sail | 263 | 288 | 386 | n.a. | n.a. | 1254[e] |
| Steam | 10,987 | 1546 | 1759 | n.a. | n.a. | 15,821[e] |
| Total | 11,250 | 1834 | 2145 | 413[f] | 3361[e] | 17,075[e] |
| *International telegraph cables (length in kilometres)* | | | | | | |
| Companies | 251,592[g] | n.a.[h] | 33,399 | 0 | 0 | 136,146 |
| Governments | 46,210[g] | n.a.[h] | 31,544 | 2683 | 14,463 | 6475 |
| Total | 297,802[g] | n.a.[h] | 64,933 | 2683 | 14,463 | 142,621 |
| *Railway density and spread* | | | | | | |
| *Track mileage open* | | | | | | |
| Per 1000 square miles | 222 | 207 | 123 | 6 | 61 | 83 |
| Per million population | 473 | 572 | 654 | 320 | 172 | 2235 |

Source: Millward 2011b.

Notes

a  Excludes S. Ireland.
b  Includes 118,249,000 metric tons of brown coal.
c  Includes 2,176,000 metric tons of brown coal.
d  Includes 157,000 metric tons of brown coal.
e  Gross tonnage.
f  1921.
g  Includes all imperial links.
h  German cables out of action, status undefined.

the second factor: early rapid industrialisation led to a massive growth of town populations which called for the participation of business and government in providing a new urban infrastructure and dealing with the appalling living conditions which emerged in Victorian Britain.[14] The mantle of responsibility for collective action fell in this case on local government. The UK central government left matters to "self-help", to local councils. Businesses, both private and municipal, were involved in building up the new environment, providing residential property, sewerage and other sanitation, constructing roads and supplying gas, water, electricity and tramway services. From the point of view of central government there were no strategic issues involved but it soon came to realise that several problems, like public health and monopoly power, could not be kept within local boundaries so legislative support followed.

The appalling living conditions of Victorian Britain have been well portrayed in novels and commentaries from Toynbee, Mrs Gaskell, Engels and Dickens onwards. They stemmed from the distinctive economic character of Britain's early industrial spurt which was not so much a matter of productivity growth as a massive shift to factory urban industry from agriculture which counted for less than 30 per cent of the labour force by 1840. Even when other countries reached Britain's 1840 income levels they still had 50 per cent more of their workforce in rural areas. Even though France and Germany, for example, experienced rapid urban growth not too long afterwards, it was Britain which first had to address the issues in a context where income levels, during the classic industrial revolution period 1760–1840, had barely risen, if at all. Hence in that period investment in local infrastructure was pitifully small with the urban capital stock growing at only 0.24 per cent per annum 1800–60, about one-third of the growth of all fixed capital.[15] Three forms of intervention followed. One was public investment in sewers, street scavenging, water supplies and other sanitary services. In addition part of the new infrastructure took the form of public enterprises in areas like electricity and gas supply. Third, there was government involvement in residential housing, mainly in the form of regulation in the nineteenth century but with direct provision in the twentieth. In none of these services was there a state monopoly. On the one hand it was not "the state" but rather local government that was involved. Nor were whole economic sectors taken over – at least in the sense that the private sector flourished in construction work, in the ownership of much of the housing stock and in running local utilities in gas, electricity and tramways. Town planning as such hardly existed and, as many historians put it, conflicts were often resolved by "property interests" – as in the railways where companies fought for access to towns, land and routes. Central government reluctantly became involved in a regulatory capacity for three reasons. The health hazard was not a private matter: cholera epidemics affected everyone, infectious diseases spread to leafy Fallowfield suburbs where the Manchester mill owners set up home whilst, in London, Members of Parliament, in session, could smell the Thames. Second, the new utilities needed rights of way – railways and water pipes across country, gas pipes and tramlines in towns – and, since local government often did not have the legal authority, it was left for rights to be granted by an Act of Parliament. Since such rights effectively gave some monopoly power, at least in the short run, that meant legislation had to specify controls on prices and profits, service quality, route configuration as well as for the engineering and financial soundness of the companies. Finally these sectors were often very capital intensive, "blind capital" would not be forthcoming so many companies sought limited liability status from Parliament. That reinforced the position of large companies since the smaller ones often could not afford the transactions cost of seeking Parliamentary approval.

In the early 1870s annual investment by local government averaged £7.4 million (at 1900 prices). Adding in private investment in housing and other local infrastructure yields a total of some £40 million or 36 per cent of all UK investment (see Table 8.5). Railway investment was declining at the end of the nineteenth century but was more than offset by rising investment in the urban infrastructure. Local authority annual investment then rose to over £40 million by the early 1900s. Neither did local government outsource this work. Building work was undertaken by the private sector but the new sewer, roads and other sanitary services, together with housing from the 1920s, were run by the local authorities who had to finance this largely out of their own resources. The local property tax (the "rates") accounted in England and Wales in 1868 for two-thirds of local authority revenues (excluding trading and borrowing) which also paid

*Table 8.5* Local government and UK investment 1870–1910 (annual average gross domestic fixed capital formation in £ millions at 1900 prices)

|  | *Local government* | *Dwellings* | *Other local infrastructure* | *Rest of economy*[a] | *Total* |
|---|---|---|---|---|---|
| 1871–75 | 7.4 | 24.1 | 8.2 | 71.7 | 111.4 |
| 1876–80 | 15.3 | 28.6 | 6.7 | 71.8 | 122.4 |
| 1881–85 | 9.0 | 23.3 | 0.8 | 82.4 | 115.4 |
| 1886–90 | 11.4 | 21.2 | 6.5 | 69.0 | 108.1 |
| 1891–95 | 19.3 | 23.9 | 10.3 | 75.2 | 128.7 |
| 1896–1900 | 27.6 | 38.1 | 13.2 | 104.8 | 183.8 |
| 1901–05 | 41.2 | 40.6 | 15.2 | 125.6 | 222.3 |
| 1906–10 | 25.2 | 30.0 | 15.9 | 105.8 | 176.9 |

Source: Feinstein 1972; Feinstein and Pollard 1988.

Notes

a Covers manufacturing, mining, quarrying, agriculture, railways, shipping, distribution and other services.

Local infrastructure is defined as gas, water and electricity supplies, transport and communications (excluding railways and shipping) and all public and social services and hence includes some central government investment, such as that by the Post Office in telecommunications, but this was very small. The figures for local government were based on those at current prices in Feinstein (1972) and converted to constant 1900 prices by assuming the local authority share of local infrastructure spending (excluding housing) at constant prices was the same as the share at current prices. There is an element of double counting from the small amounts spent by local authorities on housing which appear in both the first and second columns; the offset is a small underestimate of "other local infrastructure" in the third column which is calculated residually.

for poor relief. In Scotland it was just over one-half. Help came in the inter-war period from central government grants but throughout 1870–1939, local authorities were under strong financial pressure.[16]

The first question which arises is why sanitary services were not only financed but also directly supplied by local government. It seems a private sector barely existed. Whether such services might be financed by local government but provided by outside firms was discussed as early as the 1840s. In this case however it was not so much a matter of "outsourcing" an existing service, to use a modern phrase, as one of introducing new systems to the rapidly expanding towns. So frustrated was Edwin Chadwick that he planned in 1845 to establish the Town Improvement Company to supply services on contracts for local governments. Nothing came of it and the official view of the central government General Board of Health later was that there were not enough suitable contractors around. This service, urban drainage and sewerage, was in its infancy, and explains one of the other puzzles. Sewer technology and knowledge of optimal treatment of waste were areas of great uncertainty and the boundaries of the relevant local authorities often did not coincide with the relevant drainage areas: thus Manchester Corporation was gradually absorbing outer local government units in the basins of the Irwell and Mersey in the last decades of the nineteenth century. Alongside all this was the general slow progress in establishing governmental powers in these service areas. It was not until the early 1870s and in particular the 1875 Public Health Act that clear sanitary districts were defined and an obligation placed on local authorities to ensure good quality water supply and related public services.

A second issue is to account for the incidence and geographic spread of private and municipal enterprises (see Table 8.6). The 1875 Public Health Act *required* local authorities to ensure that adequate water supplies existed. The water supply undertakings also developed soft water and a fire-fighting capability for factory owners. Why, though, was water municipalised? Already by 1875 there were 103 water supply undertakings run by the corporations of new municipal boroughs. Municipal enterprises in gas, electricity and tramways were generally profitable but whilst water supply made large operating surpluses these were usually not enough to meet loan charges. Rather than profit, the aim seemed geared more to expanding supplies of clean water for residents as required by the Act, and municipal water supplies were generally organised and financed more like paving, refuse collection, cemeteries, bathhouses and other sanitary services.

Why not use private sector contracts? Some have argued that the large-scale schemes for taking water supplies to the new urban conurbations involved levels of finance and a degree of planning beyond the scope of private enterprise.[17] The investment requirements of the Rivington Pike scheme for Liverpool in the 1840s and the later one for Vyrnwy in Wales, the Loch Katrine project for Glasgow in the 1850s and the Thirlmere and Longdendale schemes for Manchester in the 1870s and 1880s were certainly substantial. But private enterprise had laid a route network for railways in the 1830s and 1840s equivalent to our

*Table 8.6* Number of statutory local utility undertakings in the UK 1871–1938[a]

| | Electricity | | Trams | | Gas | | Water | | |
|------|------|------|------|------|------|------|------|--------|------|
| | PR | LG | PR | LG | PR | LG | PR | MUNIC[b] | LG |
| 1871 | – | – | n.a. | n.a. | 255 | 75 | n.a. | n.a. | 250[c] |
| 1875 | n.a. | n.a. | 37[d] | 7[d] | 269[e] | 103[e] | n.a. | 127 | n.a. |
| 1879 | n.a. | n.a. | 51 | 9 | n.a. | n.a. | n.a. | n.a. | n.a. |
| 1885 | n.a. | n.a. | 129 | 27 | 364 | 160 | n.a. | 195 | n.a. |
| 1890 | n.a. | n.a. | 127 | 29 | 416 | 178 | n.a. | n.a. | n.a. |
| 1895 | 52 | 39 | 116 | 38 | 429 | 203 | n.a. | 237 | n.a. |
| 1900 | 65 | 164 | 114 | 99 | 453 | 240 | n.a. | n.a. | n.a. |
| 1905 | n.a. | n.a. | 136 | 175 | 482 | 270 | n.a. | 306 | n.a. |
| 1914 | n.a. | n.a. | 108 | 171 | 519 | 312 | 200 | 326 | 820[c] |
| 1926 | 233 | 360 | 71 | 170 | 463 | 321 | n.a. | n.a. | n.a. |
| 1934 | n.a. | n.a. | n.a. | n.a. | 412 | 314 | 173 | n.a. | 878 |
| 1938 | 208 | 373 | n.a. | n.a. | 405 | 298 | n.a. | n.a. | n.a. |

Source: Millward 2000.

Notes

a PR is the private sector, LG are local authorities, including all joint boards. The data for trams refer to the ownership of track, for electricity, to undertakings supplying electricity for light or power. S. Ireland is included before 1920.

b Undertakings owned by the corporations of municipal boroughs.

c Data probably exclude S. Ireland.

d 1876.

e 1874.

modern motorway network and the later work on lines linking the outer reaches of Wales and Scotland involved even more costly outlays on bridges, viaducts and tunnels. Rather, one might point to the institutional difficulties in the way of companies earning sufficient profit to expand supplies at a rate demanded by town councils. That is, water supply is obviously dependent on natural resources and hence, like agriculture, is liable to diminishing returns. Unless significant technical progress in storage and delivery takes place, expansion will lead to rising costs. Clearly this happened in the nineteenth century as the demands from rapid urban population growth and industrialisation exhausted the more obvious local supplies and towns had to look further afield. Estimates for 1820–1900 suggests that in London costs per thousand gallons rose by 30 per cent from 3d to 4d.[18] Relative to the prices of all other goods and services, most of which were falling, the real cost of water may have risen by about 50 per cent in the nineteenth century. For the companies to make a normal rate of return, water charges would have had to rise accordingly and large numbers of customers captured in order to exploit the economies of scale and contiguity central to keeping costs per unit down. This is where the maximum prices specified in the legislation did appear to bite. One contemporary authority suggested the maxima allowed in the 1847 Clauses Act were never high enough for the companies and so they, instead, engaged in protracted legal battles over the valuation of property to which the water rate was applied.[19] Most business customers were metered and many councils dominated by manufacturers had meter schedules which were very generous as was the "compensation" water allowed to factories operating near rivers and reservoirs subject to development in water schemes. None of this meant profit for the water companies. A great attraction of municipal operation was that it involved the finance of water services to households by rates, the tax on rateable values. By such a uniform levy, councils automatically enrolled all ratepayers on to the water undertakings' books.[20] By 1914 there were 820 local authority undertakings, some 200 statutory companies and 1339 non-statutory companies though the local authorities accounted for 80 per cent of the industry's net output. Apart from the sheer number of undertakings and the entrenched position of local authorities there were other interested parties like the Ministry of Health and the Board of Trade and a more sensible river basin structure did not emerge until the 1970s.[21]

For electricity, trams and gas different issues were involved. The trading activities of local government had mushroomed from the mid nineteenth century. Already by 1875 there were 103 municipally owned gas works in England and Wales and 312 by 1914 and the municipalities were then also running over 100 electricity supply systems and 100 tramways. These services were natural monopolies but this problem in principle was dealt with by the Parliamentary legislation which set limits on tariffs and profits. The key to explaining municipal behaviour is the endemic problem of financing the pressing demand for better sanitation and public health. The local authorities had little room for manoeuvre since they had no powers to raise income taxes as in Germany or levy duties on commodities or profits or land. Some grants and assigned revenues emerged from central government in the last decades of the century but, in general, little was done to alleviate the widely differing circumstances of the local authorities.[22] The driving force behind municipalisation was then the desire of local councils to get their hands on the surpluses of these trading enterprises and use them to "relieve the rates". This helps to explain municipalisation in Scotland where in addition the companies were cheap to buy out since the law never gave them the right to operate in perpetuity, as in England and Wales. But if it was paramount why did York, Bournemouth, Salisbury and many others refrain from extensive municipal trading? Why did Liverpool, Bristol and Hull allow private gas companies to flourish? Why did private enterprises flourish more in the south than the north?

It is important to recognise that in the early years of the century, the owners of the private companies – gas only at that stage of course – were often major local ratepayers. Together with bankers, lawyers and other professionals, they would form the local body of Improvement Commissioners or councillors. By the late nineteenth century they were a much more dispersed group as capital came from various sources and the local ratepayers were as likely to be dominated by shopkeepers.[23] In response to the rising demand for expenditures on public health, roads, policing, poor relief, education and other services, ratepayers staged revolts but also they looked for alternative revenue sources.[24] This was Joseph Chamberlain's dictum. Unless a council had substantial property income ("estates"), essential town improvements would be deferred unless some revenue other than rates was found.[25] The ports of Liverpool, Swansea, Bristol, Hull, Great Yarmouth and Southampton all had substantial income from dockside property. Hence the reason why none of these ports municipalised the local gasworks in the nineteenth century. Leeds, Manchester and Birmingham however did not have large estates and looked elsewhere so receipts from markets and gas undertakings were a useful supplement to estates in the early years whilst electricity and trams were even more attractive because the purchase clauses in Parliamentary Acts of 1870 and 1882 meant their acquisition prices would be less than for the gas companies who had unentailed property rights. Mr E. Garcke, that great student of electricity supply developments, managing director of the British Electric Traction Company and champion of the private sector, demonstrated to the Select Committee on Municipal Trading (1903) that most municipal undertakings were being run with a view to profit, and therefore he was opposed to the majority of them.[26]

Of course towns with a good rates base like Bournemouth and Eastbourne would not be under the same pressure to get their hands on trading profits even though their populations were growing. Their "urban" problems were also nothing like those of Darlington and West Bromwich and the other industrial boroughs of the north and Midlands – hence the north/south divide in the incidence of municipalisation. For a town like Chichester or Chester or Norwich, with a stagnant or only slowly growing population the pressures were even less. Some governmental units were not well suited to provide a home for utilities. London was the classic case. The formation of metropolitan undertakings was almost impossible as long as the motley collection of vestries, drainage boards and road authorities persisted. Only when London government was centralised by the 1894 Local Government Act was it possible to set in train the establishment of London County Council Tramways and the Metropolitan Water Board. Another kind of difficulty faced small towns who could ill afford the administrative costs of mounting a Parliamentary Bill needed for municipalisation. Small towns in rural areas were the least likely candidates since utilities thrived most economically in high density conditions and sufficiently large catchment areas would in any case straddle several local government boundaries. Joint municipal concerns did emerge but more common was to leave trams to the private sector and gas supplies were met by companies like East Kent Gas and South Staffordshire Gas.

A final sector where the government was strongly involved was housing. In the years before WWI its role was mainly regulation, with public investment in working class housing less than £0.5 million per annum but this had shot up to £53 million by local government in 1929, over 12 per cent of all UK investment of all kinds. By then middle class home ownership was also on the up such that the housing stock in Britain 1911–51 rose by 60 per cent as against a population increase of only 20 per cent. The quality of the housing proved to be an important determinant of health. By the 1860s mortality levels were about 30 deaths per 1000 population and, following a mid century stagnation, had started to decline. This was well before the major surge in public health investment and goes some way to support McKeown's well-known thesis that rising real incomes, from the 1840s, worked through nutrition levels and rising resistance to disease, to account for a large portion of the "lives saved".[27] The health of mothers was gaining ground rapidly and this augured well for the condition of the foetus but infant mortality remained stubbornly high: in the 1890s nearly one in five babies were dying in their first 12 months in towns like Glasgow, Bradford, Leeds, Cardiff, Preston, Leicester, Nottingham and Dundee. Infectious disease was the killer for all age groups, so that exposure was an important issue, with alleviation potentially coming from better housing and sanitation. House occupancy in Britain improved only moderately 1870–1914 from 5.0 persons per house to 4.5 and there was virtually no public spending on housing. Standards for new housing were rising and there was a plethora of regulations. It seems from studies of cross-section data and time series of mortality, that increases in the housing stock had a major statistical link with the decline of mortality. The housing variable seems to have picked up the closely associated contribution of sanitary services but it was not until after that large surge of investment in the sanitary infrastructure in the 1890s that infant mortality started its long term decline.

There were in fact considerable differences in housing density across Britain. Rents were higher in London but so were wages and the real cost of renting tended sometimes to be higher outside London. Real rents were very high in Glasgow which, given the costs of attaining certain target heating levels, induced thick walls, tenements and considerable overcrowding. The share of the population classed as living in overcrowded conditions was generally higher in Scotland (33 per cent in Edinburgh), lowest in Wales with London at 18 per cent and Leeds and Birmingham at 11 per cent.[28] Construction was an old industry, technical change was slow and there was a strong private business sector. Government was therefore wary of undermining that private building industry and its priority in the nineteenth century was in legislating for standards. Fears stemming from the epidemics of the 1830s and 1840s had prompted legislation for ventilation, drains, width of streets, occupancy of cellars but all of this was facilitating local governments not compelling them, apart from new housing where drains had to be connected to sewers. It was not until the early 1900s that the Local Government Board (a central government supervisory department) could force a local authority to demolish slum property or prohibit back-to-back houses. In the meantime the 1868 Torrens Act allowed medical officers of health to enter houses on their own initiative and permitted local authorities to demand repairs and the demolition of unsanitary dwellings. Then came the Cross Act of 1875 permitting, but again not enforcing, local authorities to demolish whole areas and build houses provided they were sold after ten years. It was not until 1903 that the Local Government Board could force recalcitrant local authorities to implement the Cross Act.

The major form of housing tenure in the nineteenth century (above 90 per cent) was that rented from private landlords who were increasingly pressured by the rise in the property tax (rates) and housing regulation. Some historians have argued landlords lacked a political voice and in the last part of the century their legal powers over tenants were being curtailed. The 1915 Increase of Rent and Mortgage Interest (War Restrictions) Act ruled that tenancies could be restricted for very specific causes, the list of which was extended in the inter-war period thereby giving more security for landlords. The Act also set controls on rent levels, the underlying drive for which was "homes for heroes", a political force which gathered strength after the war. Fears surrounding the social disruptions and revolutionary trends in Germany and Russia seem to have been the main factor behind the change of heart about government policy on housing. The Housing Act of 1919 provided local government with the power to be a major supplier of working class accommodation: not simply in the "plague spots" whose boundaries could not be easily defined but new working class rented "council" housing in the suburbs. Such an approach faced fierce opposition in some quarters and the programme stuttered initially but the 1930s saw a dramatic increase in the number of houses closed or demolished. Council housing, especially the new "model estates" like that in Wythenshawe, Manchester, flourished with subsidies mainly from the local property rate income. They existed alongside a private sector which, with caps on rents and tax relief for mortgages, saw a shift away from private rented accommodation to subsidised middle class home ownership. Both council housing and owner occupation expanded in the 1930s and after the Second World War. In 1938 rented local authority accommodation accounted for 11 per cent of housing rising to 24 per cent by 1961 whilst owner occupation had risen from 35 to 42 per cent. This structure was not to be challenged until the programme for the sale of council houses, at huge discounts, in the 1980s.

## Manufacturing in the first industrial nation

Local government was therefore, by the inter-war period 1919–39, investing strongly in the local infrastructure whilst the central government was increasingly involved in the supply of strategic goods and services like oil, airlines and the telegraph. In the latter sectors, the private business sector was not dominant in world supplies so that to gain some security of supply the government forged close links with the production process. The same thing was to happen in manufacturing and mining which underlay Britain's military and naval strength. For much of the nineteenth century Britain dominated world coal supplies and manufactured exports and felt no need to protect the sectors. By the end of the century, though outputs were still rising, Britain's dominance was being challenged and market shares were falling. The government was drawn in partly because of contemporary diagnoses that British business was not keeping up with the new management methods emerging in USA. Britain's industrial strength, relative to others, was declining yet British industry was not protected like industry in USA and Continental Europe. This was significant because it threatened to undermine Britain's relative military capacity. Also British success was heavily weighted to the classic staples of cotton, coal, shipbuilding and steel, all of which were heavily concentrated geographically, so that loss of markets implied huge structural adjustments involving high unemployment, regionally concentrated and thereby threatening social unity.

It is important therefore to understand the nature of Britain's involvement in world manufacturing and mining and whether there was something missing in its business structure and management, providing thereby an explanation for the form that state intervention took in the inter-war period. In the late nineteenth century the economy was not stagnating. British output of cotton, coal, ships and steel expanded strongly up to WWI with national output growing at nearly 2 per cent per annum and this partly explains why little was done before then. Others however were growing faster and starting to take some of Britain's markets. Figure 8.1 says it all. By the end of the 1930s Britain accounted for one-fifth of world manufactured exports, about the same as Germany and USA and quite commendable for a small island economy. The problem was that this was but one-half of its share in 1880 and the other countries' national output and output per head had been growing faster. In the 1860s Britain's GDP per head and manufacturing output per head were higher than anywhere (cf. Table 5.4). Thereafter both measures grew more slowly in Britain than in Germany and Japan and noticeably in USA which had overtaken the UK's absolute levels by the early 1900s.

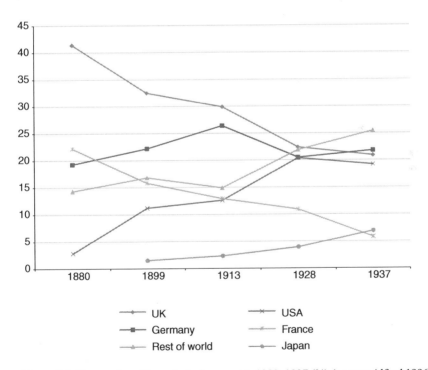

*Figure 8.1* Shares of world manfacturing exports 1880–1937 (%) (source: Alford 1996).

Note
The 1928 data exclude the Netherlands.

The traditional explanation of Britain's relative decline focused on its inability to shift away from an industrial structure characterised by labour intensive methods and small-scale firms.[29] This was the source, so the story went, of the slower growth of productivity and generated a huge literature examining British management methods and even its social structure. Some like Wiener perceived an anti-industrial spirit among Britain's upper classes creating a "cultural cordon sanitaire encircling ... technology, industry and commerce".[30] Others put more stress on the fact that Britain was the first to industrialise and developed a strong manufacturing sector with a large skilled labour force. That sunken technology proved a burden when more capital intensive methods arrived. In cotton the labour intensive "mule" spinning in Lancashire was compared unfavourably to the more capital intensive "ring" spinning in USA using unskilled but still relatively scarce labour in mills which integrated spinning and weaving. Automatic looms were widespread in USA by 1955 but accounted for only 12 per cent of UK cotton weaving. In mining the critique was about the slow rate of mechanisation: only 57 per cent of coal output was mechanically cut by 1937. Prefabricated shipping came to Japan and several other countries by the inter-war period but not until the 1960s in Britain. The story was little different for the car industry where body-shops, assembly lines and automatic transfer machines all came rather late. Britain instead, it was claimed, clung to labour intensive "craft" methods and the slow transition to more capital intensive methods was due to the presence of family firms unwilling to adopt American mass production methods. Hence yarn output man hour in cotton spinning, yarn output per man in mining etc., were lower in the UK. Single owner single product firms unwilling to expand the equity base were common in coal and cotton. Those large companies which did exist were often holding companies, providing financial links rather than integrating production like the American multiproduct multinationals.[31] The latter used assembly lines for homogeneous commodities, extensive marketing activity, strong managerial hierarchies with well developed training schemes for managers both in-house and in the growing number of business schools.

This diagnosis came open to several lines of attack. One was to point to counter examples of successful British family firms like Sainsbury's and Rowntrees, successful American family firms like Ford and British firms using mass production techniques like Lever brothers for soap. After all, the most successful sector in Britain in the twentieth century was financial services where family firms flourished (Barings, Rothschilds). Second, recent research suggests that though there were many unincorporated businesses in Britain, many of them were joint stock companies with transferable shares and limited liability and the stereotype small family firm was probably less common than was once thought.[32] There was, third, a return to the importance of factor endowments in Britain and USA.[33] That is, once one has allowed for America's abundance of land and other natural resources, there is very little left to explain. In cotton for example capital intensive ring spinning and integrated mills were not especially profitable in Britain. The major problem was competition from the low wage Far East, especially Japan. America avoided this by tariff protection of its cotton indus-try.[34] In the case of coal, output per man was 50 per cent higher in USA in 1909 but it had very large reserves of high quality coal, seams were thicker and more accessible. Quantitative estimates of these differences have been estimated to account for all the differences in output per man.[35]

Finally recent research by Broadberry suggests manufacturing did not play the overwhelming role it has often been given in accounts of Britain's relative decline and that the major differences in productivity growth across the countries of the Western world over the nineteenth and twentieth centuries lay outside the manufacturing sector.[36] National income per head was, of course, higher in Britain than elsewhere in the early nineteenth century – possibly of the order of 30 per cent higher than USA in 1820, and much higher than Germany. What is now clear is that, in manufacturing, output per employee was significantly higher in USA even at this early date. This means that the American superiority pre-ceded much of the development of managerial capitalism which Chandler (1990), Lazonick (1991) and others have invoked as the key to the success of USA. Moreover the comparative position in labour productivity across the man-ufacturing sectors of Britain, USA and indeed Germany, once it industrialised, did not significantly change over the 100 or so years from 1870. What did change were the non-manufacturing parts of the economy.

Table 8.7 indicates that output per head in manufacturing in USA was double that of the UK in 1870 and Broadberry has shown that the American lead existed in the early part of the century. This comparative productivity performance was remarkably stable over the long term. In the 1930s it was still the case that the USA figure was double that in the UK. In Germany there is not quite the same stability but labour productivity in manufacturing was about 10 per cent higher than in Britain in the 1870s and the 1930s; this was also the margin for total factor productivity. This stability was experienced against a backcloth of

*Table 8.7* Manufacturing productivity and capital intensity in UK, Germany and USA 1870–1937 (UK=100)

|  | *1870*[a] | *1889* | *1913* | *1929* | *1937* |
|---|---|---|---|---|---|
| *USA* | | | | | |
| Output per man | 204 | 196 | 209[b] | 250 | 208 |
| Capital per man | 94 | 159 | 183[b] | 173 | 151 |
| Total factor productivity | 205 | 174 | 180[b] | 218 | 235 |
| *Germany* | | | | | |
| Output per man | 100 | 95 | 119 | 105 | 100 |
| Capital per man | 60 | 71 | 105 | 67 | 73 |
| Total factor productivity | 116 | 105 | 117 | 118 | 120 |

Source: Broadberry 1993.

Notes
a The USA figures relate to 1869 and Germany to 1875.
b 1909.

considerable changes in comparative capital intensities. In the early nineteenth century, the capital–labour ratio was much higher in Britain than in Germany as one might expect. It was also however higher than USA. By the late nineteenth century the figure for USA was nearly double that in Britain though the differences in production methods were by no means straightforward. From the beginning, USA was a great user of natural resources – raw materials, land – and later of specialised resource using machinery. America saved on both labour and capital by using land and other natural resources. Initially it was only in the parts of manufacturing using very skilled labour that substitution by capital was profitable. So Britain and USA used different techniques of production to reflect their differing factor endowments. Technical progress was faster in mass production methods so the American manufacturing sector grew rapidly. The American advantage here also included a relatively homogeneous demand in a big internal market. Hence mass production techniques emerged with great scope for increases in labour productivity. It is in the twentieth century that Britain has come to adopt more capital intensive techniques with a secular trend to approximating the measured American capital intensity by the 1980s.

It is clear then that the large growth in national income per head in the nineteenth century in USA and Germany and, in particular, the process of catching up to Britain, cannot be explained by changes in comparative productivity in manufacturing. Rather it is the non-manufacturing sectors which account for USA overtaking UK national income per head levels by the turn of the century. We shall return to this in the next chapter, simply noting here that the development of transportation and the opening of the prairies was central. In the case of Germany the effects of structural change through the decline in agriculture's share was also important as we explained in Chapter 5. Even so it was not until the 1970s that Germany reached UK income levels. Both World Wars of course played a major role, with the USA gaining considerable relative advantage in these periods.[37]

## State protection and the promotion of structural change in industry

The explanation of state policies towards business in terms of ideological stances, especially in relation to laissez-faire, sees government behaviour as endemically linked to each country's history and culture. Britain in that story flourished under free enterprise in the nineteenth century and that story was underwritten by Adam Smith's embrace of free markets. Yet Britain did see extensive state intervention; it was late in coming but reflected the same pressures that others had to cope with in the nineteenth century. The output of key sectors continued to rise up to WWI with coal and cotton achieving record export levels in 1909–13. After the war, many of the cheaper cotton cloth markets were lost to Japan and India and coal to Poland, Spain and other newcomers. In the end the involvement of the state was massive, mainly through regulation and ownership of industry. The decline in Britain's share of world manufactured output and exports was significant because Britain's relative military strength was a function of its relative industrial strength, especially as compared to Germany and the deficiencies revealed during WWI only exacerbated matters. Moreover domestic unity and peace was threatened by the huge dislocations and unprecedented unemployment levels, regionally concentrated, arising from the fierce competition in the inter-war period from Europe, Japan and USA.

Although in retrospect it is clear that Britain's trading position was declining at the end of the nineteenth century, the absence of significant unemployment and wars meant pressure groups made little headway. Imports had risen from one-eighth the value of exports in 1855 to one-fifth by 1870 and to nearly one-half by 1900. Some economists like Marshall continued to argue that industry needed to be kept on its toes by competition from USA and Germany, that exporters to Britain would find other markets if Britain imposed tariffs and there were no hostile tariffs on the import of British goods vital for economic growth in other countries. A Fair Trade League was established in 1881 but had little effect and the emphasis shifted to providing some preference for Empire goods. This became part of the programme of the Tariff Reform League established in 1903 to protect industry and use customs duty to finance the welfare plans entering party programmes.[38] The League's proposals were modest, great difficulties were met in forming a united business front so that by 1913 there were still no import duties on manufactures, alcohol, wheat and mineral oil. For the rest the tariff averaged 5.6 per cent of import values, lower than most other countries.

Matters changed dramatically in the inter-war period. Direct state intervention in industry took the form of price fixing, bank aid to business, the promotion of larger business units and the more intrusive regulation of utilities. Why these forms of intervention? Here the experience of WWI, the contemporary appeal of the big corporation and the huge disharmony threatened by the very high unemployment levels all played a part. WWI had revealed strategically dangerous shortages in dyestuffs, beet sugar, oil, fertiliser and aircraft and all were protected, subsidised or regulated thereafter. In the production of explosives, poison gas, drugs and photography the UK was perceived to be behind Germany leading eventually to government promotion of Imperial Chemical Industries in 1926.[39] Electricity was becoming a key energy input to industry but was supplied by myriad small enterprises whose merger into networks became an important task of the state in the 1920s. The details of this intervention and of what followed for the railway companies after war time coordination by government will be discussed in detail later in the last section of this chapter. A second factor for the government was that the loss of exports in the 1920s led to British unemployment levels rising earlier than elsewhere and concentrated on the so-called staple industries. As Table 8.8 shows, about one-fifth of the labour force in coal, shipbuilding, iron and steel were already unemployed by 1929. In contrast, output in some sectors like electrical goods, cars, aircraft even silk and rayon expanded by over 50 per cent from 1924 to 1935.[40] Since all these industries tended to be regionally concentrated, huge disparities emerged with unemployment in 1932 in Wales at 36.5 per cent, nearly three times higher than in London and the south-east. Labour would eventually have to leave the staple industries but it required a massive structural change in the economy, impossible in the short run, and therefore constituting a toxic brew of social discontent. The third factor in the government's response was the rise of large business units in parts of electricity and motor cars as technologies and organisational methods changed, buttressed as we have seen by the apparent success of the big assembly lines in America. In Britain the 100 largest firms accounted for only 16 per cent of total employment in 1910, rising to 24 per cent by 1939.[41]

Since much of the intervention was new territory for British governments, the inter-war period policies have been seen as tentative, torn as government was between providing protection for industry and engineering wholesale reconstruction. Many businesses were granted overdrafts in the early 1920s and this involvement with industry was also new territory for British commercial banks, some of which like Williams Deacon came close to bankruptcy. The Bank of England then intervened to underwrite loans, believing as it did in the longevity of the British staple industries, free markets, the gold standard and all the other trappings of the nineteenth century. Bank aid was a short term palliative and the state, in the face of declining prices in industry and agriculture, promoted price fixing agreements. The common law had traditionally frowned on restraints of trade but this stance was disappearing as the Lord Chancellor declared that competition may be undesirable since it "may, if it is not controlled, drive manufacturers out of business, or lower wages and cause labour disturbances".[42] By the end of the 1920s, one-fifth of employment was in industries with price fixing agreements. Some were difficult to

*Table 8.8* Unemployment in Britain[a] 1929–38

|  | 1929 | 1932 | 1938 |
|---|---|---|---|
| Total registered unemployed (millions) | 1.22 | 2.75 | 1.79 |
| *% unemployed in staple industries* | | | |
| Coal | 18.2 | 41.2 | 22.0 |
| Cotton | 14.5 | 31.1 | 27.7 |
| Shipbuilding | 23.2 | 59.5 | 21.4 |
| Iron and steel | 19.9 | 48.5 | 24.8 |
| *% unemployed by region* | | | |
| Wales | 19.3 | 36.5 | 22.3 |
| Northern Ireland | 15.1 | 27.2 | 23.6 |
| Northern England | 13.5 | 27.1 | 13.8 |
| Scotland | 12.1 | 27.7 | 15.9 |
| Midlands | 9.3 | 20.1 | 7.2 |
| South-west England | 8.1 | 17.1 | 7.8 |
| London and south-east | 5.6 | 13.7 | 6.4 |

Sources: Mitchell 1988; Aldcroft and Richardson 1969; Fogarty 1945.

Note

a  The unemployment percentages relate to registered unemployed as a per cent of all insured workers. The entries for regions for 1938 relate to 1937.

mount but government subsidies helped to remove surplus capacity, as in the 1936 Spindles Act for cotton. Trade Associations had been established during the war and flourished thereafter as in steel where the British Iron and Steel Federation supported a "price umbrella" supplementing the 33 per cent import duties that were introduced, as noted earlier, in 1932.

Of course, as Tolliday said of steel, price agreements "allowed the least efficient to stay in business and the more efficient to earn inflated profits ... so that the BISF ... became the guarantor of long term organisational inertia".[43] Hence the government intervention to promote long term organisational change, in particular in the form of amalgamations. Whilst some success emerged in electricity, gas and railways, as we shall see later, for manufacturing government support was hesitant and not much was achieved. The government looked essentially to "self-help" but the bodies that emerged, like BISF, seemed to spend more time asking for protection. The National Shipbuilders' Security Ltd was formed in 1930 with the aim of buying up idle capacity. It was supported by Bank of England funds but dockyard capacity in Scotland and north-east England was reduced by only 15–20 per cent in the 1930s.

The coal industry illustrates some of the underlying difficulties. This was Britain's only primary energy source, but a massive one, dominating the world market and with a labour force of over one million. From its peak in 1911–13 domestic sales had fallen, in the face of alternative secondary fuels like gas and electricity, from 87 million tons to 67 million by 1925 with already 400 mines closed. Some attributed this to low productivity growth, in turn blamed on the large number of small companies and management inertia.[44] How big were the economies of scale in coal mining has been disputed and the labour productivity difference with USA, as already noted, can largely be explained by different geological conditions and the ageing of British pits.[45] In the 1920s, coal prices fell by 6.5 per cent per annum, voluntary marketing schemes were created but never successful, all of which lead to the 1930 Coal Mines Act. Under Part I a cartel was established with quotas – "standard tonnages" – for each company. By some measures the cartel had some success in holding coal prices against other prices, although the exporting companies, feeling the brunt of world competition, tried endlessly to evade the restrictions.[46] Unfortunately any success undermined Part II of the Act which aimed to promote reorganisation via amalgamations and closure of mines. Investigative bodies like the 1926 Samuel Commission had promoted such ideas and the Coal Mines Reorganisation Commission which was set up by the Act was required to draw up plans for amalgamations and, rather ambitiously, advanced a scheme for six big collieries based on six coalfields, later withdrawn after objections by coal owners and the labour force. Over 1930–35 there were no more amalgamations than in 1926–30 (26 schemes involving 230,000 workers). It seems the Act had some effect, but small, and certainly did not dampen the cries for nationalisation which came in 1946.

Direct state intervention of this kind was supplemented by tariff protection of manufacturing industries which became extensive in the 1930s. WWI saw quotas and related restrictions and a 33.3 per cent duty on imported luxuries, with preference for empire products, which continued after the war. Duties were then raised on glass, glue, leather, lace, pottery, paper and similar products as a byproduct of Acts passed in 1919–25 to protect industry.[47] The colonies (like Ghana) benefited more than the Dominions (Canada, Australia, New Zealand) who wanted Britain to impose high duties on non-Empire foodstuffs in exchange for high tariffs on their own non-British imports of manufactures. Little changed in the 1920s though Britain's reluctance to continue its role as hegemonic leader of free trade was not being taken up by USA. Indeed in America, hit by the Wall Street crash of 1929 and falling grain prices, the 1930 Hawley–Smoot tariff prompted the disintegration of world trade. Support in Britain from Keynes and Bevin for the policy advocated by the Dominions was followed by the 1932 Import Duties Act – a 10 per cent levy on most imports with wheat, copper and meat as the Empire exemptions. Iron and steel tariffs were raised to 33.5 per cent, as already noted, and then to 50 per cent in 1935. The Dominions' demands for higher British tariffs on non-Empire goods with preference for sectors like Canada cars were agreed at the Imperial Economic Conference in Ottawa which gave British manufacturers access to Dominion markets on tariff terms which would allow them to compete with Dominion manufacturers. The sufferers, including manufacturing sectors in other countries, attacked these policies and Denmark, Uruguay and Argentina entered agreements to minimise the loss of access to British markets as did all of Scandinavia.

Britain in the 1930s joined therefore in the disintegration of world trade as quotas, tariffs and bilateral agreements proliferated. How did British business fare so far as taxation was concerned? In the late nineteenth century, the business sector, though feeling the rise in the local government property tax ("rates", see above), was not heavily taxed by central government which relied on other sources to finance its spending on defence and debt interest. Table 8.9 shows that amongst central government revenues the share of excise taxes fell consistently 1871–1938. Customs duties also fell to 12 per cent of the total by 1935 recovering to 27 per cent by 1938. It was the receipts from income and property taxes which financed the rise of central government spending though at the end of the nineteenth century only 2.3 per cent of the population paid income tax. This was not due to any rise in business taxes. Retained profits were taxed at the standard rate and there was an excess profits duty during WWI and shortly afterwards, and a corporation tax in 1920, but both were short term expedients. Businesses were generally treated as "agents", as vehicles for income passing to individuals on whom taxes were levied. The income tax on individuals, including those on dividends, was introduced successfully, albeit painfully in Britain, by avoiding the estimation of an individual's total income. The constituent elements whether they be from rent, profit, dividends salaries were collected "at source" and by local dignitaries, officials and commoners assessing the profits of unincorporated trade and agriculture directly.[48] Business as an institution was hardly touched as a tax source for central government.

Table 8.9 UK central government revenues[a] 1871–1938 (£ million)

|  | 1871 | 1881 | 1891 | 1901 | 1913 | 1925 | 1930 | 1938 |
|---|---|---|---|---|---|---|---|---|
| 1 Customs | 20.2 | 19.2 | 19.7 | 26.6 | 33.5 | 99.3 | 119.9 | 221.6 |
| 2 Excise[b] | 24.4 | 29.7 | 35.2 | 46.3 | 48.12 | 174.2 | 180.0 | 172.5 |
| 3 Income and property taxes[c] | 8.1 | 11.4 | 15.9 | 29.4 | 47.5 | 337.7 | 294.5 | 355.4 |
| 4 Post Office[d] | 5.3 | 8.3 | 12.3 | 17.3 | 29.2 | 55.5 | 68.1 | 86.6 |
| 5 Other[e] | 7.2 | 11.3 | 13.4 | 20.7 | 30.5 | 132.7 | 152.5 | 112.6 |
| Total revenues | 68.2 | 81.9 | 96.5 | 140.2 | 188.8 | 799.4 | 815.0 | 948.7 |
| Total expenditures[f] | 67.8 | 80.6 | 93.4 | 193.3 | 184.0 | 750.8 | 711.7 | 909.4 |

Source: Mitchell 1988.

Notes
a Consolidated fund accounts of the UK, including S. Ireland before 1920. Excludes all receipts of local authorities (in revenues) and payments by local authorities (in expenditures).
b Includes stamp and motor licence duties.
c Includes land and assessment taxes (which were less than £3 million per annum), property and income taxes plus supertax.
d Includes telegraph and telephone.
e Includes death duties.
f Mainly defence and debt interest (cf. Table 8.2) plus Post Office, pensions, insurance, grants to local authorities and small amounts of economic subsidies and grants for education, arts and science.

## Problem networks: electricity and railways

Britain was so well endowed with coal in the nineteenth century and with a rail trunk network established by 1850, that there were few strategic worries about these sectors. They were of course vital inputs for the manufacturing sector and thereby contributed to Britain's industrial and therefore military strength. In the late nineteenth century, the productivity and profitability of the railway companies were declining whilst the ever-present potential monopoly power from amalgamations was becoming of increasing concern. By the end of WWI the unplanned network came under increasing scrutiny and a major reorganisation was initiated by the state. Worries also surrounded the energy sector. With ageing seams and access costly, productivity growth in the coal industry was clearly on the decline by the end of the nineteenth century whilst export markets were threatened in the 1920s as new competitors emerged. The threat to industrial strength could not be ignored so that, as already described, the inter-war period saw extensive if not always effective government intervention. Electricity by then was emerging as an important secondary fuel, especially for industry, but its structure seemed to inhibit the development of regional networks or possibly a national network to yield the levels of technical efficiency found in USA.

Electricity supply took off in the 1880s in Britain and, drawing on the experience of railways, gas and water, was subjected to significant state regulation which attracted much criticism.[49] "Notwithstanding that our countrymen have been among the first in inventive genius in electrical science", said the British Institution of Electrical Engineers in 1902, "its development in the United Kingdom is in a backward condition".[50] Many thought the legislation for tramways and electricity inhibited development, especially that of the private companies.[51] Early ventures in electricity were of course speculative and so much so as to prompt the *Birmingham Gazette* to suggest that an experiment in electric lighting "is good enough, perhaps, for speculative investment of private capital, but not good enough to justify the risking of public funds".[52] The Electric Lighting Act of 1882 gave powers to local authorities to take over private companies after 21 years (later 42) and led to complaints. The purchase clauses never applied to the power companies and it did not stop a flurry of private companies being set up, some with cables laid on streets or slung over wooden poles. The USA was progressing more quickly than Britain where in 1890 sales were still small and most generating stations had less than 0.1 megawatt capacity. The USA did not however have the same British advantages in gas and steam power. The latter was important in manufacturing and transport, and, for lighting, electricity prices could not compete with gas until about 1910.[53] A related source of concern was trams, 90 per cent of which had been electrified in USA as early as 1890. The investment needed for electricity may have appeared a risky proposition in Britain in the 1890s when the 21 year clauses on the undertakings established in the 1870s were coming to an end. The lag with the USA only lasted a short time because the municipalities took the initiative (cf. Table 8.6). Some had stepped in where private development had not been forthcoming – hilly

Halifax and Huddersfield, for example. By 1896 the municipalities had been given general permission by Parliament to operate trams as well as lay track and electric mileage rose from 45 in 1895 to 2195 in 1905/06 by which time 90 per cent of Britain's trams were electric.

Where the local authorities proved a real stumbling block was in the struggle to shift from an urban to regional focus in the production of electricity. The development of high pressure speed turbines meant unit generating costs were lower in larger stations. In addition developments in the scientific understanding of electrical current allowed supply to be transformed by stations. Interconnection of areas by grids would therefore allow more use of large generating plants and the elimination of idle capacity. Calls for greater coordination between urban areas were being made in the early 1900s and, immediately after WWI, there was much agitation for the establishment of District Boards. Following the Williamson Committee Report of 1918, the only gain was the establishment of a body, the Electricity Commissioners, to promote technical development. Another government committee was established in 1925 and reported in strong terms on the relatively high cost and low consumption of electricity in Britain, the proliferation of small plants and the need for interconnection. In the light of fears of nationalisation, the solution of setting up the Central Electricity Board (CEB) was clever.[54] Its basic functions were to construct a national grid, close down small stations and standardise electricity frequencies. But it was the institutional arrangement which was truly innovative. Certain stations were to be "selected". The CEB would buy electricity from them, transmit and then resell leaving the job of retailing to the companies and local authority undertakings. It bestowed the honour of being selected rather generously in order to oil the process of transition and research studies suggest that the best practice local authority and private generating plants were equally efficient (though with a longish "tail" of unselected municipal plants) which also would have facilitated a smooth transition.[55] The managers of the CEB were not appointed by the Treasury and all capital was raised on the stock market without a Treasury guarantee. It was this which allayed the fears, even though the reality was that it was a publicly owned enterprise since none of the stock was equity. On the face of it the Board was a success. The grid networks were set up first on a regional basis with the Board's first chairman, Duncan, experimenting in his home territory in Scotland and the national grid completed in 1933. Capital formation each year averaged £20 million and the number of consumers shot up from one million in 1920 to 9.3 million in 1938/39. With production in non-selected stations dwindling, the thermal efficiency gap with USA eliminated, the system load factor raised from 25 per cent in 1926 to 37 per cent by 1939 and the Battersea 105 megawatt station the largest in Europe, complaints were few.

By the 1930s, there was still a huge number of electricity undertakings – 581 in Table 8.6 – mainly involved in retail distribution, many with only a small turnover. In 1934 over 400 undertakings accounted for less than 10 per cent of sales, distribution costs were high and the multiplicity of boundaries prevented efficient development of networks. The trouble was local authorities accounted for 60 per cent of the undertakings and they were particularly stubborn. Not for them to give up empires and profits. A similar issue arose in the case of gas with the simplification that before the advent of natural gas in the 1970s there were no major economies of scale in production or distribution. But there were unexploited economies of scale perceived in marketing and finance. It was these factors, in conjunction with the perceived failure of arms' length regulation in the depressed economy of the 1930s, which led to the nationalisation of gas and electricity in the late 1940s.

In contrast the railway system did go through a major reconstruction into four large regional companies in 1921 but its vulnerability to the new road transport competitor and continuing financial losses also paved the way for nationalisation in 1948. The essential feature of the nineteenth century railway system (cf. Chapter 3) was private ownership with legislative regulation of fares, freight rates and safety. As in most countries, controlling prices was a continuing problem because of the complex cost structure. Very broadly, marginal costs were small so that on any route or type of traffic, fares and rates were targeted to exceed marginal costs by an amount which, aggregated across all traffic and routes, was enough to cover the joint costs of engines, coaches, wagons, signalling and track costs. The margin was usually determined by what the traffic would bear which gave the railway companies considerable scope on routes not challenged by coastal sea transport.[56] The scope for discrimination across customers lead to the stipulation in the 1854 Railway and Canal Act that no "company shall … give any undue … preference … or favour of any particular person or company". Since different customers did generate different costs, especially for freight, this requirement was easy to meet. Indeed since some railway companies did effectively "charge" some customers more by providing little help in forwarding and delivery, the Act specifically stated that all railway companies had to provide "all due and reasonable facilities for receiving and forwarding". This dimension of railway operations stemmed ultimately from their inherent natural monopoly characteristics which also facilitated collusion and amalgamations since on any routes there were rarely more than two or three lines. Parliament had some leverage because a new statute was needed for any new company. A Select Committee in 1852 actually urged Parliament to ban amalgamations but the Commons took little notice. The 1850s and 1860s saw several big amalgamations involving the North Eastern and Great Eastern railways whilst the 1870s saw much "courting" between companies on the Midlands/London lines. Such courting was banned by Parliament in 1872 and thereafter amalgamations proceeded more slowly, though "working agreements" and "conference meetings" proliferated. By 1907, 13 companies accounted for 86 per cent of track mileage and much of that was the business of the four "giants", North Western, Great Western, North Eastern and Midlands, who took two-thirds of the revenues.

By the late nineteenth century the companies were in trouble financially as their net return on capital gradually fell from 4.4 per cent in 1870 to 3.5 per cent in 1912. Although competition from steam shipping was on the increase, revenue per unit of capital was actually rising and it seems the financial problem stemmed from operating costs as real wages rose and coal prices stopped falling.[57] The railways' pricing practices and semi-monopoly positions created constant grievances which led them to placate customers and government by generous marshalling yard facilities, free insurance, despatching wagons half empty and cheap postal services. During WWI, as in most countries, investment dried up, rolling stock was run down and prices were never allowed to match rising wage and fuel bills. Operating costs were 65.2 per cent of revenues in 1913 but 104.1 per cent in 1921, meaning there was an inadequate surplus to cover interest charges. The prospects did not look good in the 1920s because, unlike other countries, manufacturing industry was losing out in foreign markets with effects on railway coal traffic which fell from 222 million tons in 1923 to 207 million in 1929. Together with the fall in other minerals and merchandise, plus the world depression from 1930, railway revenues had collapsed from £218 million in 1921 to £156 million by 1931.[58]

The government's plan in 1919 was to give financial compensation for the effects of the war and enforce a rationalisation of the company structure to generate economies of scale which would allow the companies to meet their socio-economic obligations. Thus the 1921 Railways Act reorganised the mixed bag of companies into four large regional private monopolies. To cover rising fuel and wage bills, automatic price adjustments were put in place so that a users' guarantee would insure against government subsidies. A "standard revenue" (gross profit) was set for each company: £7.1 million for Southern; £8.5 million for Great Western; £15.2 million for London North Eastern; £26.1 million for London, Midland and Scottish. These were expected to yield a net return of 4.5 per cent on capital. The scheme was optimistic and in any case undermined by a new competitor, road transport. It was moreover a new phenomenon as the four giant railway companies were now surrounded by a swarm of new, small transport firms not saddled with the railways' continuing obligations to publish fares and rates, provide services on demand, avoid undue preference and pay trade union agreed wage rates. The 1920s saw many "tramp hauliers" plying their trade throughout Britain, completely unlicensed and unregulated, and the number of motor vehicles reached 771,000 by 1924 (with horrendously high accident rates). The railway freight charging system involved 21 freight categories reflecting the value of cargo (low price per ton-mile for coal, high price for diamonds per ton-mile) but with fairly uniform prices within each category irrespective of route. The story of how the railways finished up losing traffic where they had an inherent cost advantage is common to most countries throughout the twentieth century.[59] It was not until the 1930s that legislation was introduced but the emphasis was not on liberating the railways but on constraining road transport through the licensing provisions of the 1930 and 1933 Road Traffic Acts. Indeed state policy now switched away from railways to "transport" including coordination of road and rail and it was not simply the railways that were on the agenda for public ownership but transport generally. This came after WWII, completing the revolution in state policy for industry and infrastructure.

## Notes

1 Hobson 1993.
2 On British public expenditure generally see Middleton 1996.
3 Whitaker 1991; Eloranta 2007; Eloranta and Harrison 2010; Peebles 1987.
4 Dienel and Lyth 1998.
5 Stevenson 1999.
6 Kennedy 1971, p. 741.
7 Millward 2011b.
8 Headrick 1991; Headrick and Griset 2001.
9 Fremdling 1996.
10 Silva and Diogo, 2006.
11 O'Hara 2010.
12 Ibid.
13 Laborie 2006, p. 194; Lipartito 2000, pp. 162–6; Chester 1975, pp. 16, 110, 258, 453–6.
14 For more detail on this section see Millward 2000 and 2013.
15 Williamson 1990.
16 Millward and Sheard 1995; Mitchell 1988.
17 Hassan 1985 and, much earlier, Shaw 1890 and Knoop 1912.
18 Cavalcanti 1991.
19 Silverthorne 1884.
20 Royal Commission on Water Supply 1869, pp. 246–8.
21 Hassan 1998.
22 Baugh 1992.
23 Cf. Awty 1975 for Preston, and Wilson 1990 for Chester; Hennock 1983.
24 Hennock 1963.
25 Waller 1983, p. 304; Fraser 1993, p. 262.
26 Gibbons 1901, p. 254.
27 McKeown and Record 1962.
28 Daunton 1990.
29 Habbakuk 1962.
30 Wiener 1985; Aldcroft and Richardson 1969.
31 Chandler 1990; Elbaum and Lazonick 1986; Lazonick 1991; Taylor 1961.
32 Freeman *et al.* 2012.
33 McCloskey 1981; Sandberg 1981.
34 Rose 1997; Singleton 1995. See also Chapters 3 and 9.
35 McCloskey 1981.
36 Broadberry 1993, 1994a, b; see also Maddison 1991.
37 Cf. Broadberry 1988.
38 Bairoch 1982; Marrison 1996.
39 Reader 1977; Aldcroft and Richardson 1969; Hannah 1983.
40 Pollard 1992.
41 Hannah 1983.
42 Ibid.
43 Tolliday 1986, p. 103.
44 Taylor 1961.
45 Kirby 1977; McCloskey 1981.
46 Kirby 1977.
47 Kindleberger 1989.
48 Daunton 2001, 2002.
49 The following paragraphs follow closely some paragraphs in Millward 2000 and thanks are due to Cambridge University Press for granting this author's right to automatic reprint with permission.

50 Hughes 1962, p. 38.
51 Knox 1901; Garcke 1907.
52 Jones 1983, p. 21.
53 Hannah 1979, pp. 12–16; Wilson 1993, pp. 2–3.
54 Weir Committee 1926; Hannah 1977.
55 Foreman-Peck and Waterson 1985.
56 Hawke 1969.
57 Irving 1978; Aldcroft 1974.
58 Bagwell 1974.
59 Foreman-Peck and Millward 1994.

# 9   USA 1870–1939

## Natural resources, free markets and fractured government

> Variety and conflict of laws have brought not a little conflict and confusion into our social and business arrangements.
>
> Woodrow Wilson 1889[1]

## Introduction

After the Civil War, the United States embarked on its most expansive phase of economic development, attaining world leadership by the turn of the century. Average real incomes doubled by the First World War (WWI), rose a further quarter to 1929 and then flattened out with the depression of the 1930s (Table 9.1). Whilst agricultural output and the rural population both increased in absolute terms, their share of national totals fell, representing a shift from a relatively low value added sector to high value manufacturing and services. One-half of the labour force was in agriculture in 1870, only one-quarter by 1913. Manufacturing output showed an astonishing growth, even relative to the rise in population, rising fivefold 1860–1913 and a further 44 per cent to 1929. America's endowment of minerals was outlined in Chapter 4 and the output of coal, iron ore and pig iron grew massively up to 1913 with oil expanding more in the interwar period. By 1900 already some 183 corporate giants like American Tobacco had been established as holding companies and accounted for 15 per cent of American manufacturing capacity. Accompanying the increase in large firms was the spread of markets. The population grew from 50 million in 1870 to 92 million in 1913, about 2 per cent per annum and one-half of the increase came from immigration with foreign born rising to 8 per cent of the total by 1910, declining thereafter. Extension of the rail network from 52,920 miles in 1870 to 249,709 by 1913 opened up the domestic market and routes to the exporting ports. Expressed per 1000 of the population, the length of the track was equivalent to 130 miles in 1870, doubling that by 1913 whilst telecommunications saw even bigger increases.

The interface between business and government was strongly influenced by two factors. One was the rich endowment of land and mineral resources facilitating the growth of population which itself allowed the development of a

Table 9.1 Economic development of USA 1870–1937

| | 1870 | 1913 | 1929 | 1937 |
|---|---|---|---|---|
| *General* | | | | |
| National income per head (1913=100) | 46 | 100 | 124 | 121 |
| % labour force in agriculture | 50.0 | 27.5 | 21.9 | 17.1[a] |
| Manufacturing output per head of population (1913=100) | 17[b] | 100 | 144 | n.a. |
| *Strategic* | | | | |
| Military personnel ('000) | 47 | 127 | 249 | 288 |
| Warships ('000 tons) | 175 | 824 | 721 | 1099 |
| Merchant fleet ('000 tons) | 3438 | 6555 | 14,887 | 12,382 |
| *Mineral outputs* | | | | |
| Coal (million metric tons) | 36.7 | 517.1 | 552.3 | 450.9 |
| Iron ore (mmt) | 3.89 | 62.97 | 74.20 | 72.25 |
| Pig iron (mmt) | 1.69 | 31.46 | 43.30 | 37.76 |
| Crude petroleum (mmt) | 0.70 | 33.13 | 138.1 | 172.9 |
| Natural gas (billion cubic metres) | n.a. | 16.49 | 55.27 | 70.03 |
| *Power and communications* | | | | |
| Electricity supply (kw hours per 100 population) | n.a. | 25 | 96 | 114 |
| Rail track miles per 100,000 population | 133 | 257 | 205 | 185 |
| Telegrams per 100 population | 24 | 80 | 210 | 171 |
| Telephones per 100 population | n.a. | 10 | 16 | 15 |

Sources: Tables 5.4 and 8.1 plus Annex tables, supplemented for 1937 with similar original sources.

Notes
a 1940.
b 1860.

homogeneous English speaking mass consumption market and the emergence of large corporations. Uncluttered by any remnants of feudal land ownership, it was a perfect setting for textbook free market economics. But, second, the specification of property rights and provision for social spillovers and market failures which generated a demand for more government tended to lag behind the immense surge of the private sector.[2] American government was very much founded from the bottom up, from town, to state to federation. A central element in the story was the independence of each state government, not one of which dominated. Unlike Germany, dominated by Prussia, or France and Britain's heavily centralised organs of power, USA did not have a nationally unified and homogeneous government system. As business markets extended beyond town and state boundaries and firms grew in size, the fiercely independent state governments gave way only slowly and often reluctantly to a more fully integrated national economy. Politically this generated a distrust of big business and a distrust of government which remains today.[3] The next section provides an analysis of the distinctive features of American industrial growth. Then in the third section of this chapter, government structure, expenditures and finances are discussed leading to the detailed analysis of the regulation of business at the national level in the fourth section and at the local and state levels in the fifth section in the context of the rapid urbanisation which accompanied industrialisation.

## The rise of big business and foreign trade

American economic growth was not simply a vindication of free markets. Quite apart from being shielded from foreign competition by formidable tariff barriers and transport costs, it was very much an expansion based on natural resources both renewable and non-renewable. In explaining why the American experience came to be a textbook for capitalism and to understand the growth of big business (and the reaction of politicians), the richness of its natural resource base is a key element.

The Civil War had triggered heavy tariffs on Union imports aimed at raising government revenues to finance the huge armies, supplementing a big rise in excise taxes.[4] Regressive in impact, tariffs had long been favoured by northern manufacturers such that by 1867–71 they were 46.7 per cent of the value of dutiable imports (20 per cent in 1860) and the "free list" had shrunk. Thereafter, as we shall see in more detail later, the tariff rates fell slightly to 1914 but had risen to 55.3 per cent by the early 1930s. For some historians only Russia competed with USA in the protection it afforded its industry in this period.[5] At most however it allowed American industry to develop earlier rather than, as in France, protection being vital for avoiding the annihilation which might otherwise have happened to parts of industry in the nineteenth century. In USA, large firms were rare in the earlier part of the century (cf. Chapter 4) and found mainly where labour was cheap – slave plantations, New England textiles mills using unmarried farmers' daughters. Even by the 1870s, industry was still dominated by unincorporated small firms in woodwork, metals, chemicals, printing materials. Coal fired steam power stimulated early factories in cotton textiles, flour and timber and 1850–80 saw a large increase in boots and shoes, millinery, meat packing, malt liquor, furniture, leather tanning and pig iron.[6] Employment in mining then shot up from 280,000 in 1880 to 1,068,000 by 1914 whilst the capital stock in manufacturing increased from $4.9 billion in 1879 to $36.7 billion by 1917 (1929 prices). As Figure 9.1 shows, food and related agricultural processing remained, with textiles, the biggest manufacturing sectors up to 1914 in terms of the size of capital stock though the fastest growers were in the more capital intensive sectors like iron and steel with oil refining and transport equipment the fastest in the inter-war period. Chandler saw these heavy capital goods industries, with railways, as the cradle of the big business corporation (Carnegie Steel, Armour & Co.) using continuous processing technology and exploiting declining transport costs and large markets.[7]

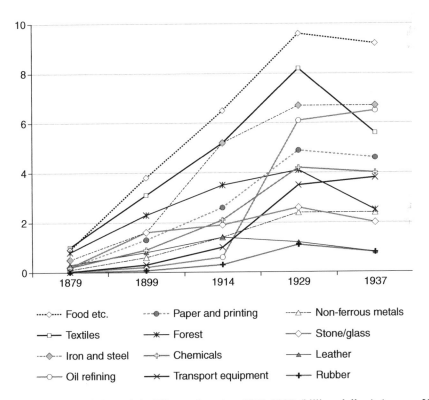

*Figure 9.1* Capital stock in US manfacturing 1879–1937 (billion dollars) (source: US Bureau of the Census 1976).

Notes
Entries for 1879 and 1899 include custom shops etc. The rest relate to factories generating $500 p.a. plus.

Markets were opened up through the development of rapid communications. Two big companies, Bell and Western Union, dominated telecommunications and they made deals with individual state governments for rights of way. Initially much was short distance with telegraph links within firms between headquarters and suburbs and used also by City councils for fire and police.[8] As lines lengthened the economic benefits were substantial: Hoag's analysis of the trade effects of the telegraph suggests that in mid nineteenth century inland America, the average information lag fell from ten days to zero.[9] Western Union dominated and, in an agreement of 1879, passed its telephone patents to the Bell company which was to stay out of telegraph. Bell initially created "patent associate" franchises for its telephone technology but capital requirements and national coordination propelled more direct involvement.[10] In 1882 it acquired the major equipment manufacturer, Western Electric, and thereafter moved relentlessly to national domination which we shall consider later. By 1913 USA had one telephone for every ten inhabitants, way above the European levels. In telegraph it lay behind the UK (with a large imperial network) and France but overtook them in the inter-war period.[11]

Most important of all for market spread was of course the railway which, in its initial stages, had been financed in a significant way by local and state governments so that by 1871, as noted in Chapter 4, they owned one-half of all railroad assets. A big inducement was the rise in property values, especially for systems less than 50 miles, which generated property tax revenues for local government whose involvement continued up to the 1890s.[12] Corruption had led to a reduced role for the state governments but the Federal government continued its land grants and it also made a $65 million loan to the Central-Pacific Union. Since annual total investment averaged around $12 billion 1862–71, most new finance by then was coming from the private sector and especially from foreign investment. Systems were being organised around connection centres like Chicago, Cincinnati, St Louis and the east coast ports, with large firms emerging: New York Central; Pennsylvania; Michigan Central. Productivity growth was huge (Table 9.2) with better coupling, airbrakes, trains, cars and locos. Rail track mileage had reached 140,000 by 1890 and increased to 350,000 by 1916, a product of three boom periods 1888–73, 1879–83 and 1888–92 after which extensive track building tailed off. Rates of return on railway investment had been declining (as in many countries) from levels of 9 per cent in the late 1860s to 6 per cent in 1907 and 4 per cent by 1914. By then bankruptcies were on the rise and investment more and more financed from internal sources. Consolidation was on the increase so that, by the early 1900s, seven groups controlled two-thirds of the mileage and accounted for 85 per cent of revenues.[13] The 1920 Transportation Act promoted further consolidation but passenger volumes declined by 30 per cent in the 1920s and investment fell in the 1930s as track was abandoned in the face of competition from road transport.

Although some like Chandler[14] saw the development of the modern industrial corporation as the main institutional channel of American economic growth, the role of natural resources was itself quite distinctive and meant the American

*Table 9.2* USA productivity by sector 1870–1937 (UK=100)

| | Output per employee | | | Manufacturing | | | GDP per head |
| | Agriculture | Transport and comunications | Utilities | Output per employee | Capital per employee | Total factor productivity | |
|---|---|---|---|---|---|---|---|
| 1870 | 100[a] | 110[a] | 56[a] | 204 | 94 | 205 | 90[a] |
| 1913 | 119[b] | 217[b] | 150[b] | 209 | 159 | 180 | 118[b] |
| 1929 | 118 | 232 | 336 | 250 | 173 | 218 | 139 |
| 1937 | 119 | 283 | 359 | 208 | 151 | 231 | 133 |

Sources: Broadberry 1993, 2006.

Notes
a 1869/71.
b 1909/11.

institutions were not necessarily appropriate for other countries. The American "manufacturing system" in the nineteenth century typically saved scarce labour by substituting natural resources, rather than capital. Lathes were often made of wood and gun stocks were manufactured by Thomas Blanchard at the Springfield Amory from sawn timber with wooden lathes and machines.[15] Interchangeable parts were introduced and the earliest successful sectors using the new technology and transport were meat packing, flour milling, malt liquor, leather tanning, pig iron. Chandlerian production was associated with a high throughput of fuel and raw materials – consider, within the business and household economies, the large petrol guzzling motor cars emerging in the early twentieth century. The American methods would have been wasteful in Europe where more labour intensive technologies for niche products represented a more optimal factor combination. American productivity in manufacturing was actually double that in Britain *before the rise of the large corporation.* It is clear from Broadberry's data (Table 9.2) that productivity in American manufacturing did not grow any faster than in British manufacturing 1870–1937. The capital/labour ratio was actually higher in Britain in the early nineteenth century, overtaken only in the latter part of the century. It was natural resources in USA that substituted for skilled labour. Productivity advance was actually highest in service sectors like transport, telecommunications, gas and electricity supplies with a big boost to agriculture from its mechanisation and falling share of the labour force.

The distinctive feature of America's industrial success was the exploitation of natural resources and how they dominated exports, a sign of the country's comparative advantage. Data for 1913, for example, show USA had very high shares of the world output of resources at the very heart of new industrial technologies: copper (56 per cent), zinc (37 per cent), coal (39 per cent), iron ore (36 per cent), lead (34 per cent), quite apart from the huge outputs of oil, phosphate, molybdenum and tungsten. Given the very high transport costs of minerals, USA was "uniquely favoured".[16] These resource advantages were reflected in the pattern of foreign trade, the underlying trends in which were hardly altered by the Civil War. Over the late nineteenth century, exports were still dominated by primary products (cotton, grain, meat, wood, tobacco, still two-thirds in 1900) even though they were becoming less dominant, as was the case also for goods of animal or vegetable origin (furs, timber products). Manufactured exports were rising and here capital and resources were complementary. The capital/labour ratio in export goods, relative to imports, was estimated by Wright as 1.61 in 1879, falling to 1.39 by 1914 as sugar refining, meat packing and other agricultural processing sectors declined in relative importance.[17] Products which intensively used non-renewable resources (pig iron, lead pipes) were estimated by Lindert to have had an export/import ratio of 2.8 in 1899 falling to 1.8 by 1914.[18] For renewable resource intensive products like wheat and timber the change was from 3.0 in 1899 to 2.0. The manufactured content of imports actually declined such that, of the total domestic consumption of manufactured goods in 1869, 14 per cent were imported, only 6 per cent in 1909 (steel 1.5 per cent), and for some products the absolute amount imported fell. We noted earlier that import tariff rates after the Civil War were double those before, and some like Eliot Brownlee have seen the retention of high duties by the Republicans as a revenue raising exercise to fund the pensions and disability payments for Union veterans.[19] With the support of farmers, southerners, middle class customers and small business, the anti-tariff movement was led, on that view, by the Democrats. Some tariff reductions were made in the 1870s but then in 1890 came the McKinley tariff raising duties on textiles, tin plate, steel rails, iron, steel (70 per cent) and wheat, though for products like wheat it was "ceremonial" since no protection was needed.[20] In some cases like steel rails, there were clear benefits to domestic industry but in general there seems little support for the infant industry argument since American industry was booming, the tariffs did not back winners (aircraft later being an exception) and much was essentially protectionist.

The textile industry was heavily protected, a factor which undermines the argument that cotton mills which used ring rather than mule spindles and which were integrated with weaving, were virtuous characteristic of American industry which Britain failed to copy.[21] This was a sector, together with apparel, which used women and children intensively. Much of the higher wage content of American exports compared to imports arose from the fact that imports had a bigger women and children labour force. The US wage differential was not, as some thought, a skill premium and indeed the rise in the women and children component of US exports throughout our period reflected the spread of this labour to canning, freezing and processing. Where skilled labour entered the foreign mix was through the superior education system which gave America a distinct edge in technology intensive products like transport equipment, machinery, professional work. Lindert estimates the export/import ratio for such products as 12.0 in 1918, a level maintained through to 1940.[22] This was how America avoided the "Dutch disease" of plentiful natural resources completely dominating exports to the disadvantage of manufactures. The capital/labour ratio in exports relative to imports continued to decline from 1.39 in 1913 to 1.05 in 1940.[23] The export/import ratio for natural resources was also falling (from 7.43 in 1913 to 3.3 by 1928), the ratio for renewable resource intensive products had fallen below 1.0 by 1935 and by 1950 for non-renewables as US became a net importer of oil.[24] By the 1930s manufactures were accounting for one-half of exports and the trend was clearly away from resource intensive products as tropical food imports rose.

The period 1913–40 had not seen much change in tariff policy. Duties were some 37.6 per cent of the value of dutiable imports in 1913 and though the Underwood Tariff of that year reduced duties, they were still amongst the highest in the world and were in any case undermined by WWI. President Wilson called for removal of all economic barriers after the war but no explicit trade policies were enunciated and the pre-war pattern remained. Indeed the fall in food prices and farmers' real incomes after the war prompted heavy lobbying, leading to the 1922 Fordney–McCumber tariff; it was billed as an emergency but to get it through Congress others had to be satisfied so the duties on manufactures were also raised, by 30 per cent. There is also evidence that negotiations on further increases had started before the 1929 Wall Street Crash and the depression and in the Hawley–Smoot tariff of 1930 the duties averaged 59.1 per cent, the highest ever for USA on some estimates.[25] Whilst the resentment of other countries was largely a depression induced response, it did not put USA in a good light, given its large holdings of gold reserves. The government tried to reclaim some respect by the Reciprocity Act and Trade Agreement Act of 1934 which lead to reductions in tariff levels but by the late 1930s American duties were still 39.8 per cent of the value of dutiable imports.

## Government structure, expenditure and finances

In 1870 the government structure was, arguably, ill fitted to cope with the massive expansion of the economy we have just described. Many contemporary observers, as well as economists later, argued against the rise in publicly provided services. Before the passage of the Air Carrier Act of 1926 establishing federal sovereignty over airspace, for example, some even opposed federal involvement, viewing aviation as a form of intra-state commerce and hence beyond Federal law.[26] "Progressives" as well as various interest groups did envisage a role for government and their voices did generate an expansion of government but the way this emerged did not prove to be the best feature of the American economy. By the late nineteenth century local government accounted for over one-half of all government spending and most town governments were active in promoting better sanitary, fire, education, police and health services. They rarely had powers to attack private monopolies in gas (like the Chicago Gas Trust), electricity, urban transit and water supply, some of which they might alternatively provide themselves as municipal enterprises (like the Cochituate Waterworks established in Boston in 1853). Regulation of business, if it existed, resided with the state governments who, although having limited tax sources initially, did have the constitutional right to regulate for anti-trust, railways, telegraph, alcohol, health and safety, marriage and later road transport and had the sole right to charter companies – Federal powers of chartering did not emerge until the 1930s. The problem was these powers varied state by state and, for some like New Jersey, business was very much a "private matter".

This created two problems. First, any flow of goods and services across state boundaries involved switching from one regulatory regime to another – food quality, rail and telecom services being classic examples of problem areas. With weak enforcement mechanisms, limited bureaucracies and sometimes vaguely expressed legislation, many issues had to be resolved in the courts, Federal in the case of inter-state issues. Some railway companies even challenged the constitutional right of the state governments to regulate at all.[27] Second, the strong independent powers of the states within a sea of free markets for goods and services, induced competition between states (as well as between towns) for business, by variation in the severity of the regulations. The danger of a "race to the bottom" was clearly present as companies sought to be chartered in for example

New Jersey with its liberal attitude to business.[28] It was as if there was an "internal market" in government and existing firms often exploited this to ward off new competition as small butchers in the eastern states tried to do when faced with competition from Chicago meat packers. The Federal government in 1870 had few powers over these matters. It had responsibility for the external affairs of the country both politically and economically in the form of tariff policy. Internally it ran the Post Office, regarded as a matter of national security and, eventually, following the Federal Reserve Act of 1912 took on the responsibility of a central bank. Its activities in selling off Federal land (Chapter 4) were huge but declining and its limited bureaucracy plus defence and war debt interest were financed largely through custom duties. Note how distant the Federal government must have seemed for a people who, before the 1860s, paid no taxes to the central government! It was however a key source of appeal for those with grievances over inter-state disputes and, as the economy expanded, the Federal government acquired more powers, a defining feature of state/business relations in our period.

How the regulatory regimes developed with respect to mining, manufacturing and national communications is discussed in the next section whilst the fifth section examines the role of regulation at the more local level in the context of rapid urbanisation, the establishment of Public Utility Commissions and the development of water supply, sanitation, gas, electricity and urban transport. Our main interest now is how the provision of government services and the way they were financed affected the business sector. The finance of local government services came largely, as noted earlier, from property taxes. By 1902 such taxes were still accounting for more than one-half of all government revenues, sales taxes 33 per cent (customs and excise, mainly Federal government) with licences, fees, etc., slightly over 10 per cent, mainly the state governments (Tables 9.3, 9.4, 9.5). Very broadly the share of customs at 13 per cent had fallen since 1860 and continued to do so in the inter-war period. Excise taxes on alcohol, tobacco etc., followed a similar trend so that by 1932 all sales taxes were only yielding 18.6 per cent. The big increase after WWI was the Federal income tax.

The different levels of American government provided different services but the structure did not change much over the period 1870–1939. The Federal government spent on defence and the associated liabilities for debt interest and veterans' pensions. Local government provided sanitation, school education, health, roads and welfare payments in the twentieth century. The state governments' main role was regulation although they did provide higher education and roads, the latter increasing strongly in the inter-war period as did their involvement in relief for unemployment and poverty whilst grants to local government accounted for 30 per cent of outlays (Table 9.5). For some economists it was wars which triggered much of the growth in government spending.[29] Federal government spending on defence was only $57 million in 1871, much on warships, reflecting the country's geographical isolation. Over the whole period 1870–1913 the defence spending burden was well below that of the other major

*Table 9.3* USA government expenditures and revenues 1870–1936

| | 1870 | 1880 | 1890 | 1902 | 1913 | 1927 | 1932 | 1936 |
|---|---|---|---|---|---|---|---|---|
| *Expenditures as % GDP* | | | | | | | | |
| Federal | 4.7 | 2.8 | 2.7 | 2.6 | 2.4 | 3.7 | 7.4 | 11.1 |
| State | 1.1 | 0.7 | 0.9 | 0.9 | 1.0 | 2.2 | 4.9 | 4.7 |
| Local | 2.6 | 2.2 | 2.8 | 4.1 | 4.6 | 5.9 | 9.2 | 4.5 |
| Total | 7.4 | 5.7 | 6.4 | 7.6 | 8.0 | 11.8 | 21.5 | 20.3 |
| *Revenue shares (%)* | | | | | | | | |
| Federal | 55.7 | 48.9 | 42.4 | 38.6 | 32.3 | 36.7 | 25.6 | 38.1 |
| State | 13.4 | 13.0 | 13.6 | 10.8 | 12.1 | 16.4 | 22.1 | 24.0 |
| Local | 31.9 | 38.1 | 44.0 | 50.7 | 55.6 | 47.0 | 52.3 | 37.9 |
| Total | 100 | 100 | 100 | 100 | 100 | 100 | 100 | 100 |
| *Types of revenues: % distribution* | | | | | | | | |
| Income tax | – | – | – | – | 1.5 | 24.3 | 14.5 | 15.8 |
| Sales tax | – | – | – | 37.5 | 29.5 | 16.5 | 18.6 | 32.0 |
| Property and user taxes | – | – | – | 51.4 | 58.7 | 50.0 | 56.2 | 38.7 |
| Charges etc. | – | – | – | 11.1 | 10.3 | 9.2 | 10.7 | 14.2 |
| Total | – | – | – | 100 | 100 | 100 | 100 | 100 |

Source: Wallis 2000; Elliot Brownlee 2000; Fishback *et al.* 2007.

Notes
Excludes grants and other transfers between different levels of government. Includes utility revenues and expenditures (Post Office, municipal enterprises, etc.).

*Table 9.4* US Federal government revenues and expenditures 1871–1938 (million dollars)

| | 1871 | 1881 | 1891 | 1901 | 1913 | 1925 | 1930 | 1938 |
|---|---|---|---|---|---|---|---|---|
| *Revenues*[a] | | | | | | | | |
| 1 Customs | 206 | 198 | 229 | 238 | 319 | 548 | 587 | 359 |
| 2 Excise[b] | 143 | 135 | 147 | 301 | 344 | 7145 | 565 | 1730 |
| 3 Income and corporation tax[c] | 3 | 0 | 0 | 5 | 0 | 1870 | 2475 | 3928 |
| 4 Other[d] | 31 | 28 | 26 | 43 | 51 | 644 | 430 | 429 |
| Total | 383 | 361 | 392 | 587 | 714 | 3640 | 4057 | 5588 |
| *Expenditures*[e] | | | | | | | | |
| 1 Army | 36 | 40 | 49 | 141 | 202 | 380 | 465 | 644 |
| 2 Navy | 19 | 26 | 26 | 61 | 133 | 346 | 374 | 596 |
| 3 Debt service | 126 | 83 | 38 | 32 | 23 | 881 | 659 | 926 |
| 4 Veterans[f] | 34 | 50 | 124 | 139 | 175 | 218 | 221 | 402 |
| 5 Other[g] | 77 | 72 | 129 | 148 | 181 | 1106 | 1600 | 4195 |
| 6 Total | 292 | 261 | 366 | 524 | 714 | 2923 | 3320 | 6764 |

Source: US Bureau of the Census 1976.

Notes
a Administrative budget.
b Mainly alcohol, tobacco, manufacturer taxes, capital stock tax and telecommunications.
c Individual income, corporation, employment, estates and gift taxes.
d Includes sale of public lands.
e Outlays of the Federal government.
f Veterans' compensation and pensions.
g Includes Post Office and interest payments by government enterprises on securities issued by the Treasury.

Table 9.5 USA state and local government revenues and expenditures 1902–38 (in 10 million dollars[a])

| | 1902 ST | 1902 LG | 1913 ST | 1913 LG | 1927 ST | 1927 LG | 1932 ST | 1932 LG | 1938 ST | 1938 LG |
|---|---|---|---|---|---|---|---|---|---|---|
| *Revenues* | | | | | | | | | | |
| 1 Income and corporation taxes[b] | 0 | – | 0 | – | 16 | – | 15 | – | 38 | – |
| 2 Property taxes[c] | – | 80 | – | 154 | – | 528 | – | 487 | – | 497 |
| 3 Excise | 3 | – | 6 | – | 45 | – | 73 | – | 167 | – |
| 4 Utility revenues | – | 6 | – | 12 | – | 40 | – | 46 | – | 110 |
| 4 Federal grants | 1 | 1 | 1 | 1 | 11 | 1 | 22 | 1 | 63 | 17 |
| 5 LG grants | 1 | – | 1 | – | 5 | – | 5 | – | 5 | – |
| 6 State grants | – | 5 | – | 9 | – | 61 | – | 8 | – | 152 |
| 7 Other | 16 | 0 | 31 | 1 | 125 | 3 | 140 | 4 | 256 | 6 |
| Total | 19 | 91 | 38 | 176 | 215 | 633 | 254 | 619 | 530 | 733 |
| *Expenditures*[d] | | | | | | | | | | |
| 1 Education | 6 | 24 | 14 | 52 | 51 | 202 | 68 | 203 | 101 | 214 |
| 2 Roads | 1 | 17 | 03 | 39 | 71 | 130 | 107 | 90 | 113 | 83 |
| 3 Public welfare | 1 | 3 | 2 | 4 | 5 | 11 | 11 | 37 | 78 | 62 |
| 4 Utility expenditure | – | 8 | – | 19 | – | 49 | – | 52 | – | 64 |
| 5 Other[e] | 11 | 44 | 20 | 82 | 79 | 245 | 103 | 256 | 215 | 268 |
| Total | 19 | 96 | 39 | 196 | 205 | 636 | 283 | 638 | 460 | 691 |

Source: US Bureau of the Census 1976.

Notes

LG = local government; ST = states.

a Thus, for example, income and corporation tax revenues for the states for 1927 totalled 160 million dollars.

b Includes road vehicle licences, employee insurance contributions, interest receipts and some property taxes.

c Includes charges and related miscellaneous revenues.

d Includes capital expenditure, grants, subsidies, debt interest.

e For LG this item includes debt interest, parks, sanitation, hospitals, police, fire protection. Debt interest was the largest ($54 × 10 million in 1938). There were some grants by LG to states but not identified here in LG outgoings (see revenues).

powers, at 0.7 per cent of GDP, as was the 1.7 per cent in the next peacetime period 1920–38 (Table 6.5). This is why total Federal expenditures were less than 3 per cent of GDP for most of the peacetime years before the great crash and depression of the 1930s (Table 9.3). There is little doubt however that the Civil War and the two World Wars boosted spending which never thereafter fell to pre-war levels. The huge armies raised in the Civil War caused Federal government spending to rise to 20 per cent of GDP by 1865. Over two-thirds came from bond issues and 15 per cent from the money supply but the rest involved higher excise taxes (alcohol, tobacco, manufactures, retail outlets, stamp duties), the need for which rose after the 1862 Homestead Act made provision for free Federal land grants. Since the excise taxes were regressive, in compensation a new Federal income tax was introduced in 1861 at 3 per cent, as well as an inheritance tax.[30] The direct taxes were later revoked but the bond issues meant a big part of Federal spending up to the 1890s was for debt interest whilst the commitment to pensions for veterans created, in some eyes, a precedent, a precursor of social insurance systems and a burden for the south since the scheme was restricted to Union veterans. The Fed also spent heavily on reconstruction in the 1860s and 1870s and its involvement in infrastructure never completely disappeared thereafter.

Income tax returned in 1913 as part of what Eliot Brownlee characterised as the most important shift in public policy in the twentieth century.[31] In fact as early as 1894 during a decade of depressed economic conditions and appeals for social welfare payments to the unemployed and poor, a modest income tax was introduced but later rejected as unconstitutional. The 16th Amendment to the Constitution led to the 1913 Underwood Act which introduced a tax of 1 per cent on corporate and personal incomes, with 6 per cent for incomes above $500 (with exemptions).

The country's involvement in WWI started formally in 1917 but because of the rise in demand from Europe for war related commodities, the economy did shift structurally, from 1915, to those sectors. Although real incomes fell 1914–16 the output of the non-farm sector rose significantly. It was 1916–18 which saw a rise in real incomes and, from April 1917, the huge rise in Federal spending. Some 20 per cent of the increase 1917–19 was financed by increases in the money supply (prices rose by 45 per cent 1914–18), 58 per cent by bond issues and 22 per cent by taxation. The War Revenues Act of 1917 introduced an excess profits tax, there were surtaxes on personal and corporate incomes and higher taxes on rail passengers and luxuries, quite apart from alcohol and tobacco to tax the "undeserving poor".[32]

The early 1920s saw some rolling back of the new state power. President Wilson had supported attacks on big corporations as economic predators and his "soak the rich" policy has been seen by some to lie behind the tax measures. He had shown that, despite the apparent "weakness of the American state", a capital intensive war could be fought successfully with democratic support providing taxes were made progressive, though his 1918 proposal for doubling taxation was rejected in 1920 by the incoming Republicans.[33] They also revoked the excess profit tax and made income tax less progressive. Many economists have viewed the Hoover administration from 1929 as fiscally active, including the initiative for the Boulder dam and other infrastructure projects. However with monetary contraction lowering confidence and raising fears of higher interest rates, the 1932 Revenue Act raised income tax, lowered exemptions and increased some surtax rates. It is also now generally accepted that, though in the New Deal the Roosevelt administration raised spending on various infrastructure sectors (see the fifth section of this chapter) and on welfare, the resultant annual deficits were not Keynesian inspired. Rather they were unintended by-products of rising unemployment and related relief payments.[34] Indeed the 1935 Revenue Act saw a graduated tax on corporations, a tax on holding companies' corporate dividends, a higher surtax and extension of the federal estate tax/inheritance taxes, quite apart from the enactment of a tax on undistributed profits in 1937. In a similar fashion, whilst the state governments did receive enhanced Federal grants to help with expenditures on roads, unemployment and other welfare payments, their constitutions circumscribed budget deficits. In addition to spending cuts for roads and public works, they had to raise sales taxes on petrol, tobacco, alcohol, soft drinks and emerging consumer durables, user charges and licences for motor cars, special taxes on inheritances, banks and rail passengers as well as a modest income tax which raised 10 per cent of state revenues as early as 1930.

## The regulation of big business

For some Americans, big business was a threat to the "liberty" promised in the constitution and in no other country did the rise of big business precede the rise of big government. In our period, in no other country of the Western World was there more economic regulation. It was uniquely extensive, active and detailed, claimed Keller, adding that nowhere else did big business grow so rapidly and see such a large government response.[35] Whether or not one agrees with some contemporaries that big business was bloated and corrupt there seems little doubt that the regulatory system was "most strongly committed to fostering small unit competition".[36] The law anticipated where problems might arise in specifying that a "public interest" existed in sectors like transport, utilities and banking and over issues like corruption, chaotic competition, monopolies and, as mass production and long distance transport emerged, product quality.[37] From the point of view of the business sector, large or small, the prevailing government structure in the two decades following the Civil War raised three problems.

Before the Civil War, as noted earlier, Americans paid no taxes to the Federal government, only limited amounts to the states, leaving local government property tax revenues as the major supplement to Federal customs duty income. Bureaucracies were therefore small and as the economy expanded the legislation that emerged often lacked an implementation mechanism so that resort was invariably made to the courts at state and federal levels. Second, state governments had meagre tax resources but major powers of regulation, quite independent of the Fed and the powers adopted varied across states creating, as Woodrow

Wilson was to say "not a little friction and confusion" (see Chapter heading). As we emphasised in the previous section, these powers covered a wide area – incorporation, commercial law, rights of way, price setting, licensing, debt, insurance – and varied strongly across states. Resistance to attempts to impose national uniformity was strong – if marriage and divorce laws could vary, so much the worse for economic matters. In some states the regulation of business behaviour was negligible, including the right to incorporate (a private matter in New Jersey); in some states such regulation was weaker than that for alcohol. In others it developed strongly in the late nineteenth century: for example New York State's Commission on Fisheries was established in 1868, Board of Health in 1880, Railroad Commission in 1882, Forest Reserve 1885, Factory Inspectorate 1886, Mine Inspectorate 1890, Public Utility Commission 1907.[38] Companies could seek out "liberal" states for registration and could in the early years evade anti-monopoly laws by converting from holding company to trust status. Troesken shows clearly how for example the Chicago Gas Holding Company (holding shares in two operating companies) had effective monopoly power in the city and in 1889 the Illinois Supreme Court ordered its dissolution.[39] The firm then transformed itself in 1891 into a stock transfer trust, entitled the Chicago Gas Company, whose trustees issued trust certificates in exchange for the shares of the owners of the two operating companies. The Board of Directors had to implement the wishes of the owners of the trust certificates but this procedure evaded the anti-trust legislation in Illinois.

The manner in which the regulatory system emerged did reflect various interest groups. Economists have often thought of the regulatory system being "captured" by the companies in the industry since state regulation might give them an easier life than unbridled competition and federal regulation might be easier than state. In fact there was a complex set of interest groups behind the movements to regulation. The Granger Association was established in 1867 to defend farmers' interests against railway companies in the context of transport costs constituting one-half of the farmers' costs. They were aggrieved at the high prices charged on routes where the railways faced little competition and sought redress via state regulation (cf. Chapter 4). Here the companies were fighting regulation and in some instances challenged the very right of states to regulate.

On top of that was the third problem, the flow of goods and services across state boundaries and hence between different regulatory systems. As late as the 1880s the Federal government had limited powers and it was this which prompted the Inter-State Commerce Act of 1887 and the 1889 Sherman Anti-Trust Act (cf. Chapter 4). The latter arose from pressure from the owners of small oil refineries feeling the pinch from Standard Oil's rapid acquisition of the bulk of the refinery capacity during the 1880s. Standard Oil had introduced rail tank cars for transport from the refineries to retail outlets which was much cheaper than the barrels used by the small refiners who complained to Senator Sherman about the rail rate discounts which Standard Oil received for using the tank cars. As the prospect of securing his anti-tank car bill diminished, Sherman plumped instead for general legislation.[40] Drawing on common law injunctions against trade restrictions, it outlawed every contract and combination in restraint of trade. It proved a powerful, lasting statement in favour of competition but was so generally worded and with no enforcement mechanism that the courts had to deal with many disputes. So also for the Inter-State Commerce Act of 1887 which outlawed unreasonable rates, pooling and price discrimination by railway companies but the lack of an enforcement mechanism left much for the courts to resolve and matters were not helped by small staff numbers in the Department of Justice.

As part of the so-called "Progressive Era", there was in the 1890s and early 1900s a general tightening up of the regulatory frameworks though the weakness of the enforcement mechanisms meant the inter-state problems did not go away. As the number of states adopting anti-trust regulations increased, many companies resorted to the New Jersey state whose government in 1889 passed a law explicitly allowing mergers in the form of holding companies. The role of Public Utility Commissions for gas, electricity, water, urban transit and related dimensions of municipal and state regulation will be discussed in the next section which focuses on urbanisation. Now attention is directed to manufacturing, mining, oil, railways and telecommunications. The 1890s saw fierce price wars in these sectors so the fragile legal and government structures were exploited to defend special interest groups as in the famous meat packing case. The innovation of refrigerated railroad cars allowed Chicago butchers to slaughter meat before despatch eastwards. A Butchers' Protection Agency was formed and insisted on local state regulation (in the east) being applied to dressed meat. The Supreme Court ruled that this was simply a protectionist argument but it did lead to the establishment of the Federal Meat Inspection Service in 1891.[41] Rail stock prices had risen after the passing of the 1887 Inter-State Commerce Act, possibly in expectation of weaker regulation but this proved wrong. In 1897 the Supreme Court ruled explicitly that collusion, price fixing and pooling were illegal though it was clear from the 1895 Sugar Trust case that the Sherman Act could not be used for "production" within states, only trade across them. Rail companies tried to avoid the restrictions on pricing and pooling by forming "freight associations" but in a 1897/98 case these were banned.

The price wars and regulatory challenges were followed by a move to mergers, sometimes financed by the issue of securities which improved access to the capital market for smaller producers but led to the emergence of dominant firms like US Steel. Prosecutions were also avoided by the establishment of holding companies like J.P. Morgan's Northern Securities Company which held stock in the Northern Pacific and Great Northern rail companies. It was not until 1904 that this was deemed to violate the Sherman Act. In the meantime the number of multi-firm mergers increased: 13 in 1895–97, 16 in 1898, 63 in 1899 and over the whole period 1895–1904 more than 1800 manufacturing firms disappeared into consolidations.[42] Staffing in the Department of Justice was strengthened during the 1901–09 Roosevelt administration as were the powers of the ICC in the 1906 Hepburn Act, leading eventually in 1910 to the Mann Elkin Act which gave the Commission the ability to set rates as opposed to simply ruling on railway practice. In this decade 11 out of the 50 largest companies in USA were investigated in government actions, none in the UK.[43]

In telecommunications, attacks on the dominance of Western Union and Bell were more muted. For telephone there was a rise in the number of non-Bell companies established, especially after the expiry of the Bell patent in 1894, and especially in rural areas where there were gaps. Associated Telegraph and Telephone had been set up in 1885 as a Bell subsidiary to develop long lines, with horizontal and vertical integration. Profit rates were high and with predatory pricing, refusing connections of independents to the long lines, legal battles and service improvements, the dominance of Bell increased. State regulators had neither the resources nor the powers to fight Bell.[44] In 1899 all Bell assets were vested in American Telegraphy and Telephone (AT&T). Policy was to loan capital or give franchises to independents or they were absorbed. Big investors like J.P. Morgan took shares in AT&T which expanded as the proportion of non-Bell companies attached to the national network rose 1907–12 from 25.6 per cent to 63.5 per cent.[45] AT&T bought out the stock of the Western Union telegraph company in 1909 but by that stage it feared Federal takeover and engaged in an extensive public relations promotion about its unifying role in the American economy, even though 98 per cent of telephone calls in 1905 were local and 95 per cent less than 100 miles. Finally in 1910 it acceded readily to the empowerment of the ICC over inter-state telegraph and telephone with a brief to generate "just and reasonable rates". Then in 1913 came the so-called Kingsbury Commitment when AT&T promised to sell Western Union, to cease the acquisition of other telephone companies and improve the access of regional independents to the long distance network. The integrated AT&T/Bell system remained intact however and the non-Bell system was by then accounting for only 5 per cent of the 21,000 exchange points.[46]

More generally, by WW1, the potential for close regulation had become more firmly embodied in the law. In 1906 the Department of Justice prosecuted two of the country's largest companies, Standard Oil and American Tobacco, leading eventually in 1911 to the Supreme Court forcing them to break up their empires. It was their huge shares of the oil refinery and tobacco markets that prompted the ruling. In the case of Standard Oil, the pressure to act came from their competitors, Kansas oil producers, a not unusual confrontation in other sectors: action against the International Paper Corporation was prompted by complaints from one of their customers, the American Newspaper Publishers Association. Then in 1914 came the Clayton Act which put some (limited) flesh on the Sherman Act's general principle by explicitly forbidding price discrimination, tying clauses and interlocking directorships, *when they reduced competition*. In the same year came the Federal Trade Commission Act essentially introducing an enforcement mechanism by empowering the FTC, with "expert machinery", to investigate firms and design instruction and guidance. WWI saw, of course, considerable government intervention even though American industry was able to cope with the full thrust of war from 1917 because, as noted earlier, it had been producing war goods for its European friends 1914–16. Internally rail traffic

increased by one-third and in 1918 the president put the US Railroads administration in charge of all lines which were however returned to private ownership
after the war and indeed the 1920s saw something of a relaxation in Federal regulation. The Transportation Act of 1920 gave the ICC powers to streamline the
rates structure and reduce "wasteful competition" and rail companies were
allowed to pool if competition was not *unduly* restricted. Reorganisation plans
however never came to anything. With the depression and the onset of road
traffic and oil pipelines, railway companies fielded 500 applications in the 1930s
for sale of property and many companies went bankrupt.[47] It was not until the
1933 Emergency Transport Act and the 1935 Motor Carriers Act that rail
rate flexibility was allowed and inter-state trucking brought under Federal
supervision.

In fact across all industries, concentration continued. Whilst in 1904, two-
thirds of manufacturing firms were incorporated (as opposed to partnerships,
proprietors etc.), that share had risen to 97.6 per cent by 1927. By 1939, over the
whole economy, one-quarter of firms were corporations accounting for 72 per
cent of business income.[48] Before the 1934 Securities Act, the Federal government had no powers over incorporation and the states hung on to their powers,
the only concession being that they could not exclude a "foreign company". In
telecommunications, concentration continued relentlessly. Despite the 1921
Willis–Graham Act explicitly condemning the consolidation of competing telephone companies, by 1930 Bell/AT&T had acquired more than 250 independent
companies and its market share had risen to 75 per cent and it accounted for 80
per cent of local exchange customers. AT&T controlled virtually all long distance services and Western Electric 92 per cent of all telephone equipment.[49]
The battle over inter-state rates (Chapter 4) continued but state regulators were
unable to control AT&T/Bell or notionally separate its assets across state boundaries. The ICC had done little since its 1910 vestment of powers and it was not
until the establishment of the Federal Communications Commission in 1934 that
a consolidated federal regulatory authority was in place. A significant shift of
emphasis was therefore taking place by the 1930s and it included (limited) measures to cope with the impact of mass marketing for cars, foodstuffs, electrical
appliances. By the 1930s, 90 per cent of the complaints to the FTC were about
deceptive *trade* practices. The FTC was poorly staffed and unable to stop some
producers switching to other supervisory bodies – like the meat packers to the
Department of Agriculture. In 1920 the Supreme Court had declared that "unfair
competition" was not well defined in the 1912 Act and that therefore the FTC
should restrict itself to fact finding and leave the definition of "unfair" to the
courts. Then in 1927 FTC versus Eastman Kodak Company case, the court ruled
that the FTC did not have the power to undo anti-competitive asset acquisition –
not until the 1960s could it do that. Typical of the broad trends up to 1940, the
Federal government had made strong inroads into the independence of the states
and the confusion of regulatory regimes but the scope for evasion and for switching regimes was still strong. The related issue was that the direct provision of
economic services by the Federal government was increasing at the same time as

the emergence, at municipal and state levels, of Public Utility Commissions in the context of rapidly rising urbanisation, providing further tests of the American government structure.

## Government, corruption and business development of the urban infrastructure

The major economic feature in the Western World 1870–1939 was industrialisation and its concomitant impact on urban life. Industrialisation had costs in the form of congested and unhealthy cities and the development of the urban infrastructure was a task that fell both on the business sector and on the government. As compared to Europe, and especially to the first industrial nation, Britain, America's problems were smaller and later. In 1880 over two-thirds of the population, 36 million, still lived in what is often called "rural territory" – settlements with fewer than 2500 inhabitants. That number rose to 57 million by 1940 but it accounted for only 43.5 per cent of the total (Table 9.6). Nor did the role of the slightly bigger towns (2500 to 4999) change much as their share remained less than 4 per cent. In contrast towns with 5000–99,000 doubled their share and those of 100,000 or more, trebled. These were massive changes but note that in 1870 the share of the population in settlements of 5000 or more was only one-half that in the UK and that, although urbanisation was thereafter more rapid than in the UK, the differing population densities remained huge. In USA, density rose from 13 persons per square mile in 1870 to 40 by 1929 but this was still only one-tenth of the UK density. So America had more room to spread its cities. Indeed land abundance had many side effects in sanitation and waste disposal. An interesting example is the "British Destructor", a motorised machine invented for disposing of waste, extensively used in Nottingham and Manchester in the twentieth century. It never took off in USA because inorganic matter could be disposed of in America's vast acres of spare land.

The other key difference was in the business/state interface. Town planning hardly existed in the nineteenth century in Europe or America but some sort of order was needed in the development of the urban infrastructure. The business sector, especially corporations and trusts, were heavily involved in the growth in USA of electricity, gas supplies, urban transit systems and waterworks.[50] These are very capital intensive sectors with significant natural monopoly elements – it was cheaper often for one firm to provide services than two or more. Private utilities applied to city or state governments for rights of way and this invariably meant that they were initially the sole supplier. Even though exclusive rights for any given area were not granted and the markets could be contested, the question then arose whether, in contracts for services, prices should be regulated. The other problem was that once a firm had made the initial investment in pipes, lines, track, reservoirs, gas plants, generating stations and trams, the costs of removal meant the assets had little second hand value; costs were indeed sunken. The firms were then at the mercy of the City Council unless all contingences could be written into the contract. In the UK these problems had, from the 1820s,

Table 9.6 USA population 1880–1940

| | Total ('000) | Distribution by size of place | | | | Foreign born ('000) | Annual inflow of immigrants ('000) |
| | | Less than 2500 (%) | 2500 to 4999 (%) | 5000 to 99,000 (%) | 100,000 plus (%) | | |
|---|---|---|---|---|---|---|---|
| 1880 | 50,155 | 71.8 | 3.2 | 12.5 | 12.5 | 3631 | 457 |
| 1890 | 62,622 | 65.2 | 3.6 | 16.3 | 14.9 | 5067 | 455 |
| 1900 | 75,994 | 60.3 | 3.8 | 17.1 | 18.7 | 5630 | 449 |
| 1910 | 91,972 | 54.3 | 4.1 | 19.5 | 22.1 | 7667 | 1042 |
| 1920 | 105,710 | 48.8 | 4.1 | 21.1 | 26.0 | 7675 | 430 |
| 1930 | 122,755 | 43.8 | 3.8 | 22.8 | 29.6 | 7647 | 242 |
| 1940 | 131,669 | 43.5 | 3.8 | 23.9 | 38.8 | 6122 | 71 |

Source: US Bureau of the Census 1976.

led to Acts of Parliament for each utility, involving national regulation of prices and service quality by central government. Each utility was, effectively, granted a local monopoly. In 1870 in USA, the Federal government did not have such powers; the states could introduce regulations whilst municipal councils who wanted to regulate had to seek powers from the state governments. Given the variation in regimes across states and the gradual spread of networks, especially in electricity and water supply, America's complex government structure generated problems just as severe in this urban context as for big business and anti-trust.

At the start of our period, in the 1870s and 1880s, most networks were small with economies of scale rarely extending beyond city boundaries. America proved especially successful in developing electricity supply, in part through its natural hydro and coal endowments. By 1913, total kilowatt hours produced per 100 population was 25 (Table 9.1), twice the level in Germany, five times that in the UK who however did close some of that gap in the inter-war period (Chapter 8). The track for electric trams expanded hugely in USA to 599 miles per million population in 1905, with Germany at 56 and the UK at 84. In part this reflected British early success and concentration on coal fired gas plants which produced 115 cubic metres per head of population in 1900, roughly four times the level in USA.[51] Waterworks and coal gas plants had existed from the very early days of industrialisation. Use of water wells and pumps had a long history but clean reliable water supplies proved vital for public health, as well as industry, in all the growing cities of the Western World but in addition America's plentiful wood supplies meant major fire risks for buildings. So waterworks were constructed as the population and industry increased. Of the 90 towns in USA with at least 2500 population, one-half had a waterworks system as early as 1830 and by 1880 this had risen to 599 out of 939 such towns.[52] The history of health diagnostics from contagion to germ theory as experienced in Britain was exported to and mirrored in USA. Supervisory health bodies emerged, the first effective one being the Metropolitan Board of Health, established by the New York legislature in 1866 and a National Board of Health was set up by the Federal government in 1879 – albeit later replaced by other bodies shortly afterwards.

Water supply affected public health as well as involving problems about natural monopoly and one option for the city council was to run the service itself. As may be seen in Table 9.7, municipal ownership of utilities was much stronger in water supply than for gas and electricity undertakings where the municipal share never exceeded 10 per cent. Electricity supply came on the scene in the 1880s but whilst accounting for one-eighth of all generating capacity at its peak, many municipal plants were in small towns and never accounted for more than 5 per cent of total electricity produced. The urban transit system took readily to the use of electricity but most of this was in private ownership. Though there are plenty of early examples of municipal ownership of water supply, like the New York Croton River project bringing supplies to the city from 1842, the shift to municipal ownership developed most strongly from the 1860s. The literature is not always very incisive in explaining causation.

*Table 9.7* Municipal ownership share of electricity, gas and water supply in USA 1870–1940 (%)

|  | Number of waterworks | Number of gas enterprises | Output of electricity supply[a] | Generating capacity of electricity[b] |
|---|---|---|---|---|
| 1870 | 47.5 | – | – | – |
| 1880 | 48.9 | – | – | – |
| 1890 | 42.9 | 0.9 | – | – |
| 1896 | 52.9 | – | – | – |
| 1900 | – | 1.7 | 4.0 | – |
| 1902 | – | – | – | 11.9[c] |
| 1910 | – | 9.5 | 3.5 | – |
| 1912 | – | – | – | 12.2 |
| 1920 | – | 4.5 | 3.5 | – |
| 1922 | – | – | – | 9.6 |
| 1924 | 70.0 | – | – | – |
| 1930 | – | – | 4.5[d] | – |
| 1932 | – | – | – | 7.8 |
| 1937 | – | – | – | 8.9 |
| 1940 | – | – | 3.0[d] | – |

Sources: Hausman and Neufeld 1990, 1999; Melosi 2000; Neufeld 2008; Troesken 1997.

Notes

a  Interpolated from Figure 1 of Hausmann and Neufeld 1999. Supply is measured in kilowatt hours. Municipal is equated as "other government and cooperatives". Total supply also covers Federal, investor owned and "other" which includes self-generation in manufacturing firms, etc.

b  Mean average of the states' kilowatt capacity (whether or not state regulation was present).

c  Note that 815 out of 3620 central stations were municipally owned, implying many had small capacity.

d  The other supplies from government were federal, equivalent to 1% in 1930 and 5% in 1940.

Through its use of natural resources, water supply is a diminishing returns industry so that unless there are big technological advances in reservoirs and distribution networks, unit costs are likely to rise with increased supply. Limited evidence suggests this was the case in the nineteenth century as more remote sites were sought for supplies. Added to this were the demands for cleaner water and controls on prices. The narratives of Jacobbson and Melosi suggest that this pressure, as in the UK, threatened profit margins and municipalisation followed in many places.[53] Troesken's study of 1890s/1900s data show distinctly lower prices in municipally owned firms many of whom proved successful in reducing disease rates for low income, often black, populations.[54] Whilst it is possible the incentive for public ownership arose from the spillover effects of improved health, Troesken thinks that the evidence points more to patronage for votes and jobs.

This leads us to wider issues concerning the shift away from municipal to state involvement in utility regulation and the establishment of Public Utility Commissions in the early twentieth century. The states had powers to regulate, including the devolvement of powers to the municipalities. Or they could do nothing. Public Utility Commissions were not the only way to regulate and it is of note that none were established in Florida, Mississippi, Iowa, Minnesota, Nebraska, South Dakota and Texas before 1960. State governments naturally came to be involved as networks spread beyond city boundaries, especially in water and electricity supply and the experience of the latter will be examined here as a significant indicator of the general trends. The early electricity enterprises were small, unknown on the stock market and largely absent in rural areas. It soon became a very capital intensive industry with the arrival of alternating current and lengthening transmission lines. Annual investments for some companies exceeded annual revenues and for the whole industry the capital/output ratio averaged ten in 1900, more than double most other sectors.[55] Many undertakings linked themselves to equipment suppliers like Thomas Houston who came to accept the securities of the electricity supply companies as payment for equipment. This effectively gave such companies a channel to national stock markets. It was also accompanied by the proliferation of holding companies with subsidiaries holding shares in the electricity supply companies. Major corporations came to the fore: Electric Bond and Shares; Edison/General Electric; Pacific Gas and Electricity. By 1915 the top ten electricity supply firms had one-quarter of industry capacity. Consolidation increased even more in the 1920s as annual investment rose from $300 million 1908–20 to $750 million in 1924–30. By 1929 the ten largest electricity systems produced three-quarters of total output. The state governments, let alone the Federal, had no powers to regulate holding companies.[56]

It was within this context that state regulation emerged and sometimes as an alternative to municipalisation. In dealing with city councils, the electricity companies had two problems. Because of their sunken costs, the revenues of the companies can be seen as a quasi-rent; a return to a factor in inelastic supply in the short run. Companies then sought contracts which gave them a very quick return or spelled out lots of contingencies. City councillors could use this bargaining power for graft, of which there is ample evidence. Patronage for jobs and higher public sector wages than the private sector have been documented in the literature.[57] In a revealing report of 1909 on municipalisation in Britain, the US National Civic Federation responded to the common assumption in USA that public ownership was corrupt and inefficient by saying it depended on the efficiency of municipal government which, said Keller, implied, "in effect a declaration that in USA it was bound to fail".[58] Even without graft, city councils might see (as in the UK cf. Chapter 8) the profits from electricity as a useful supplement to their local property tax revenues, stretched as these were by massive spending programmes: paving, sidewalks, bridges, street lighting, sewers, schools, hospitals, libraries, museums as well as loans to rail companies to give their town good connections. Whilst the debt of state governments had been a big issue early in the century now it swung to the towns. Local government debt rose from $25 million in 1840 to $82 million in 1889 and $4 billion in 1913.[59]

For the electricity companies, dealing with local government could well lead to downward pressure on prices and profits, notwithstanding that over-zealous regulation could always be challenged by the provision in the 14th Amendment

*Table 9.8* Dates of establishment of state Public Utility Commissions 1887–1934[a]

| Year | States |
| --- | --- |
| 1887 | Massachusetts |
| 1907 | Georgia, New York, Wisconsin |
| 1908 | Vermont |
| 1909 | Michigan |
| 1910 | Maryland, Michigan, New Jersey |
| 1911 | California, Connecticut, Kansas, Nevada, New Hampshire, Ohio, Washington |
| 1912 | Arizona, Oregon, Rhode Island |
| 1913 | Colorado, Idaho, Illinois, Indiana, Maine, Missouri, Montana, North Carolina, Oklahoma, West Virginia |
| 1914 | Pennsylvania, Virginia |
| 1915 | Alabama, Wyoming |
| 1917 | Utah |
| 1919 | North Dakota, Tennessee |
| 1922 | South Carolina |
| 1932 | Arkansas |
| 1934 | Kentucky, Louisiana |

Source: Troesken 1997.

Note
a New Mexico, Delaware, Florida and Mississippi commissions were established 1941–56 whilst Iowa, Minnesota, Nebraska, South Dakota and Texas did not have Public Utility Commissions before 1960.

to the Constitution which forbade governments from depriving "any person of life, liberty or property".[60] The companies did not have exclusive franchises so the threat of competition was always present. Perhaps better then to push for state regulation which might give an assured market and more stable prices. Such was the regulatory "capture" thesis of several economists. Following the establishment of a Public Utility Commission (PUC) in Massachusetts in 1887, there was a 20 year gap before some 23 states followed suit in the years 1907–13 (Table 9.8). They could set rates based on "fair values" and a "reasonable return" but because they were answerable to a larger number of customers than the ICC (which was more concerned with particular railway contracts) they came under wider public pressure. Debate continues on whether prices have been affected by different regulatory regimes but of particular concern for us here is what caused the shift in some states and not in others. The surge in the appointment of PUCs coincided with a surge in municipal ownership. In fact for electricity the latter was concentrated on small towns and a survey in 1897/98 showed private utilities had four times the capacity of municipal enterprises, though there were exceptions like Los Angeles and Detroit. Neufeld's analysis of the incidence of state regulation 1902–37 revealed that states *without* PUCs had a smaller generating capacity and smaller urban populations.[61] He suggested that a bigger urban market generated more complaints about both graft (which the companies wanted to avoid) and high prices (which the companies sought). Since the PUCs were first set up in areas with big urban markets the graft argument must have been stronger than "capture". The problem of holding companies came to be resolved by the so-called "death sentence" of the Public Utilities Holding Company Act empowering the Securities and Exchange Commission to break up inter-state holding companies and gave the Federal Power Commission power over inter-state transmission. The Act ruled against holding companies owning stock in utilities – except the heavily regulated inter-state ones.[62]

This last reform may have inhibited network development across state boundaries and attempts by the Federal government to overcome the classic inter-state problem had been going on over the whole of the first half of the twentieth century. The big utilities' use of bribes to influence regulatory outcomes and the inability to regulate the holding companies led to much debate in the 1920s. President Hoover complained about limited network spread and the need for a much wider development.[63] The Federal Power Commission had been established in 1920 but its brief had been limited to hydro-electricity. Earlier control of western irrigation schemes had been transferred to the Federal government, from state and local governments, in the 1902 National Reclamation (Newlands) Act. The first Federal multi-purpose water project was the 1906 Roosevelt Dam on the Salt River where Congress had given the Fed the power to sell "surplus power". It took another 20 years for the development of the Colorado River, leading to the Hoover dam of 1928 built by the Bureau of Reclamation covering flood control, irrigation and water supply. Such was the pressure to keep the Fed away from the electricity power business that it was only granted permission to lease "kilowatts of falling water" to the City of Los Angeles and southern California Edison company generating stations.[64] The big challenge then became Muscle Shoals, a natural barrier on the Tennessee River, a tributary of the Ohio River, itself a tributary of the Mississippi. The barrier prevented ships using the full length of the Tennessee. The construction of a dam on Muscle Shoals was completed with electricity generation to be supplied by the Alabama Power Company. Full development of the Tennessee was left to F.D. Roosevelt and in 1933 Congress passed the Tennessee Valley Act.

## Notes

1  Wilson 1889, p. 478.
2  Cf. Keller 1981.
3  McGraw 1975, 1984; Sylla 2000.
4  Hummel 2007.
5  Bairoch 1989; Wallis 2000; Lindert 2000.
6  Galambos 2000a; Atack 1985.
7  Chandler 1976, 1984, 1990.
8  Tarr *et al.* 1987.
9  Hoag 2006.
10  Vietor 1989.
11  Millward 2005.
12  Heckelman and Wallis 1997.
13  Fishlow 2000.
14  Chandler 1976, 1984, 1990.

15 Temin 1991.
16 Wright 1990.
17 Ibid.
18 Lindert 2000.
19 Eliot Brownlee 2000.
20 Bairoch 1989.
21 Rose 1997.
22 Lindert 2000.
23 Thereby explaining the paradox first raised by Leontief (1956) that by 1947 US exports were not more capital intensive than imports which many had assumed, wrongly, was the source of comparative advantage. As the text shows, resources were often a key element, complementary to capital.
24 Wright 1990; Lindert 2000.
25 Kindleberger 1989; Bairoch 1989.
26 Keller 1990.
27 Letwin 1989.
28 Fishback 2007a.
29 Higgs 2007; Hummel 2007.
30 Sylla 2000.
31 Eliot Brownlee 2000.
32 Rockoff 2005.
33 Eliot Brownlee 2000.
34 Ibid.; Fishback 2007a.
35 Keller 1981.
36 Keller 1979, p. 515.
37 McGraw 1975.
38 Troesken 1997; Sylla 2000.
39 Troesken 1995.
40 Guglielmo and Troesken 2007.
41 Ibid.
42 Letwin 1989; Lamoureaux 2000.
43 Keller 1979.
44 Vietor 1989, p. 32; McDougall 2006.
45 Lipartito 1989.
46 Keller 1990, p. 79.
47 Vietor 2000.
48 Keller 1990.
49 Vietor 1989, p. 34.
50 Also housing where standards were increasingly regulated in both Europe and America, but space precludes exploring this big topic here.
51 Mitchell 1988; Millward 2005.
52 Melosi 2000.
53 Jacobbson 2000; Melosi 2000.
54 Troesken 2001.
55 Hausman and Neufeld 2002.
56 Hausman and Neufeld 1990, 2011; Hausman 2004.
57 Troesken 1999; Guglielmo and Troesken 2007.
58 Keller 1990, p. 57.
59 Sylla 2000.
60 Troesken 1997.
61 Neufeld 2008.
62 Hausman and Neufeld 2011; Vietor 2000.
63 Keller 1990.
64 Hausman and Neufeld 1999.

# 10 Conclusions

How far has our thesis, that government relations with the business sector were dominated by considerations of external defence and internal unification, been borne out? What other factors, including ideological commitments, economic growth and cultural dimensions, were important? Whereas there is little doubt that explicit government commitments for or against planning, free trade and capitalism were present by the mid twentieth century, the argument here has been that such commitments were largely absent in the nineteenth and early twentieth centuries and cannot explain the actual government policies which emerged. Interest groups like landowners and manufacturing lobbies played a part, especially since universal suffrage emerged only at the end of our period, but rarely overrode governments' strategic policies. We are not claiming to be the first to emphasise strategic factors in government economic policy. Economic history textbooks, especially for Europe, have certainly mentioned them. What they have not done is explain systematically the differences between countries, their pervasive influence through all parts of the economy and what this means for judgements on the effectiveness of government policy. Nor has the literature established clear links between central government policies and the problems of urbanisation which faced local government. Economic growth and living standards have, quite rightly, been the areas of major interest in economic history, but if these were not prime government targets, then government effectiveness in raising growth and living standards is not an appropriate criterion for judging the relations between government and the business sector.

Two key features of government policy have been identified. The first is external defence for which a wide range of instruments were used. Since military strength required warships and armaments, later tanks and aeroplanes, reliance on foreign sources was unacceptable. Most countries, in the nineteenth century, faced overpowering competition from British manufactured exports, so tariffs and quotas were extensive. Armament manufacture was split between state enterprises and the private sector, depending on how developed was the latter. Defence spending (together with the debt interest which followed wars), dominated central government expenditures and was largely financed by regressive indirect taxes prior to the arrival of limited income and business taxes, mainly from the end of the nineteenth century. Railways were needed for troop movements, especially for journeys to borders and for carrying key commodities like coal and iron. The French planned their railway network. Many lines in Germany, Russia and Japan were publicly owned or subsidised and large parts of these countries' outputs of coal, iron and steel came from state supervised or subsidised mines and factories. Electricity supply originated as a local utility but as national networks emerged in the early twentieth century, governments started to intervene, since, like coal, it became a key resource for industry for which short run substitutes were absent. By the late nineteenth century, the electric telegraph was owned by the state (except in USA) and, into the twentieth century, the European powers subsidised or owned the embryonic airline industry and took shares in international oil companies.

Industrial protection by tariffs and quotas was a common feature and it is useful to underline why. Opening up an economy to free trade is likely to lead to a shift of resources to commodities for which the country has a comparative advantage (say cotton goods) and away from those sectors (say pottery) where it is weak. The case for free trade is the potential that the size of the gains to winners exceeds the size of the losses to losers. Gainers could compensate losers and still be in front. Since compensation is rarely paid, the extent to which a government could survive such a redistribution would depend in part on the identity of the losers so that the Junker lobby for east German farming, facing competition from Russian and American grain, could well be successful. Even more crucial was when the potential losers were in strategically sensitive sectors like the iron and steel industries in France, Germany and Russia. It is not therefore surprising that in this era of aggressive nation states facing a dominant British industrial sector, most countries opted for protection of manufacturing, with Russia and USA at the front, even though USA's geographical isolation meant it was hardly needed.

The second element is what I have labelled internal unification. Some of this was linked to particular political structures, especially to the federal dimensions in Germany and USA, to which we will return shortly. The economic problems were linked to land usage, natural monopoly conditions and urbanisation, from which neither local nor central government could escape and which threatened chaos if ignored. Industrialisation raised the demand for land for residential and industrial building and for use as conduits for communications and energy. The scarcer the land and the more dense the population the more did problems arise. On the one hand land markets in Europe never worked sufficiently well for speedy emergence of routes for the new infrastructures; rights of way were created via compulsory purchase orders, mandated by governments. Because of increasing returns to scale, in the form here of natural monopoly conditions in railways, tramways, telegraph, telephone, sewerage, gas, electricity and water supply, granting rights of way gave the first in the field a monopoly position. The sunken capital also rendered the investors vulnerable to graft seeking, opportunistic, local officials in the course of granting rights of way, lighting contracts etc. In addition, knowledge and standards about personal and public health, water supplies and sewerage, were primitive at the start of the nineteenth century so the rapidly growing conurbations, especially in UK, Germany and USA, witnessed rising death rates as air- and water-borne diseases spread. These two issues, ill health and infrastructure monopolies, affected *everyone* in urban areas and had to be confronted by local government officials, and the extension of electoral franchises tended to be earlier for local than for national constituencies. Sewerage, water supplies, street cleaning and related sanitary services were financed mainly by municipal governments and provided by them – outsourcing was limited since technical knowledge was limited and the relevant companies simply did not exist. Huge public health programmes were therefore generated and were financed in part by rising local property taxes. Since the local franchise in the nineteenth century closely matched those who paid tax, other solutions were sought. Evidence from Germany and the UK suggests that many municipal enterprises established for street markets, gas, electricity and trams were effectively "cash cows". In rural areas, away from city congestion, services were left to private utility companies. Big town councils like Berlin, Paris and Copenhagen sometimes met their financial problems not by municipalisation but by making deals with big utility companies like Paris Gas and *Deutsche Edison Gesellschaft*. Whilst most central governments would have been happy to leave all these matters to local government (to "self-help" in British parlance), they found they could not keep out. Cholera epidemics and polluted rivers meant spillover effects over wider and wider areas. Local governments sometimes did not have the legal powers to adjudicate on land rights, especially as the size of networks increased, and when local monopolies emerged in the utility sectors, price regulation by local officials threatened to generate corruption. So we find prices and service standards for businesses in housing and utilities increasingly regulated at central government level in Europe and at state and federal level in USA.

Within this broad framework we can discern distinct differences between countries, which essentially reflected geo-political considerations (political geography, political structures, resource endowments) and stage of economic development, all of which are taken as exogenous in our analysis. France and Germany both had hostile neighbours on their borders and were committed to establish good communications and a strong state presence in railways, armaments, airlines, internal telegraph and telephone. France's demography made for a stagnant population, a liability in an era of army land battles, exacerbating the weaknesses arising from the distance between its coal and iron ore deposits and from their location in the vulnerable north-east border and Lorraine regions. Hydro-electricity, oil and aeroplanes eventually eased matters but French policy was never able to overcome its strategic weaknesses in our period. Germany's problems originated in its fragmented layers of government. From 1870 the new *Reich* commenced to reduce the power of the states and cope with hostile neighbours both on eastern and on western borders. The Saar and Silesia were key industrial areas unfortunately located in sensitive border areas so Ruhr industry received special attention. Imperial ventures overseas yielded little so that Germany increasingly looked to Eastern Europe for markets and raw material supplies. In all such developments government (and especially in states like Prussia), was deeply involved with a large number of state enterprises in coal, iron, steel, railways, ports, canals, armaments and overseas trade. Nor were these a financial burden: the best evidence available suggests the *Reich* and its constituent states received a larger share of revenues from state enterprise profits than any of the other major powers. Taxation followed European patterns but government turned a blind eye to cartels as part of its support for industry.

Of the other major powers, Russia is distinguished by its long history of territorial expansion over a huge area by conquest of existing communities. Autocratic rule in a patrimonial state required, in such a large landscape, a controlled population to act as labour supply, army and tax base. It engaged in all the state intervention found in Germany but in a more hesitant fashion, fearing that industrialisation would lead to democratisation and challenge to Tsarist rule. Agriculture did progress after the Act of 1860 emancipating serfs, and industrial businesses did flourish with loans and credit support from government and foreign sources. The suppression of the unrepresented peasantry, in conjunction with the hesitant industrial policy, were key ingredients in the defeat of Tsarism in the Revolution and in WWI, heralded earlier by defeat in the 1904/05 war with Japan, a country much less hesitant in forging a path to industrialisation. Deprived of raw materials in its island setting, the Japanese government ventured into the Asian mainland, built railways, subsidised shipping and sought oil and other strategic resources. It had no contiguous hostile states and its course of action was dictated by the implicit threat from Britain, France and others, of being subjugated to mere colony status.

The UK and USA appear detached from these developments and both have been credited with a strong commitment to free trade capitalism. As an island economy, the UK had no contiguous hostile neighbours, especially with Ireland integrated after 1800. Its ingenuity, entrepreneurship and strong central administration, during the classic industrial revolution period 1760–1840, made it the dominant world industrial power by the mid nineteenth century. Free trade did imply a massive shift in the balance of the economy to industry and services but the decline in agriculture was spread out over a very long period in the context of rising agricultural output and wages. It had no need to protect its manufacturing – it was not threatened. As the first railway nation, internal communications were also, by contemporary standards, excellent and its coal output was huge. Even its international telegraph lines were left to private British companies since no other country in the nineteenth century had the industrial strength and worldwide landing rights to compete and the other powers were left dependent on British lines. Although little has been said in this book about imperial connections, it seems, from recent interpretations of the British "world system",[1] that government intervention was limited, with much reliance on the British lead in naval and mercantile power, armaments and international cables, all of which we have examined. None of this was inconsistent with what was happening elsewhere in Europe and Japan, as became apparent in the inter-war period 1919–39. Britain's loss of export markets, decline in relative industrial strength, huge regional pools of unemployment emerging as early as the 1920s and a rising presence of other major powers in the international telegraph market, led to wholesale UK government intervention. Rationalisation of the structure of industries like cotton, coal, chemicals, shipbuilding, iron and steel entered the government agenda. State enterprises, share ownership and subsidies in electricity supply, international telegraph and railways led eventually after WWII to state ownership of much of the nation's infrastructure.

By that stage Britain had come to grips with the congestion problems which early industrialisation had brought to its cities. USA had similar problems but on a smaller scale. The share of the population in small communities was larger and, as late as 1929, population density in USA was only 10 per cent of UK. The American economy was nonetheless more regulated than any of the major powers, embracing areas like anti-trust, food quality, inter-state commerce, utility pricing. Early patterns in regulating rates and tariffs for canals, railways and electricity were similar to Europe though over time the contrast between central government regulation in the UK and initially municipal regulation in USA may explain why the latter witnessed more corruption as local officials tried to exploit the vulnerability of utility companies with capital sunk in local assets. Higher level public utility regulation started in the early 1900s at state level, adding to the widespread powers of the states: anti-trust, food quality, licensing, commercial law, rights of way, price setting, debt, insurance, railways, telecoms, road transport and the sole right to charter companies. As networks expanded, inter-state flows had to be addressed, triggering a long battle to introduce Federal regulation. The ability of business to switch regulatory regimes by relocating to more business friendly states generated a culture of avoidance mirrored in today's global tax havens. The American economy did however flourish from the surge of entrepreneurship, the large internal market and excellent education system. It was well endowed in the nineteenth century with the key mineral resources at the heart of the capital goods led industrial surge of the late nineteenth century, emerging therefore in the twentieth century with a buoyant private sector but fragile government.

What other general factors emerge from the evidence? Whilst the Napoleonic code, the *corps* and *écoles* could be linked to purely strategic considerations, they did confer a special centralising feature to state/business relations in France. The next active Napoleon (III) in mid nineteenth century did promote free trade as did elements in the Prussian bureaucracy. But these explicit manifestations of commitments to free trade were short lived. Tariff protection was resisted successfully throughout the nineteenth century only in Britain where it was easier with a rapidly expanding economy and no one sector likely to lose out absolutely, apart from agriculture. Was the socialist influence strong 1815–1939? Some writers have pointed to the rise of municipal enterprise but the timing is wrong since the early bursts in Europe were in the 1850–80 period, well before the electoral success of socialist parties in the early 1900s. The retention of slavery and serfdom up to 1860 in USA and Russia did not imply non-commercial motives on the part of estate owners since both were profitable.

What proved more of a cultural and institutional commitment was the racial segregation which persisted in USA and the subservient status of much of the workforce in Russia right up to 1917.

Where the weight of evidence in favour of our core thesis breaks down is at the end of the 1815–1939 period. This, it should be emphasised, is not because of anything which happened in Russia. The 1917 Revolution and the 1920s New Economic Policy did herald more state attention to average living standards. But by the end of the 1920s it was clear that Russia was strategically vulnerable, yet again, and the whole economy was shifted to building up industrial and military strength under the rubric of Stalinist planning. For the other major powers the significant elements were the attainment of universal suffrage, the cataclysmic effects of the 1930s depression and the new political structures which emerged after WWII. This is why my book finishes in the 1930s. In the nineteenth century there was no female suffrage and economic restrictions (property qualifications for example) were widespread. Racial discrimination and a subjugated population survived for much of the twentieth century in, respectively, USA and Russia. Recent research suggests that changes in the electoral franchise have little explanatory power with respect to central government spending.[2] By the inter-war period however economic restrictions in the franchises had all but disappeared and women's suffrage was established. A considerable pressure had therefore developed to provide economic improvements for *everyone*, the need for which was dramatically underlined by the depression of the 1930s. After WWII, Japan and Germany were dismantled militarily, wars between the Western European powers had disappeared and, with the emergence of the North Atlantic Treaty Organization, defensive considerations moved up from the nation state. The General Agreement on Trade and Tariffs, the European customs area and eventually the European Economic Community meant trade could be freed up through deals which minimised internal disruptions as the economic strengths of each country changed. The Cold War involving Russia, USA and NATO brought new parameters to the state/business interface. Strategic factors perhaps became less important in government domestic policy but that is another story.

## Notes

1 Cf. Darwin's incisive analyis (2009) of the "Empire Project", p. 39 and elsewhere.
2 Aidt *et al.* 2006.

# Annex

Table A1 Land areas of the major powers 1820–1951 ('000 square miles)

|      | France[a] | Germany[b] | Japan[c] | Russia[d] | UK[e] | USA[f] |
|------|-----------|------------|----------|-----------|-------|--------|
| 1820 | 213       | 108        | 163      | 6775      | 142   | 1788   |
| 1870 | 213       | 198        | 163      | 7643      | 142   | 3022   |
| 1913 | 208       | 204        | 163      | 8379      | 142   | 3022   |
| 1929 | 213       | 172        | 163      | 8176      | 117   | 3022   |
| 1951 | 213       | 137        | 183      | 8600      | 117   | 3022   |

Notes and sources

a The area of France is taken to be 212,900 square miles ($m^2$) (as given in *Whitaker's Almanac* for 1924), except for 1913 when Alsace and Lorraine were in Germany and a figure of 207,218 $m^2$ is used, as in the 1910 Almanac.

b The 1820 entry relates to Prussia in 1815. In Fischer *et al.* (1982, p. 35), the area of Prussia is given as 282,261 $km^2$ for 1841. Deducting Hohenzollern (1148 $km^2$) gives 280,132 or 108,124 $m^2$. *Whitaker's Almanac* for 1910 records the area of the German Empire as 203,827 $m^2$ which is used for 1913. This includes 5622 $m^2$ for Alsace and Lorraine which is deducted to yield a figure for 1870 of 198,235 $m^2$. For 1929 the figure of 172,300 $m^2$ is used as in *Whitaker's Almanac* for 1924. The 1951 entry includes East and West and is 137,105 $m^2$, from *Whitaker's Almanac* for 1960.

c The area of Japan is taken to be 162,655 $m^2$ for 1820–1929 as given in *Whitaker's Almanac* for 1910. For 1951 it is 182,700 $m^2$ as in *Whitaker's Almanac* for 1960.

d The area of the Russian empire was 8,379,044 $m^2$ according to the 1910 *Whitaker's Almanac* and this is used for 1913. Berelowitch *et al.* (1998, pp. 493, 504) give the area as 19.8 million $km^2$ for 1867 which is used for 1870 (1 $km^2$ = 0.386 $m^2$). They also state that population density in 1810 was 2.4 persons per $km^2$ and the population was 42 million which yields an area of 6,775,000 $m^2$ which is used for 1820. Lorimer (1946, p. 29) gives the area of USSR as 8,176,000 $m^2$ in 1924 and this figure is used here for 1929. The 1960 *Whitaker's Almanac* gives the area of the USSR as 8,599,766 $m^2$ which is used for 1951 and therefore includes areas like Latvia and Byelorussia which were part of USSR but are not part of the Russian Federation.

e The area of the UK comprises Britain (that is England, Wales and Scotland, 89,715 $m^2$) plus Northern Ireland (5462 $m^2$) and, before 1921, S. Ireland (27,136 $m^2$). See Mitchell (1988).

f The USA data are from US Bureau of the Census 1976 and relate to the gross area including inland lakes. In the period 1821–69 (cf. Gallman 2000, p. 12) all of Texas, Oregon and the Mexican secession (1,204,700 $m^2$) was absorbed together with the Gadsen Purchase (45,553 $m^2$, southern parts of Arizona and New Mexico). Alaska (590,884 $m^2$) was purchased in 1868 but did not become a state until 1958. Similarly Hawai (6449 $m^2$) was purchased in 1890 but did not become the 50th state until 1959.

*Table A2* Population of the major powers[a] 1820–1952 (millions)

| Year | France | Germany | Japan | Russia | UK[b] | USA |
|------|--------|---------|-------|--------|-------|-----|
| 1820 | 30.7 | 15.1[c] | 31.0 | 50.0[d] | 21.2 | 9.6 |
| 1870 | 38.4 | 39.2 | 34.4 | 82.0[d] | 31.4 | 39.9 |
| 1913 | 39.8 | 67.0 | 51.7 | 162.8[d] | 45.6 | 97.2 |
| 1929 | 41.2 | 64.7[e] | 63.2 | 172.0 | 45.7 | 121.8 |
| 1951 | 42.2 | 68.9 | 84.3 | 183.2 | 50.6 | 154.9 |

Sources: Berelowitch *et al.* 1998; Fischer *et al.* 1982; Maddison 1991, 1995, 2003; Mitchell 1988.

Notes

a Contemporary borders. See Table A1.

b The population of Britain (i.e. England, Wales and Scotland) was 14.0 million in 1820, 23.8 (1870), 35.5 (1913), 44.4 (1929), 48.9 (1951). The population of all Ireland was 6.7 million (1820), 5.4 (1870), 4.3 (1913). Together they comprised the UK but, after 1921, only N. Ireland whose population was 1.24 million in 1929 and 1.27 in 1951. The population of S. Ireland was 2.94 in 1929 and 2.96 in 1951. See Mitchell 1988.

c Prussia 1820. See Fischer *et al.* (1982, p. 39) (Prussia less Hohenzollern, 61,500).

d The Russian Empire, including Poland and Finland. The entries for 1820 and 1870 were interpolated from the graph on p. 493 of Berelowich *et al.* 1998. The 1913 entry relates to 1914.

e Relates to 1935 territory of the Reich.

*Table A3* Gross domestic product per head 1820–1951 (modern boundaries, 1990 international Geary-Khamis $)[a]

|      | France | Germany | Japan | Russia | UK | USA |
|------|--------|---------|-------|--------|-----|-----|
| 1820 | 1135 | 1077 | 669 | 688 | 1706 | 1257 |
| 1870 | 1876 | 1839 | 737 | 943 | 3190 | 2445 |
| 1913 | 3485 | 3648 | 1387 | 1488 | 4921 | 5301 |
| 1929 | 4710 | 4051 | 2026 | 1386 | 5503 | 6899 |
| 1951 | 5553 | 4206 | 2126 | 2806 | 7123 | 10,116 |

Source: Maddison 2003.

Note

a In general, the data relate to 2003 boundaries except Russia which covers the territory of the former USSR in 1989. For Germany the entries for 1820–1913 relate to 1870 frontiers (i.e. do not include Alsace-Lorraine), the 1929 entry to 1936 frontiers.

*Table A4* Distribution of employees by sector 1820–1950 (%)[a]

|  | France | Germany | Japan | Russia | UK | USA |
|---|---|---|---|---|---|---|
| *1820* |  |  |  |  |  |  |
| Agriculture | 61.0[b] | 64.0[b] | – | – | 37.6 | 70.0 |
| Industry | – | – | – | – | 32.9 | 15.0 |
| Services | – | – | – | – | 29.5 | 15.0 |
| *1870* |  |  |  |  |  |  |
| Agriculture | 49.2 | 49.5 | 70.1[c] | 81.0 | 22.7 | 50.0 |
| Industry | 27.8 | 28.7 | – | – | 42.3 | 24.4 |
| Services | 23.0 | 21.8 | – | – | 35.4 | 25.6 |
| *1913* |  |  |  |  |  |  |
| Agriculture | 41.1 | 34.6 | 60.1 | 70.0 | 11.7 | 27.5 |
| Industry | 32.3 | 41.1 | 17.5 | – | 44.1 | 29.7 |
| Services | 26.6 | 24.3 | 22.4 | – | 44.1 | 42.8 |
| *1930* |  |  |  |  |  |  |
| Agriculture | 35.6 | 29.0 | 49.4 | – | 6.0 | 21.9 |
| Industry | 33.3 | 40.4 | 20.8 | – | 46.5 | 33.6 |
| Services | 31.1 | 30.6 | 29.7 | – | 47.5 | 47.2 |
| *1950* |  |  |  |  |  |  |
| Agriculture | 28.3 | 22.2 | 48.3 | 46.0 | 5.1 | 12.9 |
| Industry | 34.9 | 43.0 | 22.6 | 29.0 | 9.0 | 44.9 |
| Services | 36.8 | 34.8 | 29.1 | 25.0 | 45.8 | 53.5 |

Sources: Maddison 1995, Table 2.5; Buyst and Franaszek 2010 for France, Germany, UK 1930; Mitchell 2003b and c for Japan 1870 and 1930 and USA 1930; Dennison and Simpson 2010, p. 149 for France and Germany 1820 and Russia 1870.

Notes
a Dashes indicate data not available. Coverage may vary since some sources use the "employed population" and others the "economically active population". Agriculture includes forestry and fishing. Industry covers manufacturing, extraction, construction and energy. The data relate to contemporary boundaries except as follows: Russia 1913–50 relates to the territory of the former USSR in 1989; for Germany the entry for 1820 relates to Prussia, for 1870–1913 to 1870 frontiers (i.e. does not include Alsace-Lorraine), 1930 to 1936 frontiers and 1950 to 2003 frontiers.
b Interpolated from 1775 and 1845 figures for Prussia and France in Dennison and Simpson (2010, p. 149).
c 1872.

*Table A5* Coal output of the major powers[a] 1820–1951 (million metric tons)

| Year | France | Germany[b] | Japan | Russia | UK | USA[c] |
|---|---|---|---|---|---|---|
| 1820 | 1.1 | 1.3 | n.a. | n.a. | 17.7 | 0.3 |
| 1870 | 13.3 | 32.0 | 0.2 | 0.7 | 112.1 | 36.7 |
| 1913 | 40.8 | 277.3 | 21.3 | 36.1 | 292.0 | 517.1 |
| 1929 | 55.0 | 337.9[d] | 34.4 | 40.0 | 262.0 | 552.3 |
| 1951 | 55.0 | 358.3 | 44.7 | 282.0 | 225.8 | 522.8 |

Sources: Mitchell 2003a, b and c.

Notes
a Contemporary borders. See Table A1.
b Includes brown coal.
c Includes hard bituminous, brown bituminous and anthracite.
d Excludes Upper Silesia and Saarland.

*Table A6* Output of iron ore and pig iron: the major powers[a] 1820–1951 (in '000 metric tons)

| Year | | France | Germany | Japan | Russia | UK | USA[b] |
|------|------|--------|---------|-------|--------|-----|--------|
| 1820 | Iron ore | 830[c] | 175[d] | n.a. | n.a. | n.a. | n.a. |
|      | Pig iron | 113[c] | 85[e] | n.a. | 135[f] | 374 | 1805 |
| 1870 | Iron ore | 2614 | 2918 | n.a. | n.a. | 14,602 | 3893 |
|      | Pig iron | 1178 | 1261 | n.a. | 359 | 6059 | 1692 |
| 1913 | Iron ore | 21,918 | 28,608 | 17[g] | 9537 | 16,254 | 62,975 |
|      | Pig iron | 5207 | 16,761 | 243 | 4641 | 10,425 | 31,463 |
| 1929 | Iron ore | 50,728 | 6374 | 88[g] | 7997 | 13,427 | 74,200 |
|      | Pig iron | 10,300 | 13,240 | 1112 | 4021 | 7711 | 43,298 |
| 1951 | Iron ore | 35,207 | 12,923[h] | 600[g] | 44,926 | 15,014 | 118,375 |
|      | Pig iron | 8750 | 11,039 | 3227 | 21,909 | 9824 | 65,746 |

Sources: Mitchell 2003a, b and c.

Notes
a Contemporary borders. See Table A1.
b Iron ore measured as crude weight, rather than Fe content.
c 1819 for pig iron and 1835 for iron ore.
d 1822.
e 1823.
f Covers 50 provinces of European Russia, excluding Poland, Finland and the Caucasus.
g Gross weight for 1913, Fe content subsequently.
h Covers West Germany only.

*Table A7* Output of metals (non-ferrous) and minerals in Western Europe[a] and Japan 1870–1951 ('000 metric tons)

|  | 1870 | 1913 | 1929 | 1951 |
|---|---|---|---|---|
| *France* | | | | |
| Bauxite | n.a. | 309 | 678 | 1146 |
| Potash | – | – | 492 | 872 |
| *Germany* | | | | |
| Copper | 207 | 942 | 29 | 8.5[b] |
| Lead | 106 | 145 | 60.5 | 50.4[c] |
| Potassium salts | 292 | 11,957[d] | 13,328 | 10,847[c] |
| Potash | – | – | – | 1409[b] |
| Zinc | 367 | 773 | 142.5[e] | 75.3[c] |
| *Japan* | | | | |
| Copper | 2.1[f] | 6.7[f] | 75[f] | 43[f] |
| Chromium | n.a. | n.a. | 3 | 14 |
| Gold | 0.0001[g] | 0.0055 | 0.0104 | 0.0059 |
| Manganese[h] | 1[i] | 18[j] | 3 | 68 |
| Mercury[k] | n.a. | 0.001[l] | 0.025 | 0.064 |
| Molybdenum[m] | n.a. | n.a. | n.a. | 0.054 |
| Silver[n] | 0.0027 | 0.146 | 0.176 | 0.170 |
| Sulphur | 48[o] | 59 | 62 | 93 |
| Tungsten | n.a. | n.a. | 0.023 | 0.100 |
| Zinc | n.a. | 34 | 18 | 68 |
| *UK* | | | | |
| Copper | 7.3[p] | – | – | – |
| Lead | 74.6 | 18.4 | 18.0 | 4.2[q] |
| Tin | 10.4[p] | 5.4 | 18.0 | 4.2 |

Sources: Mitchell 2003 a and c.

Notes

a  Contemporary borders. See Table A1. Dashes mean the amount was negligible relative to world supplies.

b  Mainly East Germany.

c  Wholly West Germany.

d  Includes Alsace and Lorraine.

e  Excludes eastern Upper Silesia but includes non-crude as well as crude ore.

f  Smelter production. 1870 entry relates to 1874.

g  1874.

h  Mn content.

i  1888.

j  Gross weight.

k  Hg content.

l  1911.

m  Mo content.

n  Metal content. 1870 entry relates to 1874 production at the refinery stage; later entries to content of mined ores.

o  1875.

p  Data for 1870 suggest 3.0 metric tons of tin were sold and also 7600 metric tons of copper were sold publicly in Devon and Cornwall.

q  Includes metal from lead concentrates.

*Table A8* Output of metals (non-ferrous) and minerals in Russia 1870–1951 ('000 metric tons)

| | 1870 | 1913 | 1929 | 1951 |
|---|---|---|---|---|
| *Metals* | | | | |
| Copper ores | 99.2[a] | 1117.1 | 540.7[b] | n.a. |
| Refined copper | 5.05 | 33.1 | 35.5 | 255[c] |
| Lead | 1.63 | 1.53 | 5.49 | 144[cd] |
| Zinc ore | 0.08[a] | 37.95 | 1.47[b] | n.a. |
| Zinc produced | 3.09 | 2.95 | 3.01 | 123[d] |
| Manganese ore | n.a. | 1250 | 1410[d] | 3380[e] |
| Platinum | 4.0[a] | 4.91 | 2.04[e] | n.a. |
| *Minerals* | | | | |
| Gold | 0.035[a] | 0.062 | 0.031[e] | n.a. |
| Silver produced[f] | 0.015[a] | 0.004 | 0.013[b] | n.a. |
| Soda ash | 1.32 | 160.0 | 238.7 | 748.6[e] |
| Asbestos (in million shingles) | n.a. | 9 | 51.3 | 546.4[e] |

Sources: Thanks are due to Olya and Nat Moser and Peter Gatrell for supplying me with data and guidance to the following sources. Kafengaus 1994 for 1870–1929 copper, zinc ore, platinum, gold, silver; Zaleski 1971 for 1929 soda ash and 1980 for refined copper 1950. Nutter 1962 for refined copper, zinc produced, manganese ore (confirmed in Zaleski 1980), soda ash (confirmed in Zaleski 1971 for 1929 entry and Zaleski 1980 for 1950 entry) and lead (where Kafengaus has 1.37 for 1913 and 1.027 for 1926/27).

Notes
a  1887
b  1926/27
c  1950
d  Estimate
e  1917
f  Belikovyy, metal dore.

*Table A9* USA output of metals (non-ferrous) and minerals 1870–1951 ('000 metric tons)

|  | 1870 | 1913 | 1929 | 1951 |
|---|---|---|---|---|
| *Metals* | | | | |
| Bauxite[a] | * | 214 | 372 | 1878 |
| Copper[b] | 13 | 560 | 905 | 842 |
| Lead | n.a. | 438 | 588[b] | 352[b] |
| Manganese | 5.8[c] | 4 | 27 | 48 |
| Mercury[d] | 1.044 | 0.688 | 0.815 | 0.251 |
| Molybdenum[e] | * | 0.001 | 1.771 | 17.217 |
| Tungsten[f] | n.a. | 664 | 358 | 2709 |
| Vanadium[g] | n.a. | 6.592 | 4.418 | 2.758 |
| Zinc[b] | n.a. | 375 | 657 | 618 |
| *Minerals* | | | | |
| Asbestos | n.a. | n.a. | 2.9 | 47 |
| Gold[h] | 0.075 | 0.134 | 0.064 | 0.062 |
| Potash[i] | * | 1 | 53 | 1228 |
| Silver[h] | 0.385 | 2.314 | 1.893 | 1.237 |
| Sulphur[j] | 1 | 499 | 2400 | 5365 |

Source: Mitchell 2003b.

Notes

\* Negligible.

a  1913 data relate to shipments, 1929 to production or shipments, 1951 to production of dried bauxite equivalent.

b  Estimated recoverable content of domestically mined ores. For copper it is the Cu content for zinc Zn.

c  Mn content. 1870 entry relates to 1880 shipments of ore of more than 40% Mn content, 1913–51 to 35%+ content.

d  Hg content.

e  Mo content.

f  $WO_3$ content.

g  V content.

h  Production at refinery stage 1870; thereafter content of mined ore. Silver is metal content.

i  Relates to $K_2O$ content and excludes ferro-alloys.

j  Excludes ferro-alloys. The 1870 entry relates to 1880.

*Table A10* Oil and gas production of the major powers[a] 1870–1951 (crude petroleum in '000 metric tons and natural gas in million cubic metres)

| Year | | France | Germany | Japan | Russia | UK | USA |
|------|-----|--------|---------|-------|--------|-----|------|
| 1870 | Oil | 0 | 0 | 0.6[b] | 33 | 0 | 701 |
|      | Gas | 0 | 0 | n.a. | n.a. | 0 | n.a. |
| 1913 | Oil | 0 | 121 | 252[c] | 10,281 | 0 | 33,126 |
|      | Gas | 0 | 0 | 14[d] | 29 | 0 | 16,486[c] |
| 1929 | Oil | 75 | 103 | 278 | 13,684 | 0 | 138,104 |
|      | Gas | 0 | 0 | 29 | 331 | 0 | 55,274[e] |
| 1951 | Oil | 291 | 1367 | 336 | 42,253 | 46 | 303,754 |
|      | Gas | 282 | 84[f] | 83 | 6252 | 0 | 211,159 |

Sources: Mitchell 2003a, b and c.

Notes
a Contemporary borders. See Table A1.
b 1879. Includes Taiwan.
c Includes Taiwan
d 1916.
e Marketed production.
f Covers only West Germany and excludes natural gas from oil wells.

*Table A11* Electricity supply in the major powers 1913–51 (net gigawatt hours)[a]

| Year | France | Germany | Japan | Russia | UK | USA |
|------|--------|---------|-------|--------|-----|------|
| 1913 | 1.80 | 8.0[b] | 1.14 | 2.04 | 2.5[c] | 24.75[d] |
| 1929 | 15.60 | 30.66[b] | 15.12 | 6.22 | 16.98 | 116.75 |
| 1951 | 38.15 | 75.19[b] | 47.86 | 104.02 | 69.37[b] | 433.36 |

Sources: Mitchell 2003a, b and c.

Notes
a Contemporary borders. See Table A1. "Net" means after deducting power used in generating stations.
b Gross output.
c Rough estimate of sales.
d 1912.

*Table A12* Electricity supply and population: major powers[a] 1913–51 (net kilowatt hours per 100 population)

| Year | France | Germany | Japan | Russia | UK | USA |
|------|--------|---------|-------|--------|-----|------|
| 1913 | 5 | 12[b] | 2 | 1.2[c] | 6[d] | 25[e] |
| 1929 | 38 | 47[b] | 24 | 4 | 37 | 96 |
| 1951 | 90 | 109[b] | 57 | 57 | 137[b] | 280 |

Sources: see Tables A1, A2 and A11.

Notes
a Contemporary borders. "Net" means after deducting power used in generating stations.
b Gross output.
c 1913 electricity supply divided by 1914 population.
d Rough estimate of sales.
e 1912. Population was 95.3 million.

*Table A13* Merchant fleets of the major powers 1820–1951 (net registered weight in '000 metric tons)[a]

| Year | France | Germany | Japan | Russia | UK | USA |
|------|--------|---------|-------|--------|----|----|
| 1820 | 680[b] | 265[c] | n.a. | n.a. | 2439 | 1260[d] |
| 1870 | 1072 | 939 | 16[d] | 260[e] | 5691 | 3438[d] |
| 1913 | 1582 | 3320 | 1528 | 783[e] | 12,120 | 6841[d] |
| 1929 | 2007 | 2402 | 3862 | 437[d] | 11,369 | 14,987[d] |
| 1951 | 3367[f] | 1099[g] | 2182 | 2222[d] | 10,955 | 27,496[d] |

Sources: Mitchell 2003a, b and c.

Notes

a  Contemporary borders. See Table A1. "Net" means after deducting cargo weight.
b  1838.
c  1829.
d  Gross tonnage. For Japan 1870, the data refer to all non-wooden vessels owned by Japanese citizens.
e  Excludes vessels less than 25 tons and all Finland.
f  Gross capacity of vessels 100 tons or more.
g  The data for East Germany excludes vessels less than 60 net tons.

*Table A14* Length of railway track open: major powers[a] 1820–1951 (miles)

| Year | France | Germany | Japan | Russia | UK[b] | USA |
|------|--------|---------|-------|--------|-------|-----|
| 1820 | 11[c] | 0 | n.a. | 17[d] | 27 | 23[e] |
| 1870 | 9658 | 11,728 | 18[f] | 6668 | 13,395[g] | 52,920[e] |
| 1913 | 25,332 | 39,380 | 6568 | 43,591 | 20,270 | 249,769 |
| 1929 | 26,283 | 36,152 | 12,840 | 47,782 | 20,281 | 249,424 |
| 1951 | 25,600 | 30,955 | 17,124[h] | 73,195 | 19,356 | 223,419 |

Sources: Mitchell 1988, 2003a, b and c.

Notes

a  Contemporary borders. See Table A1.
b  Britain, that is, excludes all Ireland.
c  1828.
d  Relates to average length of line open, excluding local lines. Later data relate to all lines, end year. The 1820 entry relates to 1838.
e  Railways operated, which includes some double counting. The data refer to railways owned. The 1820 entry relates to 1830.
f  1872.
g  1871.
h  Includes tramlines.
1 mile = 1.6094 kilometres.

*Table A15* Railway track and population: major powers[a] 1820–1951 (rail track miles per 100,000 population)

| Year | France | Germany | Japan | Russia | UK[b] | USA |
|------|--------|---------|-------|--------|-------|-----|
| 1820 | 0.1[c] | 0 | n.a. | 0.1[de] | 0.2 | 0.2[f] |
| 1870 | 25 | 30 | 0.1[g] | 8[d] | 51[h] | 133[f] |
| 1913 | 64 | 59 | 13 | 27[di] | 49 | 257 |
| 1929 | 64 | 56 | 20 | 28 | 46 | 205 |
| 1951 | 61 | 45 | 20[j] | 40 | 40 | 144 |

Sources: see Tables A1, A2 and A14.

Notes
a Contemporary borders. See Table A1.
b Britain only, i.e. excludes all Ireland.
c 1831.
d Excludes local lines and relates to average length of line open during the year. Later entries relate to all lines at year end.
e 1838 track length divided by population estimate for 1838 of 58 million interpolated from Berelowitch *et al.* (1998, p. 493).
f Railways operated, which includes some double counting. After 1870, the data refer to railways owned. The 1820 entry relates to 1830.
g 1872 track divided by 1872 population.
h 1871.
i 1913 track divided by 1914 population.
j Includes tramlines.

*Table A16* Railway track spread: major powers[a] 1820–1951 (rail track miles per 1000 square miles of territory)

| Year | France | Germany | Japan | Russia | UK | USA |
|------|--------|---------|-------|--------|-----|-----|
| 1820 | 0.1[b] | 0 | n.a. | 0.01[c] | 0.3 | 0.01[d] |
| 1870 | 45 | 59 | 0.1[e] | 0.8 | 149[f] | 17[d] |
| 1913 | 122 | 193 | 41 | 5.2 | 226 | 83 |
| 1929 | 123 | 209 | 79 | 5.8 | 226 | 82 |
| 1951 | 121 | 226 | 94[g] | 8.5 | 216 | 74 |

Sources: see Tables A1 and A14.

Notes
a Contemporary borders.
b 1828
c Excludes local lines and relates to average length of line open during the year. Later entries relate to all lines at year end.
d Railways operated, which includes some double counting. After 1870, the data refer to railways owned. The 1820 entry relates to 1830.
e 1872.
f 1871.
g Includes tramlines.

*Table A17* Communications of the major powers[a] 1870–1951 (millions of telegrams, telephone calls and telephones)

| Year | | France | Germany | Japan | Russia | UK | USA |
|------|--|--------|---------|-------|--------|-----|-----|
| 1870 | Telegrams | 5.66[b] | 8.66 | 0.011[c] | 2.72 | 8.6[d] | 9.2[e] |
| 1913 | Telegrams | 52.2[bf] | 52.3[f] | 32.88[g] | 97.65 | 87.1 | 75[e] |
|      | Telephone calls | 430[f] | 2518[f] | n.a. | n.a. | 872 | n.a. |
|      | Telephones | 0.31[bf] | 1.43[f] | 1.82[h] | n.a. | n.a. | 9.54 |
| 1929 | Telegrams | 48.39 | 30.9 | 64.77[g] | n.a. | 71.0 | 256 |
|      | Telephone calls | 782 | 2599 | n.a. | n.a. | 1323 | n.a. |
|      | Telephones | 1.02 | 3.18[i] | 0.66[h] | 0.86[j] | n.a. | 19.77 |
| 1951 | Telegrams | 24.79 | 33.8[k] | 99.32 | n.a. | 62.0 | 204 |
|      | Telephone calls | 1729 | 2933[k] | n.a. | n.a. | 3492 | n.a. |
|      | Telephones | 2.52 | 3.08[l] | 1.74 | n.a. | 5.72 | 45.64 |

Sources: Mitchell 2003a, b and c.

Notes

a  Contemporary borders. See Table A1. International telephone and telegraph calls are counted twice, that is, once for sending and once for receipt.
b  1870 and 1913 entries exclude official and radio telephones. The 1913 entry relates to 1914.
c  Excludes official telegrams and receipt of international telegrams.
d  Excludes 1 January to 4 February.
e  Relates to number of Western Union Telegraph messages handled. The 1913 entry relates to 1911.
f  Alsace and Lorraine included in Germany not France.
g  International telegrams counted only once, as sent.
h  Lines connected.
i  Excludes Saarland.
j  1935.
k  Excludes Saarland and West Berlin.
l  Data for East Germany include principal connections only.

*Table A18* Density of telecommunications of the major powers[a] 1870–1951 (telegrams per 100 population and telephones in use per 100 population)

| Year | | France | Germany | Japan | Russia | UK | USA |
|------|------|--------|---------|-------|--------|-----|-----|
| 1870 | Telegrams | 14.9[b] | 22.1 | 0.03[c] | 3.3[d] | 27.4[e] | 24.1[f] |
| 1913 | Telegrams | 131.2[bg] | 78.1[g] | 63.6[h] | 60.0[d] | 191.0 | 79.9[f] |
| | Telephones | 0.78[bg] | 2.1[g] | 3.5[i] | n.a. | n.a. | 9.8 |
| 1929 | Telegrams | 117.5 | 47.8[j] | 102.5[h] | n.a. | 155.4 | 210 |
| | Telephones | 2.5 | 4.9[j] | 1.0[i] | 0.5[k] | n.a. | 16.2 |
| 1951 | Telegrams | 58.7 | 49.1[l] | 117.8 | n.a. | 122.5 | 131.7 |
| | Telephones | 6.0 | 4.5[m] | 2.1 | n.a. | 11.3 | 29.5 |

Sources: Tables A2 and A17.

Notes

a  Contemporary borders. See Table A1. International telegraph messages are counted twice, that is, once for sending and once for receipt.

b  Excludes official and radio telephones. The 1913 entry relates to 1914 (French population 39.8 million).

c  Excludes official telegrams and receipt of international telegrams.

d  Population for 1870 interpolated from Berelowitch *et al.* (1998, p. 493) and includes Russian Poland and Finland. The population data used for 1913 relate to 1914.

e  Excludes 1 January to 4 February.

f  Relates to number of Western Union Telegraph messages handled. The 1913 entry relates to 1911.

g  Alsace and Lorraine included in Germany not France.

h  International telegrams counted only once, as sent.

i  Lines connected.

j  Population data refer to the 1929 population of the area of the Reich in 1935.

k  1935 when the population of the USSR was 179.6 million.

l  Telegram data exclude Saarland and West Berlin.

m Data for East Germany include principal connections only.

# Bibliography

Aidt, T., Dutta, J. and Loukoianova, E. (2006), "Democracy comes to Europe: Franchise Extension and the Fiscal Outcomes 1830–1939", *European Economic Review*, 50(2), 245–83.

Aitken, H.G.J. (ed.), (1959), *The State and Economic Growth*, New York: SSSRC.

Aldcroft, D.H. (1969), *British Railways in Transition*, London: Macmillan.

Aldcroft, D.H. (1974), *Studies in British Transport History*, Newton Abbott: David and Charles.

Aldcroft, D.H. and Richardson, H.W. (1969), *The British Economy 1870–1939*, London: Macmillan.

Alford, W.E. (1996), *Britain in the World Economy since 1880*, London: Longman.

Allen, G.C. (1962), *A Short Economic History of Modern Japan*, London: Unwin.

Allen, G.C. (1965), "The Industrialisation of the Far East", in Habakkuk, H.J. and Postan, M. (eds), *The Cambridge Economic History of Europe: Volume VI: The Industrial Revolutions and After: Incomes, Population and Technological Change*, Cambridge: Cambridge University Press.

Allen, R.C. (2010), *The British Industrial Revolution in Global Perspective*, Cambridge: Cambridge University Press.

American Telegraph and Telephone (AT&T), (1913), *Telephone and Telegraph Statistics of the World*.

Anchordoguy, M. (2001), "Nippon Telegraph and Telephone Company (NTT) and the Building of a Telecommunications Industry in Japan", *Business History Review*, 75(3), 507–41.

Andersson-Skog, L. (1996), "From State Railway Housekeeping to Railway Economics: Swedish Railway Policy and Economic Transformation after 1920 in an Institutional Perspective", *Scandinavian Economic History Review*, XLIX, 23–42.

Andersson-Skog, L. (1999), "Political Economy and Institutional Diffusion.: The Case of the Swedish Railways and Telecommunications up to 1950", in Anderson-Skog, L. and Krantz, O. (eds), *Institutions and the Transport and Communications Industries*, Canton, MA: Science History Publications.

Anderson-Skog, L. and Krantz, O. (eds), (1999), *Institutions and the Transport and Communications Industries*, Canton, MA: Science History Publications.

Andic, S. and Veverka, A. (1963), "The Growth of Government Expenditure in Germany since the Unification", *Zeitschaft fuer des gesampte Finanzwesen*, n.f. 23, Stuttgart.

Aoki, E. (1993), "Policy: Developing an Independent Transportation Technology (1910–1921)", and "Policy: Consolidating the Transportation system (1922–1937)", in Yamamoto, H. (ed.), *Technological Innovation and the Development of Transportation in Japan*, New York: United Nations University Press.

Atack, J. (1985), "Industrial Structure and the Emergence of the Modern Industrial Corporation", *Explorations in Economic History*, 22(1), 29–52.

Attali, J. and Stowdze, Y. (1977), "The Birth of the Telephone and Economic Crisis: The Slow Development of Monologue in French Society", in de Sola Pool, I. (ed.), *The Social Impact of the Telephone*, Cambridge, MA: MIT Press.

Awty, B.W. (1975), "The Introduction of Gas Lighting to Preston", *Transactions of the History Society of Lancashire and Cheshire*, 125, 84–100.

Babkov, A. (1912), "National Finances and the Economic Evolution of Russia", *Russian Review*, I(3), 170–91.

Bagwell, P.S. (1974), *The Transport Revolution from 1770*, London: Batsford.

Bairoch, P. (1982), "International Industrialisation Levels from 1750 to 1980", *Journal of European Economic History*, 11, 269–333.

Bairoch, P. (1989), "European Trade Policy, 1815–1914", in Mathias, P. and Pollard, S. (eds), *The Cambridge Economic History of Europe: Volume VIII: The Industrial Economies: The Development of Economic and Social Policies*, Cambridge: Cambridge University Press.

Bairoch, P. (1998), "Une Nouvelle Distribution des Populations: Villes et Campagnes", in Bardet, J.-P. and Dupâquier, J. (eds), *Histoire des Populations de l'Europe 1999: Vol. 2: La Révolution Démographique, 1750–1914*, Paris, Fayard.

Balderston, T. (1993), *The Origins and Course of the German Economic Crisis 1923–32*, Berlin: Hainde and Spener.

Balderston, T. (2010), "The Economics of Abundance: Coal and Cotton in Lancashire and the World", *Economic History Review*, 63(3), 569–90.

Bardet, J-P. (1998), "La France en Declin", in Bardet, J.-P. and Dupâquier, J. (eds), *Histoire des Populations de l'Europe 1999: Vol. 2: La Révolution Démographique, 1750–1914*, Paris, Fayard.

Bardet, J-P. (1999), "La France: La Fin d'une Singularité?", in Bardet, J.-P. and Dupâquier, J. (eds), *Histoire des Populations de l'Europe 1999: Vol. 3: Les Temps Incertain, 1914–1998*, Paris, Fayard.

Bardet, J.-P. and Dupâquier, J. (eds), (1998), *Histoire des Populations de l'Europe1999: Vol 3: Les Temps Incertain, 1914–1998*, Paris, Fayard.

Bardet, J.-P. and Dupâquier, J. (eds), (1998), *Histoire des Populations de l'Europe1999: Vol 2 La Révolution Démographique, 1750–1914*, Paris, Fayard.

Barjot, D. (2011), "Public Utilities and Private Initiative: The French Concession Model in Historical Perspective", *Business History*, 53(5), 782–800.

Barker, T.S. and Savage, C.I. (1974), *An Economic History of Transport*, London: Heinemann.

Barnett, C. (1986), *The Audit of War: The Illusions and Realities of Britain as a Great Nation*, London: Macmillan.

Barrett, S.D. (2006), "Privatisation in Ireland", in Köthenbürger, M., Sinn, H.-W. and Whalley, J. (eds), *Privatisation Experiences in the European Union*, Cambridge, MA: MIT Press.

Barrett, S.D. (2007), "Transforming Air Transport in Ireland", in Clifton, J., Fuentes, D. and Comin, F. (eds), *Transforming Public Enterprise in Europe and the Americas: Networks, Integration and Transnationalisation*, Basingstoke: Palgrave.

Baugh, G.C. (1992), "Government Grants in Aid of the Rates in England and Wales 1889–1990", *Bulletin of the Institute of Historical Research*, 65, 215–37.

Baumol, W.J. (ed.), (1980), *Public and Private Enterprise in the Mixed Economy*, New York: Macmillan.

Baykov, A. (1954), "The Economic Development of Russia", *Economic History Review*, 2nd Series, vii, 137–49.

Berelowitch, W., Dupâquier, J. and Gieystzor, I. (1998), "L'Europe Orientale", in Bardet, J.-P. and Dupâquier, J. (eds), *Histoire des Populations de l'Europe 1999: Vol. 2: La Révolution Démographique, 1750–1914*, Paris, Fayard.

Bertho-Lavenir, C. (1978), "The Telephone in France 1879–1979: National Characteristics and International Influences", in Maintz, R. and Hughes, T.P, (eds), *The Development of Large Technical Systems*, Boulder CO: Frankfurt and Westview Press.

Black, C.E. (1960), *The Transformation of Russian Society: Aspects of Social Change Since 1861*, Cambridge, MA: Harvard University Press.

Blackwell, W.L. (1968), *The Beginnings of Russian Industrialisation 1800–1860*, Princeton, NJ: Princeton University Press.

Blackwell, W.L. (ed.), (1974), *Russian Economic Development between Peter the Great and Stalin*, New York: Franklin Watts Inc.

Blanchard, M. (1969), "The Railway Policy of the Second Empire", in Crouzet, F., Chaloner, W.H. and Stern, W.M. (eds), *Essays in European Economic History 1789–1914*, London: Edward Arnold.

Blum, J. (1961), *Lord and Peasant in Russia from the Ninth to the Nineteenth Century*, Princeton, NJ: Princeton University Press.

Blum, J. (1978), *The End of the Old Order in Rural Europe*, Princeton, NJ: Princeton University Press.

Boiteux, M. (1957), "Le Tarif Vert d' Électricité de France", *Revue Française de l'Énergie*, 82, 137–151, reprinted in English in Nelson, J.R, (ed.), (1964), *Marginal Cost Pricing in Practice*, Englewood Cliffs, NJ: Prentice-Hall.

Bongaerts, J.C. (1985), "Financing Railways in the German states 1840–60: A Preliminary View", *Journal of European Economic History*, 14, 331–45.

Borchardt, K. (1973), "Germany 1700–1914", in Cipolla, C. (ed.), *The Fontana Economic History of Europe: The Emergence of Industrial Societies: Parts 1 and 2*, Glasgow: Fontana Collins.

Borchardt, K. (1991), *Perspectives on Modern German Economic History*, Cambridge: Cambridge University Press.

Bowen, R.H. (1950), "Rise of Modern Industry: The Roles of Government and Private Enterprise in German Industrial Growth 1870–1914", *Journal of Economic History*, 10(supplement), 68–81.

Bradley, S. and Hausman, J. (eds), (1989), *Future Competition in Telecommunications*, Cambridge, MA: Harvard Business School Press.

Brady, R.A. (1943), "The Economic Impact of Imperial Germany: Industrial Policy", *Journal of Economic History*, 3(December Supplement), 108–23.

Bressler, H.J. (1922), "The French Railway Problem", *Political Science Quarterly*, XXXVII, 211–28.

Broadberry, S., Federico, G. and Klein, A. (2010), "Sectoral Developments, 1870–1914", in Broadberry, S.N. and O'Rourke, K.H. (eds), *The Cambridge Economic History of Modern Europe*, Cambridge: Cambridge University Press, Volume II.

Broadberry, S.N. (1988), "The Impact of the World Wars on the Long Run Economic Performance of the British Economy", *Oxford Review of Economic Policy*, 4(1), 25–36.

Broadberry, S.N. (1993), "Manufacturing and the Convergence Hypothesis: What the Long Run Data Show", *Journal of Economic History*, 53(4), 772–95.

Broadberry, S.N. (1994a), "Technological Leadership and Productivity Leadership in Manufacturing since the Industrial Revolution: Implications from the Convergence Debate", *Economic Journal*, 104(423), 291–302.

Broadberry, S.N. (1994b), "Comparative Productivity in Britain and American Manufacturing during the Nineteenth Century", *Explorations in Economic History*, 31(4), 521–8.

Broadberry, S.N. (1997a), "Anglo-German Productivity Differences 1870–1990: A Sectoral Analysis", *European Review of Economic History*, 1(2), 247–68.

Broadberry, S.N. (1997b), *The Productivity Race: British Manufacturing in International Perspective*, Cambridge: Cambridge University Press.

Broadberry, S.N. (1998), "How did the United States and Germany Overtake Britain? A Sectoral Analysis of Comparative Productivity Levels", *Journal of Economic History*, 58(2), 375–407.

Broadberry, S.N. (2006), *Market Services and the Productivity Race 1850–2000: British Performance in International Perspective*, Cambridge: Cambridge University Press.

Broadberry, S.N. and Ghosal, S. (2002), "From the Counting House to the Modern Office: Explaining Comparative Productivity Performance in Services since 1870", *Journal of Economic History*, 62(4), 967–98.

Broadberry, S.N. and Harrison, M. (eds), (2005), *The Economics of World War I*, Cambridge: Cambridge University Press.

Broadberry, S.N. and O'Rourke, K.H. (eds), (2010), *The Cambridge Economic History of Modern Europe* (Volume 1, 1700–1870; Volume II, 1870 to the present), Cambridge: Cambridge University Press.

Brogan, D.W. (1940), *The Development of Modern France (1870–1939)*, London: Hamish Hamilton.

Brooks, B.C. (1916), "Municipalisation of the Berlin Electrical Works", *Quarterly Journal of Economics*, 30, 188–94.

Buyst, E. and Franaszek, P. (2010), "Sectoral Developments, 1914–45", in Broadberry, S.N. and O'Rourke, K.H. (eds), *The Cambridge Economic History of Modern Europe*, Cambridge: Cambridge University Press, Volume II.

Byatt, I.C.R. (1978), *The British Electrical Industry 1815–1914*, Oxford: Oxford University Press.

Cain, P.J. (1973), "Private Enterprise or Public Utility? Output, Pricing and Investment in English Railways", *Journal of Transport History*, 1, 9–28.

Caldwell, B. (ed.), (2007), *The Collected Works of F.A. Hayek: Volume II: The Road to Serfdom; Text and Documents: The Definitive Edition*, Chicago, IL: University of Chicago Press.

Cameron, R.E. (1958), "Economic Growth and Stagnation in France 1815–1914", *Journal of Modern History*, XXX(1), 1–13.

Cameron, R.E. (1961), *France and the Economic Development of Europe 1880–1914: Conquests of Peace and Seeds of War*, Princeton, NJ: Princeton University Press.

Cameron, R.E. (ed.), (1967), *Banking in the Early Stages of Industrialisation: A study in Comparative History*, Oxford: Oxford University Press.

Cardot, F. (ed.), (1987), *1880–1980: Une Siècle de l'Électricité dans le Monde*, Paris: Presses Universitaires de France.

Caron, F. (1979), *An Economic History of Modern France*, London: Methuen.

Caron, F. (1987), "The Evolution of the Technical System of Railways in France", in Maintz, R. and Hughes, T.P, (eds), *The Development of Large Technical Systems*, Boulder CO: Frankfurt and Westview Press.

Caron, F. and Cardot, F. (ed.), (1991), *Histoire Générale de l'Electricité en France: Tome Premier: 1881–1918: Espoirs et Conquêtes*, Paris: L'Association pour L'Histoire de l'Électricité en France, Fayard.

Carr, E.H. and Davies, R.W. (1969), *A History of Soviet Russia: Foundations of a Planned Economy 1926–1929: Volume 1*, Harmondsworth: Penguin.

Carré, J.-J., Dubois, P. and Malinvaud, E. (1975), *French Economic Growth*, Stanford, CA: Stanford University Press.

Carreras, A. and Josephson, C. (2010), "Aggregate Growth, 1870–1914: Growing at the Production Frontier", in Broadberry, S.N. and O'Rourke, K.H. (eds), *The Cambridge Economic History of Modern Europe*, Cambridge: Cambridge University Press, Volume II.

Carsten, F.L. (1989), *A History of the Prussian Junkers*, Aldershot: Scolar Press.

Cavalcanti, J. (1991), "Economic Aspects of the Provision and Development of Water Supply in Nineteenth Century Britain", PhD thesis, University of Manchester.

Chadeau, E. (2000), "The Rise and Decline of State-Owned Industry in Twentieth Century France", in Toninelli, P.A. (ed.), *The Rise and Fall of State Owned Enterprise in the Western World*, Cambridge: Cambridge University Press.

Chadwick, E. (1859), "Results of Different Principles of Legislation and Administration in Europe: Of Competition for the Field, as compared with Competition within the Field, of Service", *Journal of the Royal Statistical Society*, 22, 381–420.

Chandler, A.D. Jr (1976), "The Development of Modern Management Structure in the US and UK", in Hannah, L. (ed.), *Management Strategy and Business Development: An Historical and Comparative Study*, London: Macmillan.

Chandler, A.D. Jr (1984), "The Emergence of Managerial Capitalism", *Business History*, 58, 473–503.

Chandler, A.D. Jr (1990), *Scale and Scope: The Dynamics of Industrial Capitalism*, London: Belknap Press of Harvard University.

Chandler, A.D. and Daems, H. (eds), (1980), *Managerial Hierarchies*, Cambridge: Cambridge University Press.

Chesnais, J.-C. (1999), "La Fécondité au XXe siècle: Une Baisse Irrégulière, mais Profunde et Irresistible", in Bardet, J.-P. and Dupâquier, J. (eds), *Histoire des Populations de l'Europe 1999: Vol. 3: Les Temps Incertain, 1914–1998*, Paris, Fayard.

Chester, Sir N. (1975), *The Nationalisation of British Industry 1945–51*, London: HMSO.

Chick, M. (2002), "Le Tarif Vert Retrouvé: The Marginal Cost Concept and the Pricing of Electricity in Britain and France 1945–73", *Energy Journal*, 23(1), 97–116.

Chick, M. (2006), "The Marginalist Approach and the Making of Fuel Policy in France and Britain, 1945–72", *Economic History Review*, LIX(1), 143–67.

Cipolla, C. (ed.), (1973), *The Fontana Economic History of Europe: The Emergence of Industrial Societies: Parts 1 and 2*, Glasgow: Fontana Collins.

Cipolla, C. (ed.), (1976), *The Fontana Economic History of Europe: Contemporary Economies: Parts 1 and 2*, Glasgow: Collins.

Clapham, J.H. (1961), *The Economic Development of France and Germany 1815–1914*, Cambridge: Cambridge University Press.

Clapham, J.H. (1964), *The Economic History of Britain: Vol I*, Cambridge: Cambridge University Press.

Clark, C. (2009), *Kaiser Wilhelm II: A Life in Power*, London: Penguin.

Clarke, J.J. (1977), "The Nationalisation of War Industries in France, 1935–37: A Case study", *Journal of Modern History*, 49, 411–30.

Clifton, J., Fuentes, D. and Comin, F. (eds), (2007), *Transforming Public Enterprise in Europe and the Americas: Networks, Integration and Transnationalisation*, Basingstoke: Palgrave.

Coale, A.J. and Treadway, R. (1986), "A Summary of the Changing Distribution of Overall Fertility, Marital Fertility, and the Proportion Married in the Provinces of Europe", in A.J Coale and S.C. Watkins (eds), *The Decline of Fertility in Europe*, Princeton, NJ: Princeton University Press.

Coleman, D.C. (ed.), (1969), *Revisions in Mercantilism*, London: Methuen.

Conrad, A.F. and Meyer, J.R. (1958), "The Economics of Slavery in the Ante-Bellum South", *Journal of Political Economy*, 66(April), 93–130.

Copeland, M.T. (1912), *The Cotton Manufacturing Industry of the United States*, Cambridge, MA: Harvard University Press.

Crafts, N.F.R. (1977), "Industrial Revolution in England and France: Some Thoughts on the Question 'Why was England First?'", *Economic History Review*, 30(3), 421–41.

Crafts, N.F.R. (1984), "Economic Growth in France and Britain", *Journal of Economic History*, Oxford: Clarendon Press.

Crafts, N.F.R. (1985), *British Economic Growth during the Industrial Revolution*, Oxford: Clarendon Press.

Crawcour, E.S. (1997), "Industrialisation and Technological Change 1885–1920", in Yamamura, K. (ed.), *The Economic Emergence of Modern Japan*, Cambridge: Cambridge University Press.

Crisp, O. (1959), "The State Peasants under Nicholas I", *Slavonic Review*, xvi, 387–412.

Crisp, O. (1967), "Banking in the Industrialization of Tsarist Russia, 1860–1914", in Cameron, R.E. (ed.), *Banking in the Early Stages of Industrialisation: A Study in Comparative History*, Oxford: Oxford University Press.

Crisp, O. (1972), "The Pattern of industrialization in Russia 1700–1914", in Léon, P., Crouzet, F. and Gascon, R. (eds), *L'Industrialisation en Europe au XIXe Siècle*, Paris: Centre National de la Recherche Scientifique.

Crisp, O. (1976), *Studies in the Russian Economy before 1914*, London: Macmillan.

Crisp, O. (1978), "Labour and Industrialisation in Russia", in Mathias, P. and Postan, M.M. (eds), *The Cambridge Economic History of Europe: Volume VII: The Industrial Economies: Capital, Labour, Enterprise*, Cambridge: Cambridge University Press, Part 2.

Crompton, G.W. (1985), "'Efficient and Economical Working?' The Performance of the Railway Companies 1923–33", *Business History*, 27(2), 222–37.

Crompton, G.W. (1989), "Squeezing the Pulpless Orange: Labour and Capital on the Railways in the Inter-War Period", *Business History*, 31, 66–83.

Crouzet, F. (1972), "Western Europe and Great Britain: Catching-up in the First Half of the nineteenth Century", in Youngson, A.J. (ed.), *Economic Development in the Long Run*, London: Allen and Unwin.

Crouzet, F., Chaloner, W.H. and Stern, W.M. (eds), (1969), *Essays in European Economic History 1789–1914*, London: Edward Arnold.

Darwin, J. (2009), *The Empire Project: The Rise and Fall of the British World-System 1830–1970*, Cambridge: Cambridge University Press.

Daudin, G., Morys, M. and O'Rourke, K.H. (2010), "Globalisation, 1870–1914", in Broadberry, S.N. and O'Rourke, K.H. (eds), *The Cambridge Economic History of Modern Europe*, Cambridge: Cambridge University Press, Volume II.

Daunton, M. (1990), "Housing", in Thompson, F.M.L. (ed.), *The Cambridge Social History of Britain 1750–1950: Volume 2: People and their Environment*, Cambridge: Cambridge University Press.

Daunton, M. (ed.), (2000), *Cambridge Urban History of Britain: Vol. III, 1840–1950*, Cambridge: Cambridge University Press.

Daunton, M. (2001), *Trusting Leviathan: The Politics of Taxation in Britain, 1799–1914*, Cambridge: Cambridge University Press.

Daunton, M.S. (2002), *Just Taxes: The Politics of Taxation in Britain, 1914–79*, Cambridge: Cambridge University Press.

David, P. (1970), "Learning by Doing and Tariff Protection: A Reconsideration of the Ante Bellum United States Cotton Textile Industry", *Journal of Economic History*, 30, 521–601.

David, P.A., Gutman, H.G., Sutch, R., Temin, P. and Wright, G. (1976), *Reckoning with Slavery: A Critical Study in the Quantitative History of American Negro Slavery*, Oxford: Oxford University Press.

Davies, R.W. (1989), "Economic and Social Policy in the USSR", in Mathias, P. and Pollard, S. (eds), *The Cambridge Economic History of Europe: Volume VIII: The Industrial Economies: The Development of Economic and Social Policies*, Cambridge: Cambridge University Press, Part I.

Davies, R.W. (ed.), (1991), *From Tsarism to the New Economic Policy: Continuity and Change in the Economy of the USSR*, Ithaca, NY: Cornell University Press.

Davis, C.M. (1999), "Russia: A Comparative Economic Systems Interpretation", in Foreman-Peck, J. and Federico, G. (eds), *European Industrial Policy: The Twentieth Century Experience*, Oxford: Oxford University Press.

Dawson, W.H. (1916), *Municipal Life and Local Government in Germany*, London: Longmans, Green and Co.

Dennison, T. and Simpson, J. (2010), "Agriculture", in Broadberry, S.N. and O'Rourke, K.H. (eds), *The Cambridge Economic History of Modern Europe*, Cambridge: Cambridge University Press, Volume I.

Dennison, T. (2011), *The Institutional Framework of Russian Serfdom*, Cambridge: Cambridge University Press.

Dienel, H-L. and Lyth, P.J. (eds), (1998), *Flying the Flag: European Commercial Air Transport since 1945*, Basingstoke: Macmillan.

Dobbin, F. (1994), *Forging Industrial Policy: The United States, Britain and France in the Railway Age*, Cambridge: Cambridge University Press.

Domar, E. (1970), "The Causes of Slavery or Serfdom: A Hypothesis", *Journal of Economic History*, XXX, 18–22.

Domar, E. and Machina, M.J. (1984), "On the Profitability of Russian Serfdom", *Journal of Economic History*, XLIV, 919–55.

Dormois, J.-P. (1999), "France: The Idiosyncracies of *Voluntarisme*", in Foreman-Peck, J. and Federico, G. (eds), *European Industrial Policy: The Twentieth Century Experience*, Oxford: Oxford University Press.

Dougall, H.H. (1933), "Railway Rates and Rate Making in France since 1921", *Journal of Political Economy*, XXXV, 289–333.

Doukas, K. (1938), "Ownership, Management and Regulation of Electric Undertakings in France", *George Washington Law Review*, VI(2), 147–70 and 282–312.

Doukas, K. (1939), "Armaments and the French Experience", *American Political Science Quarterly*, 33, 279–91.

Doukas, K. (1945), *The French Railroads and the State*, New York: Columbia Press.

Dowd, T. and Dobbin, F. (2001), "Origins of the Myth of Neo-liberalism: Regulation in the First Century of US Railroading", in Magnusson, L. and Ottosson, J. (eds), *The State, Regulation and the Economy: An Historical Perspective*, Cheltenham: Edward Elgar.

Dunham, A.L. (1941), "How the First French Railways were Planned", *Journal of Economic History*, I, 12–25.

Dunlavy, C.A. (2001), "Bursting through State Limits. Lessons from American Railroad History", in Magnusson, L. and Ottosson, J. (eds), *The State, Regulation and the Economy: An Historical Perspective*, Cheltenham: Edward Elgar.

Dunlavy, C.N. (1992), *Politics and Industrialisation: Early Railroads in USA and Prussia*, Princeton, NJ: Princeton University Press.

Dupriez, L.H. (ed.), (1955), *Economic Progress*, Louvain: International Economic Association.

Earle, E.M. (ed.), (1950), *Modern France*, Princeton, NJ: Princeton University Press.

Einaudi, M. (1948), "Nationalisation in France and Italy", *Social Research*, 15(1), 22–43.

Elbaum, B. and Lazonick, W. (eds), (1986), *The Decline of the British Economy*, Oxford: Clarendon Press.

Eliot Brownlee, W. (2000), "The Public Sector", in Engerman, S.L. and Gallman, R.E. (eds), *The Cambridge Economic History of the United States*, Cambridge: Cambridge University Press, Volume III.

Eloranta, J. (2007), "From the Great Illusion to the Great War: Military Spending Behaviour of the Great Powers, 1870–1913", *European Review of Economic History*, II(2), 255–83.

Eloranta, J. and Harrision, M. (2010), "War and Disintegration, 1914–1950", in Broadberry, S.N. and O'Rourke, K.H. (eds), *The Cambridge Economic History of Modern Europe*, Cambridge: Cambridge University Press, Volume II.

Engerman, S.L. (1973), "Some Considerations Relating to Property Rights in Man", *Journal of Economic History*, 33, 43–65.

Engerman, S.L. and Gallman, R.E. (eds), (2000), *The Cambridge Economic History of the United States (Volume II, The Long Nineteenth Century; Volume III: The Twentieth Century)*, Cambridge: Cambridge University Press,

Esper, T. (1978), "The Condition of the Serf Workers in Russia's Metallurgical Industry 1800–1861", *Journal of Modern History*, 50, 660–679.

Esper, T. (1980), "Hired Labor in the Metallurgical Industry of the Urals during the Late Serf Period", *Jarbücher Für Geschichte Osteuropas*, 28, 62–70.

Esper, T. (1981), "The Incomes of Russian Serf Iron Workers in the Nineteenth Century", *Past and Present*, 93, 137–59.

Evans, R.J. (1990), *Death in Hamburg: Society and Politics in the Cholera Years 1830–1910*, Oxford: Clarendon Press.

Falk, W. and Pittack, H. (1986), "Publicly Owned Enterprises and Forms of Participation of the State in Private Enterprise in Germany before 1933", in Zamagni, V. (ed.), *Origins and Development of Publicly Owned Enterprises*, University of Florence, Ninth International Economic History Conference, Section B111.

Falkus, M.E. (1972), *The Industrialisation of Russia 1700–1914*, London: Macmillan.

Feinstein, C.H. (1972), *National Income, Expenditure and Output in the United Kingdom 1865–1965*, Cambridge: Cambridge University Press.

Feinstein, C.H. and Pollard, S. (eds), (1988), *Studies in Capital Formation in the UK, 1750–1920*, Oxford: Oxford University Press.

Feldenkirchen, W. (1999), "Germany: The Invention of Interventionisms", in Foreman-Peck, J. and Federico, G. (eds), *European Industrial Policy: The Twentieth Century Experience*, Oxford: Oxford University Press.

Fenoaltea, S. (1981), "The Slavery Debate: A Note from the Sidelines", *Explorations in Economic History*, 18, 304–8.

Ferguson, N. (1994), "Public Finance and National Security: The Domestic Origins of the First World War Revisited", *Past and Present*, 142, 141–68.

Fernandez, A. (1999), "Les Lumières de la Ville: L'Administration Municipale à l'Épreuve de l' Électrification", *Vingtième Siècles Revue d'Histoire*, 62, 107–22.

Figes, O. (1997), *A People's Tragedy: The Russian Revolution 1891–1924*, London: Pimlico.

Figes, O. (2011), *Crimea: The Last Chance*, London: Penguin.

Finger, M. and Künneke, R. (eds), (2011), *International Handbook for the Liberalisation of Infrastructures*, Basingstoke: Edward Elgar.

Fischer, W. (1960), "The German Zollverein: A Case study in Customs Union", *Kyklos*, 65–88.

Fischer, W. (1963), "Government Activity and Industrialisation in Germany (1815–70)", in Rostow, W.W. (ed.), *The Economics of Take-Off into Sustained Growth*, London: Macmillan.

Fischer, W., von Krengel, J. and Wietog, J. (1982), *Sozialgeschichtliches Arbeitsbuch Band: Materiales zur Statistik des Deutsche en Bundes 1815–1870*, Beck München: Verlag C.H.

Fishback, P. (2007a), "Government and the Economy", chapter 1 of Fishback, P. (ed.), *Government and the American Economy: A New History*, Chicago, IL: University of Chicago Press.

Fishback, P. (2007b), "The Progressive Era", chapter 10 of Fishback, P. (ed.), *Government and the American Economy: A New History*, Chicago, IL: University of Chicago Press.

Fishback, P. (2007c), "The New Deal" chapter 13 of Fishback, P. (ed.), *Government and the American Economy: A New History*, Chicago, IL: University of Chicago Press.

Fishback, P. (ed.), (2007), *Government and the American Economy: A New History*, Chicago, IL: University of Chicago Press.

Fishlow, A. (2000), "Internal Transportation in the Nineteenth and Twentieth Centuries", in Engerman, S.L. and Gallman, R.E. (eds), *The Cambridge Economic History of the United States*, Cambridge: Cambridge University Press, Volume II.

Floud, R. and Johnson, P. (eds), (2004a), *The Cambridge Economic History of Britain: Volume I: Industrialisation, 1700–1860*, Cambridge: Cambridge University Press.

Floud, R. and Johnson, P. (eds), (2004b) *The Cambridge Economic History of Britain: Volume II: Economic Maturity 1860–1939*, Cambridge: Cambridge University Press.

Floud, R. and McCloskey, D. (eds), (1981), *The Economic History of Britain since 1700: Vol. I: 1700–1860*, Cambridge: Cambridge University Press.

Floud, R. and McCloskey, D. (eds), (1994), *The Economic History of Britain: Volume 2: 1860s to the 1970s*, Cambridge: Cambridge University Press.

Floud, R., Humphries, J. and Johnson, P. (eds), (2013), *The Economic History of Britain, 1700–2010*, Cambridge: Cambridge University Press, Volumes 1 and 2.

Fogarty, M.P. (1945), *The Prospects of the Industrial Areas of Great Britain*, London: Methuen.

Fogel, R.W. and Engerman, S. (1974), *Time on the Cross: The Economics of American Negro Slavery*, 2 volumes, Boston, MA: Little Brown and Company.

Fohlen, C. (1973), "France 1700–1914", in Cipolla, C. (ed.), *The Fontana Economic History of Europe: The Emergence of Industrial Societies*, Glasgow: Fontana Collins, Part 1.

Fohlen, C. (1976), "France 1920–70", in Cipolla, C. (ed.), *The Fontana Economic History of Europe: Contemporary Economies*, Glasgow: Collins, Part 1.

Fohlen, C. (1978), "Entrepreneurship and Management in France in the Nineteenth Century", in Mathias, P. and Postan, M.M. (eds), *The Cambridge Economic History of Europe: Volume VII: The Industrial Economies: Capital, Labour, Enterprise*, Cambridge: Cambridge University Press, Part I.

Fontvieille, L. (1976), "Évolution et croissance de l'Etat français de1815 á 1969", *Économies et Sociétés*, 10.

Ford, A.G. (1989), "International Financial Policy and the Gold Standard 1870–1914", in Mathias, P. and Pollard, S. (eds), *The Cambridge Economic History of Europe: Volume VIII: The Industrial Economies: The Development of Economic and Social Policies*, Cambridge: Cambridge University Press.

Foreman-Peck, J. (1985), "Competition and Performance in the UK Telecommunications Industry", *Telecommunications Policy*, September, 215–29.

Foreman-Peck, J. (1987), "Natural Monopoly and Railway Policy in the Nineteenth Century", *Oxford Economic Papers*, 39, 699–718.

Foreman-Peck, J. (1989a), "L'État et le Développment du Reseau de Telecommunications en Europe à ses Débuts", *Histoire, Économie, Société*, 4, 383–402.

Foreman-Peck, J. (1989b), "Competition, Cooperation and Nationalisation in the Early Telegraph Network", *Business History*, 31(3), 81–102.

Foreman-Peck, J. and Federico, G. (eds), (1999), *European Industrial Policy: The Twentieth Century Experience*, Oxford: Oxford University Press.

Foreman-Peck, J. and Millward, R. (1994), *Public and Private Ownership of British Industry 1820–1990*, Oxford: Oxford University Press.

Foreman-Peck, J. and Waterson, M. (1985), "The Comparative Efficiency of Public and Private Enterprise in Britain: Electricity Generation between the World Wars", *Economic Journal*, 95(Supplement), 83–95.

Fraser, H. (1993), "Municipal Socialism and Social Policy", in Morris, R.J. and Rodger, R. (eds), *The Victorian City: A Reader in British Urban History: 1820–1914*, London: Longman.

Freedman, C.E. (1965), "Joint Stock Business Organisation in France 1807–67", *Business History Review*, XXXIX, 184–204.

Freeman, M., Pearson, R. and Taylor, J. (2012), *Shareholder Democracies? Corporate Governance in Britain and Ireland before 1850*, Chicago, IL: University of Chicago Press.

Fremdling, R. (1979), "Railroads and German Economic Growth: A Leading Sector Analysis with a comparison to the USA and GB", *Journal of Economic History*, XXXVII, 583–604.

Fremdling, R. (1980), "Freight Rates and the State Budget: The Role of the Nationalised Prussian Railways 1880–1913", *Journal of European Economic History*, 9(1), 21–39.

Fremdling, R. (1996), "Anglo-German Rivalry in Coal Markets in France, the Netherlands and Germany 1850–1913", *Journal of European Economic History*, 25(3), 399–446.

Fremdling, R. (1999), "The Prussian and Dutch Railway Regulation in the Nineteenth Century", in Anderson-Skog, L. and Krantz, O. (eds), *Institutions and the Transport and Communications Industries*, Canton, MA: Science History Publications.

Fremdling, R. and Knieps, G. (1993), "Competition, Regulation and Nationalisation: The Prussian Railway System in the Nineteenth Century", *Scandinavian Economic History Review*, XLI(1), 129–54.

Fridensen, P. and Strauss, A. (eds), (1987), *Le Capitalisme Francaise*, Paris: Libraiarie Artheme, Fayard.

Frost, R.L. (1981), *Alternating Currents: Nationalised Power in France 1946–70*, Ithaca, NY: Cornell University Press.

Gabel, D. (1994), "Competition in a Network Industry: The Telephone Industry 1894–1910", *Journal of Economic History*, 54(3), 543–72.

Galambos, L. (2000a), "State-Owned Enterprise in a Hostile Environment: The US Experience", in Toninelli, P.A. (ed.), *The Rise and Fall of State Owned Enterprise in the Western World*, Cambridge: Cambridge University Press.

Galambos, L. (2000b), "The US Corporate Economy in the Twentieth Century", in Engerman, S.L. and Gallman, R.E. (eds), *The Cambridge Economic History of the United States*, Cambridge: Cambridge University Press, Volume III.

Gallman, R.E. (2000), "Economic Growth and Structural Change in the Long Nineteenth Century", in Engerman, S.L. and Gallman, R.E. (eds), *The Cambridge Economic History of the United States*, Cambridge: Cambridge University Press, Volume II.

Garcke, E. (1907), *Manual of Electrical Undertakings*, London: publisher not known.

Gatrell, P. (1986), *The Tsarist Economy 1850–1917*, London: Batsford.

Gatrell, P. (1994), *Government, Industry and Rearmament in Russia, 1900–1914*, Cambridge: Cambridge University Press.

Gatrell, P. (2012), "The Russian Fiscal State, 1600–1914", in O'Brien, P. and Yun-Casalillo, B. (eds), *The Rise of the Fiscal State in Eurasia*, Cambridge: Cambridge University Press.

Gatrell, P. and Davies, R.W. (1991), "The Industrial Economy", in Davies, R.W. (ed.), *From Tsarism to the New Economic Policy: Continuity and Change in the Economy of the USSR*, Ithaca, NY: Cornell University Press.

Geiger, R. (1984), "Planning the French Canals: The Becquez Plan of 1820–1922", *Journal of Economic History*, 44, 329–39.

Genovese, E. (1965), *The Political Economy of Slavery: Studies in the Economy and Society of the Slave South*, New York: Pantheon Books.

Gershenkron, A. (1955), "Social Attitudes, Entrepreneurship and Economic Development", in Dupriez, L.H. (ed.), *Economic Progress*, Louvain: International Economic Association.

Gershenkron, A. (1960), "Russia: Patterns and Problems of Economic Development, 1861–1958", in Black, C.E. *The Transformation of Russian Society: Aspects of Social Change since 1861*, Cambridge, MA: Harvard University Press.

Gershenkron, A. (1963), "The Early Phases of Industrialisation in Russia: Afterthoughts and Counterthoughts", in Rostow, W.W. (ed.), *The Economics of Take-Off into Sustained Growth*, London: Macmillan.

Gershenkron, A. (1965), "Agrarian Policies and Industrialisation: Russia 1861–1917", in Habakkuk, H.J. and Postan, M. (eds), *The Cambridge Economic History of Europe: Volume VI: The Industrial Revolutions and After: Incomes, Population and Technological Change*, Cambridge: Cambridge University Press.

Gershenkron, A. (1966a), *Economic Backwardness in Historical Perspective*, Cambridge, MA: Harvard University Press.

Gershenkron, A. (1966b), *Bread and Democracy in Germany*, New York: Howard Fertig.

Gibbons, H.J. (1901), "The Opposition to Municipal Socialism in England", *Journal of Political Economy*, 9, 243–59.

Gillet, M. (1969), "The Coal Age and the Rise of Coalfields of the North and the Pas de Calais", in Crouzet, F., Chaloner, W.H. and Stern, W.M. (eds), *Essays in European Economic History 1789–1914*, London: Edward Arnold.

Giuntini, A., Hertner, P. and Nunez, G. (eds), (2004), *Urban Growth on Two Continents in the Nineteenth and Twentieth Centuries: Technology, Networks, Finance and Public Regulation*, Granada: Editorial Comares, S.L.

Glass, D.V. (1967), *Population Policies and Movements in Europe*, London: Cass.

Goldscheid, R. (1966), "The Political Economy of Public Finance and the Industrialisation of Prussia, 1815–66", *Journal of Economic History*, 26, 484–97.

Goodrich, C. (1960), *Government Promotion of American Canals and Railroads 1800–1890*, New York: Columbia University Press.

Goodwin, C.D. (ed.), (1991), *Economics and National Security: A History of their Interaction*, Durham, NC: Duke University Press.

Goubert, G.P. (1988), "The Development of Water and Sewerage Systems in France 1850–1950", in Tarr, J.A. and G. Dupuy, G. (eds), *Technology and the Rise of the Networked City in Europe*, Philadelphia, PA: Temple University Press.

Goubert, G.P. (1989), *The Conquest of Water: The Advent of Health in the Industrial Age*, Princeton, NJ: Princeton University Press.

Gournay, C. de (1988), "Telephone Networks in France and Great Britain", in Tarr, J.A. and G. Dupuy, G. (eds), *Technology and the Rise of the Networked City in Europe*, Philadelphia, PA: Temple University Press.

Gourvish, T.R. (1980), *Railways in the British Economy 1830–1914*, London: Macmillan.

Gourvish, T.R. (ed.), (2003), *Business and Politics in Europe, 1900–1970*, Cambridge: Cambridge University Press.

Greasley, D. (1990), "Fifty Years of Coal Mining Productivity: The Record of the British Coal Industry before 1939", *Journal of Economic History*, 50(4), 877–902.

Greasley, D. (1995), "The Coal Industry: Images and Realities on the Road to Nationalization", in Millward, R. and Singleton, J. (eds), *The Political Economy of Nationalisation in Britain 1920–5*, Cambridge: Cambridge University Press.

Gregory, P.R. (1982), *Russian National Income 1885–1913*, Cambridge: Cambridge University Press.

Gregory, P.R. (1991), "The Role of the State in Promoting Economic Development: The Russian Case and its Implications", in Sylla, R. and Toniolo, G. (eds), *Patterns of Industrialization*, London: Routledge.

Gregory, P.R. (1994), *Before Command: An Economic History of Russia from Emancipation to the First Five Year Plan*, Princeton, NJ: Princeton University Press.

Gregory, P.R. (2004), *The Political Economy of Stalinism*, Cambridge: Cambridge University Press.

Grossman, G. (1973), "Russia and the Soviet Union", in Cipolla, C. (ed.), *The Fontana Economic History of Europe: The Emergence of Industrial Societies*, Glasgow: Fontana Collins, Part 2.

Guglielmo, M. and Troesken, W. (2007), "The Gilded Age", in Fishback, P. (ed.), *Government and the American Economy: A New History*, Chicago, IL: University of Chicago Press.

Gunston, W.H. (1933), "Telephone Development of the World at the End of 1932", *Telegraph and Telephone Journal*, 56, 56–8.

Gutman, H.G. (1975), *Slavery and the Numbers Game: A Critique of Time on the Cross*, Champaign, IL: University of Illinois Press.

Habbakuk, H.J. (1962), *American and British Technology in the Nineteenth Century*, Cambridge: Cambridge University Press.

Habakkuk, H.J. and Postan, M. (eds), (1965), *The Cambridge Economic History of Europe: Volume VI: The Industrial Revolutions and After: Incomes, Population and Technological Change*, Cambridge: Cambridge University Press.

Hackett, J. and Hackett, A. (1963), *Economic Planning in France*, Cambridge, MA: Harvard University Press.

Hannah, L. (ed.), (1976), *Management Strategy and Business Development: An Historical and Comparative Study*, London: Macmillan.

Hannah, L. (1977), "A Pioneer of Public Enterprise: The Central Electricity Generating Board and the National Grid", in Supple, B. (ed.), *Essays in British Business History*, Oxford: Clarendon Press.

Hannah, L. (1979), *Electricity before Nationalisation*, London: Macmillan.

Hannah, L. (1983), *The Rise of the Corporate Economy*, London: Methuen.

Harada, K. (1993), "Policy and Railroads: Transportation in the Period of Railroad Priority (1892–1909)", in Yamamoto, H. (ed.), *Technological Innovation and the Development of Transportation in Japan*, New York: United Nations University Press.

Hardach, K. (1976), "Germany 1914–70", in Cipolla, C. (ed.), *The Fontana Economic History of Europe: Contemporary Economies*, Glasgow: Collins, Part 1.

Harley, C.K. (2004a), "Trade: Discovery, Mercantalism and Technology", in Floud, R. and Johnson, P. (eds), *The Cambridge Economic History of Britain: Volume II: Economic Maturity 1860–1939*, Cambridge: Cambridge University Press.

Harley, C.K. (2004b), "Trade, 1870–1939: From Globalization to Fragmentation", in Floud, R. and Johnson, P. (eds), *The Cambridge Economic History of Britain: Volume II: Economic Maturity 1860–1939*, Cambridge: Cambridge University Press.

Harley, C.K. and McCloskey, D. (1981), "Foreign Trade: Competition and the Expanding International Economy", in Floud, R. and McCloskey, D. (eds), *The Economic History of Britain: Volume 2: 1860s to the 1970s*, Cambridge: Cambridge University Press.

Harley, K. (1992), "International Competitiveness of the Antebellum American Cotton Textile Industry", *Journal of Economic History*, 52, 559–84.

Harrison, M. (1991), "The Peasantry and Industrialization", in Davies, R.W. (ed.), *From Tsarism to the New Economic Policy: Continuity and Change in the Economy of the USSR*, Ithaca, NY: Cornell University Press.

Hassan, J.A. (1985), "The Growth and Impact of the British Water Industry in the Nineteenth Century", *Economic History Review*, 38(4), 531–47.

Hassan, J.A. (1998), *A History of Water in Modern England and Wales*, Manchester: Manchester University Press.

Hausman, W.J. (2004), "Webs of Influence and Control: Personal and Financial Networks in the Formative Years of the US Electric Power Industry", *Annales Historiques de l'Électricité*, 2(June), 53–67.

Hausman, W.J. and Neufeld, J.L. (1990), "The Structure and Profitability of the US Electric Utility Industry at the turn of the Century", *Business History*, 32(2), 225–43.

Hausman, W.J. and Neufeld, J.L. (1999), "Falling Water: The Origins of Direct Federal Participation in the US Electric Utility Industry, 1902–1933", *Annals of Public and Cooperative Economics*, 70(1), 49–74.

Hausman, W.J. and Neufeld, J.L. (2002), "The Market for Capital and the Origins of State Regulation of Electric Utilities in the United States", *Journal of Economic History*, 62(4), 1050–73.

Hausman, W.J. and Neufeld, J.L. (2011), "How Politics, Economics and Institutions Shaped Electric Utility Regulation in the United States: 1879–2009", *Business History*, 53(5), 723–46.

Hawke, G.R. (1969), "Pricing Policy of Railways in England and Wales before 1881", Reed, M.C. (ed.), *Railways in the Victorian Economy: Studies in Finance and Economic Growth*, Newton Abbott: David and Charles.

Headrick, D.R. (1991), *The Invisible Weapon: Telecommunications and International Politics 1951–1945*, Oxford: Oxford University Press.

Headrick, D.R. and Griset, P. (2001), "Submarine Telegraph Cables: Business and Politics", *Business History Review*, 75(3), 543–78.

Heckleman, J. and Wallis, J.J. (1997), "Railroads and Property Taxes", *Explorations in Economic History*, 34, 77–99.

Hedin, L.-E. (1967), "Some Notes on the Financing of the Swedish Railways 1860–1914", *Economy and History*, X, 3–37.

Henderson, W.O. (1958), *The State and the Industrial Revolution in Prussia 1740–1870*, Liverpool: Liverpool University Press.

Henderson, W.O. (1961), "The Rise of the Metal and Armaments Industries in Berlin and Brandenburg 1712–1795", *Business History*, 3(2), 63–74.

Henderson, W.O. (1975), *The Rise of German Industrial Power 1834–1914*, London: Temple Smith.

Hennock, E.P. (1963), "Finance and Politics in Urban Local Government in England 1835–1900", *Historical Journal*, 6(2), 212–25.

Hennock, E.P. (1983), *Fit and Proper Persons*, London: Arnold.

Hennock, E.P. (2000), "The Urban Sanitary Movement in England and Germany 1838–1914: A Comparison", *Continuity and Change*, 15(2), 269–96.

Hentschel, V. (1989), "German Economic and Social Policy, 1815–1939", in Mathias, P. and Pollard, S. (eds), *The Cambridge Economic History of Europe: Volume VIII: The Industrial Economies: The Development of Economic and Social Policies*, Cambridge: Cambridge University Press.

Higgs, R. (2007), "The World Wars", in Fishback, P. (ed.), *Government and the American Economy: A New History*, Chicago, IL: University of Chicago Press.

Hirschfield, A. (1973), "The Role of Public Enteprise in the French Economy", *Annals of Public and Collective Economy*, 44, 225–69.

Hoag, C. (2006), "The Atlantic Cable and Capital Market Information Flows", *Journal of Economic History*, 66(2), 342–53.

Hobsbawn, E.J. (1962), *The Age of Revolution*, London: Wiedenfeld and Nicolson.

Hobsbawn, E.J. (1990), *Nations and Nationalism since 1870: Programme, Myth and Reality*, Cambridge: Cambridge University Press.

Hobson, J.M. (1993), "The Military Extraction Gap and the Wary Titan: The Fiscal Sociology of British Defence Policy 1870–1913", *Journal of European Economic History*, 22(2), 461–502.

Hoffman, W.G. (1963), "The Take-Off in Germany", in Rostow, W.W. (ed.), *The Economics of Take-Off into Sustained Growth*, London: Macmillan.

Horn, N. and Kocka, K. (eds), (1979), *Recht und Entwicklung der Gros Unternehmen im 19 und fruhen 20. Jahrhundert*, Gottingen: Vandenhoeck and Ruprecht.

Howe, F. (1913), *European Cities at Work*, New York: Charles Scribner's & Sons.

Hughes T.P. (1962), "The British Electrical Industry Lag: 1882–88", *Technology and Culture*, 3, 27–44.

Hughes, T.P. (1969), "Technological Momentum in History: Hydrogenation in Germany 1898–1933", *Past and Present*, 44, 106–32.

Hughes, T.P. (1977), "Technology as a Force for Change in History: The Effort to Form a Unified Electric Power Sfystem in Weimar Germany", in Mommsen, H. (ed.), *Industrielles System und politische Entwicklung under Weimarer Republik*, Dusseldorf: Droste Verlag.

Hughes, T.P. (1983), *Networks of Power: Electrification in Western Society 1880–1930*, Baltimore, MD: Johns Hopkins Press.

Hughes, T.P. and Pinch, T. (1987), *The Social Construction of Technological Systems*, Cambridge, MA: MIT Press.

Hummel, J.R. (2007), "The Civil War and Reconstruction", in Fishback, P. (ed.), *Government and the American Economy: A New History*, Chicago, IL: University of Chicago Press.

Huss, M.-M. (1988), "Pronatalism and the Popular Ideology of the Child in Wartime France: The Evidence of the Picture Postcard", in Wall, R. and Winter, J. (eds), *The Upheaval of War*, Cambridge: Cambridge University Press.

Hyldtoft, O. (1994), "Modern Theories of Regulation: An Old Story: Danish Gasworks in the Nineteenth Century", *Scandinavian Economic History Review*, XLII(1), 29–53.

Hyldtoft, O. (1995), "Making Gas: The Establishment of the Nordic Gas systems, 1800–1870", in Kaijser, A. and Hedin, M. (eds), *Nordic Energy Systems: Historical Perspectives and Current Issues*, Canton, MA: Science History Publications.

Irving, R.J. (1978), "The Profitability and Performance of British Railways 1870–1914", *Economic History Review*, 31, 36–66.

Jacobson, C.D. (2000), *Ties that Bind: Economic and Political Dilemmas of Urban Utility Networks 1800–1990*, Pittsburg, PA: University of Pittsburg Press.

Joint Select Committee of the House of Lords and the House of Commons (1902–03), *Report on Municipal Trading*, Parliamentary Papers 1900 VII and 1903 VII, London: HMSO.

Jones, G. and Zeitlin, J. (eds), (2008), *Oxford Handbook of Business History*, Oxford: Oxford University Press.

Jones, L.J. (1983) "Public Pursuit and Private Profit: Liberal Businessmen and Municipal Politics in Birmingham, 1845–1900", *Business History*, 25(3), 240–59.

Kafengaus, L.B. (1994), *Evolutsiia promeyshlennovo proizvodstva Rosii [Evolution of Russian Industrial Production]*, Moscow: Epifaniya.

Kahan, A. (1965), "Continuity in Economic Activity and Policy during the Post-Petrine Period in Russia", *Journal of Economic History*, 25(1), 61–85.

Kahan, A. (1966), "The Costs of Westernisation in Russia: The Gentry and the Economy in the Eighteenth Century", *Slavic Review*, 75(1), 40–66.

Kahan, A. (1967), "Government Policies and the Industrialisation of Russia", *Journal of Economic History*, 27(4), 460–77.

Kahk, J. and Ligi, H. (1975), "The Peasant Household in Estonia on the Eve of Industrialisation", *Studia Historiae Oeconomicae*, 10, 133–44.

Kaijser, A. and Hedin, M. (eds), (1995), *Nordic Energy Systems: Historical Perspectives and Current Issues*, Canton, MA: Science History Publications.

Kaser, M.C. (1978), "Russian Entrepreneurship", in Mathias, P. and Postan, M.M. (eds), *The Cambridge Economic History of Europe: Volume VII: The Industrial Economies: Capital, Labour, Enterprise*, Cambridge: Cambridge University Press, Part 2.

Keefer, P. (1996), "Protection against a Capricious State: French Investment and Spanish Railroads, 1845–1875", *Journal of Economic History*, 56(1), 170–92.

Keizo, S. (ed.), (1958), *Japanese Society in the Meija Era*, Tokyo: Obunsha.

Keller, M. (1979), "Public Policy and Large Enterprises: Comparative Historical Perspective", in Horn, N. and Kocka, K. (eds), *Recht und Entwicklung der Gros Unternehmen im 19 und fruhen 20. Jahrhundert*, Gottingen: Vandenhoeck and Ruprecht.

Keller, M. (1981). "The Pluralist State: American Economic Regulation in Comparative Perspective", in McCraw, T.K. (ed.), *Regulation in Perspective: Historical Essays*, Cambridge, MA: Harvard University Press.

Keller, M. (1990), *Regulation and the New Economy: Public Policy and Economic Change in America 1900–1933*, Cambridge, MA: Harvard University Press.

Kemp, T. (1989), "Economic and Social Policy in France", in Mathias, P. and Pollard, S. (eds), *The Cambridge Economic History of Europe: Volume VIII: The Industrial Economies: The Development of Economic and Social Policies*, Cambridge: Cambridge University Press.

Kennedy, P.M. (1971), "Imperial Cable Communications and Strategy, 1870–1914", *English Historical Review*, 86(241), 728–52.

Kennedy, P.M. (1988), *The Rise and Fall of Great Powers: Economic Change and Military Conflict from 1500 to 2000*, London: Harper Collins.

Keyder, C. (1985), "State and Industry in France", *American Economic Review*, 72(2), 308–14.

Kinder, H. and Hilgemann, W. (2003), *The Penguin Atlas of World History: Volume II: From the French Revolution to the Present*, London: Penguin.

Kindleberger, C.P. (1989), "Commercial Policy between the Wars", in Mathias, P. and Pollard, S. (eds), *The Cambridge Economic History of Europe: Volume VIII: The Industrial Economies: The Development of Economic and Social Policies*, Cambridge: Cambridge University Press, Part I.

Kirby, M.W. (1977), *The British Coal Mining Industry 1870–1946*, London: Macmillan.

Kirby, M.W. (1992), "Institutional Rigidities and Economic Decline: Reflections on the British Experience", *Economic History Review*, 45, 637–60.

Knoop, D. (1912), *Principles and Methods of Municipal Trading*, London: Macmillan.

Knox, V. (1901), "The Economic Effects of the Tramways Act of 1870", *Economic Journal*, 11, 492–510.

Kocka, J. (1978), "Entrepreneurs and Managers in German Industrialisation", in Mathias, P. and Postan, M.M. (eds), *The Cambridge Economic History of Europe: Volume VII: The Industrial Economies: Capital, Labour, Enterprise*, Cambridge: Cambridge University Press, Part 1.

Kocka, J. (1980), "The Rise of the Modern Industrial Enterprise in Germany", in Chandler, A.D. and Daems, H. (eds), *Managerial Hierarchies*, Cambridge: Cambridge University Press.

Köthenbürger, M., Sinn, H.-W. and Whalley, J. (eds), (2006), *Privatisation Experiences in the European Union*, Cambridge, MA: MIT Press.

Kovacic, W.E. and Shapiro, C. (2000), "Antitrust Policy: A Century of Economic and Legal Thinking", *Journal of Economi Perspectives*, 14(1), 43–60.

Kuhl, A. (ed.), (2002a), *De Munizipalsozialismus in Europa*, Munchen: Oldenberg Verlag.

Kuhl, A. (2002b), "Le Debat sur le Socialisme Municipal en Allemagne avant 1914 et la Municipalisation de l' Électricité", in Kuhl, A. (ed.), *De Munizipalsozialismus in Europa*, Munchen: Oldenberg Verlag.

Kuisel, R.F. (1973), "Technocrats and Public Economic Policy: From the 3rd to the 4th Republic", *Journal of European Economic History*, 2, 53–99.

Kuisel, R.F. (1981), *Capitalism and the State in Modern France*, Cambridge: Cambridge University Press.

Laborie, L. (2006), "A Missing Link: Telecommunication Networks and European Integration", in Leuten, E. van and Kaijser, A. (eds), *Networking Europe: Transnational Infrastructure and the Shape of Europe 1850–2000*, Sagamore Beach, MA: Watson.

Laffut, M. (1983), "Belgium", in O'Brien, P.K. (ed.), *Railways and the Economic Development of Europe*, Oxford: Macmillan.

Lamoureaux, N.R. (2000), "Entrepreneurship, Business Organization and Economic Concentration", in Engerman, S.L. and Gallman, R.E. (eds), *The Cambridge Economic History of the United States*, Cambridge: Cambridge University Press, Volume II.

Landes, D.S. (1949), "French Entrepreneurship and Industrial Growth in the Nineteenth Century", *Journal of Economic History*, IX, 45–61.

Landes, D.S. (1950), "French Business and the Businessman: A Social and Cultural Analysis", in Earle, E.M. (ed.), *Modern France*, Princeton, NJ: Princeton University Press.

Landes, D.S. (1965), "Japan and Europe: Contrasts in Industrialisation", in Lockwood, W.W. (ed.), *The State and Economic Enterprise in Japan*, Princeton, NJ: Princeton University Press.

Lange, O. (1936), "On the Economic Theory of Socialism", *Review of Economic Studies*, 4(1), 53–71 and 4(2), 123–42.

Lanthier, P. (1979), "Les Dirigeants de Grands Enterprises Éléctricique en France 1911–73", in Levy-Leboyer, M. (ed.), *Le Patronal de la Seconde Industrialisation*, Paris: Les Editions Ouvrières.

Larroque, D. (1988), "Economic Aspects of Public Transit in the Parisian Area", in Tarr, J.A. and Dupuy, G. (eds), *Technology and the Rise of the Networked City in Europe*, Philadelphia, PA: Temple University Press..

Laue, T. (1960), "The State and the Economy", in Black, C.E. (ed.), *The Transformation of Russian Society: Aspects of Social Change Since 1861*, Cambridge, MA: Harvard University Press.

Lazonick, W. (1991), *Business Organisation and the Myth of the Market Economy*, Cambridge: Cambridge University Press.

Lebergott, S. (1984), *The Americans: An Economic Record*, New York: Norton & Co.

Lee, W.R. (ed.), (1979), *European Demography and Economic Growth*, London: Croom Helm.

Lefranc, G. (1929/30), "The French Railroads 1823–42", *Journal of Economic and Business History*, II, 299–331.

Lenin, V.I. (1905), "The Fall of Port Arthur", in V.I. Lenin, *Collected Works*, volume 8, London: Lawrence and Wishart.

Léon, P., Crouzet, F. and Gascon, R. (eds), (1972), *L'Industrialisation en Europe au XIXe Siècle*, Paris: Centre National de la Recherche Scientifique.

Leonard, C. and Ljundberg, J. (2010), "Population and Living Standards, 1870–1914", in Broadberry, S.N. and O'Rourke, K.H. (eds), *The Cambridge Economic History of Modern Europe*, Cambridge: Cambridge University Press, Volume II.

Leontief, W. (1956), "Factor Proportions and the Structure of American Trade: Further Theoretical and Empirical Analysis", *Review of Economics and Statistics*, 38, 386–407.

Lequin, Y. (1978), "Labour in the French Economy since the Revolution", in Mathias, P. and Postan, M.M. (eds), *The Cambridge Economic History of Europe: Volume VII: The Industrial Economies: Capital, Labour, Enterprise*, Cambridge: Cambridge University Press, Part I.

Lerner, A. (1944), *The Economics of Control*, London: Macmillan.

Letwin, W. (1989), "American Economic Policy, 1865–1939", in Mathias, P. and Pollard, S. (eds), *The Cambridge Economic History of Europe: Volume VIII: The Industrial Economies: The Development of Economic and Social Policies*, Cambridge: Cambridge University Press.

Leuten, E. van and Kaijser, A. (eds), (2006), *Networking Europe: Transnational Infrastructure and the Shape of Europe 1850–2000*, 51–60. Sagamore Beach, MA: Watson.

Levy-Leboyer, M. (1978), "Capital Investment and Economic Growth in France 1820–1930", in Mathias, P. and Postan, M.M. (eds), *The Cambridge Economic History of Europe: Volume VII: The Industrial Economies: Capital, Labour, Enterprise*, Cambridge: Cambridge University Press, Part I.

Levy-Leboyer, M. (ed.), (1979), *Le Patronal de la Seconde Industrialisation*, Paris: Les Editions Ouvrières.

Levy-Leboyer, M. (1980), "The Large Corporation in Modern France", in Chandler, A.D. and Daems, H. (eds), *Managerial Hierarchies*, Cambridge: Cambridge University Press.

Levy-Leboyer, M. (1994), "Introduction", "Panorama de l' Électrification: De la Grande Guerre à la nationalisation" and "Une réussite inachevée", in Levy-Leboyer, M. and Morsel, H. (eds), *Histoire de l'Électricité en France: Vol. II: L'Interconnection et Le Marché, 1919–46*, Paris: L'Association pour l'Histoire de l'Electricité en France, Fayard.

Levy-Leboyer, M. and Morsel, H. (eds), (1994), *Histoire de l'Électricité en France: Vol. II: L'Interconnection et Le Marché, 1919–46*, Paris: L'Association pour l'Histoire de l'Electricité en France, Fayard.

Leyen, A. von der (1926), "The German Federal Railway Company", *Annals of Collective Economy*, II, 321–45.

Lindert, P. (2000), "US Foreign Trade and Trade Policy in the Twentieth Century", in Engerman, S.L. and Gallman, R.E. (eds), *The Cambridge Economic History of the United States*, Cambridge: Cambridge University Press, Volume III.

Lipartito, K. (1988), "The Telephone in the South: A Comparative Analysis, 1877–1920", *Journal of Economic History*, 48(2), 419–21.

Lipartito, K. (1989), "System Building on the Margin: The Problem of Public Choice in the Telephone Industry", *Journal of Economic History*, 49(2), 323–36.

Lipartito, K. (2000), "Failure to Communicate: British Telecommunications and the American Model", in Zeitlin, J. and Herrigel, G. (eds), *Americanisation and its Limits: Reworking US Technology and Management in Post-War Europe and Japan*, Oxford: Oxford University Press.

Lipsey, R.E. (2000), "US Foreign Trade and the Balance of Payments 1800–1913", in Engerman, S.L. and Gallman, R.E. (eds), *The Cambridge Economic History of the United States*, Cambridge: Cambridge University Press, Volume II.

Lively, R.A. (1955), "The American System", *Business History Review*, 29(1), 81–96.

Lockwood, W.W. (1965a), "Japan's New Capitalism", in Lockwood, W.W. (ed.), *The State and Economic Enterprise in Japan*, Princeton, NJ: Princeton University Press.

Lockwood, W.W. (ed.), (1965b), *The State and Economic Enterprise in Japan*, Princeton, NJ: Princeton University Press.

Lorimer, F. (1946), *The Population of the Soviet Union: History and Prospects*, Geneva: League of Nations.

Lübbers, T. (2004), "Is Cartelisation Profitable? A Case Study of the Rhenish Westphalian Coal Syndicate, 1893–1913", *Preprints of the Max Planck Institute of Research on Collective Goods*, March, Bonn.

Lucas, N. (1985), *Western European Energy Policies*, Oxford: Clarendon Press.

Lyashchenko, P.I. (1949), *History of the National Economy of Russia to the 1917 Revolution*, New York: Macmillan.

McCloskey, D.N. (1981), *Enterprise and Trade in Victorian Britain: Essays in Historical Economics*, London: Allen and Unwin.

McCraw, T.K. (1975), "Regulation in America: A Review Article." *Business History Review*, 49(2), 159–83.

McCraw, T.K. (ed.), (1981), *Regulation in Perspective: Historical Essays*, Cambridge, MA: Harvard University Press.

McDougall, R. (2006), "Long Lines: AT&T's Long Distance Network as an Organisational and Political Strategy", *Business History Review*, 80(2), 297–327.

McGraw, T.K. (1984), "Business and Government: The Origins of the Adversary Relationship", *California Management Review*, 26(2), 33–52.

Mackay, J.P. (1976), *Tramways and Trolleys: The Rise of Urban Transport in Europe*, Princeton, NJ: Princeton University Press.

Mckendrick, N. and Outhwaite, R.B. (eds), (1986), *Business Life and Public Policy: Essays in Honour of D.C. Coleman*, Cambridge: Cambridge University Press.

McKeown, T. and Record, R.G. (1962), "Reasons for the Decline in Mortality in England and Wales during the Nineteenth Century", *Population Studies*, 16, 94–122.

MacMahon, A.W. and Dittmar, W.R. (1939/40), "Autonomous Public Enterprise: The German Railways", *Political Science Quarterly*, Part I (LIV December 1939, 481–513), Part II (LV March 1940, 25–52), Part III (LV June, 176–98).

Macpherson, W.J. (1987), *The Economic Development of Japan c. 1868–1941*, London: Macmillan.

Maddison, A. (1991), *Dynamic Forces in Capitalist Development*, Oxford: Oxford University Press.

Maddison, A. (1995), *Monitoring the World Economy 1820–1992*, Paris: Organisation for Economic Cooperation and Development.

Maddison, A. (2003), *The World Economy: Historical Statistics*, Paris: Organisation for Economic Cooperation and Development.

Magnusson, L. (2009), *Nation, State and the Industrial Revolution: The Visible Hand*, London: Routledge.

Magnusson, L. and Ottosson, J. (eds), (2001), *The State, Regulation and the Economy: An Historical Perspective*, Cheltenham: Edward Elgar.

Maintz, R. and Hughes, T.P. (eds), (1978), *The Development of Large Technical Systems*, Boulder, CO: Frankfurt and Westview Press.

Malanima, P. (2010), "Urbanisation", in in Broadberry, S.N. and O'Rourke, K.H. (eds), *The Cambridge Economic History of Modern Europe*, Cambridge: Cambridge University Press, Volume I.

Marburg, T.F. (1964), "Government and Business in Germany: Public Policy towards Cartels", *Business History Review*, 38(1), 78–101.

Marczewski, J. (1963), "The Take-Off Hypothesis and French Experience", in Rostow, W.W. (ed.), *The Economics of Take-Off into Sustained Growth*, London: Macmillan.

Margairaz, M. (1998), "Companies under Public Control in France 1900–1950", in Whiteside, N. and Salais, R. (eds), *Governance, Industry and Labour Markets in Britain and France*, London: Routledge.

Marriott, J.A.R. and Robertson, C.G. (1946), *The Evolution of Prussia: The Making of an Empire*, Oxford: Clarendon Press.

Marrison, A. (1996), *British Business and Protection 1903–1932*, Oxford: Clarendon Press.

Maschke, E. (1969), "Outline of the History of German Cartels from 1873 to 1914", in Crouzet, F., Chaloner, W.H. and Stern, W.M. (eds), *Essays in European Economic History 1789–1914*, London: Edward Arnold.

Masuda, H. (1993), "Policy and Coastal and River Transport: Transportation in Transition (1868–1891)", "Coastal Transport: Transportation in the Period of Railroad Priority (1892–1909)" and "Inland Shipping: Transport in the Postwar Recovery Period

(1946–1954)", in Yamamoto, H. (ed.), *Technological Innovation and the Development of Transportation in Japan*, New York: United Nations University Press.

Mathias, P. and Pollard, S. (eds), (1989), *The Cambridge Economic History of Europe: Volume VIII: The Industrial Economies: The Development of Economic and Social Policies*, Cambridge: Cambridge University Press.

Mathias, P. and Postan, M.M. (eds), (1978), *The Cambridge Economic History of Europe: Volume VII: The Industrial Economies: Capital, Labour, Enterprise*, Cambridge: Cambridge University Press, Parts 1 and 2.

Matthews, D. (1985), "Rogues, Speculators and Competing Monopolies: The Early London Gas Companies, 1812–1860", *London Journal*, 2, 39–50.

Matthews, D. (1987), "Technology Transfer in the Late 19th Century Gas Industry", *Journal of Economic History*, XLVII(4), 967–80.

Melosi, M.V. (2000), *The Sanitary City: Urban Infrastructure in America from Colonial Times to the Present*, Baltimore, MD: John Hopkins University Press.

Messager, R. (1988), "Municipalities and Managers: Heat Networks in Germany", in Tarr, J.A. and G. Dupuy, G. (eds), *Technology and the Rise of the Networked City in Europe*, Philadelphia, PA: Temple University Press.

Metzer, J. (1974), "Railroad Development and Market Integration: The Case of Tsarist Russia", *Journal of Economic History*, XXXIV(3), 529–50.

Metzer, J. (1976) "Railroads in Tsarist Russia: Direct Gains and Implications", *Explorations in Economic History*, 13(1), 85–111.

Meyer, H.R. (1906), "Municipal Ownership in Germany", *Journal of Political Economy*, 14, 553–67.

Middleton, R. (1996), *Government versus the Market: The Growth of the Public Sector, Economic Management and British Economic Performance*, Cheltenham: Edward Elgar.

Mierzejewski, A.C. (1990), "The German National Railway Company between the World Wars: Modernisation or Preparation for War?" *Journal of Transport History*, 11, 40–60.

Mierzejewski, A.C. (1995), "Payment and Profits: The German National Railway Company and Reparations 1924–32", *German Studies Review*, 18, 65–85.

Mierzejewski, A.C. (1996), "The German National Railway Company confronts its Competitors 1920–39", *Business and Economic History*, 25, 89–102.

Mierzejewski, A.C. (1999), *The Most Valuable Asset of the Reich: A History of the German National Railway*, 2 volumes, Chapel Hill, NC, and London: University of North Carolina Press.

Milhaud, E. (1939), "The Nationalisation of the Aeronautical Industry in France and its Immediate Consequences", *Annals of Collective Economy*, XV, 223–51.

Millward, R. (1982), "An Economic Analysis of the Organization of Serfdom in Eastern Europe", *Journal of Economic History*, 42(3), 513–48.

Millward, R. (1984), "The Early Stages of European Industrialisation: Economic Organisation under Serfdom", *Explorations in Economic History*, 21(4), 406–28.

Millward, R. (1990), "Productivity in the UK Services Sector: Historical Trends 1856–1985 and Comparison with USA 1950–85", *Oxford Bulletin of Economics and Statistics*, 52(4), 423–36.

Millward, R. (1991), "The Market Behaviour of Local Utilities in Pre-World War I Britain: The Case of Gas", *Economic History Review*, XLIV, 102–27.

Millward, R. (1997), "The 1940s Nationalisations in Britain: Means of Production or Means to an End?" *Economic History Review*, 50(2), 209–34.

Millward, R. (2000), "The Political Economy of Urban Utilities in Britain 1840–1950", in Daunton, M. (ed.), *Cambridge Urban History of Britain: Vol. III, 1840–1950*, Cambridge: Cambridge University Press.

Millward, R. (2005), *Private and Public Enterprise in Europe: Energy, Telecommunications and Transport* c.*1830–1990*, Cambridge: Cambridge University Press.

Millward, R. (2007), "La Distribution de L'Eau dans les Villes en Grande-Bretagne au XIXe et XXe Siècles: Le Gouvernement Municipal et le Dilemme des Compagnies Privées", *Histoire, Economie et Société*, 26(2), 111–28.

Millward, R. (2008), "Business and the State", in Jones, G. and Zeitlin, J. (eds), *Oxford Handbook of Business History*, Oxford: Oxford University Press.

Millward, R. (2011a), "The Institutional Economic History of Infrastructure Industries c1830–1990: Ideology, Technology, Geo-politics?" in Finger, M. and Künneke, R. (eds), *International Handbook for the Liberalisation of Infrastructures*, Basingstoke: Edward Elgar.

Millward, R. (2011b), "Geo-politics versus Market Structure Interventions in Europe's Infrastructure Industries c. 1830–1939", *Business History*, 53(5), 673–87.

Millward, R. (2011c), "Public Enterprise in the Modern Western World: An Historical Analysis", *Annals of Public and Collective Economics*, 82(4), 375–98.

Millward, R. (2013), "The Growth of the Public Sector", in Floud, R., Humphries, J. and Johnson, P. (eds), *The Economic History of Britain, 1700–2010*, Cambridge: Cambridge University Press, volume 2.

Millward. R. and Sheard, S. (1995), "The Urban Fiscal Problem 1870–1914: Government Expenditure and Finances in England and Wales", *Economic History Review*, XLVIII(3), 501–35.

Millward, R. and Singleton, J. (eds), (1995), *The Political Economy of Nationalisation in Britain 1920–5*, Cambridge: Cambridge University Press.

Millward, R. and Ward, R. (1993), "From Private to Public Ownership of Gas Undertakings in England and Wales, 1851–1947: Chronology, Incidence and Causes", *Business History*, 35(3), 1–21.

Milward, A.S. and Saul, S.B. (1973), *The Economic Development of Continental Europe 1780–1870*, London: Allen and Unwin.

Milward, A.S. and Saul, S.B. (1977), *The Development of the Economies of Continental Europe 1850–1914*, Cambridge, MA: Harvard University Press.

Mitchell, B.R. (1988), *British Historical Statistics*, Cambridge: Cambridge University Press.

Mitchell, B.R. (2003a), *International Historical Statistics: Europe 1750–2000*, London: Macmillan.

Mitchell, B.R. (2003b), *International Historical Statistics: The Americas: 1750–2000*, London: Macmillan.

Mitchell, B.R. (2003c), *International Historical Statistics: Africa, Asia and Oceania 1750–2000*, New York: Stockton.

Mitsuhaya, K. (1958), "Development of Transportation and Communication Systems", in Keizo, S. (ed.), *Japanese Society in the Meija Era*, Tokyo: Obunsha.

Moch, J. (1953), "Nationalisation in France", *Annals of Collective Economy*, XXIV, 97–111.

Mokyr, J. (2009), *The Enlightened Economy: An Economic History of Britain 1700–1850*, New Haven, CT: Yale University Press.

Mokyr, J. and Voth, H.-J. (2010), "Understanding Growth in Europe 1700–1870: Theory and Evidence", in Broadberry, S.N. and O'Rourke, K.H. (eds), *The Cambridge Economic History of Modern Europe*, Cambridge: Cambridge University Press.

Mommsen, H. (ed.), (1977), *Industrielles System und politische Entwicklung under Weimarer Republik*, Dusseldorf: Droste Verlag.

Morris, R.J. and Rodger, R. (eds), (1993), *The Victorian City: A Reader in British Urban History: 1820–1914*, London: Longman.

Morrison, H. (1933), *Socialisation and Transport*, London: Constable.

Morsel, H. (1987), "L'hydro-électricité en France: du patronal disperse a la direction nationale (1902–46)", in Fridensen, P. and Strauss, A. (eds), *Le Capitalisme Francaise*, Paris: Libraiarie Artheme, Fayard.

Mulert, O. (1929), "The Economic Activities of German Municipalities", *Annals of Collective Economy*, V, 209–76.

Murphy, T.E. (2006), "Old Habits Die Hard (Sometimes): What Can Departement Heterogeneity Tell Us about the French Fertility Decline?" Annual Conference of the Economic History Society, New Researchers Session II/B, Reading, UK.

Nakamura, T. (1997), "Depression, Recovery and War 1920–45", in Yamamura, K. (ed.), *The Economic Emergence of Modern Japan*, Cambridge: Cambridge University Press.

Nelson, J.R. (ed.), (1964), *Marginal Cost Pricing in Practice*, Englewood Cliffs, NJ: Prentice-Hall.

Neufeld, J.L. (2008), "Corruption, Quasi-Rents and the Regulation of Electric Utilities", *Journal of Economic History*, 68(4), 1059–97.

Niertz, N. (1998), "Air France: An Elephant in an Evening Suit", in Dienel, H-L. and Lyth, P.J. (eds), *Flying the Flag: European Commercial Air Transport since 1945*, Basingstoke: Macmillan.

Noreng, Ø, (1981), "State-Owned Oil Companies: Western Europe", in Vernon, R. and Aharoni, Y. (eds), *State-Owned Enterprise in Western Economies*, London: Croom Helm.

North, D. (1965), "Industrialisation in the United States", in Habakkuk, H.J. and Postan, M. (eds), *The Cambridge Economic History of Europe: Volume VI: The Industrial Revolutions and After: Incomes, Population and Technological Change*, Cambridge: Cambridge University Press.

North, D.C. (1961), *The Economic Growth of the United States, 1790–1860*, Englewood Cliffs, NJ: Prentice-Hall.

Nove, A. (1972), *An Economic History of the USSR*, Harmondsworth: Penguin.

Nutter, W. (1962), *The Growth of Industrial Production in the Soviet Union*, Princeton, NJ: Princeton University Press.

O'Brien, P.K. (ed.), (1983), *Railways and the Economic Development of Europe*, Oxford: Macmillan.

O'Brien, P.K. (1997), "Taxation, 1688–1914", *History Review*, March.

O'Brien, P.K. and Keyder, C. (1978), *Economic Growth in Britain and France 1780–1914: Two Paths to the Twentieth Century*, London: Allen and Unwin.

O'Brien, P.K. and Yun-Casalillo, B. (eds), (2012), *The Rise of the Fiscal State in Eurasia*, Cambridge: Cambridge University Press.

O'Grada, C. (1994), "British Agriculture, 1860–1914", in Floud, R. and McCloskey, D. (eds), *The Economic History of Britain: Volume 2: 1860s to the 1970s*, Cambridge: Cambridge University Press.

O'Grada, C. (1997), *A Rocky Road: The Irish Economy since the 1920s*, Manchester: Manchester University Press.

O'Hara, G. (2010), *Britain and the Sea since 1600*, London: Palgrave/Macmillan.

Oeftering, H. (1953), "The Participation of the German Federal State in Economic Enterprises", *Annals of Collective Economy*, XXIV, 271–88.

Ogilvie, S. and Overy, R. (eds), (2003), *Germany: A New Social and Economic History: Volume 3: Since 1800*, London: Hodder Arnold.

Ohkawa, K. (1957), *The Growth Rate of the Japanese Economy since 1878*, Tokyo: Kinokuniya Bookstore Co.

Ohkawa, K. and Rosovsky H. (1965), "A Century of Japanese Economic Growth", in Lockwood, W.W. (ed.), *The State and Economic Enterprise in Japan*, Princeton, NJ: Princeton University Press.

Ohkawa, K. and Rosovsky H. (1978), "Capital Formation in Japan", in Mathias, P. and Postan, M.M. (eds), *The Cambridge Economic History of Europe: Volume VII: The Industrial Economies: Capital, Labour, Enterprise*, Cambridge: Cambridge University Press, Part 2.

Oshima, H.T. (1965), "Meiji Fiscal Policy and Economic Progress", in Lockwood, W.W. (ed.), *The State and Economic Enterprise in Japan*, Princeton, NJ: Princeton University Press.

Ostergaard, G.N. (1954), "Labour and the Development of the Public Corporation", *Manchester School*, 22, 192–226.

Overy, R. (1994), *War and Economy in the Third Reich*, Oxford: Clarendon Press.

Overy, R.J. (2003a), "German Business and the Nazi New order", in Gourvish, T.R. (ed.), *Business and Politics in Europe, 1900–1970*, Cambridge: Cambridge University Press.

Overy, R.J. (2003b), "Economy and State in Germany in the Twentieth Century", in Ogilvie, S. and Overy, R. (eds), *Germany: A New Social and Economic History: Volume 3: Since 1800*, London: Hodder Arnold.

Paquier, S. and Williot, J.-P. (eds), (2005), *L'Industries du Gaz en Europe aux XIXe et XXe Siècles*, Brussels: Peter Lang.

Parker, W.N. (1959), "National States and National Development: French and German Ore Mining in the late Nineteenth Century", in Aitken, H.G.J. (ed.), *The State and Economic Growth*, New York: SSSRC.

Parris, H., Pestieau, P. and Saynor, P. (eds), (1987), *Public Enterprise in Western Europe*, Lund: Croom Helm.

Peebles, H.B. (1987), *Warshipbuilding on the Clyde: Naval Orders and the Prosperity of the Clyde Shipbuilding Industry, 1889–1939*, Edinburgh: John Donald.

Pinkney, D.H. (1957), "Money and Politics in the Rebuilding of Paris 1860–1870", *Journal of Economic History*, 17, 45–61.

Pintner, W.M. (1967), *Russian Economic Policy under Nicholas I*, Ithaca, NY: Cornell University Press.

Pipes, R. (1977), *Russia under the Old Regime*, New York: Penguin.

Pollard, S. (1981), *Peaceful Conquest: The Industrialisation of Europe 1760–1970*, Oxford: Oxford University Press.

Pollard, S. (1992), *The Development of the British Economy*, London: Edward Arnold.

Portal, R. (1965), "The Industrialisation of Russia", in Habakkuk, H.J. and Postan, M. (eds), *The Cambridge Economic History of Europe: Volume VI: The Industrial Revolutions and After: Incomes, Population and Technological Change*, Cambridge: Cambridge University Press.

Quine, M.S. (1996), *Population Politics in Twentieth Century Europe: Fascist Dictatorships and Liberal Democracies*, New York: Routledge.

Radcliffe, B. (1973), "The Building of the Paris–Saint Germain Railway", *Journal of Transport History*, 2(1), 20–40.

Ramunni, G. (1987), "L'élaboration du réseau éléctrique française: un débat technique del'entre-deux-guerres", in Cardot, F. (ed.), *1880–1980: Une Siècle de l'Électricité dans le Monde*, Paris: Presses Universitaires de France.

Ransom, R.L. (1989), *Conflict and Compromise: The Political Economy of Slavery, Emancipation and the American Civil War*, Cambridge: Cambridge University Press.

Ratcliffe, B. (1976), "Railway Imperialism: The example of the Pereires' Paris–St. Germain Company", *Business History*, 18, 66–84.

Reader, W.J. (1977), "Imperial Chemical Industries and the State 1925–45", in Supple, B. (ed.), *Essays in British Business History*, Oxford: Clarendon Press.

Reed, M.C. (ed.), (1969), *Railways in the Victorian Economy: Studies in Finance and Economic Growth*, Newton Abbott: David and Charles.

Ritschl, A. (2005), "The Pity of Peace: Germany's Economy at War, 1914–1918 and Beyond", in Broadberry, S.N. and Harrison, M. (eds), *The Economics of World War I*, Cambridge: Cambridge University Press.

Rockoff, H. (2005), "Until It's Over There: The US Economy in World War I", in Broadberry, S.N. and Harrison, M. (eds), *The Economics of World War I*, Cambridge: Cambridge University Press.

Rose, M. (1997), "The Politics of Protection: An Institutional Approach to Government: Industry Relations in the British and United States Cotton Industries 1945–73", *Business History*, 39(4), 128–51.

Rosefielde, S. and Hedlund, S. (2000), *Russia since 1980: Wrestling with Westernisation*, Cambridge: Cambridge University Press.

Rosenberg, H. (1943), "The Economic Impact of Imperial Germany: Agricultural Policy", *Journal of Economic History*, 3(December Supplement), 101–7.

Roses, J.R. and Wolf, N. (2010), "Aggregate Growth, 1913–1950", in Broadberry, S.N. and O'Rourke, K.H. (eds), *The Cambridge Economic History of Modern Europe*, Cambridge: Cambridge University Press, Volume II.

Rosovsky, H. (1953), "The Serf Entrepreneur in Russia", *Explorations in Entrepreneural History*, 6, 207–33.

Rostow, W.W. (ed.), (1963), *The Economics of Take-Off into Sustained Growth*, London: Macmillan.

Royal Commission on Water Supply (1869), *Report of the Commissioners*, London: HMSO.

Samuels, R.J. (1994), *"Rich Nation, Strong Army": National Security and the Technological Transformation of Japan*, Ithaca, NY: Cornell University Press.

Sandberg, L.G. (1981), "The Entrepreneur and Technical Change", in Floud, R. and McCloskey, D. (eds), *The Economic History of Britain: Volume 2: 1860s to the 1970s*, Cambridge: Cambridge University Press.

Schmoller, G. (1910), *The Mercantile System and its Historical Significance*, London: Macmillan.

Schneider, H.K. and Schultz, W. (1980), "Market Structure and Market Organisation in the Electricity and Gas Public Utilities of the Federal Repubic of Germany", in Baumol, W.J. (ed.), *Public and Private Enterprise in the Mixed Economy*, New York: Macmillan.

Schott, D. (ed.), (1997a), *Energy and the City in Europe: From Preindustrial Wood-Shortages to the Oil Crisis of the 1970s*, Stuttgart: VSWG-Beiheft 135, Franz Steiner Verlag.

Schott, D. (1997b), "Power for Industry: Electrification and its Strategic Use for Industrial Promotion. The Case of Mannheim", in Schott, D. (ed.), *Energy and the City in*

*Europe: From Preindustrial Wood-Shortages to the Oil Crisis of the 1970s*, Stuttgart: VSWG-Beiheft 135, Franz Steiner Verlag.

Schott, D. (2004), "Electrifying German Cities: Investments in Energy Technology and Public Transport and their Impact on Urban development 1880–1914", in Giuntini, A., Hertner, P. and Nunez, G. (eds), *Urban Growth on Two Continents in the Nineteenth and Twentieth Centuries: Technology, Networks, Finance and Public Regulation*, Granada: Editorial Comares, S.L.

Schott, D. (2005), "From Gas Light to Comprehensive Energy Supply: The Evolution of the Gas Industry in Three German Cities: Darmstadt, Mannheim, Mainz (1850–1970), in S. Paquier and J-P. Williot (eds), *L'Industries du gaz en Europe aux XIXe et XXe Siècles*, Brussels: Peter Lang.

Schremmer, D.E. (1989), "Taxation and Public Finance: Britain, France and Germany", in Mathias, P. and Pollard, S. (eds), *The Cambridge Economic History of Europe: Volume VIII: The Industrial Economies: The Development of Economic and Social Policies*, Cambridge: Cambridge University Press.

Schwob, P. (1934), "Relations between the State and the Electric Power Industry in France", *Harvard Business Review*, 13(1), 82–95.

Select Committee on the Supply of Water to the Metropolis (1821), *Report*, May.

Seton-Watson, H. (1967), *The Russian Empire 1801–1917*, Oxford: Clarendon Press.

Shaw, A. (1890), "Glasgow: A Municipal Study", *Century*, 39, 721–36.

Shaw, A. (1985), *Municipal Government in Continental Europe*, New York: Fisher Unwin.

Sherman, D. (1977), "Government Responses to Economic Modernisation in Mid Nineteenth Century France", *Journal of European Economic History*, 6, 717–36.

Silva, A.P. and Diogo, M.P. (2006), "From Host and Hostage: Portugal, Britain and the Atlantic Cables", in Leuten, E. van and Kaijser, A. (eds), *Networking Europe: Transnational Infrastructure and the Shape of Europe 1850–2000*, Sagamore Beach, MA: Watson.

Silverthorne, A. (1884), *London and Provincial Water Supplies*, London: Crosby, Lockwood & Co.

Singleton, J. (1995), "Debating the Nationalisation of the Cotton Industry, 1918–50", in Millward, R. and Singleton, J. (eds), *The Political Economy of Nationalisation in Britain 1920–5*, Cambridge: Cambridge University Press.

Smith, C.O. Jr (1990), "The Longest Run: Public Engineering and Planning in France", *American Historical Review*, 95(1990), 657–92.

Smith, T.C. (1955), *Political Change and Industrial Development in Japan: Government Enterprise, 1868–1880*, Stanford, CA: Stanford University Press.

Soderlund, E.F. (1963), "The Placing of the First Swedish Railway Loan", *Scandinavian Economic History Review*, 11, 43–59.

Stanziani, A. (2012), *Rules of Exchange: French Capitalism in Comparative Perspective, Eighteenth to Early Twentieth Centuries*, Cambridge: Cambridge University Press.

Stevenson, D. (1999), "War by Timetable? The Railway Race before 1914", *Past and Present*, 162, 163–94.

Stolper, G.F., Hauser, K. and Borschadt, K. (1967), *The German Economy: 1870 to the Present*, London: Wiedenfeld and Nicholson.

Strumilin, S. (1969), "Industrial Crises in Russia 1846–67", in Crouzet, F., Chaloner, W.H. and Stern, W.M. (eds), *Essays in European Economic History 1789–1914*, London: Edward Arnold.

Supple, B. (1973), "The State and the Industrial Revolution", in Cipolla, C. (ed.), *The Fontana Economic History of Europe: The Emergence of Industrial Societies*, Glasgow: Fontana Collins.

Supple, B. (ed.), (1977), *Essays in British Business History*, Oxford: Clarendon Press.

Supple, B. (1986), "Ideology or Pragmatism? The Nationalisation of Coal 1916–46", in Mckendrick, N. and Outhwaite, R.B. (eds), *Business Life and Public Policy: Essays in Honour of D.C. Coleman*, Cambridge: Cambridge University Press.

Supple, B. (ed.), (1963), *The Experience of Economic Growth: Case Studies in Economic History*, New York: Random House.

Supple, B. (1987), *The History of the Coal Industry: Vol. 4: 1913–46: The Political Economy of Decline*, Oxford: Clarendon Press.

Sylla, R. (2000), "Experimental Federalism: The Economics of American Government, 1789–1914", in Engerman, S.L. and Gallman, R.E. (eds), *The Cambridge Economic History of the United States*, Cambridge: Cambridge University Press, Volume II.

Sylla, R. and Toniolo, G. (eds), (1991), *Patterns of Industrialization*, London: Routledge.

Szreter, S. and Mooney, G. (1998), "Urbanisation, Mortality and the Standard of Living Debate: New Estimates of the Expectancy of Life at Birth in Nineteenth Century British Cities", *Economic History Review*, LI(1), 84–117.

Tanzi, V. and Schuknecht, L. (eds), (2000), *Public Spending in the Twentieth Century*, Cambridge: Cambridge University Press.

Tarr, J.A. and Dupuy, G. (eds), (1988), *Technology and the Rise of the Networked City in Europe*, Philadelphia, PA: Temple University Press.

Tarr, J.L., Finholt, T. and Goodman, D. (1987), "The City and the Telegraph: Urban Telecommunicaions in the Pre-Telephone Era", *Journal of Urban History*, 14(1), 38–80.

Taussig, F.W. (1888), *The Tariff History of the United States*, New York: J.P. Putnam's Sons.

Taylor, A.J. (1961), "Labour Productivity and Technological Innovation in the British Coal Industry 1850–1914", *Economic History Review*, 14, 48–70.

Temin, P. (1991), "Free Land and Federalism: A Synoptic View of American Economic History", *Journal of Interdisciplinary History*, 21(3), 371–89.

Thomas, F. (1978), "The Politics of Growth: The German Telephone System", in Maintz, R. and Hughes, T.P, (eds), *The Development of Large Technical Systems*, Boulder CO: Frankfurt and Westview Press.

Thompson, F.M.L. (ed.), (1990), *The Cambridge Social History of Britain 1750–1950: Volume 2: People and their Environment*, Cambridge: Cambridge University Press.

Thomson, D. (1958), *Democracy in France: The Third and Fourth Republics*, Oxford: Oxford University Press.

Tilly, C. (ed.), (1978), *Historical Studies of Changing Fertility*, Princeton, NJ: Princeton University Press.

Tilly, R.H. (1966), "The Political Economy of Public Finance and Prussian Industrialisation 1815–60", *Journal of Economic History*, XXVI, 484–97.

Tilly, R.H. (1978), "Capital Formation in Germany in the Nineteenth Century", in Mathias, P. and Postan, M.M. (eds), *The Cambridge Economic History of Europe: Volume VII: The Industrial Economies: Capital, Labour, Enterprise*, Cambridge: Cambridge University Press, Part I.

Tipton, F.B. (2003), "Government and the Economy in the Nineteenth Century", in Ogilvie, S. and Overy, R. (eds), *Germany: A New Social and Economic History: Volume 3: Since 1800*, London: Hodder Arnold.

Tolliday, S. (1986), "Steel and Rationalisation Policies 1918–65", in Elbaum, B. and Lazonick, W. (eds), *The Decline of the British Economy*, Oxford: Clarendon Press.

Trebilcock, C. (1981), *The Industrialisation of the Continental Powers 1780–1914*, London: Longman.

Troesken, W. (1995), "Antitrust Regulation before the Sherman Act: The Break-Up of the Chicago Gas Trust Company", *Explorations in Economic History*, 32, 109–36.

Troesken, W. (1997), "The Sources of Public Ownership: Historical Evidence from the Gas Industry", *Journal of Law, Economics and Organisation*, 13(1), 1–25.

Troesken, W. (1999), "Patronage and Public Sector Wages in 1896", *Journal of Economic History*, 59(2), 424–46.

Troesken, W. (2001), "Race, Disease and the Provision of Water in American Cities, 1889–1921", *Journal of Economic History*, 61(3), 750–76.

Tugan-Baranovsky, M.I. (1970), *The Russian Factory in the Nineteenth Century*, translated 3rd Russian edn, Homewood, IL: R.D. Irwin Inc.

US Bureau of the Census (1976), *The Statistical History of the United States: From Colonial Times to the Present*, New York: Basic Books Inc.

Valdaliso, J.M. (1996), "The Diffusion of Technological Change in the Spanish Merchant Fleet during the Twentieth Century: Available Alternatives and Conditioning Factors", *Journal of Transport History*, 12(2), 1–17.

Vernandsky, G. (1969), *A History of Russia*, New Haven, CT: Yale University Press.

Vernon, R. and Aharoni, Y. (eds), (1981), *State-Owned Enterprise in Western Economies*, London: Croom Helm.

Vietor, R.H.K. (1989), "AT&T and the Public Good: Regulation and Competition in Telecommunications, 1910–1987", in Bradley, S. and Hausman, J. (eds), *Future Competition in Telecommunications*, Cambridge, MA: Harvard Business School Press.

Vietor, R.H.K. (1990), "Contrived Competition: Airline Regulation and Deregulation, 1935–88", *Business History Review*, 64, 61–108.

Vietor, R.H.K. (2000), "Government Regulation of Business", in Engerman, S.L. and Gallman, R.E. (eds), *The Cambridge Economic History of the United States*, Cambridge: Cambridge University Press, Volume III.

Vinck, F. and Boursin, J. (1962), "The Development of the Public and Private Sectors of the Coal Mining Industry in Europe: A Comparative Study", *Annals of Public and Collective Economy*, XXXIII, 385–491.

Wall, R. and Winter, J. (eds), (1988), *The Upheaval of War*, Cambridge: Cambridge University Press.

Walle, E. van de (1978), "Alone in Europe: The French Fertility Decline Until 1850", in Tilly, C. (ed.), *Historical Studies of Changing Fertility*, Princeton, NJ: Princeton University Press.

Walle, E. van de (1979), "France", in Lee, W.R. (ed.), *European Demography and Economic Growth*, London: Croom Helm.

Waller, P.J. (1983), *Town City and Nation: England 1850–1914*, Oxford: Oxford University Press.

Wallis, J.J. (2000), "American Government Finance in the Long Run: 1790–1990", *Journal of Economic Perspectives*, Winter, 61–82.

Wallis, J.J. (2007), "The National Era", in Fishback, P. (ed.), *Government and the American Economy: A New History*, Chicago, IL: University of Chicago Press.

Wallsten, S. (2005), "Returning to Victorian Competition, Ownership and Regulation: An Empirical Study of European Telecommunications at the Turn of the Century", *Journal of Economic History*, 65(3), 693–722.

Weir Committee (1926), *Report of a Committee Appointed by the Board of Trade to Review the National Problem of the Supply of Electricity Energy*, London: Board of Trade.

Wellhöner, V. and Wixforth, H. (2003), "Finance and Industry", in Ogilvie, S. and Overy, R. (eds), *Germany: A New Social and Economic History: Volume 3: Since 1800*, London: Hodder Arnold.

Wengenroth, U. (1987), "The Electrification of the Workshop", in Cardot, F. (ed.), *1880–1980: Une Siècle de l'Électricité dans le Monde*, Paris: Presses Universitaires de France.

Wengenroth, U. (2000), "The Rise and Fall of State Owned Enterprise in Germany", in Toninelli, P.A. (ed.), *The Rise and Fall of State Owned Enterprise in the Western World*, Cambridge: Cambridge University Press.

Westwood, J.N. (1991), "The Railways", in Davies, R.W. (ed.), *From Tsarism to the New Economic Policy: Continuity and Change in the Economy of the USSR*, Ithaca, NY: Cornell University Press.

Wheatcroft, S.G. (1991), "Agriculture", in Davies, R.W. (ed.), *From Tsarism to the New Economic Policy: Continuity and Change in the Economy of the USSR*, Ithaca, NY: Cornell University Press.

Whitaker and Sons (1910, 1924, 1938, 1960), *Whitaker's Almanack*, London: Whitaker and Sons.

Whitaker, J.K. (1991), "The Economics of Defense in British Political Economy 1848–1914", in Goodwin, C.D. (ed.), *Economics and National Security: A History of their Interaction*, Durham, NC: Duke University Press.

White, C. (1987), *Russia and America: The Roots of Economic Divergence*, London: Croom Helm.

Whiteside, N. and Salais, R. (eds), (1998), *Governance, Industry and Labour Markets in Britain and France*, London: Routledge.

Wiener, M.J. (1985), *English Culture and the Decline of the Industrial Spirit 1850–1980*, London: Penguin.

Williamson, J.G. (1990), *Coping with City Growth during the British Industrial Revolution*, Cambridge: Cambridge University Press.

Williot, J.-P. (1984), "Naissance d'un Reseau Gazier á Paris au XIXème Siècle: Distribiution Gazière et Éclairage", *Histoire, Economie, Société*, 4, 569–91.

Wilson, J.F. (1993), "Competition between Electricity and Gas in Britain, 1880–1980", International Economic History Association, Pre-Conference on the Development of Electrical Energy, Paris, May.

Wilson, J.G. (1990), "Competition in the Early Gas Industry: The Case of Chester Gas Light Company", *Transactions of the Antiquarian Society of Lancashire and Cheshire*, 86, 87–110.

Wilson, Woodrow (1889), *The State: Elements of Historical and Practical Politics*, rev. edn, Boston, MA: D.C. Heath & Co., 1900.

Wolfe, M. (1969), "French Views on Wealth and Taxes from the Middle Ages to the Old Regime", in Coleman, D.C. (ed.), *Revisions in Mercantilism*, London: Methuen.

Woodruff, W. (1973), "The Emergence of an International Economy 1700–1914", in Cipolla, C. (ed.), *The Fontana Economic History of Europe: The Emergence of Industrial Societies*, Glasgow: Fontana Collins, Part 2.

Wray, W.D. (1984), *Mitsubishi and the N.Y.K., 1870–1914: Business Strategy in the Japanese Shipping Industry*, Cambridge, MA: Harvard University Press.

Wright, G. (1990), "The Origins of American Industrial Success, 1879–1940", *American Economic Review*, 80(4), 651–68.

Wright, Q. (1942), *A Study of War*, Chicago, IL: University of Chicago Press.

Wrigley, E.A. (1985), "The Fall of Martial Fertility in Nineteenth Century France: Exemplar or Exception?" *European Journal of Population*, 1(1), 31–60 and 141–77.

Yago, G. (1984), *The Decline of Transit: Urban Transportation in German and US Cities 1900–70*, Cambridge: Cambridge University Press.

Yamamoto, H. (1993a), "Traditional Transportation Systems", in Yamamoto, H. (ed.), *Technological Innovation and the Development of Transportation in Japan*, New York: United Nations University Press.

Yamamoto, H. (ed.), (1993b), *Technological Innovation and the Development of Transportation in Japan*, New York: United Nations University Press.

Yamamura, K. (1977), "Success Illgotten? The Role of Meiji Militarism in Japan's Technological Progress", *Journal of Economic History*, XXXVII(1), 113–35.

Yamamura, K. (1978), "Entrepreneurship, Ownership and Management in Modern Japan", in Mathias, P. and Postan, M.M. (eds), *The Cambridge Economic History of Europe: Volume VII: The Industrial Economies: Capital, Labour, Enterprise*, Cambridge: Cambridge University Press, Part 2.

Yamamura, K. (ed.), (1997), *The Economic Emergence of Modern Japan*, Cambridge: Cambridge University Press.

Yatsounsky, V.K. (1965), "Formation en Russia de la Grande Industrie Textile sur la Base de la Production Rurale", in *Deuxieme Conference Internationale d'Histoire Economique: Aix-en-Provence 1962*, Paris: Mouton & Co.

Yatsounsky, V.K. (1974), "The Industrial Revolution in Russia", in Blackwell, W.L. (ed.), *Russian Economic Development between Peter the Great and Stalin*, New York: Franklin Watts Inc.

Youngson, A.J. (ed.), (1972), *Economic Development in the Long Run*, London: Allen and Unwin.

Zaleski, E. (1971), *Planning for Economic Growth in the Soviet Union 1918–32*, Chapell Hill, NC: University of Carolina Press.

Zaleski, E. (1980), *Stalinist Planning for Economic Growth 1933–52*, London: Macmillan.

Zamagni, V. (ed.), (1986), "Origins and Development of Publicly Owned Enterprises", University of Florence, Ninth International Economic History Conference, Section B111.

Zauberman, A. (1976), "Russia and Eastern Europe 1920–70", in Cipolla, C. (ed.), *The Fontana Economic History of Europe: Contemporary Economies*, Glasgow: Collins, Part 2.

Zeitlin, J. and Herrigel, G. (eds), (2000), *Americanisation and its Limits: Reworking US Technology and Management in Post-War Europe and Japan*, Oxford: Oxford University Press.

Zelnik, R.E. (1965), "An Early Case of Labour Protest in St. Petersburg: The Alexandrovsk Machine Works in 1860", *Slavic Review*, 24(3), 507–20.

# Index

Page numbers in *italics* denote tables, those in **bold** denote figures.

Printed in Poland
by Amazon Fulfillment
Poland Sp. z o.o., Wrocław